Essential Guide to Cloud Cost Management

Mastering cloud cost optimization, governance, and FinOps practices

Manish Singh

www.bpbonline.com

First Edition 2026

ISBN: 978-93-78540-370

LIMITS OF LIABILITY AND DISCLAIMER OF WARRANTY

Dedicated to

My beloved wife, Asha
and
my daughter, Purvi

About the Author

Manish Singh is a cloud technology leader with over 22 years of experience in the IT industry, driving enterprise support and customer success across cloud and managed services ecosystems. Throughout his career, he has held leadership roles at cloud providers including Amazon Web Services, Google, and Oracle, where he led teams in delivering high-impact cloud solutions for enterprise clients.

A specialist in cloud architecture and IT system design, Manish has spearheaded numerous large-scale initiatives focused on cloud transformation, migration, and hybrid architectures. He is an expert in cloud financial management and FinOps practices, helping organizations optimize cloud spending while maintaining operational efficiency. He has led several cost optimization initiatives that enable enterprises to gain better visibility and maximize cloud investment value.

Based in Bangalore, Manish actively shares insights on cloud architecture and cost optimization. His published work on Amazon S3 cost optimization is widely referenced by engineers and DevOps professionals.

About the Reviewers

- **Jasanup Singh Randhawa** is a software engineer and AI practitioner with over a decade of experience building scalable, high-performance systems. In recent years, his work has increasingly focused on artificial intelligence, particularly the practical application of large language models and the evolving role of AI in modern software development. He brings a unique perspective that bridges traditional engineering with emerging AI capabilities, emphasizing how intelligent systems can augment human productivity and reshape how software is designed and delivered.

  Jasanup is deeply interested in the transformation of the engineering landscape in the age of AI—from code-centric workflows to more abstract, problem-driven approaches powered by automation and machine intelligence. He actively explores topics such as responsible AI adoption, system design in AI-first environments, and the future of developer tooling.

  With a strong academic background and extensive industry experience, Jasanup contributes thoughtful insights at the intersection of engineering and artificial intelligence. His work reflects a commitment to leveraging AI not just as a tool, but as a catalyst for innovation and meaningful technological progress.

- **Bhupendra** is a technical manager and specialist in **IT financial management** (**ITFM**) and **technology business management** (**TBM**). He is currently focused on architecting data-driven solutions using the IBM Apptio suite, including Apptio One, Cloudability, Bill of IT, and ITP. By leveraging Power BI alongside these platforms, he creates and designs sophisticated allocation methodologies that bridge the gap between technical spend and business value.

  His core passion lies in aligning ITFM and TBM frameworks to provide organizations with radical cost transparency, enabling leadership to make rapid, informed decisions. Beyond the world of financial modeling and data visualization, he is a culinary enthusiast who enjoys cooking, an avid online gamer, and a dedicated movie watcher.

Acknowledgement

I would like to express my sincere gratitude to my family and friends for their unwavering support, encouragement, and belief in me throughout the journey of writing this book. I am especially grateful to my wife, Asha, for her support, patience, and sacrifices over the past few years while I balanced professional responsibilities with writing this book. I am also thankful to my daughter, Purvi, whose presence has been a constant source of motivation and joy.

I would like to express my deep appreciation to my parents for their blessings, guidance, and values that have shaped my life and career. Their encouragement has been the foundation of all that I have achieved.

My sincere appreciation goes to BPB Publications for their guidance, expertise, and continuous support in bringing this book to fruition. The journey of refining and revising this work has been long, and I am grateful for the valuable contributions of the reviewers, technical experts, and editors whose insights helped improve the quality of this book.

I would also like to acknowledge the invaluable insights of my colleagues and co-workers from many years in the technology industry. Their feedback, mentorship, and shared experiences have been instrumental in shaping my perspective and refining my work.

Finally, I extend my sincere thanks to all the readers who have shown interest in this book. I hope the insights shared in these pages prove valuable and contribute meaningfully to your knowledge and professional growth.

Preface

Cloud adoption continues to grow as organizations migrate their workloads to cloud platforms. This trend is reflected in the steady year-on-year growth reported by leading providers such as AWS, Azure, and GCP. While security and data protection remain important priorities for organizations, managing cloud costs has become equally critical. The shift from a traditional capital expenditure model to a pay-as-you-go cloud model offers flexibility, but it also introduces challenges in controlling cloud spend, often resulting in unexpected cost increases and budget overruns.

Effective cloud cost management is not just about reducing the monthly bill. It is an ongoing process that requires a structured approach balancing cost efficiency with performance, scalability, innovation, and business growth. This book presents a comprehensive framework for cost management built on three key pillars: cost observability, cost optimization, and cost governance.

Cost observability focuses on gaining visibility into cloud usage and spending. By using native cloud tools, third-party solutions, and analytics platforms, organizations can understand cloud cost drivers and identify inefficiencies. Cost optimization involves applying strategies to reduce waste while maintaining performance and reliability. Techniques such as rightsizing resources, modernization, elasticity, and commitment-based savings help align costs with business value. Cost governance establishes the controls and guardrails needed to manage spending effectively. Through cost allocation models, policies, and a cost-aware culture, organizations can ensure financial accountability in everyday cloud operations and prevent cost overruns.

This book guides readers through the fundamentals of cloud cost management, from understanding pricing models and cost drivers to implementing optimization strategies and governance controls. It includes practical examples and real-world scenarios to demonstrate how these strategies can be applied effectively.

This book is intended for cloud engineers, architects, DevOps professionals, and IT decision-makers responsible for managing cloud spend. Whether you are new to the cloud or an experienced practitioner, this book provides practical strategies and actionable insights to strengthen your cost optimization efforts.

By the end of this book, you will be equipped to navigate the complexities of cloud cost management and develop strategies aligned with organizational priorities. I hope you find this book insightful and practical in your cloud cost management journey.

Chapter 1: Introduction to Cloud Cost Optimization—This chapter explains the fundamentals of managing costs in cloud environments. It highlights how organizations often face unexpected cost increases after moving from on-premise infrastructure to the cloud and emphasizes the need for a structured cost management approach. The chapter covers key topics such as cloud pricing models, billing components, cost drivers, and the use of Pricing Calculators to estimate the costs of deploying workloads on the cloud. It also helps the reader understand how architectural decisions impact long-term costs and why building a cost-aware culture is essential for sustainable cloud adoption and financial efficiency. By the end of this chapter, the reader will be able to navigate cloud pricing models and align technical design choices with organizational financial goals and business priorities.

Chapter 2: Gaining Visibility into Cloud Costs Using Native Tools—This chapter explains how organizations can use built-in cloud tools to understand and monitor their cloud usage and spending. It highlights the importance of cost visibility in controlling expenses and making informed financial decisions. The chapter provides a detailed overview of cost observability tools provided by cloud providers such as AWS Billing console, AWS Cost Explorer, AWS Cost and Usage Reports, and Azure Cost Management + Billing. It demonstrates how to use built-in cloud tools to track cloud usage, analyze trends, and identify cost anomalies. By the end of this chapter, the reader will be able to perform detailed cost analysis and interpret key metrics that support better technical and business decisions.

Chapter 3: Cost Visualization Dashboards—This chapter demonstrates how organizations can go beyond native cloud tools to build advanced, customized cost dashboards. It highlights the limitations of built-in tools and emphasizes the need for tailored reporting solutions as cloud environments grow. The chapter leverages AWS analytics services such as Athena and QuickSight to analyze cost and usage data, run queries, and create custom dashboards. Furthermore, it explores pre-built Cloud Intelligence Dashboards to bridge visibility gaps. By the end of this chapter, the reader will be able to build cost visualization dashboards that provide deeper insights into cloud spending and align with organizational reporting requirements.

Chapter 4: Moving from Cost Observability to Cost Optimization—This chapter marks the transition from understanding cloud costs to actively optimizing them. The chapter explains how to use native advisory tools such as AWS Trusted Advisor, Azure Advisor, and AWS Cost Optimization Hub to identify cost-saving opportunities. Furthermore, it introduces a framework for prioritizing recommendations based on return on investment and implementation effort. By the end of this chapter, the reader will be able to create a structured, data-driven cost optimization plan that balances quick wins with long-term financial sustainability.

Chapter 5: Optimizing Compute Cost—This chapter focuses on strategies to reduce costs associated with cloud compute services such as Amazon EC2 and Azure Virtual Machines. The chapter breaks down the anatomy of compute pricing and introduces key optimization levers, including instance rightsizing, elasticity, workload modernization, and commitment-based savings. The chapter also introduces tools to analyze computing usage and spending. By the end of this chapter, the reader will be able to identify optimization opportunities and develop a prioritized plan to improve compute unit cost.

Chapter 6: Optimizing Storage Cost—This chapter explores strategies to reduce costs associated with cloud storage services, which are a major contributor to overall cloud spending. The chapter explains storage pricing models and introduces key optimization techniques such as selecting the right storage type, using appropriate storage tiers, removing unused data, rightsizing volumes, and optimizing backups. It also covers tools to analyze cloud storage usage and cost patterns. By the end of this chapter, the reader will be able to identify optimization opportunities and develop a prioritized action plan to reduce storage costs while maintaining performance and compliance.

Chapter 7: Optimizing Database Cost on Cloud—This chapter focuses on strategies to manage and optimize costs associated with cloud database services, which are often the top contributors to overall cloud spending. The chapter compares self-managed and cloud-managed database models and explains key pricing components of database service, such as compute, storage, IOPS, and licensing. It introduces optimization techniques, including selecting the right database type, rightsizing instances, modernization, transitioning to serverless options, and leveraging reserved capacity. The chapter also covers tools to analyze database usage and cost patterns. By the end of this chapter, the reader will be able to identify optimization opportunities and develop a structured plan to optimize the cost of database services.

Chapter 8: Optimizing Cloud Observability Cost—This chapter addresses the often-overlooked expenses associated with monitoring and logging services such as Amazon CloudWatch, Azure Monitor, and third-party platforms. The chapter explains how large volumes of metrics and logs can lead to cost spikes as cloud environments scale. It also provides strategies to balance system visibility with cost efficiency, such as adjusting log retention, filtering data, and prioritizing critical business metrics. By the end of this chapter, the reader will be able to build a cost-efficient observability framework that maintains operational health while reducing waste and inefficiencies.

Chapter 9: Designing Cost Effective Cloud Security Architecture—This chapter focuses on optimizing the cost of cloud security services while maintaining a strong security posture. It explains how security services can become a significant contributor to cloud costs if not managed effectively. The chapter outlines the pricing models of key services such as AWS GuardDuty, WAF, and Inspector, and explains how to analyze their usage to identify cost drivers. The chapter introduces practical approaches to optimize configurations, and align security controls with actual compliance and workload requirements. It also covers tools to analyze security spending and identify key optimization levers. By the end of this chapter, the reader will be able to design a secure and cost-efficient cloud security architecture.

Chapter 10: Optimizing Data Transfer Charges on Cloud—This chapter focuses on managing and optimizing costs associated with cloud data transfer. Unlike traditional on-premises environments, where network costs are largely fixed, cloud data transfer follows a usage-based pricing model, making it important to understand and control these charges. The chapter explains different types of data transfer, including transfers across regions, availability zones, and the internet, and how each impacts overall costs. It introduces tools such as VPC Flow Logs, Amazon CloudWatch, and AWS Cost Explorer to provide visibility into data traffic patterns. The chapter also presents practical strategies to reduce **data transfer out** (**DTO**) charges without affecting system performance or scalability. By the end of this chapter, the reader will be able to design cost-efficient network architectures and implement a structured optimization plan.

Chapter 11: Establishing Cost Governance and Guardrails—This chapter shifts the focus from one-time savings to long-term financial predictability. The chapter explains how to build a robust governance framework using cost allocation strategies, tagging policies, and proactive guardrails such as budget alerts and anomaly detection. It also demonstrates how to handle unexpected cost spikes and foster a cost-aware culture where technical teams share financial accountability. By the end of this chapter, the reader will be able to implement governance mechanisms and set up guardrails that prevent bill shock while balancing financial control with cloud agility.

Chapter 12: Advancing Cost Optimization Journey with GenAI—This chapter concludes the book by bringing together the three pillars of cloud cost management—cost observability, cost optimization, and cost governance into a unified strategy. The chapter explains how organizations can apply these principles in real-world scenarios to achieve sustainable cost efficiency. It introduces generative AI tools such as Amazon Q and Microsoft Copilot, which simplify cost analysis through natural language interactions and provide actionable recommendations. The chapter also covers FOCUS, a standard that unifies billing data across cloud providers for easier multi-cloud management. By combining proven cost management strategies with emerging technologies, the reader will be able to achieve faster, smarter, and more sustainable cloud cost management.

Code Bundle and Coloured Images

Please follow the link to download the
Code Bundle and the ***Coloured Images*** of the book:

https://rebrand.ly/2sukh5i

The code bundle for the book is also hosted on GitHub at
https://github.com/bpbpublications/Essential-Guide-to-Cloud-Cost-Management.
In case there's an update to the code, it will be updated on the existing GitHub repository.

We have code bundles from our rich catalogue of books and videos available at https://github.com/bpbpublications. Check them out!

Errata

We take immense pride in our work at BPB Publications and follow best practices to ensure the accuracy of our content to provide an indulging reading experience to our subscribers. Our readers are our mirrors, and we use their inputs to reflect and improve upon human errors, if any, that may have occurred during the publishing processes involved. To let us maintain the quality and help us reach out to any readers who might be having difficulties due to any unforeseen errors, please write to us at: errata@bpbonline.com

Your support, suggestions and feedback are highly appreciated by the BPB Publications' Family.

At www.bpbonline.com, you can also read a collection of free technical articles, sign up for a range of free newsletters, and receive exclusive discounts and offers on BPB books and eBooks. You can check our social media handles below:

Instagram *Facebook* *LinkedIn* *YouTube*

Get in touch with us at: business@bpbonline.com for more details.

Piracy

If you come across any illegal copies of our works in any form on the internet, we would be grateful if you would provide us with the location address or website name. Please contact us at business@bpbonline.com with a link to the material.

If you are interested in becoming an author

If there is a topic that you have expertise in, and you are interested in either writing or contributing to a book, please visit www.bpbonline.com. We have worked with thousands of developers and tech professionals, just like you, to help them share their insights with the global tech community. You can make a general application, apply for a specific hot topic that we are recruiting an author for, or submit your own idea.

Reviews

Please leave a review. Once you have read and used this book, why not leave a review on the site that you purchased it from? Potential readers can then see and use your unbiased opinion to make purchase decisions. We at BPB can understand what you think about our products, and our authors can see your feedback on their book. Thank you!

For more information about BPB, please visit www.bpbonline.com.

Join our Discord space

Join our Discord workspace for latest updates, offers, tech happenings around the world, new releases, and sessions with the authors:

https://discord.bpbonline.com

Table of Contents

1. Introduction to Cloud Cost Optimization 1
Introduction 1
Structure 1
Objectives 1
Evolving landscape of cloud cost management 2
Introduction to cloud cost management 3
Creating a cost-aware culture 6
Primary drivers of cloud costs 6
AWS cost structure and pricing models 11
Estimating cloud spend using Pricing Calculators 16
AWS Pricing Calculator 17
Azure Pricing Calculator 20
Conclusion 23

2. Gaining Visibility into Cloud Costs Using Native Tools 25
Introduction 25
Structure 25
Objectives 25
Using native tools for cost visibility 26
Navigating your monthly AWS Billing invoice 27
AWS Billing and Cost Management dashboard 28
Managing access to AWS Billing and cost data 29
AWS Billing console, starting point for cost optimization 30
Leveraging AWS Cost Explorer to analyze usage and spend trends 32
AWS Cost Explorer pricing considerations 33
Getting started with AWS Cost Explorer 34
AWS Cost Explorer in action 35
Understanding AWS Cost and Usage Reports 38
CUR 2.0 and AWS Data Exports 40
Getting started with AWS Data Exports 41
Azure Cost Management + Billing overview 43

Introduction to Azure Cost Management + Billing overview 43
Getting started with Azure Cost Analysis 44
Understanding cost analysis dashboard 45
Customizing cost analysis views 46
Exporting cost data for further analysis 47
Bringing it all together 48
Conclusion 52

3. Cost Visualization Dashboards 53
Introduction 53
Structure 53
Objectives 53
Significance of custom cost analytics solutions 54
Integrating AWS CUR with Amazon Athena 55
Options for CUR 2.0 integration with Athena 56
Steps for CUR 2.0 integration 56
Leveraging Amazon Athena for AWS usage and spending analysis 61
Use case 1 is to identify the top spending AWS services 61
Use case 2 is to analyze Amazon S3 costs per bucket 63
Cost visualization dashboard 64
Exploring the AWS Cost and Usage dashboard 64
Getting started with the Cost and Usage dashboard 67
Dashboard customization 69
Setting alerts and notifications 69
Sharing with stakeholders 69
Building a QuickSight dashboard 69
Steps to create a QuickSight dashboard 70
Graph 1, cost by linked account 72
Graph 2, cost by service 73
Publishing and sharing dashboard 74
Other cost visualization dashboards 75
Conclusion 76

4. Moving from Cost Observability to Cost Optimization 77
Introduction 77
Structure 77

Objectives 78
Cost optimization levers 78
Eliminating waste and idle resources 78
Optimizing architecture and deployment configurations 79
Choosing the right pricing model 79
Leveraging alternative services and technologies 80
Prioritizing your cost optimization plan 80
Key factors for prioritization 81
Estimated savings potential 81
Implementation cost 82
Implementation timelines 82
Dependency management 83
Calculating ROI for cost optimization 83
Developing a prioritization framework 84
Getting started with cost optimization tools 86
Introduction to AWS Trusted Advisor 86
Accessing AWS Trusted Advisor 87
Navigating the AWS Trusted Advisor dashboard 87
Cost optimization checks in Trusted Advisor 88
Viewing and understanding recommendations 90
Getting started with Cost Optimization Hub 91
Key features of AWS Cost Optimization Hub 92
AWS Cost Optimization Hub versus AWS Trusted Advisor 92
Enabling AWS Cost Optimization Hub 93
Navigating the AWS Cost Optimization Hub 94
Cost Optimization recommendations 95
Using Azure Advisor to optimize cost 96
Navigating the Azure Advisor dashboard 97
Cost optimization recommendations 98
Implementing cost recommendations 98
Right-size or shutdown of underutilized virtual machines 99
Conclusion 99

5. Optimizing Compute Cost 101
Introduction 101

Structure....................101
Objectives....................101
Understanding compute portfolio....................102
Anatomy of cloud compute pricing....................103
Tools for analyzing compute usage and spend....................105
Reviewing compute costs using AWS Cost Explorer....................*106*
Correlating AWS Cost Explorer findings with Billing console....................*108*
Accessing granular data, cost, and usage reports....................*109*
AWS Trusted Advisor....................*109*
AWS Cost Optimization Hub....................*109*
Leveraging AWS Compute Optimizer....................*110*
Enabling Compute Optimizer....................*110*
Comparing AWS Compute Optimizer and Cost Optimization Hub....................*111*
Reviewing compute cost using Azure cost analysis....................*112*
Putting it all together....................*113*
Reviewing cost optimization levers for compute....................113
Understanding your workload characteristics....................*114*
Implementing elasticity to optimize compute cost....................*115*
Why elasticity matters....................*115*
Building elastic workloads....................*115*
Reviewing elasticity in your workload using AWS Cost Explorer....................*116*
Solutions for elasticity....................*117*
Best practices for Elastic workload design....................*117*
Compute modernization....................*118*
Instance modernization and upgrading to a newer generation....................*118*
Processor modernization, choosing the right processor architecture....................*119*
Operating system optimization....................*119*
Identifying modernization opportunities....................*120*
Quantifying modernization benefits....................*121*
Use AWS tools to accelerate modernization....................*122*
Planning your modernization journey....................*123*
Compute rightsizing....................*124*
AWS tools for compute rightsizing....................*124*
AWS Compute Optimizer side-by-side metric comparisons....................*126*
Planning your rightsizing journey....................*126*

Purchase options for compute cost optimization ... 127

Choosing a purchase option ... 128

Leveraging Spot Instances ... 128

Analyzing spot instance usage ... 129

Reserved Instances and Savings Plan ... 130

AWS Savings Plan ... 130

Analyze RI/SP coverage and utilization: ... 130

Developing a prioritized action plan ... 133

Sample prioritization framework ... 134

Conclusion ... 135

6. Optimizing Storage Cost ... 137

Introduction ... 137

Structure ... 137

Objectives ... 137

Cloud storage portfolio and charging mechanism ... 138

Understanding the cloud storage portfolio ... 138

Block storage ... 139

File storage ... 139

Object storage ... 139

Data protection and backup services ... 140

Anatomy of cloud storage pricing ... 140

Provisioned vs. consumed storage ... 140

Region-based pricing ... 141

Billing units ... 141

Purchase options, reserved capacity, and commitment-based discounts ... 142

Tiered pricing model ... 142

Backup charges ... 143

Tools for analyzing and optimizing storage usage ... 143

Reviewing storage costs with AWS Cost Explorer ... 145

Correlating Cost Explorer findings with Billing console ... 146

Accessing detailed data with Cost and Usage Reports ... 146

Using AWS Trusted Advisor for EBS optimization ... 147

Rightsizing EBS volumes with AWS Compute Optimizer ... 147

AWS Cost Optimization Hub ... 148

Amazon S3 Storage Lens 148
Amazon S3 Storage Class Analysis 150
Amazon S3 Inventory 151
Putting it all together 151
Levers for optimizing cloud storage cost 151
Choosing the right type of storage 152
Understanding access method and protocol 152
Frequency of access 152
Access pattern 153
Operation type is read or write 153
Performance metrics: Latency, IOPS, and throughput 153
Availability and durability requirements 154
Future growth and scalability 154
Removing idle resources 154
Unused EBS volumes 155
Unused S3 buckets 156
Rightsizing storage 156
Modernization of storage types 158
Case study: Transitioning from Amazon EBS gp2 volume to gp3 158
Identifying upgrade candidates 158
Modernizing I/O-optimized volumes 159
Identifying storage tier based on access patterns 160
Classifying data by access pattern 160
Transitioning data between storage tiers 161
Reducing costs from API calls 161
Analyzing API charges 161
Enable logging and monitoring 162
Optimize high-cost API calls 162
Optimizing backup-related charges 163
Understanding how snapshots are priced 163
Analyze your snapshot-related costs 163
Compare snapshot costs to volume storage 164
Implement regular snapshot clean-up 164
Use managed backup services 164
Using reserved capacity to lower storage costs 164

Developing a prioritized action plan....165
Sample prioritization framework....165
Conclusion....167

7. Optimizing Database Cost on Cloud....169
Introduction....169
Structure....169
Objectives....170
Understanding cloud database portfolios....170
Relational databases....171
Non-relational databases....171
Key-value stores....171
Document database....171
In-memory database....172
Graph databases....172
Time-series databases....172
Anatomy of cloud database pricing....172
Evaluating self-managed and cloud managed database options....173
Understanding database cost components....173
Purchase models....174
Region-based pricing....174
Instance types and sizes....174
Processor types....174
Billing units....175
Tools for analyzing database usage and spend....175
Gaining visibility into database usage and spend....177
Reviewing database cost using AWS Cost Explorer....177
Correlating Cost Explorer findings with Billing console....178
Accessing granular data using Cost and Usage Reports....180
AWS CloudWatch....180
Amazon RDS performance insights....181
Getting cost saving insights from tools....181
Optimization with AWS Trusted Advisor....181
Rightsizing recommendations with AWS Compute Optimizer....182
Centralized cost actions with AWS Cost Optimization Hub....183

Estimating and comparing costs 183
AWS Pricing Calculator 184
Putting it all together 184
Cost Optimization levers for cloud databases 185
Choosing the right database type 185
Choosing between relational and non-relational databases 185
Relational databases 186
Non-relational databases 186
Commercial vs. open-source databases 186
Commercial databases 187
Open-source databases 187
Self-managed vs. cloud-managed databases 187
Self-managed databases 188
Cloud-managed databases 188
Provisioned vs. serverless databases 188
Provisioned databases 189
Serverless databases 189
Rightsizing and modernization 189
Database rightsizing 190
Tools providing rightsizing recommendations 190
AWS Trusted Advisor 190
AWS Compute Optimizer 190
Database modernization 191
Instance modernization and upgrading to newer generations 192
Processor modernization and switching to cost-efficient architectures 192
Upgrading outdated database versions 193
Identifying modernization opportunities 193
AWS Billing console 193
AWS Cost Explorer 194
AWS Athena with CUR 194
Planning your rightsizing and modernization journey 195
Implementing elasticity 196
Evaluating elasticity with AWS Cost Explorer 196
Solutions to achieve elasticity in workload 197
AWS Instance Scheduler 197

Serverless databases 197

Autoscaling options for NoSQL databases 198

Optimizing storage and backup costs 198

Components of cloud database pricing 198

Optimizing storage costs 199

Optimizing backup costs 200

Understanding backup pricing 200

Best practices for reducing backup costs 200

Commitment-based savings 200

Checking RI coverage in AWS 201

Getting RI recommendations 201

Avoiding wastage from past RI purchases 203

Reviewing database architecture for cost optimization 203

Availability requirements 204

Resiliency requirements 204

Implementing caching layers 204

Query optimization 204

Developing a prioritized action plan 205

Sample prioritization framework 205

Conclusion 207

8. Optimizing Cloud Observability Cost 209

Introduction 209

Structure 209

Objectives 210

Understanding the cloud observability portfolio 210

Observability tools from major cloud providers 211

Amazon Web Services 211

Microsoft Azure 212

Google Cloud Platform 212

Pricing models for cloud observability services 213

Free Tier inclusions 213

Component-based pricing 214

Storage and retention costs 217

Analytics and insights charges 218

Rule evaluation 218

Regional pricing variation 218
Commitment-based savings 218
Tools for analyzing observability usage 218
AWS cost management tools 219
Reviewing observability costs with AWS Cost Explorer 219
Correlating Cost Explorer findings with Billing console 221
Accessing detailed data with Cost and Usage Reports 222
Azure tools for observability cost Analysis 223
Azure Cost Management + Billing 223
Log Analytics usage and costs 223
Putting it all together 224
Levers for optimizing cloud observability cost 224
General optimization principles 225
Right-size observability architecture 225
Environment-based configuration 225
Selecting cloud-native or third party observability tools 226
Commitment-based savings 227
Review storage strategies 227
Service-specific cost optimization strategies 227
Amazon CloudWatch optimization 227
AWS CloudTrail Optimization 230
AWS Config optimization 232
Azure Monitor and Log Analytics optimization 234
Optimizing observability costs for a food tech company 234
Developing a prioritized action plan 235
Sample prioritization framework 235
Conclusion 236

9. Designing Cost Effective Cloud Security Architecture 237
Introduction 237
Structure 238
Objectives 238
Understanding cloud security services portfolio 238
The shared responsibility model 238
Cloud provider responsibilities for cloud security 239

Organization responsibilities for security in the cloud 239

Third-party security services 240

Core categories of cloud security services 241

Identity and access management 241

Detective controls 242

Infrastructure protection 242

Data protection 243

Application security 243

Incident detection and response 243

Pricing models for cloud security services 244

Free Tier inclusions 244

Component-based pricing 245

Billing units 247

Regional price variations 247

Commitment-based savings 248

Exploring pricing of AWS security services 248

Amazon Cognito 248

Amazon GuardDuty 250

AWS Security Hub 251

AWS Shield Advanced 252

Exploring pricing of Azure Security Services 252

Tools for analyzing security services usage 254

AWS cost management tools 255

Identify security services in use 255

Reviewing security services costs with AWS Cost Explorer 256

Correlating Cost Explorer findings with Billing console 257

Accessing detailed data with Cost and Usage Reports 258

Azure tools for security services Cost Analysis 258

Identify Azure security services in use 258

Azure Cost Management + Billing 258

Putting it all together 259

Levers for optimizing cloud security services cost 260

General optimization principles 260

Right-size security architecture 261

Environment-based security configuration 262

Evaluating cloud-native and third party security tools 262
Leverage Free Tier inclusions 263
Use commitment-based savings where available 264
Pre-empt cost impact using free trials and simulations 264
Automate and archive logs efficiently 264
Service-specific cost optimization strategies 264
Identity and access management 264
Amazon Cognito optimization strategies 265
Detective controls 265
Amazon GuardDuty 266
Amazon Inspector 266
AWS Security Hub 267
Infrastructure protection 267
AWS Shield Advanced 267
Azure DDoS protection 268
AWS WAF 268
Azure Firewall 268
Data protection services 269
AWS Key Management Service 269
AWS Secrets Manager 269
Azure Key Vault 270
Developing a prioritized action plan 270
Sample prioritization framework 271
Conclusion 272

10. Optimizing Data Transfer Charges on Cloud 273
Introduction 273
Structure 273
Objectives 274
Understanding cloud data transfer charges 274
Categories of data transfer 275
Data transfer between the cloud and the Internet 275
Azure data transfer to the Internet, a comparable scenario 277
Data transfer between regions 277
Data transfer between availability zones in the same region 279
Data transfer within the same availability zone 279

Data transfer between services 280
Data transfer methods and their cost impact 280
Free Tier inclusions 281
Regional pricing variation 282
Commitment-based savings 282
Key factors influencing data transfer charges 282
Monitoring data transfer cost using native tools 283
Data transfer analysis in AWS 283
Reviewing data transfer costs with AWS Cost Explorer 284
Correlating Cost Explorer findings with Billing console 286
Accessing cost and usage data with CUR 287
SQL query 287
Reviewing operational metrics with AWS CloudWatch 289
AWS VPC Flow Logs 289
Data transfer analysis in Azure 290
Reviewing data transfer costs with Azure Cost Analysis 290
Corelating charges in the Azure Billing console 291
Reviewing operational metrics with Azure Monitor 291
Putting it all together 291
Levers for optimizing cloud data transfer charges 292
General optimization principles 292
Right-size application architecture 292
Match the right data transfer mechanism 293
Optimizing networking service costs 294
Identify and terminate Idle resources 294
Monitor data processing performed by networking services 295
Leverage Free Tier 295
Consider commitment-based savings 295
Service-specific cost optimization strategies 295
Optimizing data transfer for EC2 and Azure VMs 295
Optimizing data transfer for S3 and Azure Blob Storage 296
Elastic Load Balancing/Azure Load Balancer 296
Developing a prioritized action plan 297
Sample prioritization framework 297
Conclusion 299

11. Establishing Cost Governance and Guardrails 301
Introduction 301
Structure 302
Objectives 302
Cost governance overview 302
Objectives of cost governance 302
Factors influencing cost governance models 303
Key pillars of cost governance 303
Driving accountability through cost allocation 304
Importance of cost allocation 305
Organization and resource hierarchy 305
AWS Organizations 305
Key benefits of AWS Organizations 306
Azure resource hierarchy 306
Building a cost allocation model 307
Types of cloud costs 307
Approaches to allocating shared costs 308
Showback and chargeback 308
Tagging strategies for granular cost allocation 309
Understanding tags 309
Building a tagging model 309
Implementing tags in AWS 310
AWS Cost Categories 311
Implementing tags in Azure 312
Steps to implement tags in Azure 313
Viewing costs using tags 313
Tools for cost allocation 314
Setting up cost guardrails 314
Tracking spend against budgets 314
AWS budgets and alerts 315
AWS budgets pricing 315
Defining budget rules 315
Steps to create a budget in AWS 316
Implementing budgets in Azure 318
Steps to set up Azure budgets and alerts 318

Detecting anomalies in cloud usage and costs 320
AWS Cost Anomaly Detection 321
Azure Anomaly Detection 322
Steps to create a cost alert rule for anomaly detection 322
Viewing anomalies in cost analysis smart views 323
Comparing budgets and anomaly detection 323
Enforcing guardrails using policies 324
AWS service control policies 324
Azure Policies 324
Governing resource provisioning with AWS Service catalog 325
Handling cost spikes 325
Early detection using proactive monitoring 325
Allocating the cost to business units 326
Tracing the spike to services and features 326
Distinguishing genuine growth from misconfiguration 327
Applying optimization levers 327
Change management 328
Escalating to cloud providers 328
Updating budgets and guardrails 329
Building and updating a playbook 329
Creating a cost-aware culture 329
Conclusion 331

12. Advancing Cost Optimization Journey with GenAI 333
Introduction 333
Structure 333
Objectives 334
Indicators of effective cost optimization 334
Unit cost metrics 335
Summarizing the cost optimization framework 335
Cost observability 336
Cost optimization 337
Cloud cost governance 337
Applying the cost optimization framework in real-world examples 338
Unintended cost impact of network configuration changes 338

Duplicate logging leading to unexpected costs 339
Challenges in cost allocation across business units 341
Leveraging GenAI solutions for cost optimization 342
Amazon Q for cost optimization 342
Pricing for Amazon Q 343
Comparing traditional and GenAI-enabled cost optimization 344
Prerequisites for using Amazon Q 346
Understanding how to use Amazon Q for cost queries 346
Microsoft Copilot for cost optimization 347
Future of GenAI in cost optimization 348
Understanding FOCUS 349
Defining the FOCUS 349
Benefits of FOCUS 349
Enabling FOCUS data exports 350
Growing importance of FOCUS 352
Conclusion 352

Index 353-359

CHAPTER 1
Introduction to Cloud Cost Optimization

Introduction

Cloud adoption is experiencing steady growth, as evidenced by the increasing YoY revenue reported by leading cloud providers **Amazon Web Services** (**AWS**), **Microsoft Azure** (**Azure**), and **Google Cloud Platform** (**GCP**). While security and data protection remain a concern, managing cloud costs has become a top priority for organizations migrating to or operating within cloud environments. Many businesses experience unexpected cost escalations following migration from on-premise infrastructure to cloud environments, making cost optimization a critical focus area for the IT team. As businesses continue to leverage cloud technologies, understanding how to manage and control cloud spend becomes vital for long-term sustainability and financial efficiency. This chapter explores the fundamental aspects of cloud cost management and provides insights into optimizing cloud spend.

Structure

In this chapter, we will discuss the following topics:

- Evolving landscape of cloud cost management
- Introduction to cloud cost management
- Estimating cloud spend using Pricing Calculators

Objectives

By the end of this chapter, the readers will be able to understand the critical importance of cost management in cloud environments and identify key pricing components across major cloud platforms. Additionally, they will be able to recognize how architectural decisions and design choices can impact long-term cloud costs. They will analyze and navigate cloud cost structures and pricing models and use cloud cost calculators to estimate the financial impact of cloud workloads.

Evolving landscape of cloud cost management

To understand the importance of cloud cost management, let us explore a few hypothetical examples that underline the challenges organizations face when costs unexpectedly increase. These examples may resonate with you or your organization and offer valuable lessons on why cloud cost optimization is essential:

- **Example 1, the $100K bill shocker**: An e-commerce company had a critical application running on Azure, managed by a team of cloud engineers, DevOps professionals, and **site reliability engineering** (**SRE**) engineers. The application had performed flawlessly over the last month, meeting a high **service level agreement** (**SLA**) of 4-9's availability, and the operations team celebrated their success. However, the bill for the month presented a different view. When the finance team reviewed the monthly invoice, they were surprised to find a $100,000 increase compared to the previous month and the three-month average. The technical team was unaware of any significant increase in user traffic that could explain this spike and started investigating the cause. On detailed analysis, they found that the spike was due to the introduction of a **Network Address Translation** (**NAT**) Gateway in network flow from internal instances and incorrect routing changes, which led to a sharp increase in data transfer cost.

- **Example 2, a hidden $25K cost due to lack of communication between teams**: A fintech startup experienced a **distributed denial-of-service** (**DDoS**) attack. In response, the **Chief Information Security Officer** (**CISO**) and security team decided to increase logging levels and set up a real-time dashboard for monitoring. As part of this initiative, an engineer enabled AWS CloudTrail and integrated it with Amazon CloudWatch, with the understanding that the first copy of the management event is covered by the AWS Free Tier.

  Over the next three months, the security team successfully tracked user activity through API calls and deployed mechanisms to detect anomalies and mitigate security threats. However, during a routine financial audit, the team found that AWS CloudTrail costs had surged by $25,000 due to the management events generated. The CISO was asked to investigate why costs exceeded the Free Tier's limits and what led to this unexpected rise in spending. An analysis showed that the DevOps team was unaware that CloudTrail had already been enabled by the security team. They enabled the organization's trail for their project, which led to duplicate management events getting delivered and billed.

- **Example 3, difficulty in cost allocation across business units**: In another organization, the **Chief Technology Officer** (**CTO**) initiated a program to encourage **business units** (**BUs**) to optimize their cloud costs. To incentivize this, the CTO introduced a reward mechanism for those who could successfully reduce costs by 15%. However, the organization faced challenges in attributing costs to specific BUs. The finance team struggled to align cloud costs back to the respective units, and there were no governance and chargeback mechanisms in place to track and control expenditures effectively. With limited and overlapping accountability and no defined structure for cost management, the program failed to achieve its cost optimization goal.

These examples illustrate some of the common challenges faced by organizations in managing cloud costs. Cloud provides a flexible consumption and pricing model, but without monitoring and governance mechanisms in place, costs can spiral unexpectedly. When cloud costs spiral out of control, it triggers a cycle of back-and-forth communication between the finance team and the technical team to understand what went wrong.

Cloud cost management is not a one-time activity where you optimize your increased bills for the month and go back to the usual state; it is a continuous process that needs attention and awareness across the organization. All stakeholders—from cloud engineers to finance teams—need to understand cloud pricing models, usage patterns, and monitoring tools to effectively manage and control costs. There is a need to acknowledge the differences between operating in an On-premise environment and in a cloud environment. The processes, such as the procurement process and change management process, which worked well in the On-premise environment, need to be modified to align with the cloud consumption model.

As you think about your own organization, consider the following probing questions:

- *How are you ensuring that your cloud spending is aligned with the forecasted budget each month?*
- *Have you implemented tools for tracking, reporting, and optimizing cloud costs?*
- *How do u track daily/weekly/monthly cost changes?*
- *Did you get a notification for any cost spike or unexpected spending?*
- *How can we develop a culture of cost awareness among our technical team and finance team, as well as increase collaboration between different stakeholders working in a cloud environment?*
- *Does your organization evaluate cost impacts when making architectural decisions, designing solutions, or implementing changes?*

Organizations need to focus on creating a culture of cost awareness and implement tools and governance mechanisms to control cloud costs. This book provides guidance on these topics and will help you become proficient in cloud cost management practices.

Introduction to cloud cost management

The growth of cloud computing has changed how organizations provision, consume, and pay for IT resources. One of the drivers for businesses migrating to the cloud is the shift from a traditional **capital expenditure** (**CapEx**) model related to on-premise infrastructure, such as servers, storage, and data centers, to an **operational expenditure** (**OpEx**) model. This transition enables organizations to avoid high upfront costs and instead pay only for resources consumed, providing both cost and operational flexibility.

In addition to cost, cloud computing offers several distinct advantages over the traditional data center model, helping organizations deploy applications more efficiently and accelerate go-to-market timelines. Some core features of cloud environments are as follows:

- **Resource pooling/multi-tenant architecture**: Cloud providers operate multi-tenant platforms, where resources such as compute, storage, and networking are shared across multiple organizations. This shared infrastructure helps optimize costs by allowing providers to leverage economies of scale, delivering resources more efficiently to users.
- **On-demand self-service**: Cloud platforms allow users to provision, monitor, and manage resources through easy-to-use self-service consoles and **application programming interfaces** (**APIs**) published. This removes the dependency on IT administrators or system administrators for tasks like resource allocation, resource provisioning, etc.
- **Elasticity and scalability**: Cloud offers flexibility to scale resources up or down according to demand. During peak load, organizations can dynamically allocate additional resources to maintain application performance, and during the off-peak period, resources can be scaled down, optimizing cost efficiency.
- **Pay-as-you-go model**: With cloud, businesses pay only for the resources they consume. This consumption-based model enables organizations to optimize costs by eliminating the need for underutilized or idle resources. Cloud providers offer different billing units, such as per-second, per-minute, or per-hour billing, which ensures that organizations are charged only for what they use and for the duration that they use it.

Awareness of cloud features and understanding how they differ from the traditional data center is crucial for organizations to make the most of cloud services while keeping costs under control. However, one of the biggest challenges organizations face when migrating to the cloud is that they often bring legacy on-premise practices for capacity planning, availability, and scalability. This can lead to inefficient use of cloud resources and suboptimal cost management. Some key questions can help organizations assess their current cloud architecture and identify areas for improvement. Let us look at them in detail:

- **Is your workload leveraging the full elasticity and scalability of the cloud?**
    - *Are you running resources 24/7 on cloud, similar to traditional data center deployments, or do you take advantage of cloud elasticity and scalability?* In the data center model, capacity is often planned for peak usage, requiring a large upfront investment. However, in the cloud, resources can scale dynamically, meaning that you only need to provision for actual usage.
    - *Have you identified your peak usage hours? Does resource provisioning vary during peak load and off-peak load duration?*
    - *Do you stop non-production workloads during off-hours (e.g., 8 PM to 6 AM) or holidays to save costs?*

- **Are you paying for non-utilized or under-utilized resources?**

  Resource utilization directly impacts your cloud costs. One of the key benefits of cloud computing is the ability to pay only for the resources consumed. Organizations need to monitor resource utilization and remove idle and underutilized resources.

  - *How do you track and monitor resource usage?*
  - *What processes do you have to identify and eliminate idle and underutilized resources?*

- **Are you optimizing usage based on the cloud pricing model?**

  Understanding the billing unit for different cloud services (per second, per minute, per GB) and purchase options available (on-demand, savings plan, Reserved Instances) helps in optimizing your cloud spend. For example, Amazon S3 charges can be broken down into storage charges (GB per month), request and data retrieval charges (per 1,000 requests), and data transfer (per GB). An understanding of these billing components can help design cost-effective architectures.

  - *Does your team fully understand the billing components for every cloud service used, e.g., compute service (Amazon EC2, Lambda), storage service (Amazon S3)?*
  - *Are you aware of the billing unit for each service consumed (e.g., per-second, per-minute, per-hour) and how they impact your overall costs?*
  - *Have you performed ROI for on-demand versus other pricing models, such as Savings Plan and Reserved Instances?*

- **Do you have visibility into your cloud spend and a method for accurate forecasts?**

  Gaining visibility into cloud spend and a breakdown of costs at the resource level is essential for taking targeted actions and managing costs. Forecasting cost based on workload requirements and ensuring your monthly cloud spend is closely aligned with budgeted spend is a critical part of financial governance in the cloud.

  - *Do you have tools and processes in place to track detailed cloud expenditures, providing visibility into spending by services, resources, and business units?*
  - *How do you estimate costs for workloads, and how do you ensure that actual spending aligns with your forecasts?*
  - *What forecasting tools do you leverage to plan for monthly and yearly budgets?*

- **Are your operational processes aligned with cloud cost management best practices?**

  As organizations migrate to the cloud, cost management practices must be included in capacity planning, change management, and other governance and operational processes. Financial controllers and technical teams should collaborate to ensure that architectural decisions account for cost implications.

- *Does your organization include financial considerations in architecture design phases to assess potential cost impact?*
- *Are cost-related guardrails built into your cloud management processes, similar to security and operational guardrails?*

Creating a cost-aware culture

Many organizations focus on the availability, scalability, and security of workload on the cloud, but often neglect cost optimization. A common mistake observed is organizations reviewing the cloud bill at the end of the month and then spending hours to identify cost escalations. This reactive approach is not sustainable. Organizations must treat cloud cost management as a continuous process and focus on building and maintaining a cost-aware organizational culture. Some of the key elements of a cost-aware culture include well-defined cost governance mechanisms, including cost allocation and chargeback processes, adequate cost guardrails, and incident management processes. This culture should involve all stakeholders, including technical and financial teams, working collaboratively to manage cloud costs proactively. One approach many organizations are adopting is to create a **Cloud Center of Excellence** (**CCoE**). A CCoE is a cross-functional team that brings together experts from finance, technology, business units, and executive leadership. The CCoE helps define key usage and cost metrics and implement governance mechanisms for cloud cost management.

In summary, cloud cost management requires a good understanding of cloud features and services offered and an appreciation of fundamental differences with traditional data center models. Teams should be able to differentiate whether increased cloud costs are due to business growth and increased usage or are due to misconfigurations. Using usage and cost metrics, the team can understand the relationship between business growth and cloud costs, whether linear or non-linear, and take corrective actions as needed. By creating a cost-aware culture and close collaboration between different stakeholders, including technical and financial teams, organizations can ensure that they are maximizing value from cloud usage.

Primary drivers of cloud costs

In a traditional data center environment, the IT team typically develops a high-level architecture, performs capacity planning exercises, and works with the finance team to procure the required resources. These resources may include data center hosting space (if not already owned), servers, storage, networking devices, security hardware, and necessary application licenses. Once the hardware and software are procured, they can be used to host workloads, with costs remaining relatively stable month-to-month unless new hardware is acquired, old hardware is decommissioned, or a new application license or a support agreement is added.

In contrast, as discussed earlier, cloud platforms provide a consumption-based model, which is fundamentally different from the traditional data center approach. To effectively manage cloud cost, it is crucial to understand the key drivers and components of cloud costs and how the services consumed impact the **total cost of ownership** (**TCO**) of cloud deployments. Here are some of the primary factors to consider when assessing cloud costs:

- **Cloud service model**: Start by understanding the cloud service model you are planning to use—**infrastructure as a service** (**IaaS**), **platform as a service** (**PaaS**), or **software as a service** (**SaaS**). Each model determines how services are charged, what billing units are used, and what costs are included in the charges. For example:
    - If you are using a SaaS solution like an email service, the cloud provider may charge you per user account. This charge typically includes underlying infrastructure, licenses, and maintenance costs.
    - However, if you opt for IaaS and set up an email service using compute resources, you will be charged for the compute resources provisioned, storage resources consumed, and all related components leveraged to set up the email service. You must also procure application licenses and support agreements from the software vendor.

  Refer to the following figure to build a clearer understanding of cloud service models, which demonstrates the division between cloud provider-managed components (below the line) and customer-managed components:

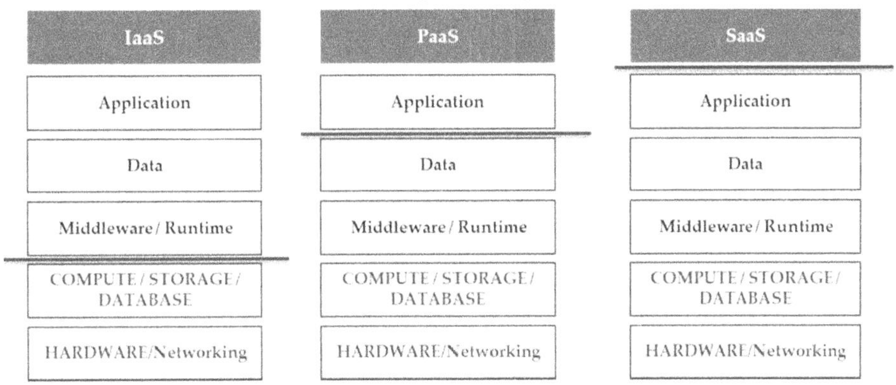

Figure 1.1: Cloud service models

- **Location-based pricing**: Cloud providers have data centers spread across the globe to help organizations meet availability, scalability, and resiliency requirements. You will come across terms like regions and availability zones. Regions are physical geographical locations where isolated data centers operate over a network. Availability zones refer to individual data centers operating over a network within a region and connected through a low-latency network. When selecting a region to deploy your workload, apart from considering factors like data residency, feature availability, and resiliency requirements, consider cost as one of the criteria. Cloud pricing varies by region. Selecting incorrect regions, along with other poor network architecture decisions for inter-region traffic, can result in excessive inter-region or inter-availability zone data transfers that significantly inflate cloud costs.

- **Services consumed and billing units**: Cloud providers are at the forefront of innovation and offer a wide array of services, each with its own billing unit. To design a cost-efficient architecture, it is crucial to break down your workload into modular components, map it to a cloud service, and analyze how each service is billed. Examples of billing units include:
    - Per-second, per-minute, or per-hour billing for compute resources.
    - Per-GB-per-month for storage services.
    - Number of requests for API calls.
    - Fixed monthly charges for some of the services deployed.

  One standard mistake organizations make when transitioning from a data center to the cloud is directly mapping the bills of materials from the data center to the cloud and failing to account for shared resources such as networking, load balancers, and security components, which can significantly impact costs. Organizations often discover missing components in their estimates only after receiving their monthly invoice from cloud providers.

- **Application licensing and support costs**: Cloud deployments often require a reassessment of application licensing and support agreements. Many software vendors have distinct licensing terms for cloud environments compared to data center deployments. Organizations must ensure compliance with these terms when migrating workloads to the cloud. Additionally, many vendors offer their software directly through cloud marketplaces, simplifying procurement and enabling usage-based billing.

- **Self-managed versus cloud-managed services**: Organizations must decide between self-managed services and cloud-managed services, as it directly impacts cost and operational complexity. When choosing between self-managed and cloud-managed services, organizations should consider several factors, such as control requirements for underlying infrastructure—server, storage, and network services, access to configuration, such as database setup configuration and logging, compliance, and vendor lock-in:
    - **Self-managed services**: The organization is responsible for deploying, managing, and maintaining the underlying infrastructure, licenses, and support agreements. For example, hosting **structured query language** (**SQL**) based databases such as Microsoft SQL Server on Azure Virtual Machines or deploying Apache Kafka on Amazon EC2.
    - **Cloud-managed services**: The cloud provider handles the above responsibilities, allowing the organization to focus on its core workloads. For example, using Azure SQL Database or Amazon Managed Streaming for Apache Kafka.

- **Scalability**: Cloud providers often offer tiered pricing, where unit costs of cloud-provided services generally decrease as resource consumption increases. When designing architecture, enterprises should consolidate consumption across business units or teams to get the advantage of scale. For example, instead of creating separate payer accounts for each team, the enterprise can create a consolidated organization structure using AWS Organization or Azure management group and provide each BU a linked account to aggregate usage and qualify for volume discounts. An appropriate organization and resource hierarchy can help in leveraging the benefits of tiered pricing models offered by cloud providers.

  Let us look at Amazon S3 pricing published on Amazon's public page to understand the tiered pricing structure :

  Note: **Pricing shown in the following figure can change, and the team should refer to the cloud provider's public pricing page for the latest information.**

Region:

US East (N. Virginia)

	Storage pricing
S3 Standard - General purpose storage for any type of data, typically used for frequently accessed data	
First 50 TB / Month	$0.023 per GB
Next 450 TB / Month	$0.022 per GB
Over 500 TB / Month	$0.021 per GB

***Figure 1.2**: Tiered pricing model*

- **Free Tier versus. paid services**: Many cloud providers, such as AWS, Azure, and Google Cloud, offer Free Tiers that allow organizations to test services during the proof-of-concept or development phase. These Free Tiers include limited usage of specific services and can significantly reduce costs during the early stages of cloud adoption. For example, AWS Free Tier offers specific services with defined limits, such as 750 hours of free EC2 usage for the first year. Refer to *Figure 1.3* to review AWS Free Tier details. Google Cloud provides free credits and access to trial resources for evaluation purposes, and the same is true with Azure:

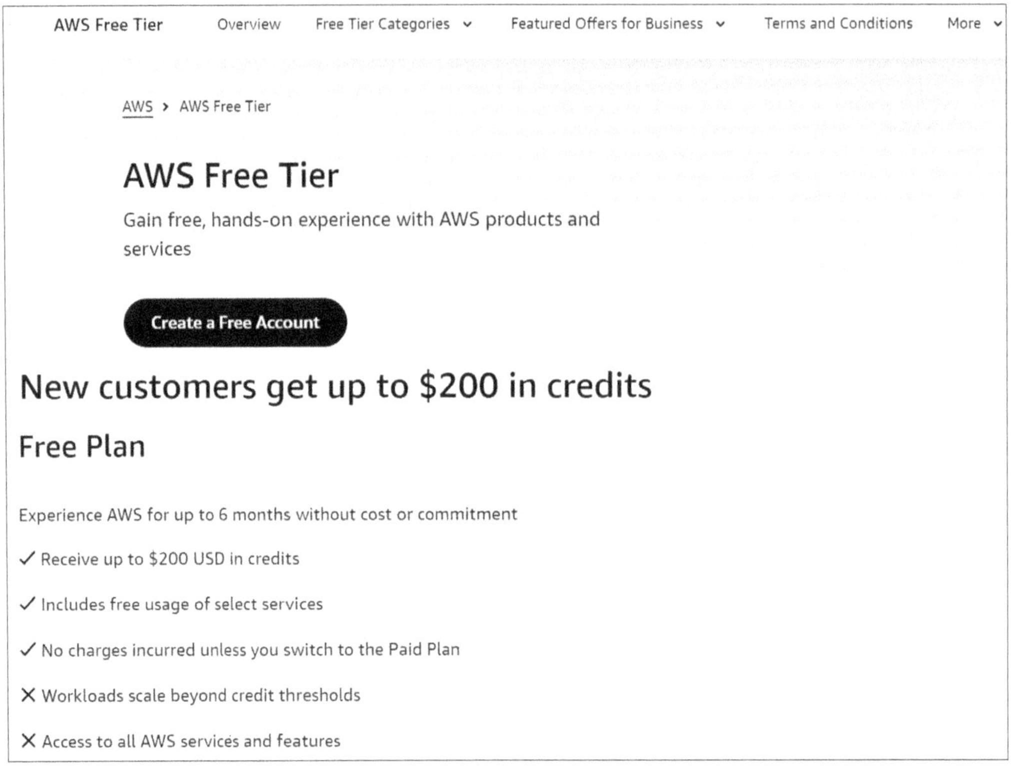

***Figure 1.3**: AWS Free Tier*

Refer to the AWS Free Tier page to understand the service limits for each service. Example, for compute service, users get 750 hours monthly of EC2 t2.micro or t3.micro instances (equivalent to running one instance continuously), with options for either Linux or Windows operating systems, including free public IPv4 addressing. Storage-wise, S3 offers 5 GB of standard storage with 20,000 GET and 2,000 PUT requests. Similarly, AWS Free Tier offers 5 GB of Amazon S3 standard storage free for 12 months, along with 20,000 GET and 2,000 PUT requests monthly. This allows new users to experience S3's secure object storage capabilities with limitations on storage space and API operations without incurring charges during the initial year.

Similar to AWS, GCP provides a Free Tier that allows users to explore and experiment with GCP services at no cost within specified monthly usage limits. It includes a 90-day free trial with $300 in credits for new users and an Always Free Tier with limited usage of key services like Compute Engine, Cloud Storage, and BigQuery. The Always Free Tier provides resources such as one e2-micro instance per month, 5 GB of standard storage. Refer to the following figure which illustrates GCP Free Tier limits:

Note: **Free Tier inclusions can change, and the user should refer to the cloud provider's Free Tier page to understand Free Tier usage limits**

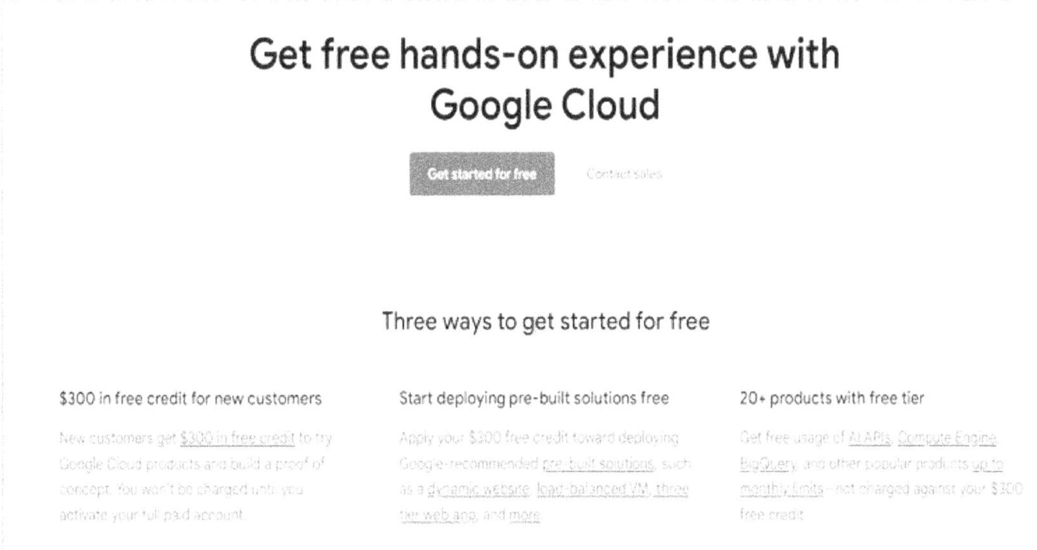

Figure 1.4: GCP Free Tier

- **Purchase options and commitment-based discounts**: Cloud providers offer various purchasing options to optimize costs compared to on-demand pricing. Organizations can evaluate their long-term requirements (e.g., 1 to 3 years) and leverage different purchase options with the required tenure to benefit from discounts offered. For example, AWS Reserved Instances and Savings Plan offer discounts over the on-demand purchase model. Many cloud providers also offer service and commitment-based discounts, and you can reach out to cloud providers for details.

  By understanding drivers impacting cloud costs, organizations can better align architecture decisions, estimate cloud costs, and develop strategies for effective cost optimization. Proactively considering these drivers will help ensure that cloud deployments and usage meet technical and financial objectives.

AWS cost structure and pricing models

This section builds on the concept discussed earlier and examines the cost structure for deploying a workload on the cloud platform. To illustrate, let us assume an organization is deploying a simple three-tier application consisting of a web tier, app tier, and **database** (**DB**) tier. The application is primarily accessed by users in India and has a data residency requirement to meet regulatory compliance. Additionally, the organization has already exhausted the AWS Free Tier and needs to estimate the cost of deploying this workload, as shown in the following figure:

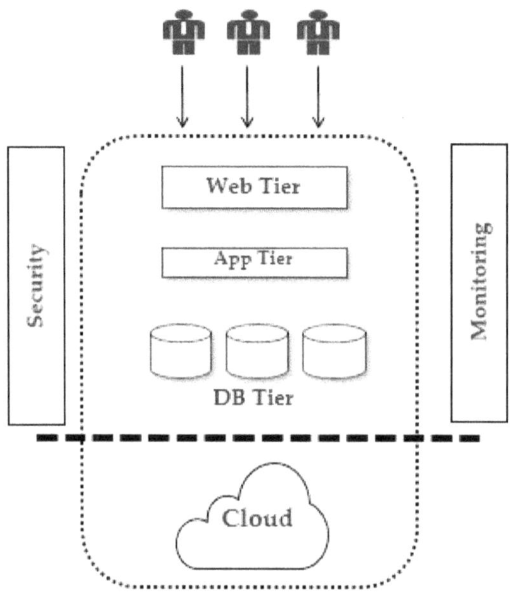

Figure 1.5: Sample three-tier application

The selection of cloud infrastructure components and their associated costs must be carefully evaluated to optimize both performance and cost-effectiveness. Let us examine some of the key architectural decisions required for deploying this three-tier application in the cloud:

- **Region selection**: Given the requirements for data residency and latency, the IT team decided to deploy the workload in an AWS region in India. AWS offers two regions in India: Asia Pacific (Mumbai) and Asia Pacific (Hyderabad). After evaluating feature availability and pricing differences, the team selected the Asia Pacific (Mumbai) region for deployment.
- **Compute services for web and app tier**: When selecting compute services for the web and app tier, AWS provides several options to match diverse workload requirements. Based on capacity planning and workload assessment, teams should select the optimal compute solution by evaluating several key factors such as whether the application is containerized or traditional, specific instance type requirements, the need for continuous availability, and anticipated resource utilization patterns. This strategic approach ensures the selected compute platform and instance size align precisely with both technical requirements and business objectives. Some commonly used compute services include:
    - **Amazon EC2**: EC2 instances are virtual servers available in various configurations optimized for different use cases. Based on capacity planning, the team can select the appropriate instance considering the **central processing unit** (**CPU**), memory, network throughput, and operating system requirements. For this workload, we selected Amazon EC2 as the compute platform as it offers the predictable

performance characteristics for our steady-state web and application tiers requirements. Additionally, EC2 provides complete control over the operating system and runtime environment, allowing our team to optimize performance and implement specific security configurations required for the application stack.

- **Serverless options**: AWS serverless services, such as AWS Lambda and AWS Fargate, enable organizations to run applications without managing the underlying virtual instances. These serverless options eliminate the need for server provisioning, maintenance, and patch management, allowing the team to focus on application code development and business logic.
- **Container services**: Teams can host containerized applications using AWS services like Amazon **Elastic Container Service** (**ECS**) or Amazon **Elastic Kubernetes Service** (**EKS**). These services offer flexibility in deploying microservice architectures.

Refer to AWS's EC2 public pricing page to determine the appropriate instance type and associated costs:

- **Database tier**: For the database tier, the organization can choose between self-managed or cloud-managed database services:
    - **Option 1, Self-Managed SQL Server on EC2**: Organizations can deploy SQL Server on Amazon EC2 instances, either **bringing their own licenses** (**BYOL model**) or opting for bundled pricing (selecting instances with OS and SQL cost included).
    - **Option 2, Amazon RDS**: It simplifies database management by handling underlying infrastructure, patching, and backups. Pricing includes licensing for SQL Server editions such as Web, Express, Standard, and Enterprise.

  Each option has different cost implications and needs to be evaluated based on workload requirements.

Refer to the following figure for a better understanding of Amazon RDS pricing:

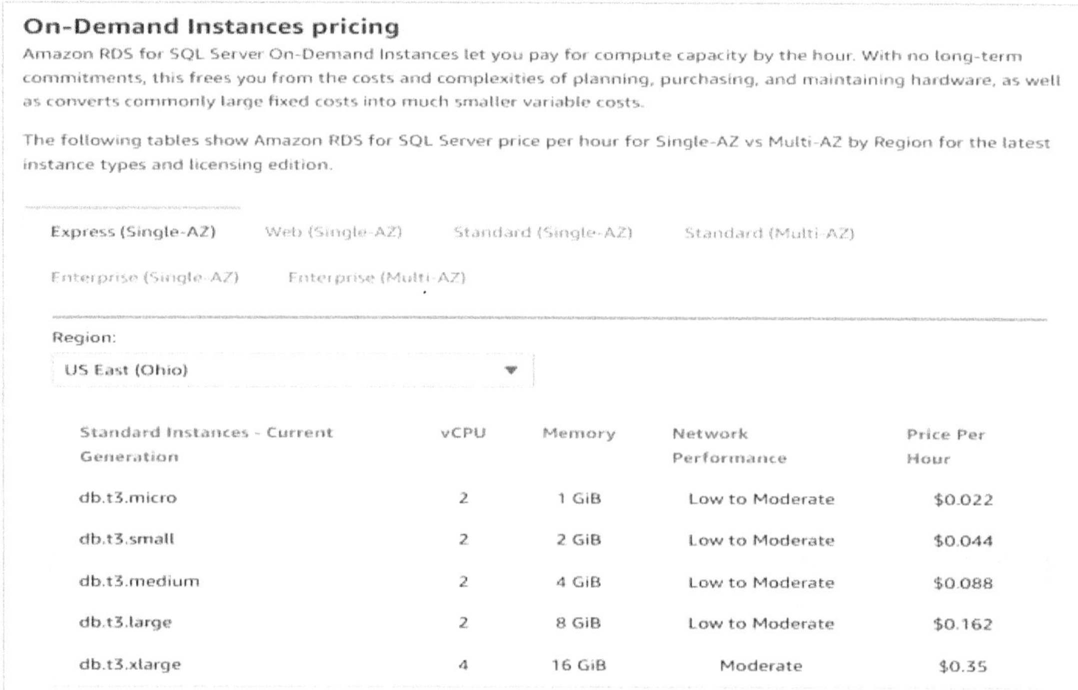

On-Demand Instances pricing

Amazon RDS for SQL Server On-Demand Instances let you pay for compute capacity by the hour. With no long-term commitments, this frees you from the costs and complexities of planning, purchasing, and maintaining hardware, as well as converts commonly large fixed costs into much smaller variable costs.

The following tables show Amazon RDS for SQL Server price per hour for Single-AZ vs Multi-AZ by Region for the latest instance types and licensing edition.

Express (Single-AZ) Web (Single-AZ) Standard (Single-AZ) Standard (Multi-AZ)

Enterprise (Single-AZ) Enterprise (Multi-AZ)

Region:

US East (Ohio)

Standard Instances - Current Generation	vCPU	Memory	Network Performance	Price Per Hour
db.t3.micro	2	1 GiB	Low to Moderate	$0.022
db.t3.small	2	2 GiB	Low to Moderate	$0.044
db.t3.medium	2	4 GiB	Low to Moderate	$0.088
db.t3.large	2	8 GiB	Low to Moderate	$0.162
db.t3.xlarge	4	16 GiB	Moderate	$0.35

Figure 1.6: Amazon RDS for SQL Server pricing

- **Additional services to consider**: Beyond compute and database resources, the following services should be factored for cost analysis, as these services are required to make application production-ready:
  - **Storage services**: AWS offers various storage solutions, including block storage, file storage, and object storage. Pricing differs based on storage type, capacity, **input/output operations per second (IOPS)**, throughput, and availability requirements. Architects need to evaluate storage requirements and pricing elements and select the right storage type from the AWS storage portfolio. For instance, Amazon **Elastic Block Store (EBS)** pricing is based on GB data stored and performance requirements, while S3 pricing depends on GB data stored and the selected storage tier. Refer to the following figure to understand the pricing of EBS storage:

Region:

US East (Ohio)

Amazon EBS Volumes

With Amazon EBS, you pay only for what you provision. The pricing for Amazon EBS volumes is listed below.

Volume Type	Price
General Purpose SSD (gp3) - Storage	$0.08/GB-month
General Purpose SSD (gp3) - IOPS	3,000 IOPS free and $0.005/provisioned IOPS-month over 3,000
General Purpose SSD (gp3) - Throughput	125 MB/s free and $0.040/provisioned MB/s-month over 125
General Purpose SSD (gp2) Volumes	$0.10 per GB-month of provisioned storage
Provisioned IOPS SSD (io2) - Storage	$0.125/GB-month
Provisioned IOPS SSD (io2) - IOPS	$0.065/provisioned IOPS-month up to 32,000 IOPS
	$0.046/provisioned IOPS-month from 32,001 to 64,000 IOPS
	$0.032/provisioned IOPS-month for greater than 64,000 IOPS
Provisioned IOPS SSD (io1) Volumes	$0.125 per GB-month of provisioned storage AND $0.065 per provisioned IOPS-month
Throughput Optimized HDD (st1) Volumes	$0.045 per GB-month of provisioned storage
Cold HDD (sc1) Volumes	$0.015 per GB-month of provisioned storage

***Figure 1.7**: Storage—EBS pricing*

- **Network charges**: Understand different network charges associated with workload, such as the following:
  - Public IP charges for attaching to EC2 instances.
  - Data transfer costs (e.g., between instances across availability zones or regions).
  - **Virtual private network** (**VPN**) costs for secure remote access.
- **Load balancers**: AWS provides load balancer options such as **Application Load Balancer** and **Network Load Balancer** (**NLB**) for your workload deployments. Each has distinct features and pricing structures. Select the appropriate load balancers as per workload requirements.
- **Security services**: Depending on compliance and regulatory requirements, organizations can deploy various security services such as **AWS Shield Advanced** for DDoS protection or **Amazon GuardDuty** for threat detection. Each security service has its own billing unit, with some services getting charged on a monthly basis while some are charged based on usage or data ingested.
- **Tools for monitoring and operations**: AWS offers native tools like **Amazon CloudWatch** for monitoring, **AWS Systems Manager** for operations, and a set of tools for cost management. These tools may have both free and paid tiers, depending on usage. You can evaluate their features and choose between the tools available in the market or the native tools and services provided by AWS.

- **Application licensing and support costs**: Organizations need to account for software licensing and support costs for the application being deployed, which can be procured either directly from vendors or via the AWS Marketplace.
- **AWS purchase options**: AWS services like EC2 and RDS offer multiple purchase options that can significantly optimize costs. The default on-demand purchase option can be 30-40% more expensive than other options. One of the key decision elements is to use an on-demand pricing model or leverage another pricing model, such as Reserved Instances, to optimize cost.
    - **Amazon EC2 purchase options**: On-demand pricing, spot instances, Savings Plan, and Reserved Instances for long-term commitments.
    - **Amazon RDS pricing options**: On-demand instances and Reserved Instances (for long-term savings).

This section provided an overview of cloud cost structures and emphasized how architectural decisions directly impact overall costs. While AWS was used to illustrate how applications can be broken down into different services to understand cost components, the same approach applies to other cloud platforms, such as Microsoft Azure and Google Cloud. For workloads deployed across these platforms, it is important to identify equivalent services and review their respective pricing models to ensure cost efficiency. In the upcoming chapters, we will explore comparable services from different cloud providers and examine the cost structure.

Given the rapid pace of innovation across AWS, Azure, and Google Cloud, organizations should continuously review new services from their chosen provider to modernize their workloads and achieve better price-performance ratios.

Estimating cloud spend using Pricing Calculators

Accurate cost estimation is critical for organizations planning to deploy workloads on the cloud. A well-calculated estimate ensures that the monthly invoice aligns closely with budgeted expenses, minimizing unexpected variances. Cloud providers offer Pricing Calculators to help businesses estimate costs, evaluate service and pricing options, and assess the financial impact of various deployment choices. For example, Pricing Calculators can help compare costs between different instance types, storage solutions, and pricing models such as on-demand and Reserved Instances.

The initial step in estimating cloud spend is to break down the high-level architecture into modular components and map them to relevant cloud services. Once this mapping is complete and capacity planning has been conducted, the details can be put into the Pricing Calculator for a monthly cost estimate.

AWS Pricing Calculator

The AWS Pricing Calculator provides insights to help organizations make informed decisions about workload deployment on AWS. Let us use the calculator to estimate the cost of deploying the three-tier application discussed earlier. For this demonstration, we will assume the on-demand purchase option.

Here is a sample configuration:

- **Region**: Asia Pacific (Mumbai)
- **Web tier**: 2 EC2 instances (2 vCPU, 4 GB RAM, Linux)
- **App tier**: 2 EC2 instances (4 vCPU, 8 GB RAM, Linux)
- **Database tier**: Amazon RDS (SQL Server, Enterprise Edition)
- **Storage**: 50 GB EBS per instance, 500 GB Amazon S3
- **Data transfer**: 1 GB/hour outbound from the Web Tier
- **Load balancer (LBR)**: 1

Follow these steps to use the AWS Pricing Calculator:

1. **Access the tool**: Open the **AWS Pricing Calculator** by going to AWS public pages or at **https://calculator.aws/#/**.
2. **Create an estimate**: Click **Create estimate** to begin:

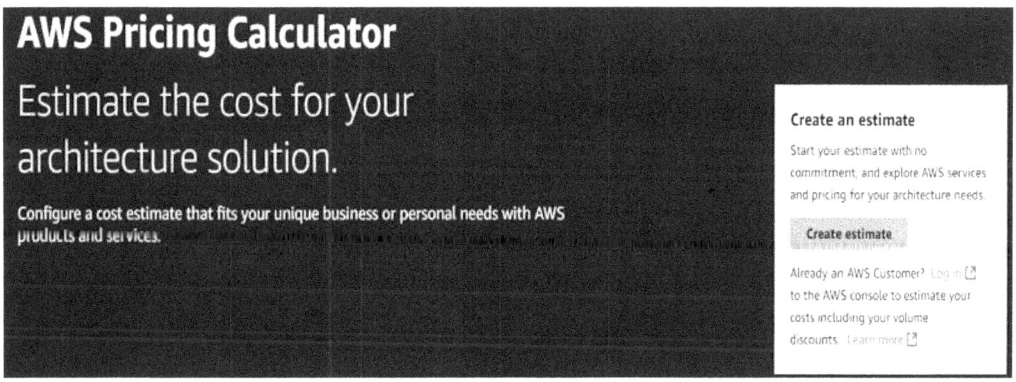

Figure 1.8: AWS Pricing Calculator

3. Configure compute services:
   a. Select the **Asia Pacific (Mumbai)** region.
   b. Add EC2 instances for the web and app tiers, choosing the appropriate instance types and on-demand pricing.
   c. Include associated services such as EBS storage and data transfer costs.

The following figure shows how you can select and configure various services to calculate your total deployment costs:

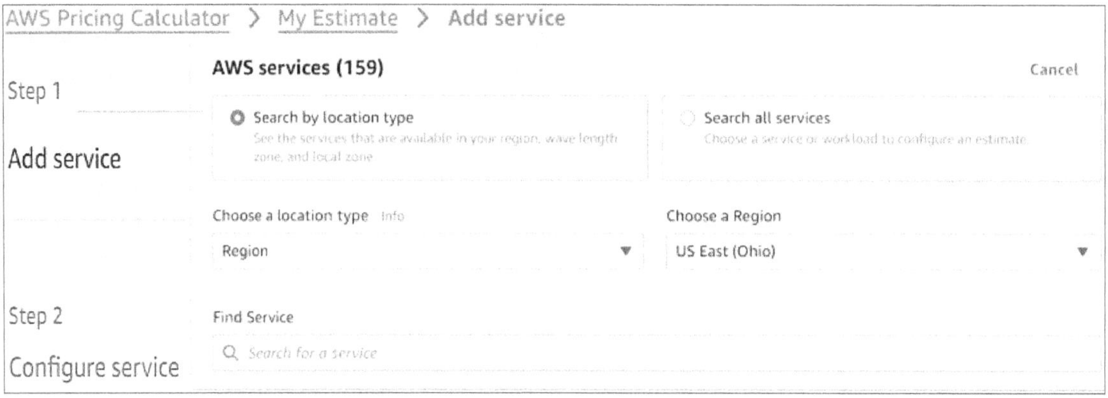

***Figure 1.9**: Pricing Calculator and adding service details*

On the **Add service** page, search for **EC2** service and then select **Configure**. You will be asked to enter details for the service selected (Amazon EC2 in this instance), such as:

- Region
- Operating system
- **Tenancy**: Shared, dedicated instances, dedicated hosts
- Number of instances to be launched
- Instance family and instance size
- Purchase options

You can also add related services such as Amazon EBS, data transfer, and detailed monitoring by providing related service details. A snapshot showing some of the EC2 service details to be added is shown in the following figure:

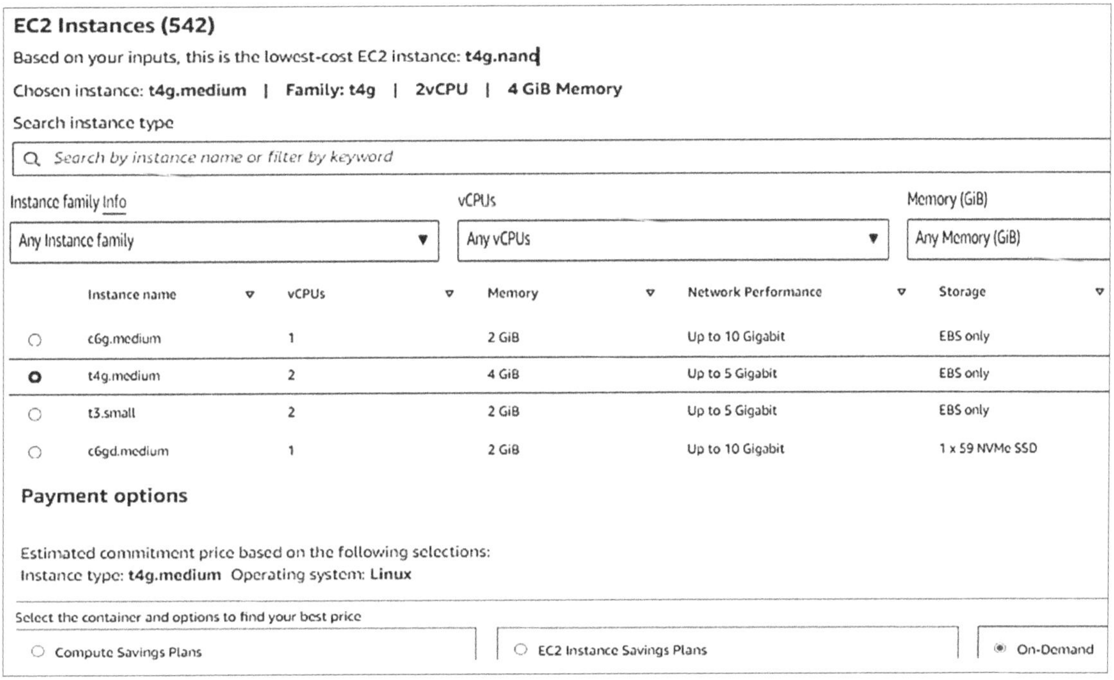

Figure 1.10: Pricing Calculator EC2 service configuration

4. Once you add all the details, you will be able to view the total upfront cost and total monthly costs. Let us add more services, such as a database, by selecting **Save and add service**.

    - **Add database**: Add Amazon RDS for the database tier, specifying the SQL Server edition and instance type.
    - **Add other services**: Add storage (Amazon S3) and other required services like Load Balancer.
    - **View summary**: After configuring all services, click **View Summary** to review monthly and annual cost breakdowns by service. Use the **Edit** option to adjust inputs as needed.

    The detailed cost breakdown allows teams to analyze the financial impact of their workload deployment and make adjustments to optimize costs.

5. **Export or share the estimate**: The estimate can be exported in formats like **comma separated values** (**CSV**), PDF, or **JavaScript Object Notation** (**JSON**), or shared with team members for collaboration.

    As shown in the following figure, the AWS Pricing Calculator provides a comprehensive estimate summary that breaks down estimated expenses across all selected services:

***Figure 1.11**: Estimate summary of Pricing Calculator*

Azure Pricing Calculator

Azure Pricing Calculator helps organizations estimate costs for workloads deployed on Azure. This free Pricing Calculator helps answer questions like *What will be the total cost of running a workload on Azure*? and supports budgeting and financial planning for Azure consumption.

Refer to the following steps to use the Azure Pricing Calculator:

1. **Access the tool**: Visit the Azure website and navigate to the pricing section to open the Azure Pricing Calculator.
2. **Select products**: Based on the high-level architecture, select Azure services. For example:
   a. Add **virtual machines (VMs)** for the web and app tiers: select **Virtual Machines** and click **Add to estimate**.

Refer to the following figure to search for the product to be added:

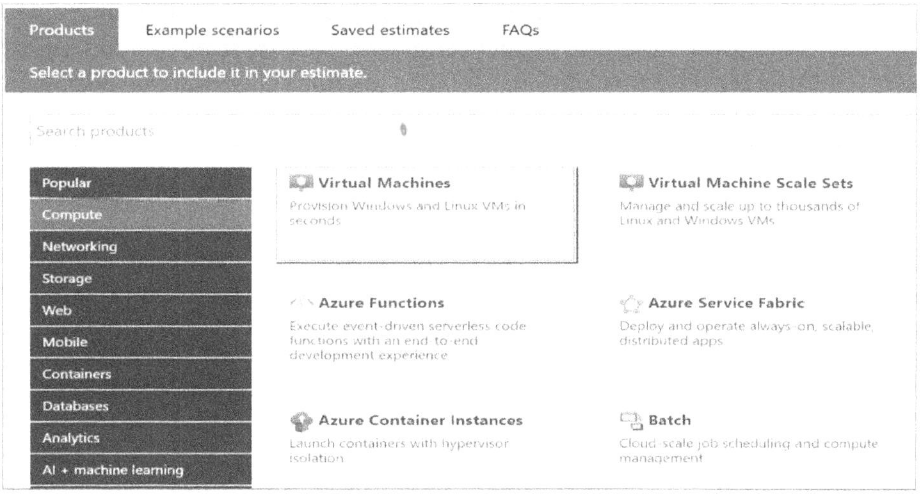

Figure 1.12: *Azure Pricing Calculator*

Similar to the AWS Pricing Calculator, when you select **Virtual Machines**, you will be asked to enter related service details such as:

- Region
- OS
- Instance family and size
- Number of VMs
- Savings options, etc.

Refer to the following figure

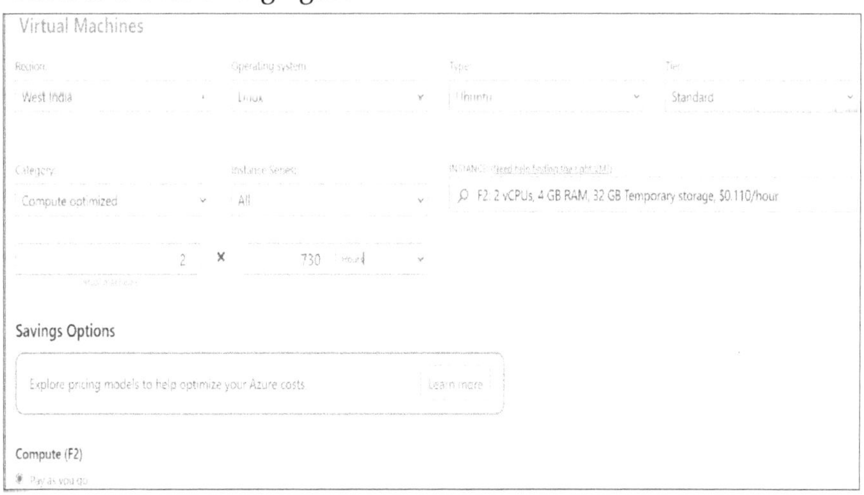

Figure 1.13: *Adding VM details for web tier and app tier*

b. **Add database tier**: Azure SQL—select **Azure SQL Database** and click **Add to estimate**. In the **Azure SQL Database** section of the **Estimate Page**, provide details such as **Region, Purchase Model, Compute Tier, Hardware Type, Instance type,** and **Disaster Recovery** options. Refer to the following figure to add Azure SQL to the estimate:

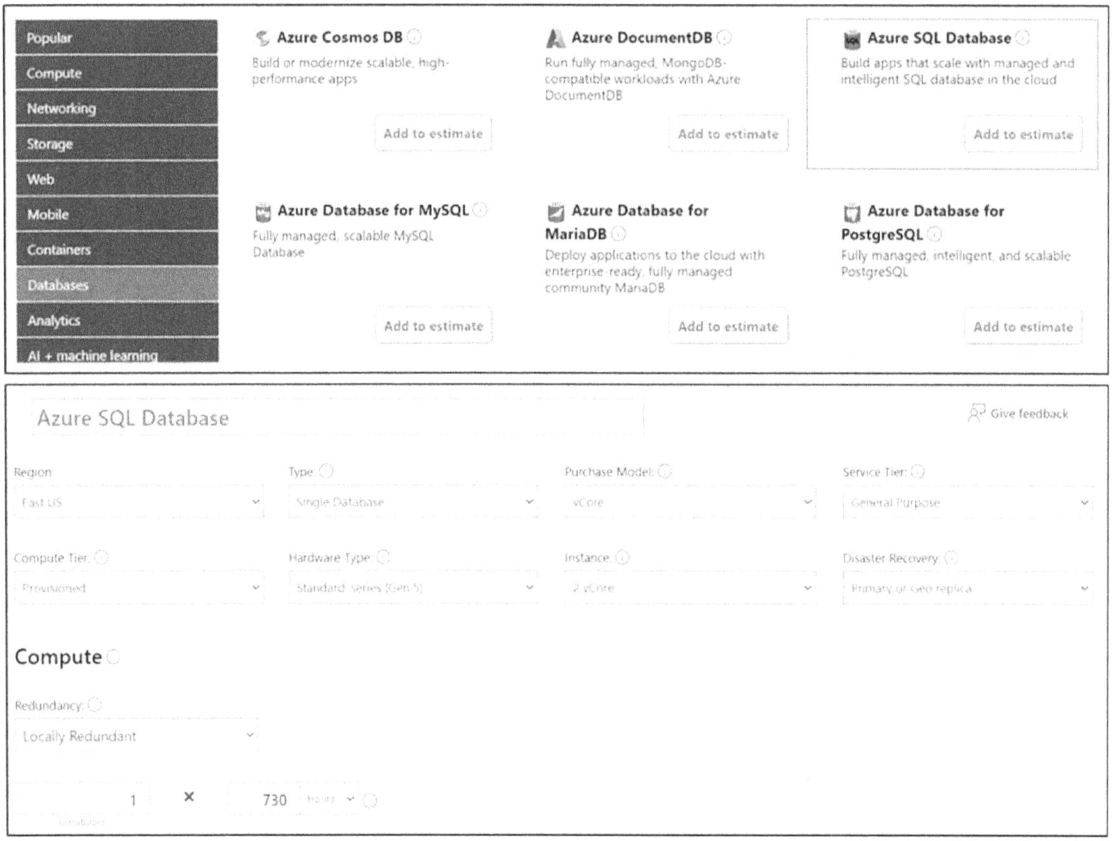

Figure 1.14: Estimating Azure SQL Cost

c. Add other services to the estimate, such as Storage—Managed Disks, Networking—Load Balancers, or Application Gateways.

3. **Review costs**: Once all products are added, scroll down to view the estimated monthly cost.

4. **Adjust and export**: Change parameters like currency or export the estimate to an Excel sheet for further analysis.

Conclusion

For organizations starting their journey on the cloud, understanding the basics of cloud cost management is essential. This includes identifying cost drivers, billing components, and pricing models. Aligning architectural decisions with cloud service features is critical to managing costs effectively. The organization also needs to understand that cost optimization is not a one-time activity and needs to create a cost-aware culture. Throughout this chapter, we have seen how effective cloud cost management requires collaboration across the organization. When technical teams and financial stakeholders work together, organizations can better monitor, control, and optimize their cloud investments, ensuring sustainable cost management for the long term.

In the next chapter, we will explore native cloud cost management tools such as AWS Cost Explorer, AWS Billing console, AWS Data Exports, Azure Cost Management + Billing, and Azure Cost Analysis. These tools provide real-time visibility into cloud spending, helping organizations track actual usage, identify cost anomalies, and analyze historical trends across their cloud deployments. By leveraging these native tools, teams can gain actionable insights to improve cost efficiency and maintain better control over their cloud budgets.

Join our Discord space

Join our Discord workspace for latest updates, offers, tech happenings around the world, new releases, and sessions with the authors:

https://discord.bpbonline.com

CHAPTER 2
Gaining Visibility into Cloud Costs Using Native Tools

Introduction

In *Chapter 1, Introduction to Cloud Cost Optimization,* we discussed how cloud cost management has become critical for organizations migrating their infrastructure and applications to the cloud. One key aspect of effective cost management is gaining visibility into cloud spending. This visibility is essential for understanding and controlling cloud expenses and serves as a cornerstone for informed budgeting and optimization strategies. Without proper insight, organizations struggle to control expenses, allocate budgets effectively, and optimize their cloud usage. This chapter focuses on some of the native cost management tools offered by leading cloud providers such as AWS and Microsoft Azure to help organizations gain better visibility into their cloud usage and spend.

Structure

In this chapter, we will discuss the following topics:

- Using native tools for cost visibility
- Navigating your monthly AWS Billing invoice
- Leveraging AWS Cost Explorer to analyze usage and spend trends
- Understanding AWS Cost and Usage Reports
- Azure Cost Management + Billing overview
- Bringing it all together

Objectives

By the end of this chapter, the readers will understand when and how to leverage various cost management services to track, analyze, and optimize cloud expenses. They will learn to navigate and utilize some of the native tools from AWS and Azure. The chapter strengthens their understanding of AWS Billing console, **AWS Cost Explorer**, **Azure Cost Management**

+ Billing, etc., enabling them to conduct detailed spending analysis and interpret crucial cost metrics that drive business decisions. The readers will also learn how to set up and configure AWS **Cost and Usage Reports** (**CUR**) for granular, resource-level cost tracking. The understanding of native cost management tools will set up a foundation for cost optimization strategies as we continue on our journey of cloud cost optimization.

Using native tools for cost visibility

Different stakeholders within an organization have varying requirements for cloud spend visibility. For executives such as CxOs and IT heads, high-level insights into overall cloud costs, monthly trends, and expenditure by business units are essential. These metrics help in strategic planning, resource allocation, and long-term budgeting. For instance, executives often rely on **year-over-year** (**YoY**) or **quarter-over-quarter** (**QoQ**) comparisons to forecast future spending and adjust business priorities accordingly.

Finance teams, on the other hand, focus on the granular details of monthly invoices, billing structures, and cost fluctuations. They require granular information about service usage, pricing tiers, and any unusual spending patterns that might indicate billing anomalies or require investigation, such as potential billing errors. Similarly, department heads have more focused requirements, primarily concerning their specific area of operations. For example, a manufacturing department head would be particularly interested in the costs associated with applications and services supporting their manufacturing processes rather than the entire organization's cloud spending.

From a technical team perspective, cloud engineers and DevOps teams require detailed visibility into individual resource costs, utilization levels, and performance metrics. These insights enable them to identify inefficiencies, such as over-provisioned resources or idle services, and implement optimization measures to reduce costs significantly.

The complexity of cloud billing and the diverse needs of different organizational roles necessitate comprehensive visibility into cloud spending patterns. To address these requirements, major cloud providers offer native tools and dashboards that provide extensive visibility into cloud spending. Examples include AWS Cost Explorer, Microsoft Azure Cost Management + Billing (Cost Analysis), and Google Cloud's Cost Management platform. These tools provide features such as:

- Granular breakdowns of costs by service and resource.
- Usage trends and forecasting capabilities.
- Budgeting tools with alerts and notifications.
- Metrics for resource utilization.
- Recommendations for cost-saving opportunities.

While these native tools serve as an excellent starting point for achieving visibility, they may not always meet the organization's specific reporting needs. Businesses with complex multi-cloud environments or unique reporting requirements may supplement native tools with third-party solutions or custom-built reporting frameworks.

In the following sections, we will build a comprehensive understanding of native cost visibility tools, starting with AWS Billing and AWS Cost Explorer before turning to the Azure Cost Management + Billing service.

Navigating your monthly AWS Billing invoice

The monthly billing invoice from a cloud provider is a crucial document for the finance team and executives. It provides a detailed breakdown of cloud usage, associated charges, and any applicable discounts and credits. Understanding these invoices is essential for tracking cloud spending, ensuring budget alignment, and identifying spending anomalies. Let us explore some key components of a cloud billing invoice and understand how they help organizations manage cloud expenses effectively:

- **Monthly usage and charges**: Organizations using cloud services consume multiple resources, such as virtual machines (Amazon EC2), storage, and networking. The billing invoice provides visibility into these services, breaking down consumption based on billing units. For example, it shows the total running hours of EC2 instances, the amount of storage used in gigabytes per month, and data transfer volumes for network-related charges. This breakdown helps organizations understand how much cloud resources they are consuming and what they pay for.
- **Pricing units and cost calculations**: Cloud providers use different pricing models, including Free Tiers and paid plans. The invoice helps determine whether an organization's consumption stays within the Free Tier limits or exceeds them. Beyond the Free Tier, most cloud services follow a tiered pricing model where unit costs decrease as usage increases. Finance teams can analyze the cost per unit of service and compare it with their cloud provider agreements to ensure pricing accuracy. Finance teams can easily verify if charges in the billing invoice align with their negotiated rates and agreements.
- **Recurring and subscription-based charges**: Many organizations subscribe to third-party applications from a cloud marketplace. These subscriptions typically incur recurring monthly charges. Monthly invoices capture all recurring charges, including marketplace subscriptions, Reserved Instances monthly payments, and monthly support charges. This helps organizations in tracking their ongoing financial commitment.
- **One-time charges and upfront payments**: Certain cloud services require one-time payments or upfront costs. For example, when purchasing a Reserved Instance for a one—or three-year term, there is an option for partial or full upfront payment, which will be reflected in the next billing cycle. Similarly, some third-party services from the cloud marketplace offer one-time licensing fees. The invoice will reflect these charges, helping the finance team account for all expenses and differentiate between recurring and one-time costs.

- **Credits and discounts**: Cloud providers often offer credits and discounts based on long-term contracts, migration incentives, or promotional offers. The organization may receive credits for testing new services or discounts based on its spending commitment. The invoice provides a view of all applied credits and discounts, allowing businesses to ensure they are receiving the expected cost reductions as per their cloud provider agreement.

Billing invoices summarize an organization's cloud spending, similar to an on-premise IT bill of materials. They highlight which services contribute the most to overall cost and are a starting point for deeper cost analysis. By carefully reviewing invoices, an organization can identify spending trends, validate pricing agreements, and explore opportunities for cost optimization.

AWS Billing and Cost Management dashboard

The AWS Billing and Cost Management dashboard is a centralized platform for organizations to track and manage their cloud spending. It combines various financial management features in a user-friendly interface, making it easier to monitor spending, analyze costs, and plan budgets effectively. You can access AWS Billing and Cost Management, as shown in *Figure 2.1*, by logging into the AWS Management Console, clicking on your account name in the top right corner, and then selecting Billing and Cost Management from the dropdown menu.

The dashboard is divided into key sections, each serving a specific purpose:

- **Billing and payments**: This section provides access to monthly invoices, allowing users to view detailed bills, download invoices in PDF format, and maintain billing records for compliance and analysis. It also manages payment methods and tracks AWS credits, including promotional discounts.

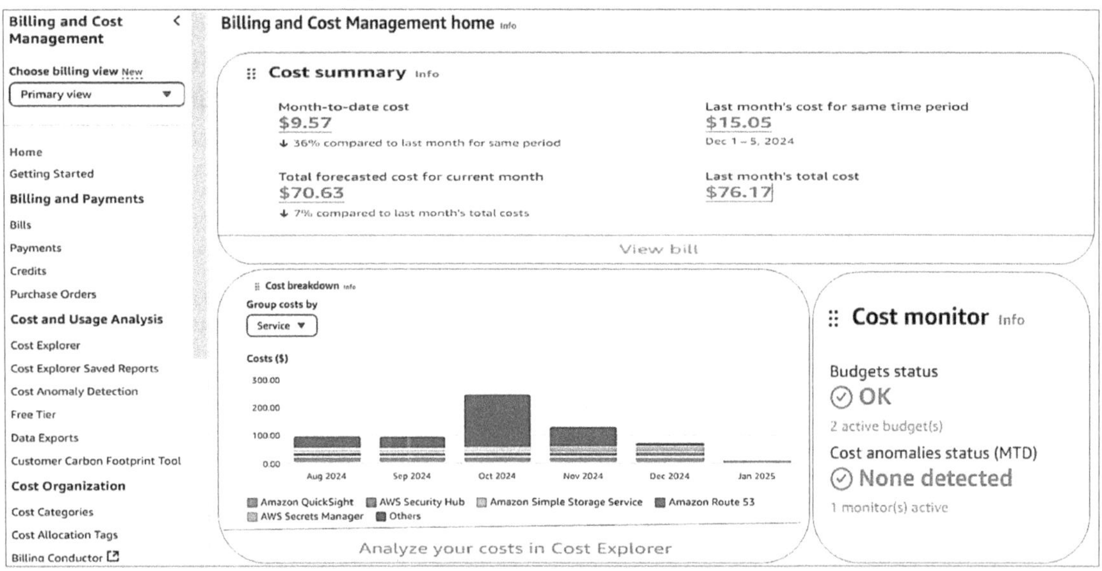

Figure 2.1: Billing and Cost Management overview

- **Cost and usage analysis**: This section provides detailed insights into cloud spending. Organizations can analyze service costs, resource utilization, and account-level expenses using tools like **AWS Cost Explorer**. It also supports data exports in **comma-separated values (CSV)** format, enabling integration with other systems for deeper analysis.
- **Cost organization**: AWS offers cost-tracking tools like cost allocation tags and consolidated billing. Users can assign tags to monitor expenses by project, department, or application. Additionally, consolidated billing allows organizations to manage multiple accounts under a single payment structure, simplifying cost tracking. Cost categories enable further customization by grouping expenses based on business needs.
- **Budgets and planning**: This section helps organizations proactively manage cloud expenses by setting budgets based on cost or usage metrics. A notification system alerts stakeholders when spending approaches or exceeds defined thresholds, enabling timely interventions and cost control measures.
- **Preferences and settings**: Users can configure payment preferences, tax settings, invoice options, and cost management features to align with their organizational policies.

The AWS Billing and Cost Management homepage has multiple visualizations that provide immediate insights into your cloud spending patterns and resource usage. Some of the key views are as follows:

- **Cost summary**: Displays current and forecasted costs to help plan future expenses.
- **Cost breakdown**: This shows spending trends across top AWS services over six months.
- **Cost monitor**: Budget tracking capabilities, providing status updates and alerts when spending limits are approached.
- **Saving opportunities**: Identifies potential cost optimization strategies by analyzing usage patterns.

The customizable homepage allows users to adjust views and metrics based on their specific monitoring needs.

Managing access to AWS Billing and cost data

Billing and cost information in AWS is confidential and should not be accessible to all users. Exposing this data could give malicious actors insights into your services, potentially revealing your region, account details, and system architecture. By default, only the root user (account owner) can view and manage billing data, while IAM users do not have access unless expressly granted.

There are two mechanisms to grant access to billing data:

- **Service control policies** (**SCPs**) for organization-wide controls.
- AWS account owners can grant IAM users or roles access to billing and cost data by enabling IAM access to billing and attaching the necessary IAM policies.

IAM users can only access billing information if the account owner activates IAM access and assigns the proper permissions. The AWS documentation provides detailed instructions on setting this up.

AWS Billing console, starting point for cost optimization

The AWS Billing console serves as a launchpad for organizations to begin their cost optimization journey. It provides detailed insights into AWS spending, helping users analyze costs, track usage trends, and identify optimization opportunities. Some of the key features of the AWS Billing console:

- Access to current and historical billing data.
- Track spending patterns across different periods.
- Identify high-cost services and linked accounts.
- Analyze service-specific charges, including billing units (e.g., per running hour, per GB).
- Pricing unit vs. expected contract pricing.
- Regional usage and associated costs.

To analyze your AWS charges, navigate to the **Billing** page by selecting **Bills** under the AWS Billing and Cost Management dashboard. This page provides a monthly view of your chargeable costs, along with a breakdown of AWS service usage charges and AWS Marketplace purchases. By default, the dashboard displays month-to-date costs, but you can select a different billing period using the dropdown at the top-right corner. Refer to the following figure:

Figure 2.2: AWS Billing console overview

Some key data to focus on are:

- **AWS estimated bills summary**: This section provides an overview of:
  - Billing period and account ID
  - Bill status (issued/pending)
  - Total charges
- **Highest estimated costs by service and region**: This section highlights top-spending services and areas, making it easier to identify cost movers.
- **Charges by service**: This is the first tab in the Billing console page and provides a breakdown of costs by AWS service, helping you analyze:
  - Top services by spend.
  - Any new services being adopted in the month.
  - Distribution of service usage by region.
    - **Example**: To analyze Amazon EC2 costs, expand the EC2 section, as shown in *Figure 2.3*. The charges are segregated by region. The cost breakdown includes total running hours, billing units (per hour), and pricing per unit.

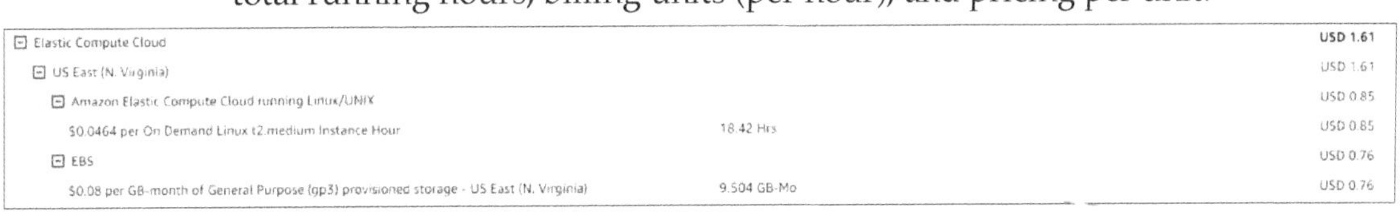

Figure 2.3: AWS Billing and EC2 charge overview

- **Charges by account (for management accounts)**: This section provides visibility into spending across all linked accounts in an AWS Organization. It helps identify which linked accounts are incurring the highest charges.
- **Downloading invoices**: To download invoices:
    - Navigate to the **Invoices** tab.
    - Select the billing period.
    - Download the PDF invoice, which includes charges by service and discounts applied.
    - You can also view and download Tax Invoices from the **Tax Invoices and Additional Documents** section.

The AWS Billing console provides high-level insights into cloud spend and helps in the initial analysis and tracking of cloud expenses effectively. Regularly reviewing your bills can help detect anomalies, optimize spending, and improve cost efficiency across AWS environments.

Leveraging AWS Cost Explorer to analyze usage and spend trends

AWS Cost Explorer and Billing console serve different purposes in managing and analyzing AWS spending, though they complement each other in providing a comprehensive cost management solution. While AWS Billing and monthly invoices provide insights about charges, unit pricing, and applied discounts, AWS Cost Explorer offers a more interactive and analytical approach to cost management. Here is a summary of the two tools:

- **Billing console**: This tool is primarily used by finance teams to view total charges, payment details, and applied discounts, ensuring that the right costs are allocated and accounted for. They help track spend per billing unit, pricing per unit, and verify if scaling discounts, credits, or contractual pricing have been applied.
- **AWS Cost Explorer**: This tool is designed for IT engineers and cloud professionals who need deeper cost insights. Instead of just summarizing charges, it provides an intuitive graphical interface to analyze spend across multiple dimensions, such as service type, linked accounts, and regions.

Let us look into some of the features provided by AWS Cost Explorer:

- **In-depth cost analysis**: AWS Cost Explorer makes complex cost data easy to understand through visual displays and analyzes spending patterns.
- **Data export for offline analysis**: Allows downloading cost and usage data in CSV format for further processing and integration with external tools.

- **Looking into the future**: AWS Cost Explorer enables you to forecast spend for the next 3 to 12 months based on historical usage trends. These forecasts help organizations set budgets, create alerts, and manage financial planning proactively.
- **Granular data**: Cost Explorer supports hourly, daily, and monthly data granularity, helping users understand cost spikes, peak usage periods, and outliers.

AWS Cost Explorer pricing considerations

Before leveraging AWS Cost Explorer, it is important to understand its pricing structure. There are two key factors that can impact Cost Explorer pricing:

- **Lookback period**: The default historical data retention is 14 months, but it can be extended to 38 months for deeper trend analysis, such as year-over-year or quarter-on-quarter comparisons.
- **Data granularity**: Cost Explorer supports hourly, daily, and monthly data granularity. While monthly and daily granularity are free, Hourly granularity is a paid option that supports retaining up to 14 days of past data. Charges depend on the number of usage records generated. For example, running one EC2 instance for 24 hours generates 24 usage records (hourly data), incurring charges accordingly. Hourly granularity helps identify business peak usage trends and detect unexpected cost spikes (outliers).

  To enable extended lookback periods or hourly data granularity, go to the **Preferences** section in **AWS Cost Explorer**. The interface will display the applicable charges before activation, as illustrated in the following figure:

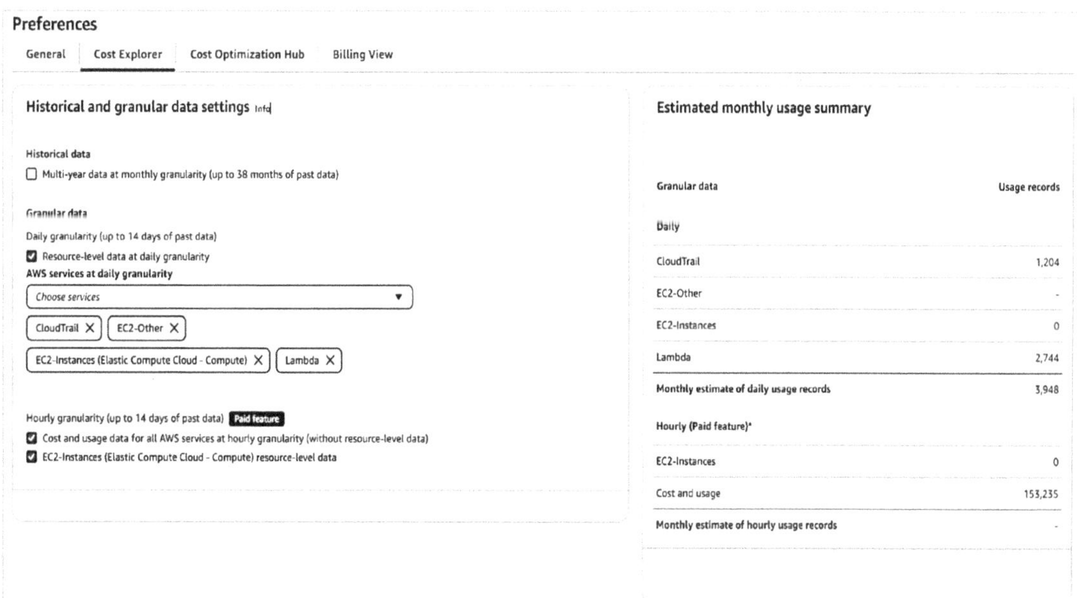

***Figure 2.4**: AWS Cost Explorer preferences*

For detailed pricing, refer to the AWS Cost Explorer pricing page.

Getting started with AWS Cost Explorer

There are two options to easily access AWS Cost Explorer:

- **Option 1**: Navigate through the **Billing and Cost Management** console and select **Cost Explorer** under the **Cost and Usage Analysis** section.
- **Option 2**: Type `Cost explorer` in the AWS Services search bar.

Refer to *Figure 2.5* for guidance on both launch options:

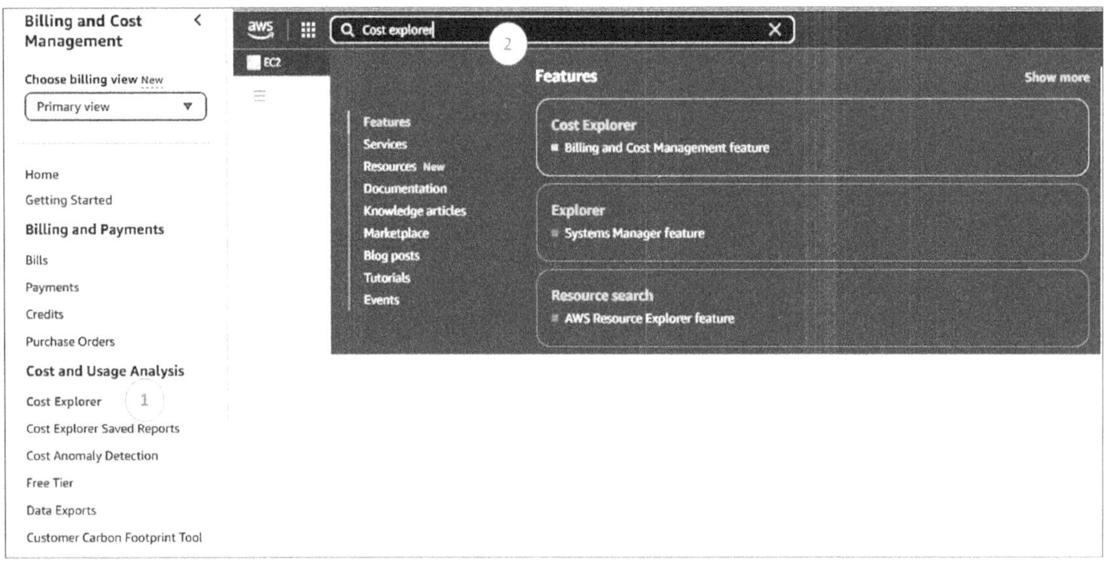

***Figure 2.5**: Launching AWS Cost Explorer*

You can customize your analysis using the report parameters available when accessing AWS Cost Explorer. Let us review some of the report parameters available:

- **Date range**: Select past or future dates for forecasting (default: the last six months). This parameter can be changed to the appropriate duration of the analysis.
- **Granularity**: Choose hourly, daily, or monthly data.
- **Group by dimensions**: Analyze costs by service, linked account, region, API, etc. This parameter helps find the cost trend according to the Dimension selected.
- **Filters**: Narrow down results by selecting specific services or accounts. For example, to analyze EC2 spending for a particular account, set the **Service** filter to **EC2-Instances** and set **Linked account** filter to the account that you want to check:

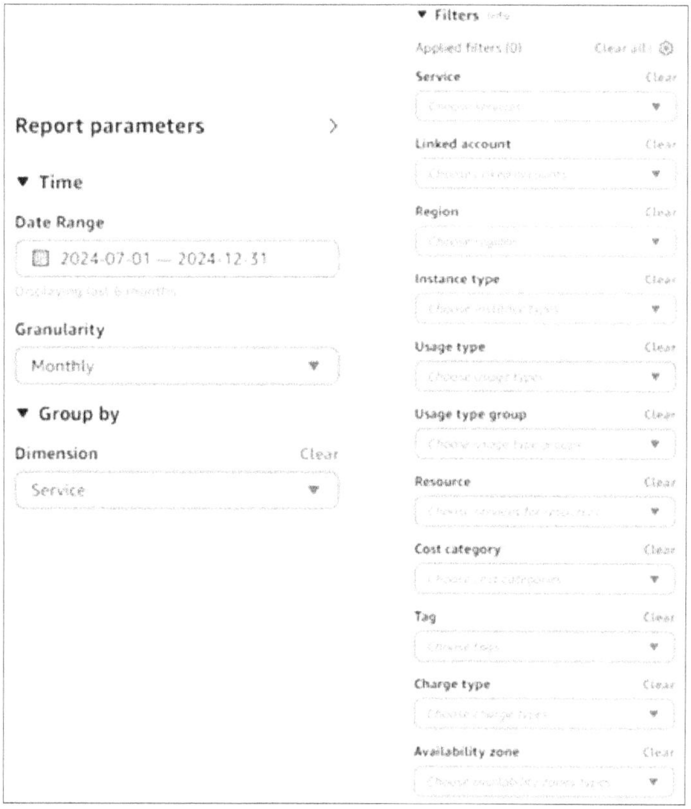

Figure 2.6: *Cost Explorer and the report parameters*

The Cost Explorer page consists of two main sections:

- **Cost and usage graph**: A visual representation of spending trends based on selected filters.
- **Cost and usage breakdown**: A detailed table showing actual cost data and can be downloaded as a CSV file.

Once you have set up a report by selecting the required report parameters, you can save it for later reference. Select **Save to Report Library** and provide the name of the report to identify the saved report. The report will be available in the **Reports** section of the Cost Explorer tool for easy access.

AWS Cost Explorer in action

Let us look at some examples on how to use AWS Cost Explorer to get insights into cloud usage and spend, and understand any trends from the data generated:

- **Example 1, identifying top AWS services used**: You would like to find the top 5 services used by your organization that contribute the most to the monthly bill. The report can be generated by selecting the report parameter:
  - o **Set time range**: Last six months (customize as per requirement)
  - o **Set group by**: Service

This report helps you understand which services contribute the most to AWS Costs:

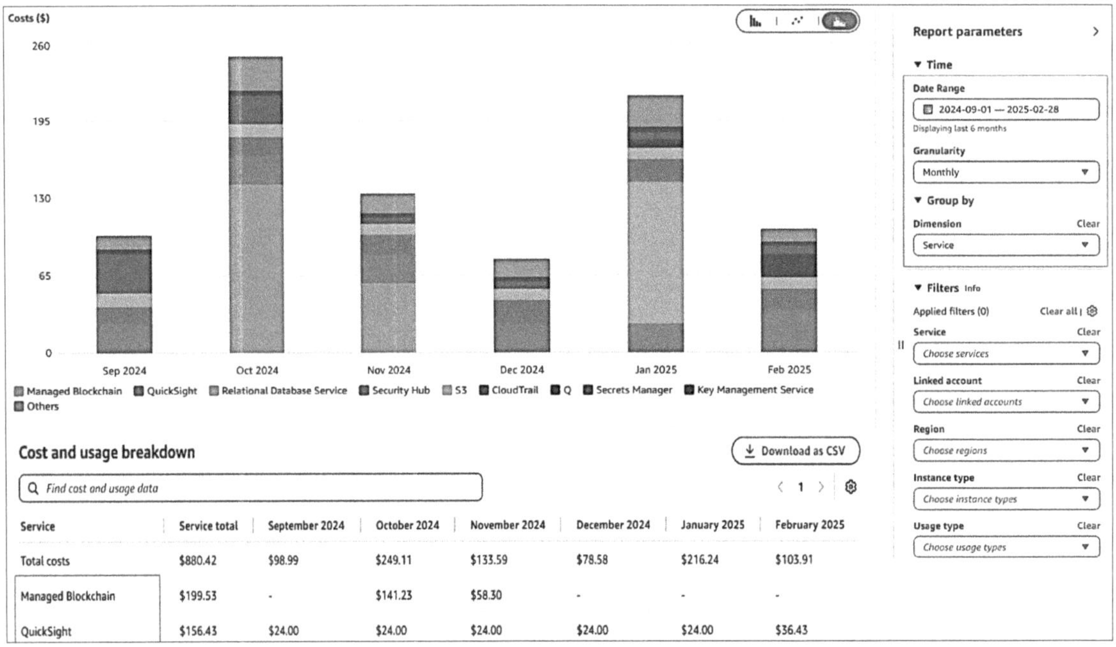

***Figure 2.7**: Spend by service*

- **Example 2, understanding regional usage**: You want to build on example 1 and understand where the organization's resources are deployed. Also, verify if any unexpected regions are being used, indicating anomalies. To check where most of your AWS resources are deployed, modify the **Report** parameter as outlined in the following points and figure:
  - o **Set time range**: Last 6 months (customize as per requirement)
  - o **Change group by**: Region

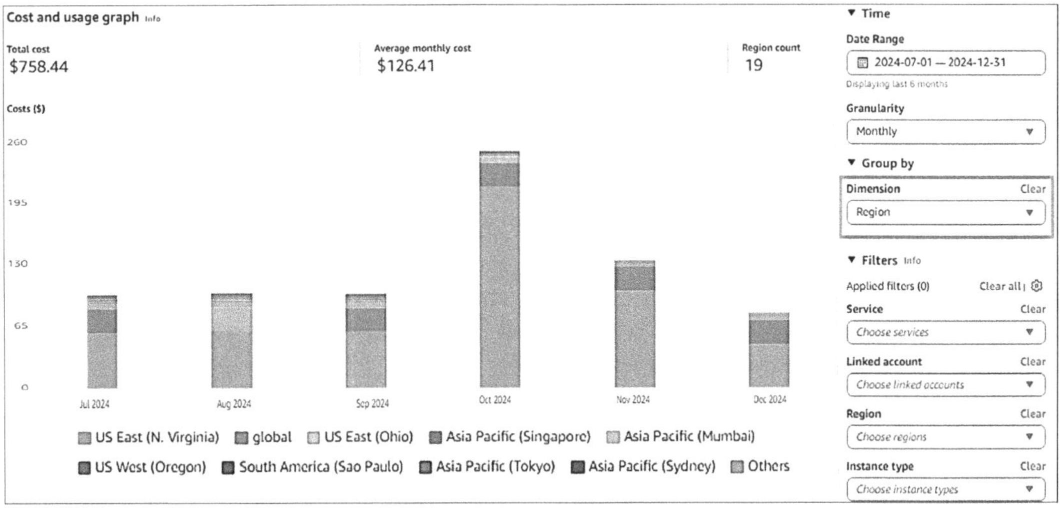

Figure 2.8: Spend by region

An unexpected region in the report could indicate a security misconfiguration or an unauthorized deployment.

- **Example 3, exploring US East (Virginia) region**: You noticed that US-East (Virginia) incurs most of the charges and would like to explore spending in this region. To analyze spending within a specific region (e.g., US-East, Virginia):
  - Set **Region** filter to US-East-1
  - Set **Group by** to service

  This helps in identifying services used in the US East (Virginia) region and associated charges, as shown in the following figure:

Figure 2.9: Top services in a region

AWS Cost Explorer is a powerful tool for analyzing AWS spending, identifying trends, and forecasting future costs. By leveraging its report parameters and filtering options, organizations can optimize cloud costs, detect anomalies, and make data-driven decisions.

Understanding AWS Cost and Usage Reports

In the previous section, we saw how AWS Cost Explorer provides visualization and reporting capabilities to help analyze spending as well as customize the visualization by selecting appropriate report parameters. AWS CUR is a comprehensive financial reporting tool that provides the most detailed view of AWS cost and usage data, offering significant advantages over AWS Cost Explorer. Some of the key features of AWS CUR are as follows:

- **Granular data**: CUR provides cost and usage data at hourly, daily, or monthly intervals, allowing for detailed analysis.
- **Cost breakdown**: It categorizes costs by AWS product, resource, and tags, making it easier to allocate expenses and dive into spend data from different dimensions.
- **Export to Amazon S3**: The report is stored in an S3 bucket in either CSV or Parquet for long-term storage and provides integration with third-party analytics tools.
- **Integration with AWS analytics services**: CUR supports native integration with Amazon Athena and Amazon QuickSight, making it easier to query and visualize the data.
- **Frequent updates**: The report is updated up to three times a day, ensuring access to near real-time cost data.
- **Well-defined data dictionary**: CUR includes a structured data dictionary that helps users analyze cost data using **structured query language** (**SQL**) queries or other analytics tools:

Let us explore the key differences between AWS Cost Explorer and AWS CUR and their ideal use cases:

Feature	AWS Cost Explorer	AWS CUR
Purpose	Designed to visualize cost and usage data through different visualization options. Provides interactive charts and filters to customize visualization as per user requirements.	Provides a comprehensive dataset with a detailed resource-level view of AWS costs and usage data, designed for advanced analysis, reporting, and data integration.
Data granularity	Provides aggregated data (For example, daily or monthly by service, account, or tag). Resource-level details are limited.	Provides a granular level of billing data, including resource-level details such as resource IDs, resource type, operation types, and pricing-related details.

Feature	AWS Cost Explorer	AWS CUR
Visualization	Includes built-in charts and dashboards for trend analysis, forecasting, and anomaly detection.	Does not provide visualization natively. Data must be analyzed using external tools such as Amazon Athena, Amazon QuickSight, or third-party BI tools.
Customization level	Offers limited customization options as filters and groupings are predefined within the console.	Supports detailed and customized reporting capabilities. Users can query, join, and model data to create customized reports and analytics pipelines.
Data retention	Retains up to 38 months of historical cost and usage data within the AWS Billing console.	Data is delivered to an Amazon S3 bucket and can be stored indefinitely for long-term retention and analysis.
Data export	Allows exporting datasets to CSV format for offline analysis, though limited to summarized data.	Exports complete billing and usage data in CSV or Parquet format to Amazon S3 at defined intervals.
Integration with AWS services	Limited to visualization within AWS Billing and Cost Management.	Deep integration with AWS data and analytics services such as S3, Athena, Redshift, and QuickSight for querying and advanced analysis.
Ease of use	Console-based UI, which is suitable for finance, procurement, and operations users for quick insights.	Requires technical knowledge and SQL/BI expertise to process and analyze large datasets.
Ideal for	Quick insights and high-level cost visibility.	Detailed, long-term financial and operational analysis.

Table 2.1: AWS Cost Explorer versus AWS CUR

Let us examine a sample CUR file that highlights some of the recorded fields:

identity/LineItemId	identity/TimeInterval	bill/InvoiceId	bill/InvoicingEntity	bill/BillingEntity	bill/BillType
xlw	2024-09-01T00:00:00Z/2024-0'		Amazon Web S	AWS	Anniversary
nxr	2024-09-01T00:00:00Z/2024-0'		Amazon Web S	AWS	Anniversary
tuw	2024-09-01T00:00:00Z/2024-0'		Amazon Web S	AWS	Anniversary

bill/PayerAccountId	bill/BillingPeriodStartDate	bill/BillingPeriodEndDate	lineItem/UsageAccountId	lineItem/LineItemType	lineItem/UsageStartDate	lineItem/UsageEndDate
2.2	2024-09-01T0(	2024-10-01T0(	2.27064E+11	Usage	2024-09-01T00:00:0C	2024-09-01T0
2.2	2024-09-01T0(	2024-10-01T0(	3.38385E+11	Usage	2024-09-01T00:00:0C	2024-09-01T0
2.2	2024-09-01T0(	2024-10-01T0(	5.07085E+11	Usage	2024-09-01T00:00:0C	2024-09-01T0

Figure 2.10: CUR extract

In summary, we can conclude that:

- AWS Cost Explorer is ideal for quick cost visualization and trend analysis, while AWS CUR offers deeper resource-level insights, custom reporting options, and long-term cost analysis.
- Organizations looking for customized reports, such as executive summaries, advanced reporting requirements, or integration capabilities with **business intelligence** (**BI**) tools will find CUR to be a powerful solution.

CUR 2.0 and AWS Data Exports

AWS has enhanced its cost and usage reporting capabilities by introducing CUR 2.0 and AWS Data Exports. CUR 2.0 is built on legacy CUR and offers a more consistent and predictable schema. CUR 2.0 has added new columns and nested a few columns to reduce data sparsity. AWS Data Exports complements this by providing a better way to export costs and usage data in the format organizations want and with precisely the data they want to export. This helps in maintaining data pipeline stability and ensuring sensitive information remains protected.

Some of the key features provided by AWS Data Exports are listed here:

- **SQL capabilities**: AWS Data Exports enables users to export selected columns using column selection and row filtering. This helps maintain consistency in data exports, ensuring the stability of existing data pipelines even if the CUR schema changes or new columns are introduced by AWS in the future. It also supports custom formatting requirements and helps align CUR data to the specific format needed by the data pipeline.
- **Data management capabilities**: AWS Data Exports helps optimize dataset sizes, reduce processing overhead, and improve overall performance. Organizations can filter out sensitive cost data or exclude data from specific accounts, ensuring compliance with security protocols and data governance requirements. Additionally, the features can be leveraged to create customized views for different business units, making it easier for organizations to track and manage costs across various departments.
- **Compatibility**: AWS Data Exports supports both the legacy CUR and CUR 2.0, providing backward compatibility.
- **S3 export**: Data can be easily exported to Amazon S3 buckets for further processing and long-term retention.
- **Integration**: The service integrates seamlessly with AWS native data analytics tools such as QuickSight, simplifying the development of customized dashboards.

This enhanced structure makes cost and usage data more accessible and manageable for organizations of all sizes, while allowing customization of exports according to specific business needs.

Getting started with AWS Data Exports

In this section, we will guide you through the process of using AWS Data Exports to create a recurring CUR. You can launch the **Data Exports** feature from the **Billing and Cost Management** section of the AWS Management console. Refer to *Figure 2.11*, and click **Create** to begin generating the export:

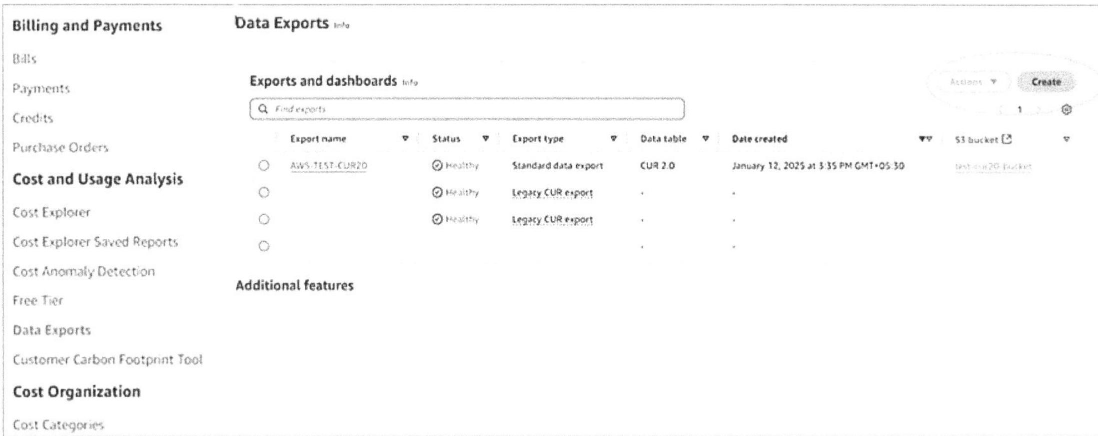

***Figure 2.11**: Data Export overview*

There are three export types you can choose from, each designed for different use cases:

- **Standard data export**: This option provides three distinct export types with separate data tables:
    - **CUR 2.0**: The new mechanism for detailed AWS cost and usage data.
    - **Cost Optimization recommendations**: Exports data from the AWS Cost Optimization Hub, providing insights to help reduce costs.
    - **FOCUS 1.0 with AWS columns**: This export includes data in the FOCUS 1.0 format, added with AWS-specific columns.
- **Cost and usage dashboard powered by QuickSight**: This option exports CUR data and automatically deploys a QuickSight dashboard. The result is a pre-built dashboard that your organization can use for in-depth analysis.
- **Legacy data export**: Many organizations still require the original CUR format for their pipelines and existing analytics solutions. This option supports exporting legacy data in the traditional CUR format, ensuring compatibility with older data pipelines.

The following figure illustrates the three **AWS Data Exports** options available:

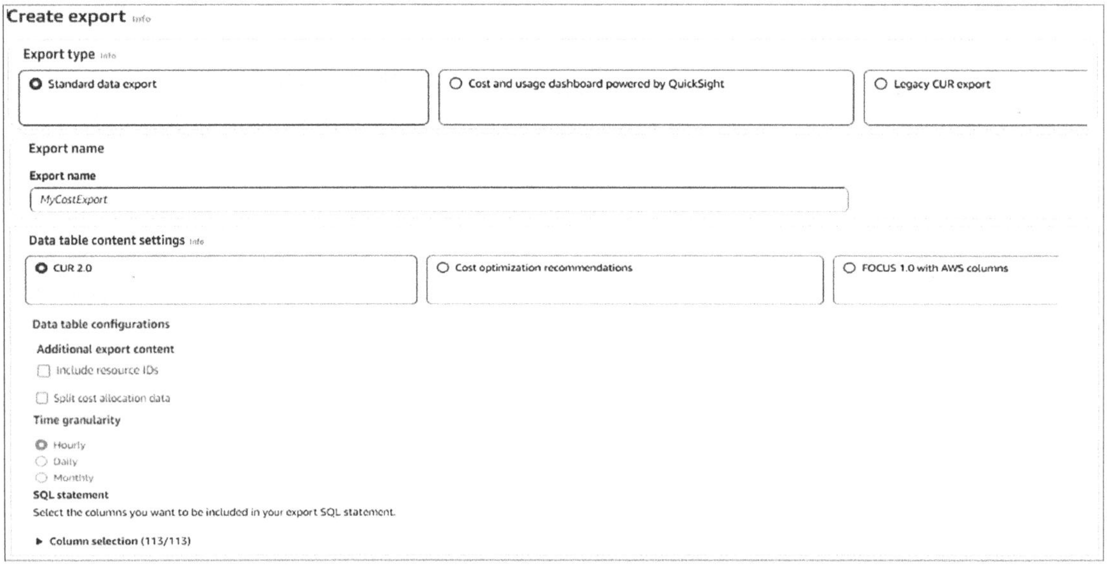

Figure 2.12: *Creating an export*

Let us start by creating a standard data export by following these steps:

1. **Export name**: Provide a name for your report. This will help you easily reference and manage your exports.
2. **Data table content setting**: Select **CUR 2.0** as the data table format. This ensures you are using the most up-to-date cost and usage data.
3. **Additional export conditions**: Opt to **Include resource IDs**. Including resource IDs helps map costs to individual resources, making your data more granular and actionable.
4. **Time granularity**: Specify the level of granularity for your report. You can select **Hourly**, **Daily**, or **Monthly**. For this walkthrough, select **Hourly** to explore the most granular data.
5. **Column selection**: Data Exports provides this feature to export only the required data. Choose the columns that you need for your data pipeline. You can edit this selection later. The column selection generates an SQL query, which will help customize the data export.
6. **Data export delivery options**: Select the data exporting format. You can choose between Parquet or GZIP (text/CSV). These formats are optimized for storage and analytics. For this walkthrough, select the Parquet format.

7. **S3 Bucket**: Specify the S3 bucket where the CUR 2.0 data will be exported.
8. Once all the details are provided, click **Create** to initiate the export. After the report is generated, you can review it in the **Exports and Dashboard** section. It will highlight the following:
    a. **Export Name**: The unique name you provided for the export.
    b. **Export Type**: The type of export chosen (e.g., **Standard Data Export**, **Cost and Usage Dashboard**, or **Legacy Data Export**).
    c. **Creation Date**: The date the export was created.
    d. **Last Refreshed Date**: The most recent update to the export data.
    e. **S3 Bucket Location**: The location of the S3 bucket where the data was exported.
9. Click on the **Export Name** to review the details provided while creating the export.
10. If you need to make any changes to your export, you have the following options:
    a. Select the **Export Name** of the report you want to edit.
    b. From the **Actions** dropdown, click **Edit** to make adjustments to the export settings.

    In the next chapter, we will explore other export options, such as the Cost and Usage dashboard (provided by QuickSight).

Azure Cost Management + Billing overview

Just as AWS offers a set of tools and services to track and analyze cloud spend, Microsoft Azure provides a cost management service known as **Azure Cost Management + Billing**. The features provided by Azure Cost Management + Billing help organizations track their Azure spending, set budgets, and optimize costs through features like Cost Analysis, Exports, and detailed Billing insights.

In this section, we will look at Azure Cost Management + Billing, with a particular focus on the Cost Analysis tool. Cost Analysis is an interactive platform that offers detailed visualizations and breakdowns of Azure usage and cost. Whether you need to monitor expenses by resource, service, or location, Azure Cost Analysis enables users to make data-driven decisions to optimize cloud spending and improve financial efficiency. For a comprehensive understanding, refer to *Figure 12.13*.

Introduction to Azure Cost Management + Billing overview

Azure Cost Management + Billing provides a centralized hub for managing and tracking Azure costs. Some of the key features are as follows:

- **Cost analysis**: Track and analyze costs across Azure subscriptions, resource groups, or billing accounts.
- **Billing**: Detailed usage and invoice information.
- **Budgets**: Set budgets and alerts to keep spending under control.
- **Exports**: Export cost data for in-depth analysis and visualization through Power BI or Excel tools.

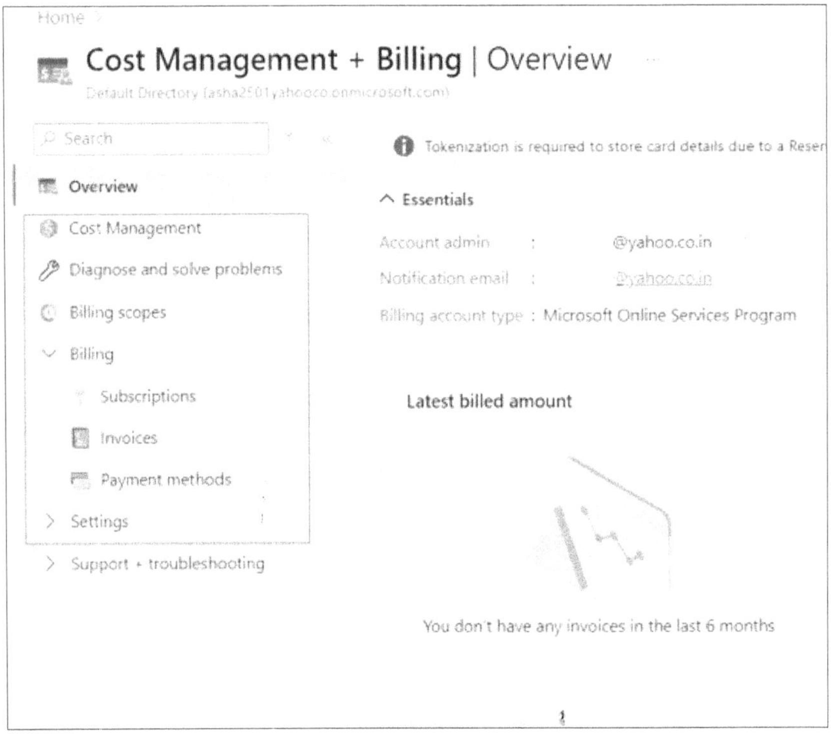

Figure 2.13: Azure Cost Management + Billing console

Getting started with Azure Cost Analysis

Follow these steps to get started with Azure Cost Analysis:

1. Search for **Cost Management + Billing** in the Azure console. The **Cost Management + Billing** section contains several tools and features for cost tracking, analysis, and billing insights.
2. Select **Cost Analysis** under the **Cost Management** section in the Azure portal.
3. **Choose your scope for analysis**: You can choose from a subscription, resource group, or billing account, depending on the level of detail you need.

4. **Views**: By default, the view will display **Accumulated Costs** for the current month. This view helps get an overview of the total costs associated with your selected scope.
5. Azure Cost Analysis has several predefined views, such as **Cost by Resource** and **Daily Costs**. Each view offers customization options to tailor the data presentation to your needs.

Understanding cost analysis dashboard

The cost analysis dashboard provides an interactive and intuitive way to visualize your cloud spending. Some of the key visuals include the following:

- **Cost by service**: This view shows which Azure services drive costs (e.g., virtual machines, storage, networking). It helps you pinpoint high-cost services and assess if they are being used efficiently.
- **Cost by resource group**: This view allows you to track costs associated with specific projects or applications. This is particularly useful for organizations that organize their resources into different resource groups based on teams or departments.
- **Cost by location**: Useful for multi-region deployments to compare spending by Azure region.
- **Usage trends**: The usage trends graph displays historical usage patterns. This can help identify cost spikes and areas where resource utilization can be optimized.

The following figure provides an overview of the Azure Cost Analysis dashboard, highlighting key cost insights and features:

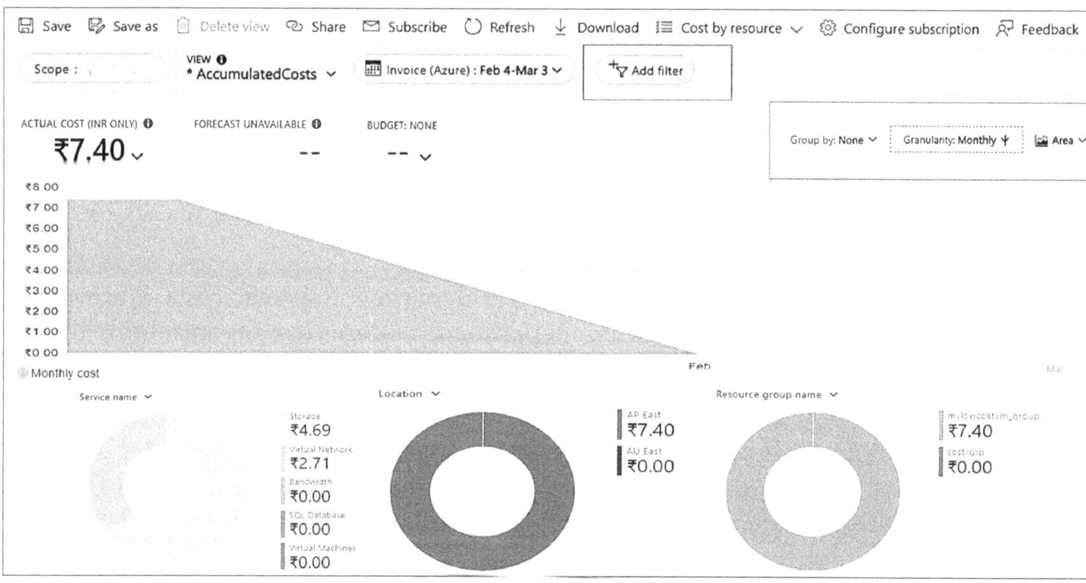

Figure 2.14: Azure Cost Analysis dashboard

Customizing cost analysis views

Azure provides several options for customizing the cost analysis dashboard to align with visualization requirements. Let us look at them in detail:

- **Group by**: You can group data by various criteria such as Service Name, Location, Resource Group, or Meter Category. This allows for a more granular view of where costs are accumulating.
- **Date range**: You can select a predefined date range (Last 7 days, Last 30 days) or specify a custom date range to focus on specific time periods for analysis.
- **Visualization type**: Azure offers various visualization formats, including Area, Bar Chart, Line Graph, and Table View. Choose the one that best fits your data analysis requirements.
- **Filters**: To narrow down your analysis, you can apply filters to focus on specific services, resources, or cost categories. This is especially helpful when you want to zoom in on particular cost drivers.

Refer to the following list, which outlines different examples:

- **Example 1**: Organization wants to analyze Azure compute costs. To focus on costs related to Azure compute services, follow the given steps:
  1. Open **Cost Management + Billing** (search for `Cost Management`).
  2. Under **Cost Management**, click **Cost analysis**. The default view shows costs for your selected scope (subscription/billing account). Confirm the scope at the top-left and change it if needed.
  3. Set the time range in the top bar (For example – Last 7 or 30 days, This Month, This Quarter, or Custom date range).
  4. Choose the granularity—Daily/Monthly
  5. Click the **Add filter** option. In the filter list, find the service name and select **Virtual Machines**. This will restrict the view to compute related charges.
  6. You can use **Export and Download CSV** to export the filtered results for offline analysis or to feed into a spreadsheet/BI tool.
- **Example 2**: In this example, we will analyze department-specific costs. Suppose you want to analyze costs for a specific department within your organization. You can filter by tag and use key-value pairs to isolate costs related to that department. Follow the steps to get the cost related to a specific tag:
  1. In the **Add filter** option, choose **Tags**. You will see a list of tag keys; select the relevant key (For example, **Department**). If not, use the generic **Tags** filter and type the key name.
  2. Choose the value you want (For example, **Finance**). The cost view will now be restricted to only resources that have a tag of **Department = Finance**.

Exporting cost data for further analysis

For more advanced cost analysis, Azure allows you to export your cost data to other platforms like Power BI, Excel, or CSV for deeper insights. To export cost data, follow these steps:

1. Go to the **Cost Management + Billing** section.
2. Under the **Cost Management** section in the left sidebar, select **Exports**.
3. Create a new export by clicking the **+ Create** or **Schedule Export** and select **Create your own export**.
4. In the **New export** form, fill in the basic details and click **Next**.
    - **Name**: Enter a descriptive name for your export (e.g., **`Monthly-Cost-Export`**)
    - **Type of data**: Cost and usage details (actuals)
    - **Frequency**: One time, Daily, or Monthly
5. Provide storage account details and output format (CSV or Parquet).
6. Review the information provided and click **Create**.
7. The exported data will be available in CSV format, allowing you to analyze and visualize it in your preferred tool:

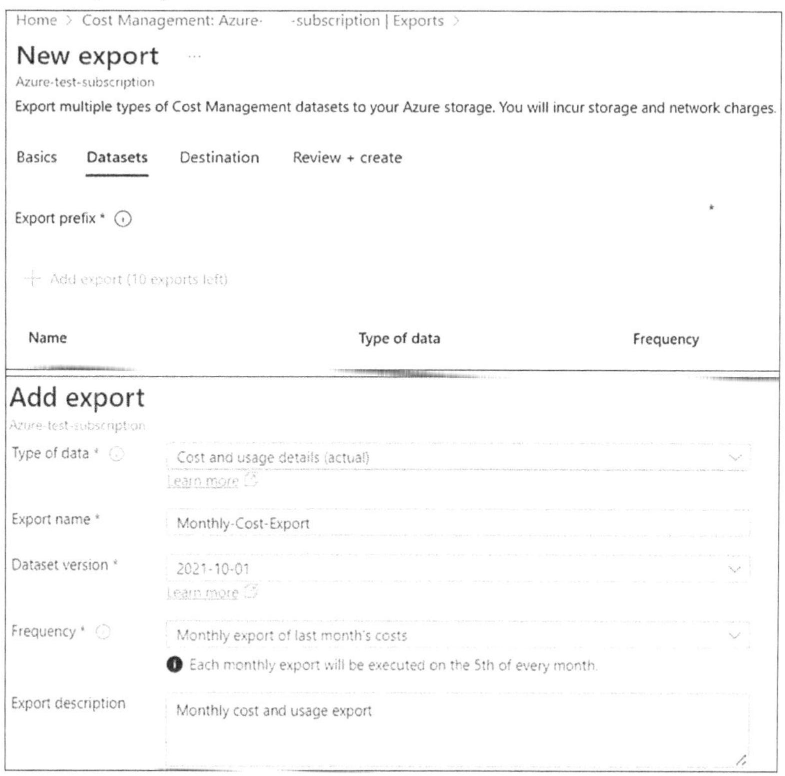

Figure 2.15: Azure exports

Bringing it all together

In this chapter, we will explore how an organization can begin its journey toward cost optimization by leveraging cloud provider native tools for getting insights into cloud cost. To provide context, let us revisit an example from the preceding chapter, where a fintech startup faced an unexpected spike in its AWS CloudTrail spend. The company's CISO was tasked with investigating why the costs exceeded the Free Tier limits and what factors contributed to this sudden rise in spending. CISO can start by leveraging a set of cost visibility tools provided by AWS and summarized in the following figure:

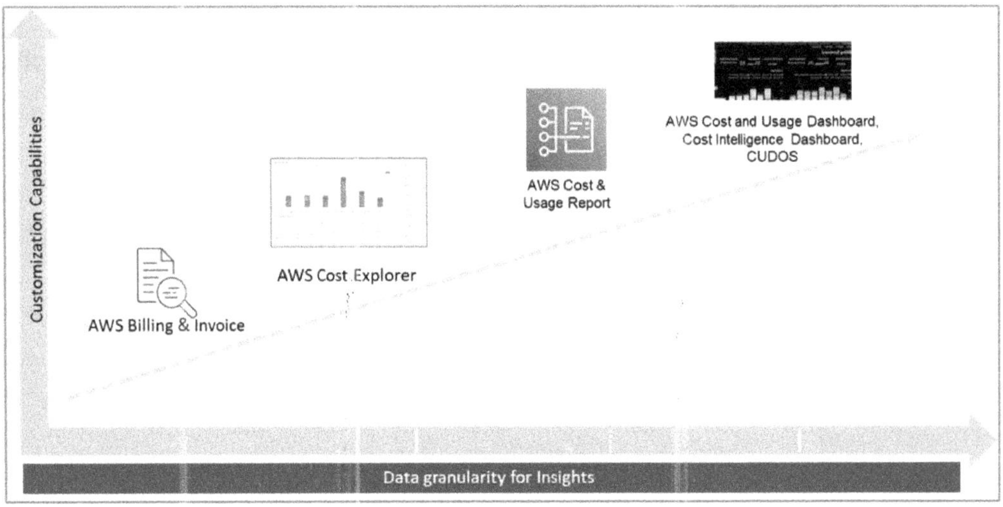

Figure 2.16: Tool matrix

CISO can start performing analysis and get a detailed look at spend and usage by following the steps as given here:

1. **Spend analysis using AWS Billing**: The first place the CISO should start when analyzing the unexpected spike in AWS CloudTrail costs is the **AWS Billing Dashboard** under the **Billing and Cost Management** section in the **AWS Management** console. AWS Billing provides a comprehensive overview of the organization's usage and spend, including **key performance indicators (KPIs)** such as:

    a. **Billing unit**: The unit of measurement for the service (e.g., hours, requests, data volume).

    b. **Price per unit**: The cost associated with each billing unit.

    c. **Monthly spend**: The total cost incurred over the billing cycle.

    The **Charges by Service** tab breaks down costs by individual AWS services and is further segregated by region. To investigate the CloudTrail spend, the CISO can expand the CloudTrail **Service** section, which will provide key details:

a. **Charges by Region**: Identifying which AWS region incurred the highest CloudTrail costs. For example, it could show that the **US East** (**N. Virginia**) region accounted for most of the CloudTrail charges.

b. **Charges by Instance, Feature, or API call**: This helps pinpoint which AWS CloudTrail features, instances, or API calls contributed to the costs.

c. **Usage quantity**: Shows the quantity of CloudTrail usage based on the billing unit, which can be helpful in comparing usage across different periods. It will also help if we have exceeded Free Tier limits.

d. **Price per unit**: How much the organization is charged per billing unit, as shown in the following figure:

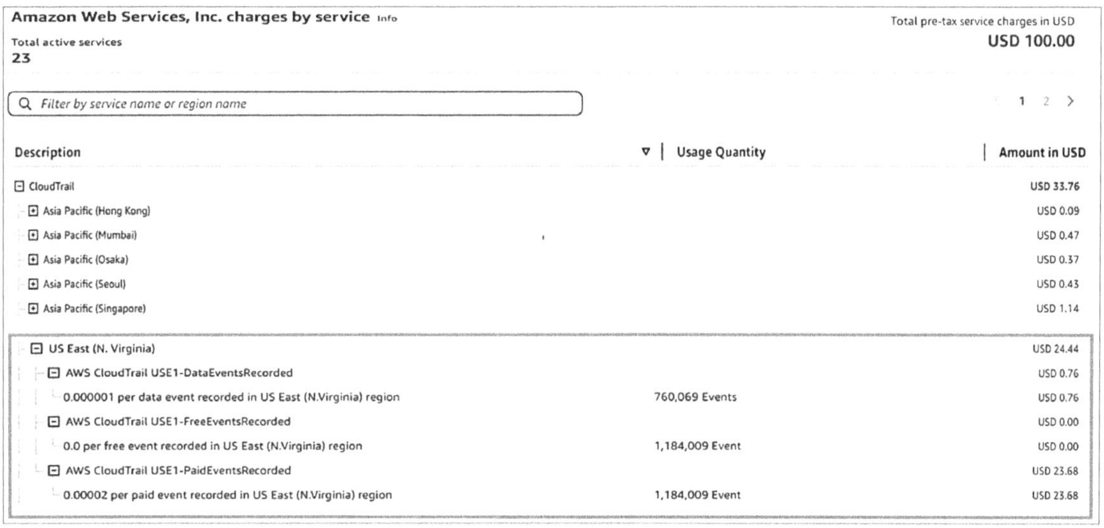

***Figure 2.17**: Analyzing CloudTrail spend with Billing console*

At this stage, the CISO will find that most of the charges are related to the **AWS CloudTrail USE1-PaidEventsRecorded** and **AWS CloudTrail USE1-DataEventsRecorded** services in the **US East (N. Virginia)** region.

2. **Comparing usage and spending with previous months using AWS Cost Explorer**: To better understand the cause of the cost spike, the next step is to compare the current month's usage and spending with those from the previous month. By conducting this comparative analysis, the CISO can determine the following:

   - *Are these charges recurring or incurred by the CloudTrail service in the current month, indicating changes performed in the environment?*
   - *Which API calls are responsible for this spike?* **AWS CloudTrail USE1-PaidEventsRecorded** or **AWS CloudTrail USE1-DataEventsRecorded** (data events or management events)

This can be done using the AWS Cost Explorer, which provides powerful tools for visualizing spending trends. Follow these steps:

a. Go to AWS **Cost Explorer** from the AWS Management Console.

b. Set the **Date Range** to include both the current and the previous month for comparison.

c. Set the **Granularity** to **Monthly** to see monthly trends.

d. In the **Group By** section, select **Usage Type**, as you want to analyze costs based on usage type (e.g., **Paid Events Recorded** or **Data Events Recorded**).

e. Under **Filter**, select **Service** and filter by **CloudTrail** to focus on CloudTrail-specific costs.

Cost Explorer will generate a visualization showing how CloudTrail usage and spend changed from month to month. This breakdown, as shown in *Figure 2.18*, will provide insights into which services or usage patterns caused the unexpected increase in costs:

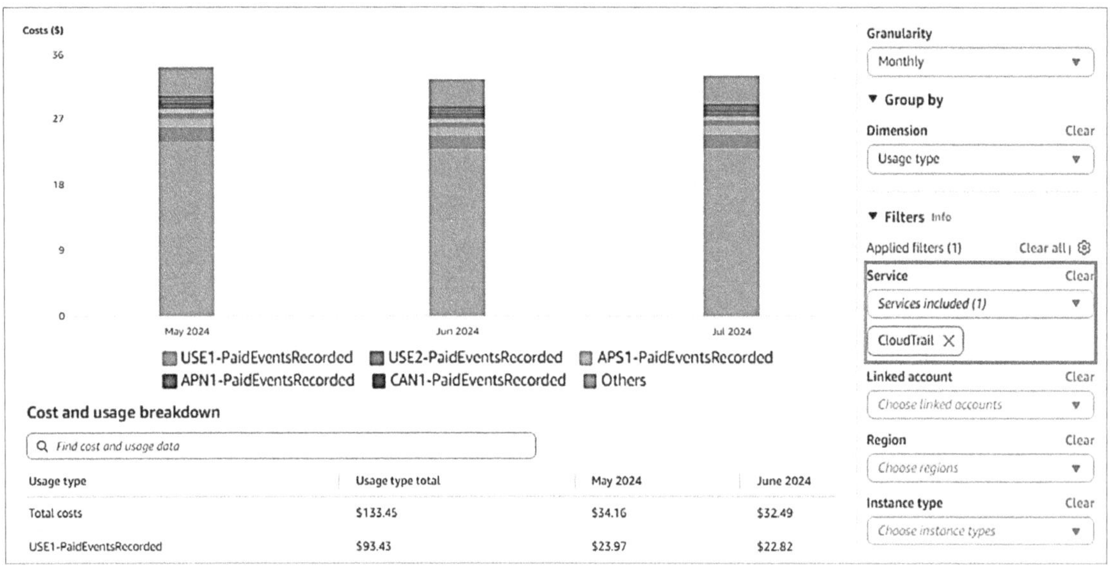

Figure 2.18: Analyzing CloudTrail spend with Cost Explorer

3. **Detailed resource-level analysis using CUR:** Once the CISO has identified the areas of concern using the **AWS Billing** Dashboard and **AWS Cost Explorer**, the next step is to gain more detailed, resource-level insights. This is where CUR comes in. The CUR is an essential tool for tracking and analyzing AWS usage and spending at a granular level. The report can be exported to Amazon S3 for storage and then used with powerful analytics tools like Amazon Athena and Amazon QuickSight to create custom dashboards and reports.

To use the CUR effectively, follow these steps:

a. **Export the CUR to S3**: The report can be set up to run periodically (e.g., daily or monthly) and export the data to an S3 bucket.

b. **Analyze the Data**: Use Athena to run queries against the CUR data stored in S3, or use QuickSight to visualize the cost and usage data. Both tools allow the CISO and other stakeholders to dive deeper into the cost breakdown and identify specific resources or usage patterns driving the cost increases.

In the next chapter, we will explore different Cost and Usage Dashboards, including how to build custom dashboards for more effective cost monitoring. The snapshot of the cost intelligence dashboard is given in the following figure:

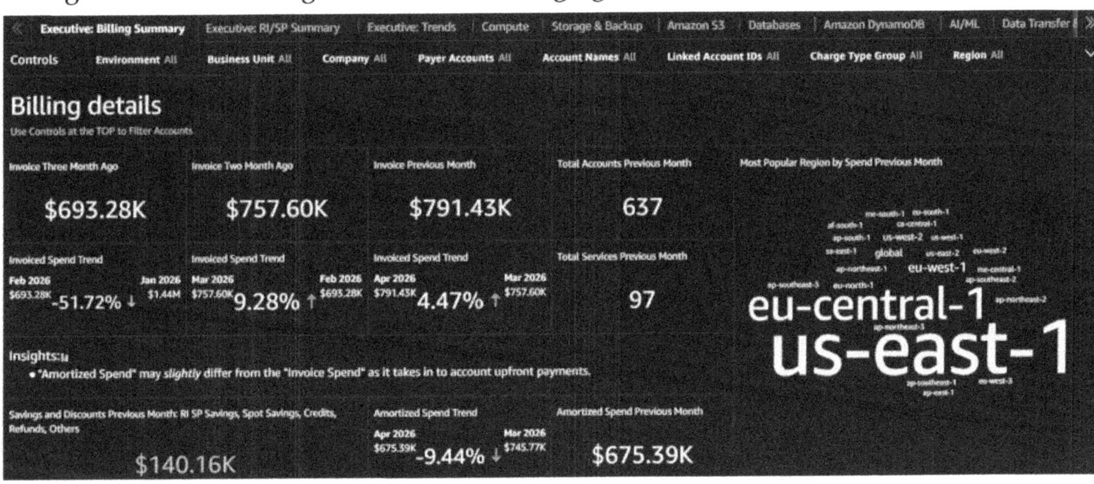

Figure 2.19: Analyzing CloudTrail spend with QuickSight Dashboard

By using AWS native cost management tools like **AWS Billing**, **AWS Cost Explorer**, and the **AWS CUR**, organizations can identify patterns in usage and spending, allowing them to take informed actions toward cost optimization. For the fintech startup in our example, the insights gained through these tools would enable the CISO to pinpoint the exact cause of the CloudTrail cost spike and take appropriate steps to optimize future usage.

The concept of leveraging various AWS native tools to analyze usage and cost can be similarly extended to Azure and Google cloud native tools.

Here are the main key takeaways and points to remember from this chapter:

- Native cost management tools from cloud providers such as AWS and Azure offer features for diverse cost observability needs, from basic monitoring to advanced reporting.
- **AWS Billing console** serves as the foundation for cost management, providing detailed breakdowns of charges, usage patterns, and billing units across services and regions.

- **AWS Cost Explorer** offers interactive visualization and analysis capabilities, enabling trend analysis, forecasting, and customizable reporting for up to 38 months of historical data.
- **AWS CUR** delivers the most granular view of cost data, with near real-time updates and integration capabilities with analytics services like Amazon Athena and QuickSight.
- Access management is crucial for billing data, as only root users have default access, while IAM users need explicit permissions to view and manage cost information.
- **Azure Cost Management + Billing** provides similar capabilities as tools provided by AWS, allowing organizations to track costs across subscriptions, resource groups, and analyze data through customizable views and visualizations.
- Regular monitoring and analysis using cost management tools helps detect cost anomalies, optimize spending, and make data-driven decisions for cloud cost management.

Conclusion

Cloud providers offer a range of cost management tools to help organizations monitor their usage and optimize their cloud spending. In this chapter, we explored some of the native tools provided by AWS and Azure, highlighting how these tools provide valuable visibility into cost and usage, aiding organizations in their cost optimization journey. The native cost management services offered by AWS, Azure, and Google serve as a strong foundation for any organization starting to focus on cloud cost optimization.

However, it is important to recognize that each tool has its own set of features, visibility options, and customization limitations. Organizations need to assess their specific observability and reporting requirements and match them with the capabilities of the native cost management tools. Where gaps exist, they may need to develop custom dashboards to fully meet their visibility needs.

In the next chapter, we will explore some of the dashboards built on cost and usage data exported from native tools. We will also help you learn building your own cost visualization dashboard leveraging analytics tools such as Amazon QuickSight.

CHAPTER 3
Cost Visualization Dashboards

Introduction

In the previous chapter, we explored native tools that provide detailed visibility into cloud usage and spending. Cloud providers such as **Amazon Web Services** (**AWS**), Azure, and Google Cloud offer native tools like AWS Cost Explorer, Azure Cost Management, and Google Cloud's Cost Management platform that provide visibility into usage and spending, helping organizations monitor and optimize their cloud expenses.

In most cases, these built-in solutions meet organizations' basic financial visualization needs. However, as cloud environments grow in complexity, businesses often require more advanced and customized insights that go beyond the standard visualization dashboards and reports provided by cloud providers.

In this chapter, we will explore how to extract and analyze cloud cost data beyond native dashboards. We will learn how to process usage and spend data using AWS analytics services and run **structured query language** (**SQL**) queries to perform deep cost analysis. Additionally, we will create a sample dashboard from scratch that visualizes key cloud cost metrics, providing a more tailored approach to financial tracking and optimization.

Structure

In this chapter, we will discuss the following topics:

- Significance of custom cost analytics solutions
- Integrating AWS CUR with Amazon Athena
- Cost visualization dashboards

Objectives

By the end of this chapter, the readers will understand how to use AWS analytics services to analyze cost and usage data exported from AWS native tools. You will learn to create custom dashboards that meet your organization's reporting needs. You will also learn how to use SQL queries for deeper insights into your AWS spending patterns.

By mastering these topics, you can create insightful, data-driven reports and visualizations per the organization's cost management needs.

Significance of custom cost analytics solutions

Many organizations require deeper analysis and flexible reporting aligned to their specific operational and financial structures. This includes the ability to query cloud cost and usage data using SQL, integrate data into existing analytics pipelines, and create custom dashboards based on business needs.

For instance, the finance team may need a detailed breakdown of multi-account spending, while the engineering team might require more granular resource-level cost tracking integrated with operational data. The need for deeper insights into cost and usage data can be because of varied business requirements, such as:

- Integration with internal financial systems and enterprise reporting tools.
- Detailed analysis of resource utilization patterns.
- Correlation of spending data with business metrics and **key performance indicators** (**KPIs**), such as the retail organization looking for cloud cost per order.
- Custom allocation models for chargebacks.
- Specialized reporting for compliance and governance.

To meet these requirements, businesses often build their own reporting solutions using cloud-native data processing and analytics services. Cloud providers facilitate this by offering features that allow organizations to export billing and usage data. For example, AWS provides **Cost and Usage Reports** (**CUR**), which enable businesses to export comprehensive cost data to an *Amazon S3* bucket.

Once stored in the Amazon S3 bucket, this data can be ingested into analytics services such as Amazon Athena (a serverless query service that analyzes S3 data using standard SQL statements), Amazon QuickSight [a **business intelligence** (**BI**) service for creating interactive dashboards and visualizations], or loaded into Amazon Redshift (a fully managed, petabyte-scale data warehouse service for analyzing business data). These services then allow organizations to run advanced queries, generate customized reports, and visualize spending trends in a format that aligns with their internal requirements. The data available in the Amazon S3 bucket can also be used to implement machine learning models for cost prediction.

Refer to the following figure to understand how cost and usage data can be integrated with different AWS services:

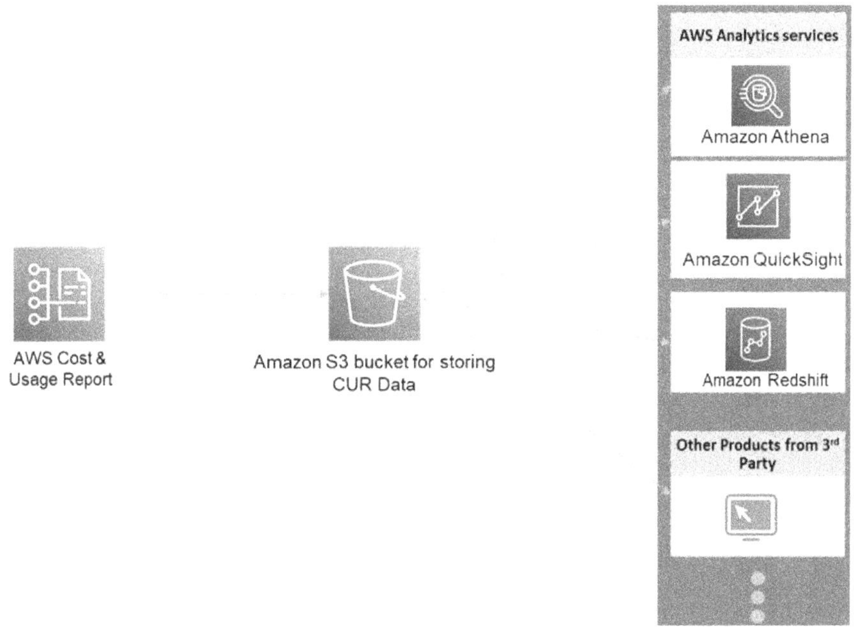

***Figure 3.1**: Analyzing cost and usage data*

Similar capabilities exist in Azure with Azure Cost Management exports and in Google Cloud through billing export to BigQuery. This exported data serves as a foundation for building customized analytics solutions.

Developing customized dashboards using BI solutions requires technical knowledge and an in-depth understanding of analytics and visualization services. A detailed walkthrough of BI tools across all major cloud providers is beyond the scope of this book. We will use AWS BI services and demonstrate the process of building a simple dashboard. This example will help readers understand how developers can create advanced dashboards for deeper cost insights.

Integrating AWS CUR with Amazon Athena

In the previous chapters, we explored the AWS Data Exports feature under Billing and Cost Management to export CUR data to an Amazon S3 bucket. The CUR 2.0 report comprehensively details AWS usage and associated charges, offering insights beyond native AWS Cost Management tools. However, manually downloading and analyzing CUR data using Excel or other tools can be cumbersome and time-consuming. Since CUR data is stored in the Amazon S3 bucket, it can be integrated with AWS analytics services like Amazon Athena, Amazon QuickSight, Amazon Redshift, or third-party analytics solutions.

Amazon Athena is an interactive query service that enables organizations to analyze CUR data using SQL queries without requiring data extraction or transformation. Athena is integrated with AWS Glue Data Catalog, which can crawl the S3 data source storing CUR data and generate table definitions, making querying more efficient.

Options for CUR 2.0 integration with Athena

There are two primary options to integrate CUR 2.0 data with Amazon Athena:

- **Option 1, AWS CloudFormation Template**: AWS provides a pre-built CloudFormation template to automate CUR 2.0 integration with Amazon Athena.
- **Option 2, AWS Glue Crawler**: This method involves setting up an AWS Glue Crawler to discover CUR data and create Athena tables and partitions.

In this section, we will follow the second option and set up AWS Glue Crawler to integrate CUR 2.0 data with Amazon Athena.

Steps for CUR 2.0 integration

In the previous chapter, under the section *Getting Started with AWS Data Exports,* we reviewed steps for creating a standard data export with the CUR2.0 option. Before proceeding with the integration of CUR 2.0 with Athena, ensure the following export settings while configuring CUR 2.0 (standard data export):

1. **Compression type and file format**: Parquet.
2. **File versioning**: Overwrite the existing data export file.

The following figure shows the options to be selected when creating a standard data export from the **AWS Data Exports** page:

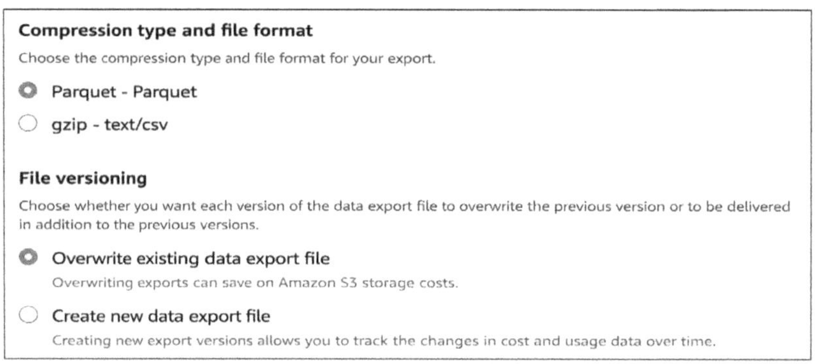

Figure 3.2: *Pre-requisite for CUR 2.0 integration*

Once the pre-requisite is completed and verified, follow these steps:

1. **Launch Amazon Athena**: Open the Amazon Athena service in the AWS Management Console. Access Athena Query Editor and choose Trino SQL as the query engine (This is the default for most regions).
2. **Set up AWS Glue Crawler**: The team can create a table in Athena by using Glue Crawler to catalog the CUR 2.0 data.

3. **Launch AWS Glue Crawler workflow**: Select **AWS Glue Crawler** from **Create** a table option to initiate the crawler workflow.

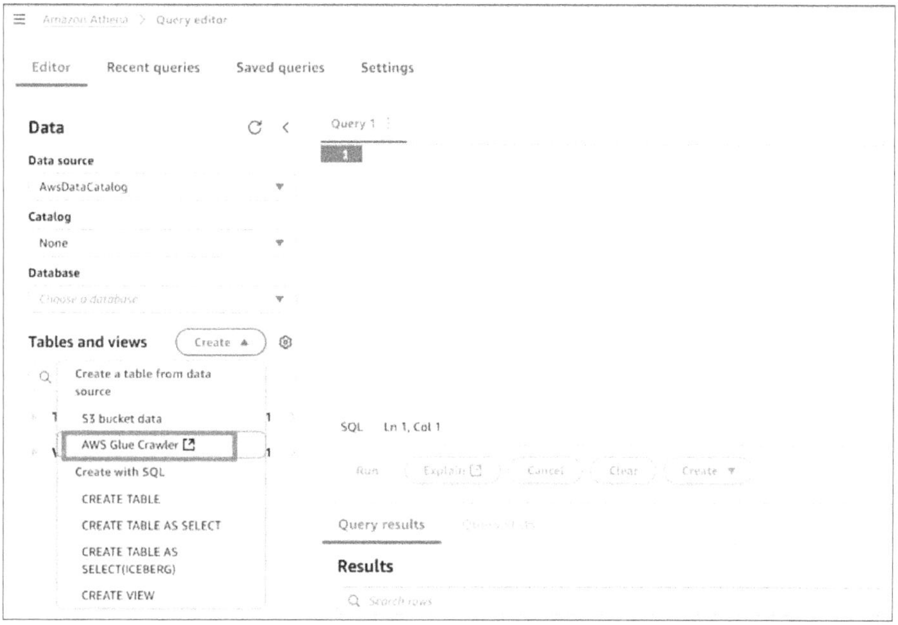

Figure 3.3: Launching AWS Glue Crawler

4. **Create and configure the Crawler**: Open the **AWS Glue** console and navigate to **Crawlers**. Click **Create crawler**, as shown in the following figure:

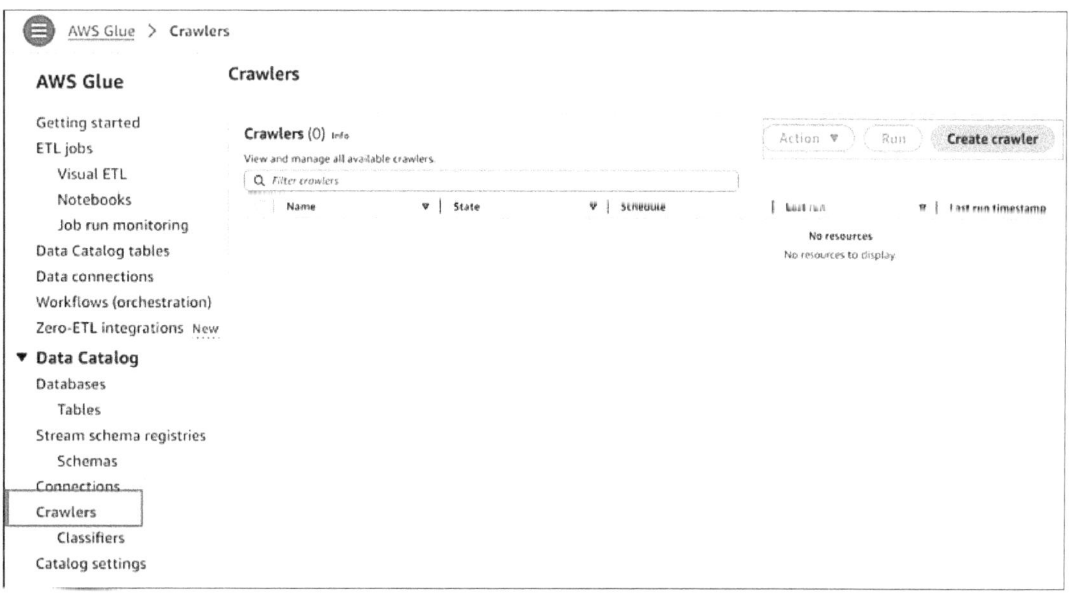

Figure 3.4: Create crawler

a. Provide the name of the crawler, e.g., **`cur20-crawler`**, and click **Next**, as shown in the following figure:

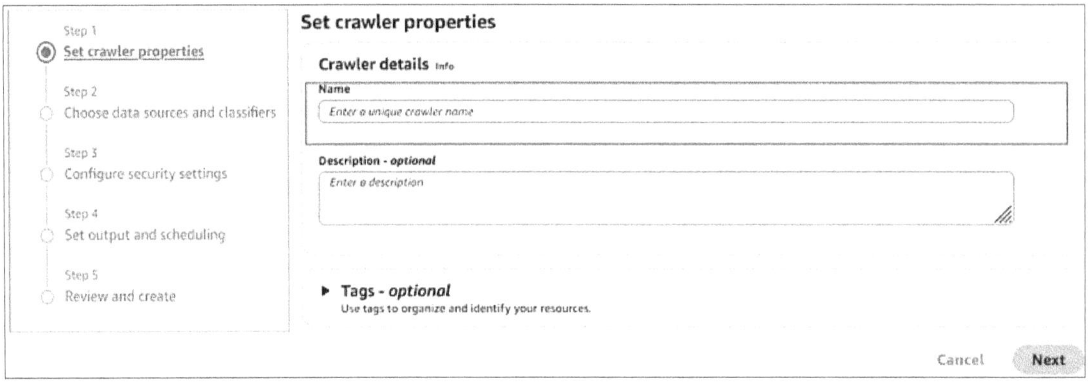

Figure 3.5: Provide Crawler details

b. Choose **Add a Data Source** and specify the S3 bucket location where CUR 2.0 data is stored, where the format is **`s3://<bucket-name>/<prefix>/<export-name>/data`**, as shown here:

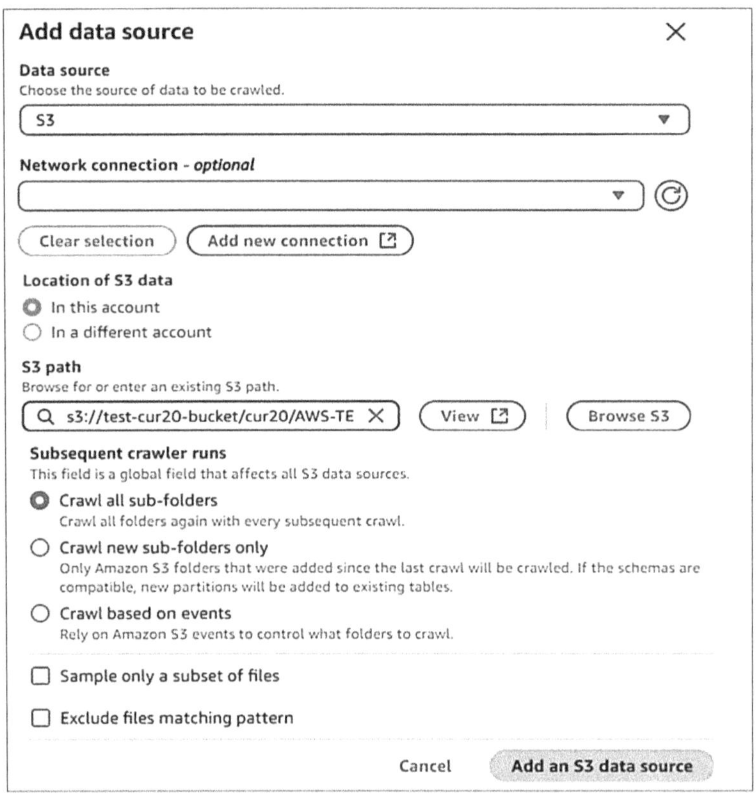

Figure 3.6: Creating Glue Crawler

5. **Configure IAM role for the crawler**: Assign an IAM role that allows the crawler to access the CUR S3 bucket. Either create a new IAM role or select an existing one. If you are selecting an existing IAM Role, ensure the IAM role has the following permissions:
   a. AWSGlueServiceRole
   b. S3 Read Access to the CUR bucket

   Refer to the following image for permission-related issues, and verify IAM role configurations:

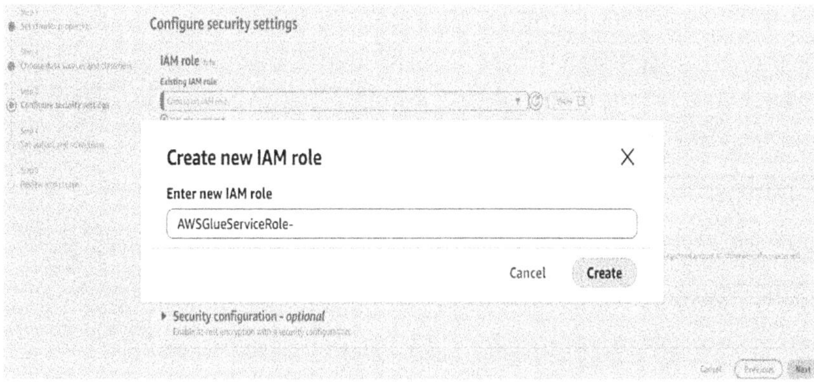

Figure 3.7: IAM role for crawler

6. **Define database and table configuration**:
   a. Specify the database name where the CUR data should be stored.
   b. If the database does not exist, create a new one, as shown in the following figure:

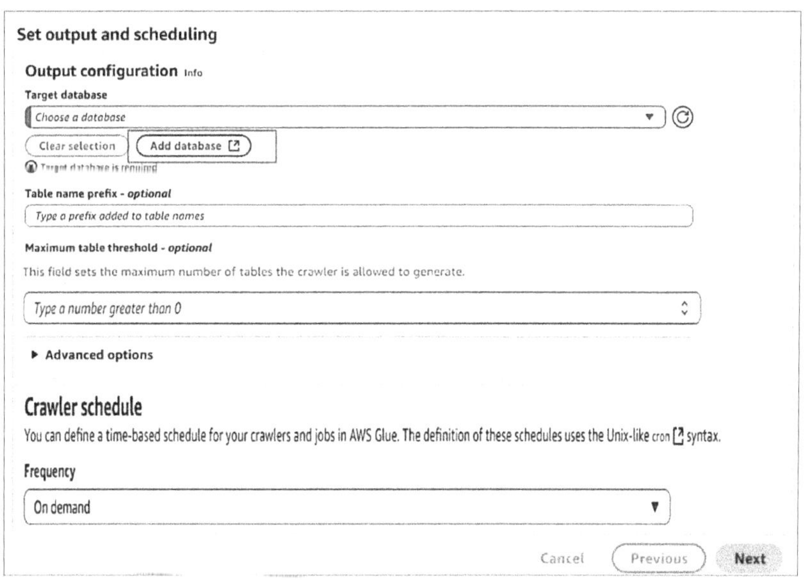

Figure 3.8: Provide database and scheduling details

7. **Set crawler schedule**: Choose the frequency of the crawler run. Consider setting up scheduled crawler runs to maintain updated data:
   a. On-demand
   b. Scheduled (Hourly/Daily/Weekly/Monthly)
   c. Custom (Cron Expression)
8. **Review and create the crawler**:
   a. Review the crawler settings and create the crawler.
   b. Once created, navigate to the crawler list and run the crawler by selecting **Run crawler**. The crawler may take several minutes to complete, depending on the data volume.
9. **Verify table creation in Athena**:
   a. After the crawler run is successful, check the logs for any errors.
   b. Open Amazon Athena, refresh the database list, and locate the newly created CUR tables.
10. **Run a test query**:
    a. **Set up query result location**: Before running queries, ensure you have configured an S3 location for query results in Athena settings.
    b. Select the table created by the Glue Crawler.
    c. Click **Preview Table** to execute a sample query. The successful execution of the SQL Query indicates that the CUR20 data has been successfully integrated with Athena for deeper insights, or
    d. Run the query in the Athena console.

```
SELECT * FROM your_athena_db.cur20_table LIMIT 10;
```

Tips: **Replace `your_athena_db.cur20_table` with your actual table name**

The following figure shows the Athena console and results from **Preview Table** operations. If you encounter an error requesting an S3 bucket location for query results, specify an appropriate S3 bucket in the Athena settings:

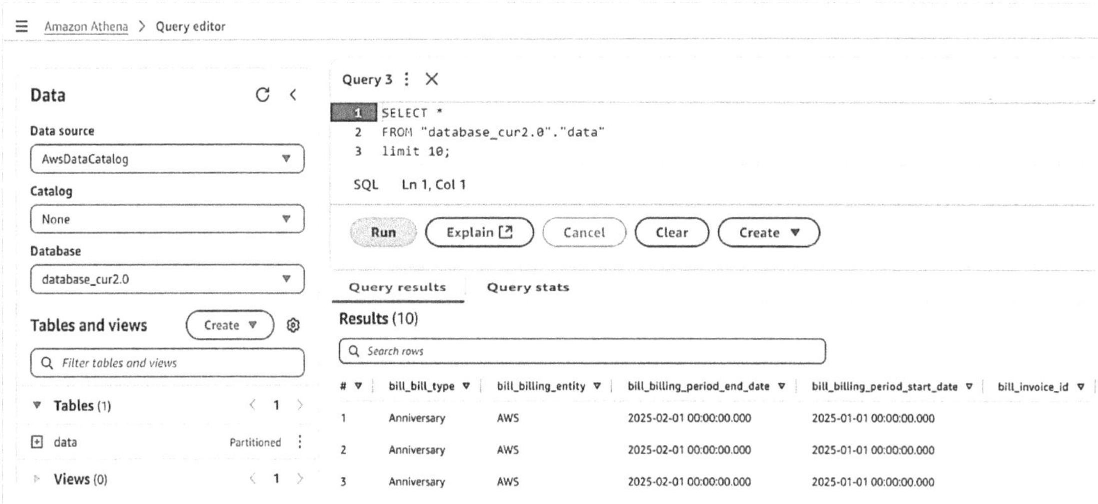

Figure 3.9: Results of the preview table

Leveraging Amazon Athena for AWS usage and spending analysis

Once the CUR is successfully integrated with Amazon Athena, teams can use SQL queries to analyze AWS spending, understand trends, and gain insights into usage patterns. To begin, open **Amazon Athena**, navigate to the database where the CUR data is stored, and explore the tables. The data dictionary provided in the AWS documentation can help understand column definitions and stored values.

This section will use Amazon Athena and SQL queries for some basic use cases. Users can write advanced queries using SQL to get detailed cost level information, including resource level details.

Use case 1 is to identify the top spending AWS services

A common cost analysis requirement is understanding which AWS services contribute the most to overall spending. In the previous chapter, we saw how to use the **AWS Billing console** and the **AWS Cost Explorer** to identify the top AWS services contributing to overall spending.

Let us write a sample query to get a list of the top 10 AWS services ranked by their cost within a specified billing period.

Before writing queries, familiarize yourself with key CUR columns:

- **line_item_product_code**: Service identifier
- **line_item_unblended_cost**: Cost incurred

- **line_item_resource_id**: Specific resource identifier
- **bill_billing_period_start_date**: Start of billing period

The following code outlines a SQL query of the top spending services:

```
SELECT
    line_item_product_code AS Service,
    ROUND(SUM(line_item_unblended_cost), 2) AS Service_cost,
    DATE_FORMAT(bill_billing_period_start_date, '%Y-%m') AS BillingMonth
FROM your_athena_db.cur20_table
WHERE bill_billing_period_start_date >= DATE '2024-12-01'  -- Start Date
    AND bill_billing_period_start_date < DATE '2025-01-15'  -- End Date
    AND line_item_unblended_cost > 0
GROUP BY
    line_item_product_code,
    DATE_FORMAT(bill_billing_period_start_date, '%Y-%m')
HAVING
    SUM(line_item_unblended_cost) > 0
ORDER BY
    BillingMonth,
    Service_cost DESC
LIMIT 10;
```

The following figure shows sample results from running the query:

#	Service	Service_cost	BillingMonth
1	AmazonRDS	15.55	2025-01
2	AmazonQuickSight	10.45	2025-01
3	AWSSecurityHub	8.3	2025-01
4	AmazonS3	4.06	2025-01
5	AWSSecretsManager	2.81	2025-01
6	AmazonEC2	1.88	2025-01
7	awskms	1.74	2025-01
8	AmazonMacie	1.42	2025-01
9	AmazonGuardDuty	1.22	2025-01
10	AWSCostExplorer	1.04	2025-01

***Figure 3.10**: Top services by spend*

Here are a few key insights from the Query:

- **Service**: The top AWS service name (e.g., EC2, S3, Lambda) ranked by cost.
- **Service_cost**: The total unblended cost in USD.
- **BillingMonth**: The month in which the charges were incurred.

By analyzing this output, businesses can track major cost drivers, optimize service usage, and adjust budgets accordingly.

Tips:

- **Replace `your_athena_db.cur20_table` with your actual table name.**
- **Modify the date range based on your analysis period.**
- **Refer to the Athena pricing page for understanding the cost of running Athena queries based on the volume of data scanned.**

Use case 2 is to analyze Amazon S3 costs per bucket

AWS S3 costs can vary based on storage usage, retrieval patterns, and API calls. The following query retrieves the cost per S3 bucket for a given period:

The following code outlines a SQL query of the cost per S3 bucket:

```
SELECT
    line_item_resource_id AS bucket_name,
    ROUND(SUM(line_item_unblended_cost), 2) AS total_cost,
    DATE_FORMAT(bill_billing_period_start_date, '%Y-%m') AS billing_month
FROM your_athena_db.cur20_table
WHERE line_item_product_code = 'AmazonS3'
    AND bill_billing_period_start_date >= DATE '2024-01-01'
    AND bill_billing_period_start_date < DATE '2025-01-15'
GROUP BY
    line_item_resource_id,
    DATE_FORMAT(bill_billing_period_start_date, '%Y-%m')
HAVING
    SUM(line_item_unblended_cost) > 0
ORDER BY
    total_cost DESC
LIMIT 20;"
```

The results are shown here for reference:

#	bucket_name	total_cost	billing_month
1	01064:storage-lens/S3-lens-dashboard	1.67	2025-01
2	emrtestmantam	0.51	2025-01
3	aws-athena-query-results-us-east-1	0.5	2025-01
4	aws-cloudtrail-logs-sec-assessment	0.29	2025-01
5	cur-bucket-	0.27	2025-01
6	cloudtrail-awslogs-	0.25	2025-01

***Figure 3.11**: Cost per S3 bucket*

Here are a few key insights:

- **bucket_name**: The name of the S3 bucket incurring costs.
- **total_cost**: The total unblended cost associated with the bucket.
- **billing_month**: The billing period during which the cost was recorded.

This query helps identify expensive S3 buckets, allowing teams to optimize storage tiers, adjust lifecycle policies, or monitor unnecessary data retention.

Using Amazon Athena, AWS users can gain granular insights into their cost and usage data without setting up a complex data pipeline.

Cost visualization dashboard

Amazon QuickSight is a cloud-based BI service that enables users to create visualizations and gain insights from data. It supports various data sources and allows organizations to build interactive, easy-to-use dashboards. One of its valuable applications is visualizing AWS cost and usage data. By leveraging QuickSight, users can track spending patterns, analyze trends, and optimize resource allocation efficiently.

Exploring the AWS Cost and Usage dashboard

The Cost and Usage dashboard, available under AWS Data Exports, offers a pre-configured, easy-to-deploy solution for analyzing AWS billing data. This dashboard provides a high-level overview and detailed insights into cost and usage patterns, enabling organizations to make informed financial and operational decisions. It can be shared with key stakeholders, such as finance teams, executives, and technical teams, ensuring transparency and efficient cost management.

Some key features of the Cost and Usage dashboard are listed here:

- **Quick deployment**: The dashboard can be easily deployed through AWS Data Exports, eliminating the need for manual deployment and dashboard creation steps.
- **Pre-built visuals**: These come with pre-built charts and graphs, saving time and effort when creating reports from scratch.
- **Based on AWS CUR 2.0**: The dashboard is powered by the latest version of AWS's CUR 2.0, ensuring accurate and detailed cost tracking.
- **Customizable views**: Users can modify and tailor the dashboard to meet specific business requirements.
- **Automated alerts**: Users can set up alerts for specific cost thresholds, ensuring proactive cost management.
- **Report sharing capabilities**: The dashboard can be shared with relevant teams to ensure transparency and improve budgeting strategies.

Refer to the following steps to configure the cost and usage dashboard:

1. **Creating a QuickSight account**: Before deploying the Cost and Usage dashboard, a QuickSight account is required. If you do not have a QuickSight account, create a new account:
    a. Log in to the **AWS Management** console.
    b. Launch QuickSight from the **Service** console and sign up for an account.
    c. Complete the setup by providing a QuickSight username and linking it to your AWS account, as shown in the following figure:

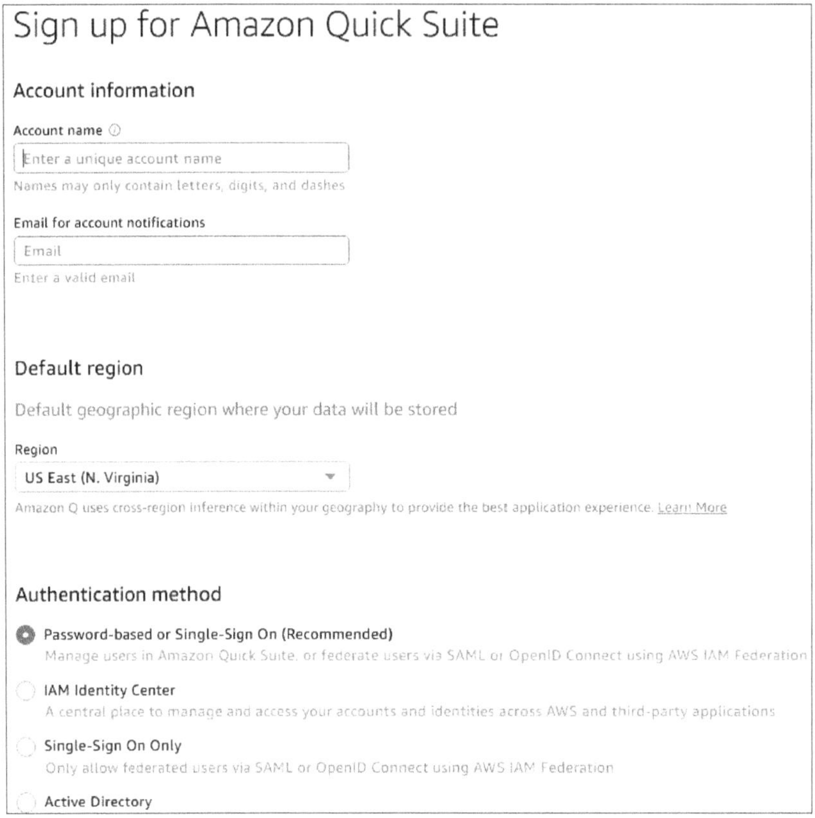

Figure 3.12: Create QuickSight account

2. **Configuring the Cost and Usage dashboard**:
   a. Navigate to **AWS Data Exports** under **Billing and Cost Management**.
   b. Click **Create Export** and select **Cost and Usage Dashboard (powered by QuickSight)**.
   c. Provide the required details:
      i. **Export name**: An identifier for your export.
      ii. **QuickSight username**: Username created in *Step 1*.
      iii. **S3 bucket details**: Specify an Amazon S3 bucket where the cost and usage data will be stored.
      iv. **Service role name**: Assign the appropriate IAM role that grants QuickSight permission to access the S3 bucket.
   d. Click **Create Export** to initiate the process. The dashboard deployment takes a few minutes.

Once created, it may take up to 24 hours for the visualization to be fully populated with cost and usage data. *Figure 3.13* shows some of the parameters to be provided when creating an export.

3. Accessing the Cost and Usage dashboard:

    a. Log in to your QuickSight account.

    b. Navigate to the **Dashboards** section.

    c. Locate and open the Cost and Usage dashboard deployed in the previous step:

***Figure 3.13**: Creating a Cost and Usage dashboard powered by QuickSight*

Getting started with the Cost and Usage dashboard

AWS Data Export, Cost and Usage dashboard, powered by QuickSight, represents a significant advancement over the traditional Cost Explorer, offering enterprises a more comprehensive and actionable approach to cloud financial management. While **AWS Cost Explorer** provides basic cost visualization and trend analysis, its insights are limited to predefined filters and views that require users to manually correlate multiple charts to identify optimization opportunities. The Cost and Usage dashboard enables resource-level visibility, allowing deeper insights into usage patterns, **Reserved Instances** (**RI**), and **Savings Plan** (**SP**) coverage. The dashboards include hundreds of pre-built visualizations to help users detect anomalies, identify spending trends, and uncover cost optimization opportunities with minimal manual effort. Let us review the Cost and Usage dashboard by going to the QuickSight account, selecting the dashboard from the left pane, and launching the required dashboard. The dashboard contains multiple tabs that provide insights into AWS spending:

Figure 3.14: Cost and Usage dashboard

The following list outlines a few key sections:

- **Executive summary**: A high-level view of AWS spending, including trends, budget variance, and key cost drivers.
- **Month-on-month trends**: Tracks spending trends over time, helping businesses identify monthly spending patterns and anomalies.
- **Service-specific cost insights**: Detailed breakdowns of cost and usage across various AWS services, including these options:
    - **Compute services**: EC2, AWS Fargate, and AWS Lambda usage and cost trends.
    - **Storage services**: Amazon EBS, Amazon S3, and file storage solutions (e.g., EFS, FSx).
    - **Database services**: Cost insights for Amazon RDS, Amazon DynamoDB.
    - **Networking and data transfers**: Analysis of AWS data transfer costs and network expenses.
    - **AI/ML services**: Spending patterns for AWS AI and machine learning services.
    - **Monitoring and observability**: Insights into costs associated with AWS CloudWatch, AWS X-Ray, and other monitoring tools.
    - **End-user computing**: Cost tracking for Amazon Workspaces and related services.

This comprehensive breakdown enables organizations to pinpoint high-cost areas, including resource-level details, and optimize resource utilization accordingly.

Dashboard customization

Users can customize the Cost and Usage dashboard as per their needs. QuickSight provides a **Save As** option, allowing users to create a copy of the default dashboard and modify it. Customization options include the following:

- Adding or rearranging visuals.
- Creating new reports focusing on specific cost categories.
- Adding filters to drill down into region-specific or service-specific costs.

Setting alerts and notifications

QuickSight allows users to set up alerts for cost thresholds. By configuring alarms, users can receive notifications when spending exceeds predefined limits, enabling proactive budget management.

Sharing with stakeholders

Dashboards can be shared with team members, ensuring that finance, executive, and technical teams have access to cost insights. Permissions can be configured to restrict access based on user roles.

The AWS Cost and Usage dashboard is a useful tool that provides deep insights into AWS spend. By leveraging Amazon QuickSight, businesses can effectively track, analyze, and optimize cloud costs. With its pre-built visuals, customization options, and stakeholder collaboration features, the dashboard helps organizations enhance cost efficiency and make informed financial decisions.

Building a QuickSight dashboard

In the preceding section, we explored how to use the **AWS Cost and Usage** dashboard to leverage pre-built visualizations for analyzing cloud expenditure and sharing cost insights with stakeholders. However, for more advanced customization or to build a completely new dashboard, QuickSight enables users to create visualizations from scratch. This section provides step-by-step guidance on how to develop a QuickSight dashboard to visualize AWS cost and usage data, starting with setting up prerequisites, creating a data source, and designing visualizations.

Before building a QuickSight dashboard, the following setup must be completed:

1. Leverage **AWS Data exports** to create an export of the AWS CUR to an Amazon S3 bucket. In *Chapter 2, Gaining Visibility into Cloud Costs Using Native Tools,* refer to the section, *Getting started with AWS Data Exports,* for detailed instructions. Ensure the exported data is stored in Parquet or CSV format.

2. As per the instructions given in the preceding section, *Steps for CUR 2.0 integration*, integrate CUR with Amazon Athena:
    a. Use AWS Glue to create a table in Amazon Athena.
    b. Run Athena queries to validate data availability.
3. Create a QuickSight account with required permissions.
4. Configured IAM permissions for QuickSight to access required services:
    a. Go to **QuickSight Service** in the **AWS** console.
    b. Select **Manage QuickSight** from the navigation menu.
    c. Under **Security & permissions**, click **Manage** AWS permissions and grant access to Athena and S3:

***Figure 3.15**: Granting permissions to Amazon QuickSight*

After completing these prerequisites, follow the steps mentioned in the upcoming subsection to develop a QuickSight dashboard.

Steps to create a QuickSight dashboard

Follow these steps to create a data source in QuickSight:

1. Open Amazon QuickSight and navigate to the QuickSight console.
2. From the QuickSight home page, click **Datasets** in the left menu.
3. Select **New Dataset** and choose **Amazon Athena** as the data source.
4. In the **Create a Data Source** window:
    a. Enter a **Data source name** (e.g., `cur20-custom-dashboard`).
    b. Choose the appropriate **Athena workgroup** (default is primary unless a custom workgroup is created).

c. Click **Validate Connection** and then **Create data source**:

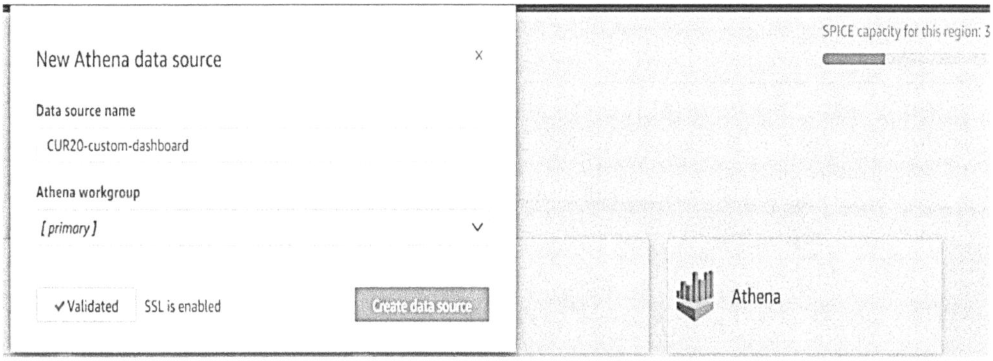

Figure 3.16: Creating a data source

5. Once the data source is created, select the appropriate Athena database and table containing cost data. Refer to the integration of Cost and Usage report with Athena for details:

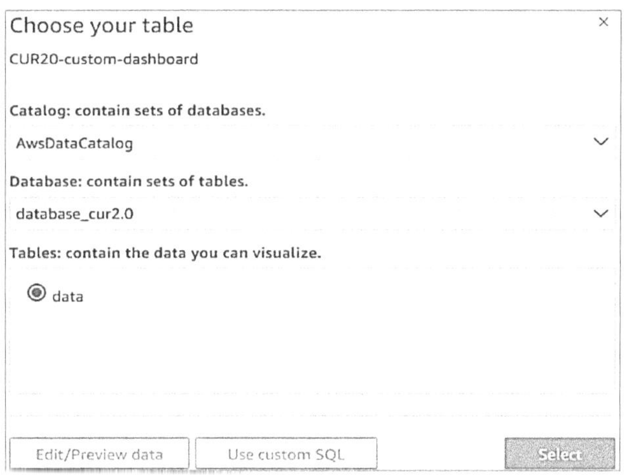

Figure 3.17: Creating a data source—Database details

6. Configure data import settings. Before you create a dataset, choose whether data should be loaded into SPICE for faster analysis (SPICE is a paid feature) or Query directly from the database.

   a. Choose **Direct Query**, then select **Visualize**.

   b. After completing this step, a dataset is created and ready for visualization.

7. **Creating an Analysis in QuickSight**: In this step, we will create an analysis and then publish it for users to access.

   a. Navigate to the **Analyses** tab in QuickSight and click **Create New Analysis**.

b. Select the dataset created in the previous step.

c. Click **Use in Analysis** to begin building visualizations. We will be creating two graphs: Cost by linked account and cost by services.

8. Adding visuals to the dashboard.

Now that the dataset is available, the next step is to create different visual representations of AWS Cost and Usage data. Refer to the next section on steps to create two different visualizations in QuickSight.

Graph 1, cost by linked account

Follow these steps to create the 1st visual in the dashboard:

1. Click **Add Visual** and select **Vertical Bar Chart**.
2. Configure the graph as follows:
   a. **X-axis**: `line_item_usage_account_id` (represents AWS linked accounts).
   b. **Y-axis**: `line_item_unblended_cost` (shows the cost associated with each linked account).
3. Click the pencil icon to rename:
   a. **X-axis label**: Account ID
   b. **Y-axis label**: Cost
4. Update the chart title to **Cost by Linked account**. The visualization will look like the following figure:

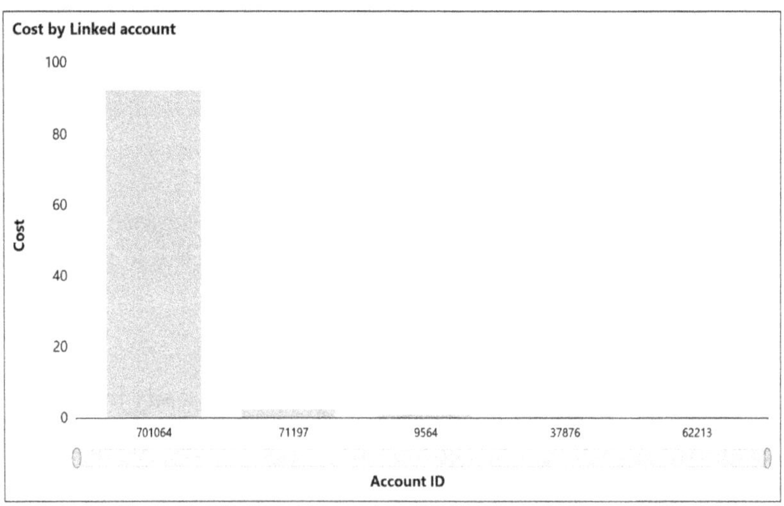

Figure 3.18: Cost by Linked account

Graph 2, cost by service

Follow these steps to add 2nd visual to the dashboard:

1. Click **Add Visual** and select **Horizontal Bar Chart**.
2. Configure the graph as follows:
    a. **Y-axis**: `line_item_product_code` (represents AWS services).
    b. **X-axis**: `line_item_unblended_cost` (shows the cost per service).
3. Click the pencil icon to rename:
    a. **X-axis label**: Cost
    b. **Y-axis label**: Services
4. Update the chart title to **Cost by services**. The visualization will look like the following figure:

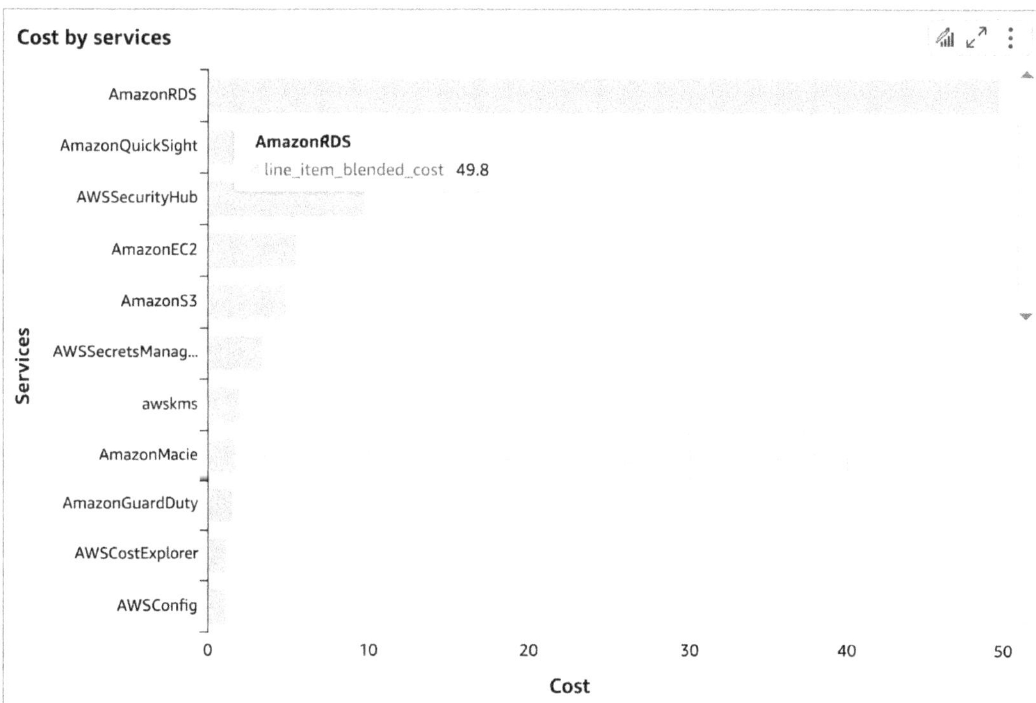

Figure 3.19: Cost by service

By using these two graphs, stakeholders can gain insight into spending across AWS accounts and services.

Publishing and sharing dashboard

An analysis is a read-and-write version of visualizations and datasets. Users can modify visuals, apply filters, and explore data. A dashboard is a read-only version that can be shared with stakeholders. It allows them to interact with filters, but they cannot make any changes to the visualizations or the dataset.

1. Click the **Publish** icon from the **Analysis** page.
2. Enter a dashboard name (e.g., **`Sample-CUR20-dashboard`**).
3. Click **Publish dashboard** to finalize:

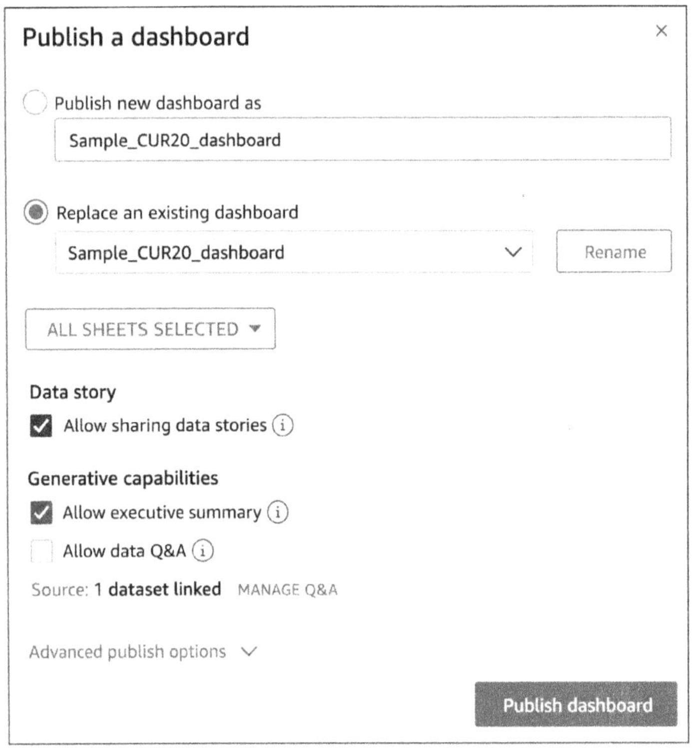

***Figure 3.20**: Publish dashboard*

Once the dashboard is published, you can start using it for analysis or sharing with other stakeholders for usage. The sample dashboard developed in the section will look similar to the following figure:

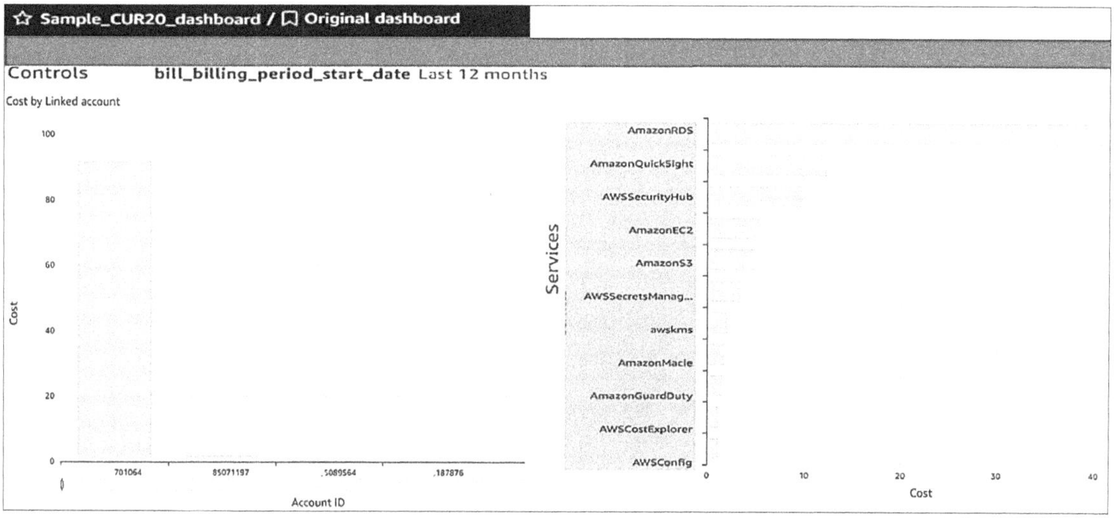

Figure 3.21: Sample dashboard published

Building a QuickSight dashboard from scratch provides organizations with insights into AWS cost and usage trends. This section outlines the key steps, from setting up prerequisites to creating and customizing a QuickSight dashboard. Whether using pre-built visuals or designing custom dashboards, AWS QuickSight empowers organizations with data-driven cost optimization strategies.

Other cost visualization dashboards

In addition to the AWS Data Exports—Cost and Usage dashboard powered by Quicksight, there are other pre-built cost visualization dashboards provided by the AWS builder community that offer deeper insights into cloud expenditure. One such dashboard is **Cloud Intelligence Dashboards** (**CID**), an open-source framework developed by AWS builders. CID offers a comprehensive view of AWS cost and usage data, making it a valuable tool for financial and technical teams. These dashboards are designed to provide high-level summaries as well as detailed, resource-level insights, helping organizations monitor cloud costs and optimize their spending efficiently. Organizations can leverage pre-built dashboards offered by AWS or the AWS Builder community, eliminating the need to develop cost visualization solutions from scratch.

To explore CID, users can visit **workshop.aws** and search for CID to find various available dashboards and deployment steps. Financial teams can leverage these dashboards to analyze monthly, quarterly, and annual AWS expenditures, ensuring better budget planning and cost tracking. Meanwhile, technical teams benefit from detailed resource-level breakdowns, enabling them to identify cost drivers and optimize resource utilization.

Some of the key benefits of CID include the following:

- **Ease of deployment**: CID dashboards can be deployed quickly using either the command line or AWS CloudFormation templates, ensuring minimal setup time. The organization saves an expensive development cycle to build a dashboard from scratch.
- **Resource-level visibility**: These dashboards provide granular cost insights, including visibility into RI and SP usage.
- **Multiple data source support**: CID dashboards integrate with various AWS data sources, including the CUR, Compute Optimizer, and AWS Trusted Advisor, providing a holistic view of AWS costs.
- **Pre-built visualizations**: The dashboards have hundreds of pre-built visualizations and machine learning-driven insights, allowing users to easily identify trends, detect anomalies, and receive cost optimization recommendations.

Organizations leveraging CID can enhance their cost management strategies, ensuring better forecasting, budgeting, and optimization. These dashboards provide historical insights and help organizations implement proactive cost control measures by identifying potential optimization opportunities.

Conclusion

Effective **cloud financial management** (**CFM**) requires organizations to have clear visibility into their cloud usage and costs. AWS offers a variety of cost management tools that help organizations analyze and monitor their cloud expenses. These tools include native AWS tools and dashboards, third-party analytics platforms, and pre-built cost visualization dashboards like CID. Organizations can start with AWS-native cost tools, evaluate pre-built dashboards, and customize or build their own dashboards to align with their specific visibility and reporting requirements.

Gaining visibility into cloud usage and spending is the first step toward successful cloud financial management. In the previous chapters, the focus has been on cost visualization and gaining insights into cloud spend. In the next chapter, we will shift our focus to cost optimization strategies, exploring tools and techniques that help organizations reduce costs while maintaining performance and efficiency.

CHAPTER 4
Moving from Cost Observability to Cost Optimization

Introduction

Cloud cost increases with increased usage during high-traffic events such as Black Friday or New Year's sales. Similarly, migrating new workloads to the cloud or adopting new cloud services can contribute to an increase in monthly costs. To understand spending fluctuations effectively, organizations must analyze cost trends using cost observability tools and correlate them with business events and metrics.

In *Chapter 3, Cost Visualization Dashboards*, we explored cost observability tools such as AWS Cost Explorer and Azure Cost Management + Billing to analyze cloud usage and spending. We also discussed creating custom cost observability dashboards as per organizational needs. This chapter shifts focus from cost observability to cost optimization by leveraging native advisory tools like AWS Trusted Advisor and Azure Advisor. These advisory tools provide actionable recommendations to optimize cloud costs and improve overall efficiency.

An ideal cost optimization strategy ensures that unit costs decrease as cloud usage grows. Unit costs represent cloud spend per relevant business metric—such as cost per transaction, per ride, per flight, or per insurance policy sold. Tracking and reporting unit costs offer a more accurate measure of cloud efficiency, helping businesses distinguish between cost increases due to growth versus misconfigurations or inefficiencies.

Structure

In this chapter, we will discuss the following topics:

- Cost optimization levers
- Prioritizing your cost optimization plan
- Getting started with cost optimization tools

Objectives

By the end of this chapter, the readers will be able to develop a structured approach to evaluate and prioritize cost optimization opportunities. They will learn to create a data-driven implementation plan that balances quick wins with long-term savings. Additionally, the readers will be able to effectively utilize native cloud provider advisory tools to identify resource wastage and optimization potential while gaining deeper insights into AWS Cost Optimization opportunities using AWS Cost Optimization Hub.

Cost optimization levers

Cloud cost optimization requires a strategic approach, as there are hundreds of levers organizations can pull to reduce spending. However, these levers can be broadly categorized into four key areas, as shown in the following figure:

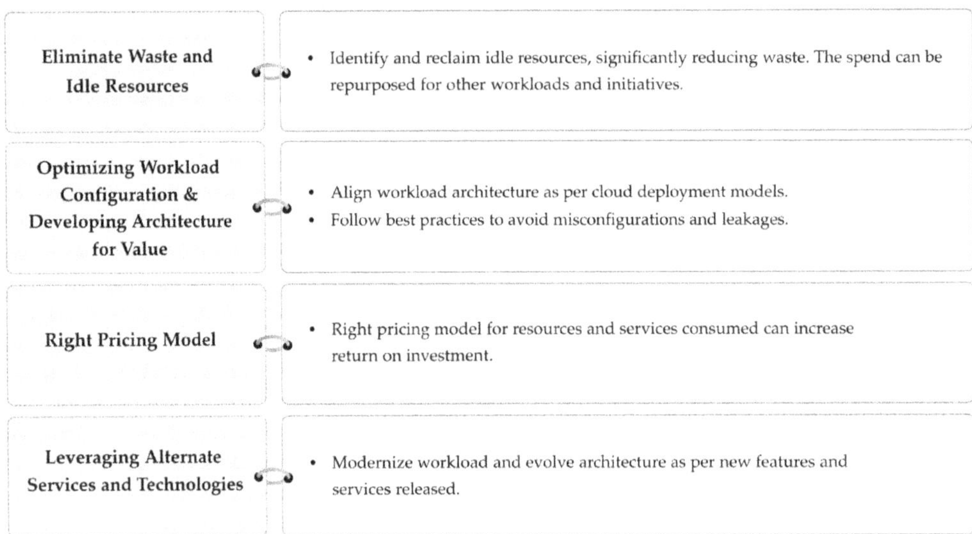

***Figure 4.1:** Cost optimization levers*

Eliminating waste and idle resources

This is a common challenge as organizations scale their cloud footprint. Over time, organizations deploy hundreds of **virtual machines** (**VMs**), storage volumes, and network devices to support various workloads. However, many of these resources may remain underutilized or entirely idle. For example:

- Unattached storage volumes incur costs without serving any workload.
- VMs running at less than 2% **central processing unit** (**CPU**) or memory utilization, indicating over-provisioning.

These inefficiencies often arise due to the following factors:

- Overprovisioning to accommodate peak loads.
- Redundant systems deployed beyond their necessity.
- Inadequate resource lifecycle planning, such as a lack of proper decommissioning practices when workloads are no longer needed.

Regular reviews using cloud monitoring and cost observability tools can help identify and reclaim idle resources, significantly reducing waste.

Optimizing architecture and deployment configurations

Suboptimal configurations can lead to unnecessary cost increases. To effectively manage cloud costs, it is crucial to identify and address suboptimal configurations that can lead to unnecessary expenses. The following list outlines a few examples of suboptimal configurations:

- Misconfigured network routing can cause excessive data transfer charges.
- Inefficient backup or retention policies can lead to inflated storage costs.

Regular configuration reviews can ensure that services are set up optimally. Additionally, designing architecture with a cost lens can lead to cost savings, such as:

- Migrating workloads from VMs to serverless architectures, reducing compute costs.
- Evaluating the trade-offs between self-hosted and fully managed cloud services based on specific workload requirements. While managed services can reduce operational overhead and licensing expenses in many scenarios, self-hosted solutions may be more cost-effective for certain workloads with existing investments.

Choosing the right pricing model

Cloud providers offer multiple pricing options, and selecting the right pricing model can significantly impact cost:

- **On-demand instances**: These are flexible but the most expensive.
- **Commitment-based pricing**: Reserved Instance or Savings Plan offers significant discounts for long-term commitment.
- **Spot instances**: Provide 75-90% savings over on-demand pricing, but are best suited for non-critical, short-lived workloads.

Organizations can achieve substantial cost reduction by aligning workload deployment with the appropriate pricing model. For instance, development and test instances might benefit from spot instances, while production workloads might be better suited for a commitment-based pricing model.

Leveraging alternative services and technologies

Organizations often follow a lift-and-shift migration strategy when moving workloads to the cloud. However, cloud providers continuously release new services and features that may offer better performance and cost efficiency. By proactively assessing emerging cloud capabilities, organizations can refine their architectures and adopt more cost-efficient alternatives over time.

Businesses should regularly perform the following to optimize costs:

- Consider modernization opportunities beyond initial lift-and-shift migrations.
- Evaluate newly launched cloud services and features for potential cost savings.
- Consider alternative compute, database, or storage services that may offer better pricing.
- Explore managed services to reduce operational overhead and lower the total cost of ownership.
- Evaluate multi-cloud and hybrid cloud strategies when developing their architectural framework. These approaches can yield architectures that optimize cost efficiency while aligning more effectively with specific workload requirements and business objectives.

By focusing on these four key cost optimization levers, organizations can proactively manage cloud cost, ensuring optimal resource utilization, efficient architecture, and the right pricing model. In the next section, we will explore how to prioritize cost optimization recommendations for maximum impact.

Prioritizing your cost optimization plan

In the cost optimization journey, once engineers have analyzed cloud spending using monitoring tools and identified the key cost drivers, the next critical step is to determine how to optimize those costs. In later sections, we will examine specific tools that help identify cost-saving opportunities across various services. However, the biggest challenge organizations face is prioritizing a number of cost optimization recommendations coming from different tools. There can be hundreds of cost-saving recommendations across various services, making it overwhelming to decide where to start.

To implement optimizations effectively, businesses must develop structured sprint cycles and project plans that maximize savings with minimal effort and in the shortest time possible. This raises the key question: *how do we prioritize cost optimization actions to achieve the greatest impact with the least effort?* and we will try to give guidance on approaching this problem statement.

Key factors for prioritization

Several factors influence the prioritization of cost optimization recommendations. The following sections discuss key factors in great detail.

Estimated savings potential

The first step in prioritization is quantifying the potential savings from implementing a given recommendation. This requires a deep understanding of cloud services, billing units, and pricing models:

- **Example 1**: In this example, we look at unused storage volumes. The cloud native advisory tool identifies five unattached Amazon **Elastic Block Store** (**EBS**) volumes that are not being used by any EC2 instances and recommends deleting the volumes. To calculate the monthly savings from decommissioning them, the engineer must check the following:
    - The size and pricing of each volume.
    - Whether the volume will be required in the future.
    - Snapshot cost for backup before deleting the volume.

  Using the preceding information, the engineer can calculate potential cost savings achievable by identifying and removing unattached Amazon EBS volumes. Most of the cloud native advisory tools provide cost optimization recommendations accompanied by estimated potential savings, enabling organizations to prioritize implementation efforts based on financial impact.

- **Example 2, recommendation on snapshot clean-up**: In this example, we look at optimizing snapshot storage costs. A cloud-native advisory tool highlights that the organization is spending $5,000 per month on snapshot storage. Further analysis reveals that 90% of the snapshots are older than 30 days, prompting a recommendation to delete them or implement a snapshot lifecycle management policy. Before implementing this recommendation, the engineer must evaluate the following:
    - **Billing structure for snapshot storage**: Determine whether snapshots are incremental or full copies and how it is charged.
    - **Impact of deletion on costs**: Check if deleting older snapshots will directly reduce costs or simply redistribute data blocks to parent snapshots. This can be analyzed by understanding the relationship between full and incremental snapshots.
    - **Estimating cost savings**: If direct cost reduction is unclear, analyze relevant metrics like the data change rate to assess potential savings.
    - Compliance or business requirement for longer data retention.

Using this information, the engineer can determine the feasibility and effectiveness of snapshot cleanup in optimizing storage costs.

Implementation cost

The optimization benefits from implementing the recommendation should be weighed against implementation complexity and associated costs. Before implementing cost optimization recommendations, organizations should evaluate the following factors to ensure that the benefits outweigh the implementation challenges:

- **Associated cost**: Some recommendations may lead to additional costs during implementation. For example, an Analysis of data access patterns may suggest moving 100GB of data from the Amazon S3 Standard tier to S3 Glacier archival storage to save on storage costs. However, moving data from one storage tier to another storage tier can incur API calls and data transfer-related charges. The associated costs need to be reviewed and factored into any implementation decision.
- **Effort hours required**: Estimating the effort required for implementation is essential. For example, decommissioning five EBS volumes may require minimal effort, while migrating a workload from virtual machines like EC2 to a serverless model could involve significant engineering effort and testing.
- **Skills and resource availability**: Implementing some of the cost-saving recommendations may require specialized expertise. For example, moving to a serverless model may require specialized skills and knowledge of services like AWS Lambda. Organizations need to validate the availability of relevant skills before developing a plan to implement the suggested changes.
- **Competing priorities and ongoing projects**: These may limit the engineering team's bandwidth to focus on the implementation of Cost Optimization recommendations.

Implementation timelines

Some of the cost-saving recommendations can be implemented immediately, while others require long-term planning. It is important to note that the implementation timelines for cost savings recommendations can vary from organization to organization, depending on the organization's internal processes, extent of service usage, and technical complexity. Let us look at some examples:

- **Quick wins (Minimal effort and can be implemented in short timelines)**:
    - Decommissioning unused resources (VMs, disks, snapshots).
    - Purchasing **Reserved Instances** (**RI**) or Savings Plan to lower resource costs.
- **Medium-term projects**:
    - Storage tier optimization
    - Backup policy modifications
    - Auto-scaling implementation

   - Right-sizing existing resources
- **Long-term optimization strategies**:
   - Rearchitecting applications to move from virtual machines to serverless.
   - Database migrations

Understanding implementation timelines ensures that the teams focus on low-effort, high-impact changes first while planning for long-term cost-saving strategies.

Dependency management

Some cost-saving recommendations may be conflicting or dependent on other recommendations. Understanding these dependencies helps prioritize an action plan to maximize savings.

For example, an engineer shared two recommendations to optimize the cost for EC2 instances. Let us look at them in detail:

- 10% of EC2 instances are underutilized and should be rightsized or decommissioned.
- The organization should purchase a Savings Plan to lower EC2 costs.

If the team commits to a Savings Plan first based on the current EC2 usage, and then later decommissions instances, the organization will still have to pay for the committed hours, negating the expected cost savings from decommissioning or rightsizing of EC2 instances.

The best approach in this scenario would be to right-size and decommission instances first, understand the usage post-decommissioning and right-sizing, and then purchase a Savings Plan based on the new, optimized instance count.

Calculating ROI for cost optimization

Once estimated savings and implementation costs are determined, organizations should calculate the potential **return on investment** (**ROI**):

ROI = [Estimated savings from recommendations] – [Implementation and associated cost]

Ensure that potential savings outweigh the effort and associated costs. If the ROI is positive, the optimization recommendation can be included in the sprint cycle. However, optimization recommendations should be analyzed at both a granular and a holistic level:

- **Granular level**: Analyzing cost impact for specific resources (e.g., a single EC2 instance).
- **Holistic level**: Evaluating impact across the entire cloud infrastructure (e.g., optimizing all EC2 instances).

A small change (like rightsizing a single VM) might not seem significant, but applying the change across hundreds of instances could result in substantial savings.

Developing a prioritization framework

To streamline prioritization, organizations can assign weights to key factors and calculate a **priority score** (**Pi**) as per the calculation:

$$Pi = Wa \times Wb \times Wc$$

Let us break this down:

- **Wa**: Potential ROI
- **Wb**: Skills and bandwidth availability
- **Wc**: Implementation timelines

The higher the Pi score, the higher the priority for the recommendation given.

For example, let us take an example to understand the weightage system used in the calculation of Pi.

The metrics used to assign weightage will vary by organization and need to be customized. To understand this, let us assume an organization has designed a sample weightage system as detailed in the table below. Wa, Wb, and Wc are assumed to have three different weights based on implementation priority—1, 2, and 3 (1 is the least favorable for implementation, 3 is the most favorable for implementation):

Factor	Weight	Criteria
Wa (ROI) based on monthly savings potential	1	<$1000
	2	$1000-$5000
	3	>$5000
Wb (skills and bandwidth availability)	1	No bandwidth available/Not a priority
	2	Limited bandwidth
	3	Full availability
Wc (implementation timelines)	1	>=4 weeks
	2	2-4 Weeks
	3	<1 week

***Table 4.1**: Sample weightage system*

Now, assume the team has got 3 cost savings recommendations from **AWS Trusted Advisor** and a cloud consultant. We will use Pi and the sample weightage system given in *Table 4.1* to develop a sprint cycle for the three different cost-saving recommendations received:

- **Recommendation 1**: Decommission unused EC2 instances:
  - **Monthly savings**: $7,500 (Wa = 3)
  - Devops team bandwidth is available to implement the recommendations (Wb = 3)

    - **Implementation time**: 5 days (Wc = 3)
    - **Priority score**: $Pi = Wa*Wb*Wc = 3 \times 3 \times 3 = 27$
- **Recommendation 2**: Storage tier optimization:
    - **Monthly savings**: $5,500 (Wa = 3)
    - Limited bandwidth as storage specialist is working on another project (Wb = 2)
    - **Implementation time**: 3 weeks (Wc = 2)
    - **Priority score**: $Pi = 3 \times 2 \times 2 = 12$
- **Recommendation 3**: Database instance right-sizing:
    - **Monthly savings**: $800 (Wa = 1)
    - No bandwidth of database SME currently available (Wb = 1)
    - **Implementation time**: 1 weeks (Wc = 3)
    - **Priority score**: $Pi = 1 \times 1 \times 3 = 3$

Recommendations with higher Pi should be implemented first, while lower priority scores can be scheduled for later implementation. In this example, the team would prioritize decommissioning unused EC2 instances (Pi is 27), followed by storage tier optimization (Pi is 12), and finally database instance right-sizing (Pi is 3). This prioritization framework can help organizations develop effective sprint cycles for cost optimization initiatives.

The same data can be plotted on an XY graph, where the X-axis represents implementation complexity (time and effort) and the Y-axis shows potential savings. Recommendations in the top-left quadrant (high savings, low complexity) represent the ideal quick wins that should be prioritized first. The bottom-right quadrant (low savings, high complexity) contains items that might be deprioritized or reconsidered. Engineers can use the approach defined to balance short-term and long-term cost-saving initiatives. The team can start with quick wins that have high priority scores and then systematically track progress on long-term cost optimization recommendations, ensuring continuous improvement in cost efficiency while aligning with organizational capabilities and priorities.

Let us look into a sample graph showing recommendations across impact and complexity, which can help finetune short- and long-term strategy:

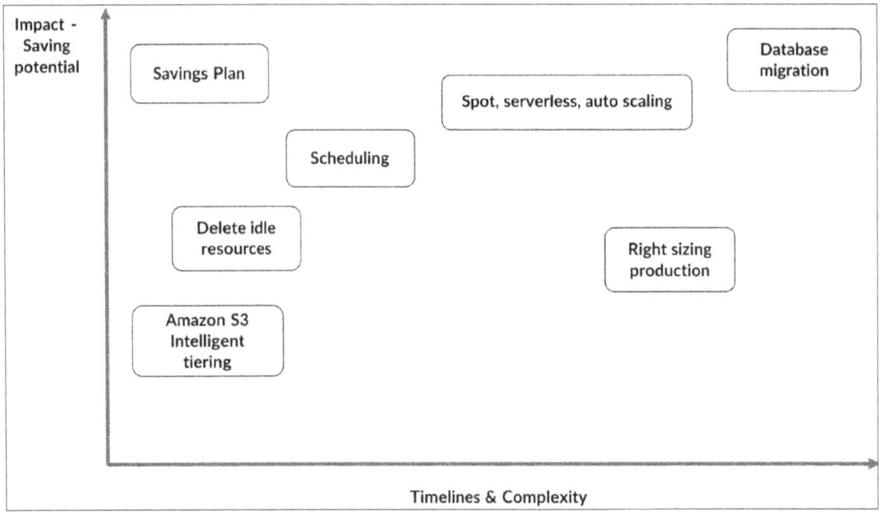

Figure 4.2: *Impact and complexity graph*

Getting started with cost optimization tools

As organizations scale their cloud infrastructure, managing costs becomes increasingly complex. While cost optimization strategies can yield significant savings, identifying where to focus requires reliable data and insights. There are two primary approaches to identifying areas for cost savings:

- **Manual review**: Cloud teams can analyze various service metrics and correlate with spend data to identify inefficiencies and misconfigurations—such as idle virtual instances, underutilized storage, or costly network routes.
- **Native cloud tools**: Cloud providers offer tools like AWS Trusted Advisor and Azure Advisor, which analyze different metrics from services and generate cost-saving recommendations.

In this section, we will explore native cloud tools like AWS Trusted Advisor, Azure Advisor, and AWS Cost Optimization Hub to get cost-saving recommendations based on best practices.

Introduction to AWS Trusted Advisor

AWS Trusted Advisor is a cloud optimization tool that inspects AWS resources and provides recommendations based on AWS best practices. These recommendations span six key categories, helping organizations improve cost efficiency, security, performance, fault tolerance, service limits, and operational excellence. Trusted Advisor continuously evaluates the AWS environment and resources provisioned, highlighting underutilized resources, misconfigurations, and security vulnerabilities. By following its recommendations, organizations can enhance performance, increase security, and reduce unnecessary spending.

Accessing AWS Trusted Advisor

AWS Trusted Advisor is available to all AWS customers, but the level of checks depends on the organization's support plan. To use AWS Trusted Advisor, the user needs to have appropriate IAM permissions that allow them to list and view Trusted Advisor recommendations and details of impacted resources.

The scope of AWS Trusted Advisor checks as per the AWS support plan subscription, is illustrated in the following table:

AWS support plan	Trusted Advisor access
Basic and developer support	Core security checks and service quota checks
Business, enterprise support, or Unified Operations	Full access to all Trusted Advisor checks

Table 4.2: *Trusted Advisor access*

If your organization is on the basic or developer support plan, you will need to upgrade to a business or enterprise support plan to access all cost optimization features of AWS Trusted Advisor. However, it is important to note that these higher-tier support plans involve additional costs and should be evaluated against the potential savings. Organizations need to conduct a cost benefit analysis to ensure the investment in an upgraded support plan delivers sufficient value to offset the increased support expenses.

Navigating the AWS Trusted Advisor dashboard

You can launch the Trusted Advisor dashboard by following these steps:

1. Sign in to the **AWS Management** console.
2. Search for `Trusted Advisor` in the AWS search bar.
3. Open the **Trusted Advisor** console to view recommendations, as shown in the following figure:

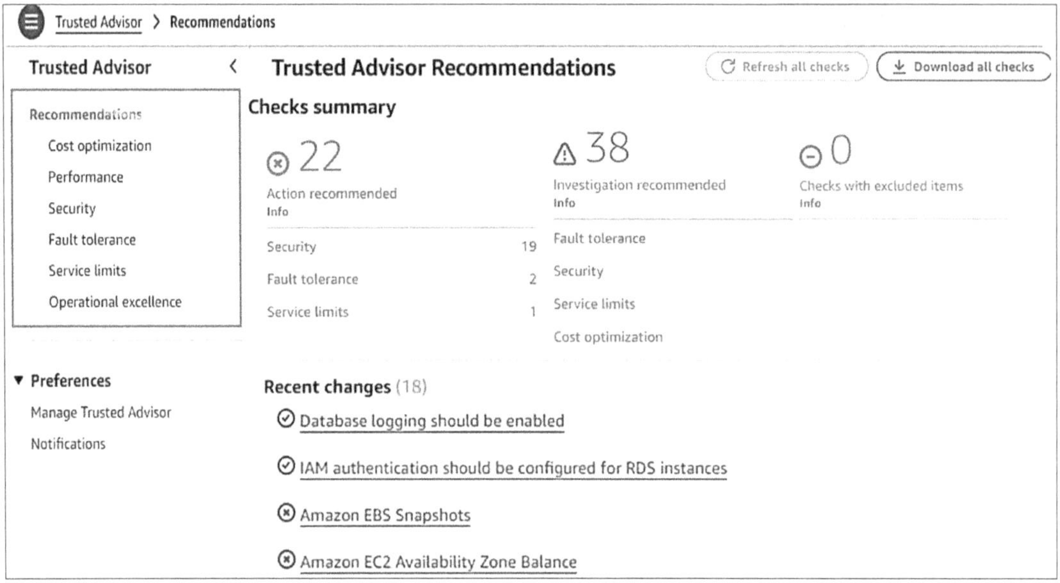

***Figure 4.3**: Trusted Advisor console*

Trusted Advisor provides an at-a-glance summary of findings across different categories, displaying the following:

- **Action recommended (Critical Issue)**: Immediate action recommended.
- **Investigation recommended (Warning)**: Investigation required to determine impact.
- Checks with excluded items.

You will find recommendations split across six categories:

- Cost optimization
- Performance
- Security
- Fault tolerance
- Service limits
- Operational excellence

In this chapter, we will focus on the cost optimization category, which provides potential monthly savings estimates and lists cost-related findings.

Cost optimization checks in Trusted Advisor

Trusted Advisor evaluates AWS usage and flags areas where organizations may overspend or underutilize resources. Click **Cost optimization** from the left pane of the AWS Trusted

Advisor console to launch the **Cost optimization** category page of **Trusted Advisor**, as shown in the following figure:

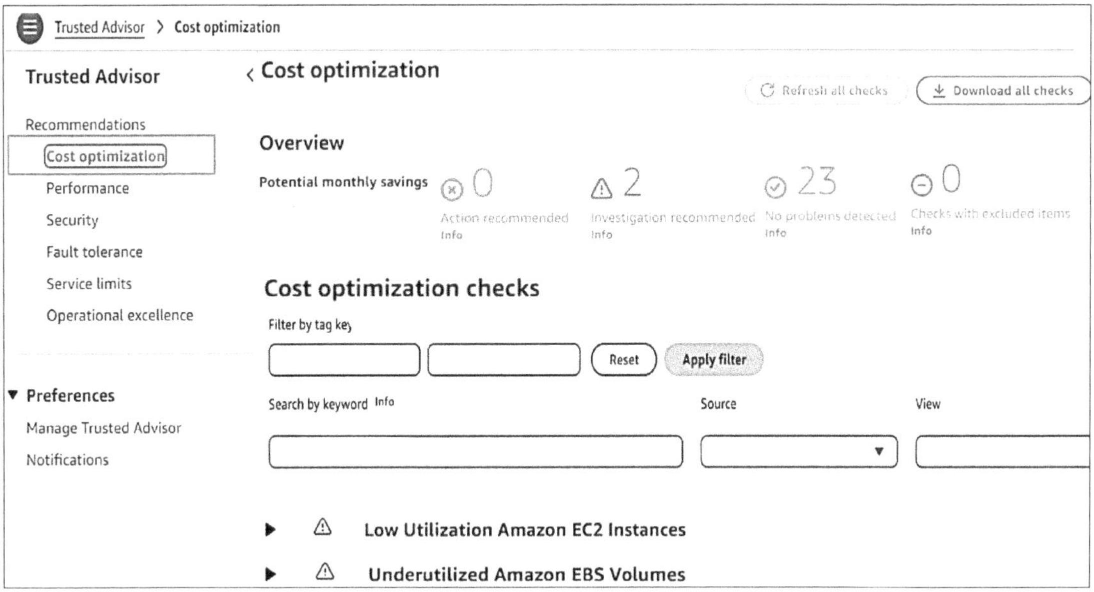

Figure 4.4: Trusted Advisor and cost category

AWS Trusted Advisor offers more than 30 cost optimization checks, with selected examples illustrated in the following figure:

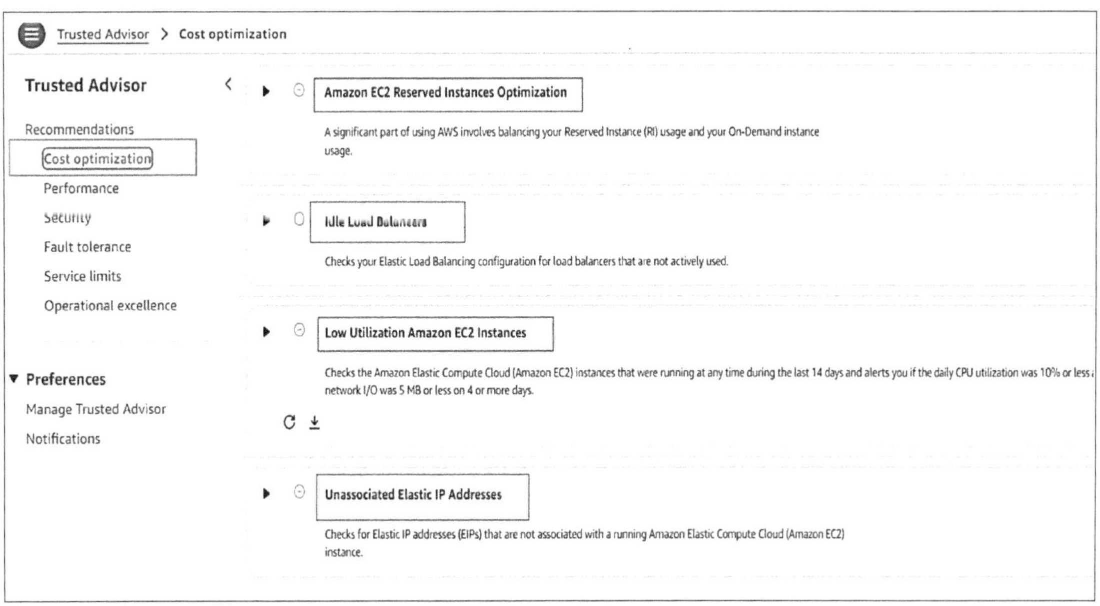

Figure 4.5: AWS Trusted Advisor and checks

Let us review some of the cost optimization-related checks:

- **Low utilization of Amazon EC2 instances**: Identifies EC2 instances running with low CPU utilization (≤10%) and minimal network activity over the last 14 days. The organization can then make a decision to rightsize instances to a smaller compute size or terminate unused instances to eliminate unnecessary costs.
- **Underutilized Amazon EBS volumes**: Identifies EBS volumes with very low read / write activity. These volumes can be deleted after taking snapshots or downsized to save cost.
- **Unassociated Elastic IP addresses**: Elastic IP addresses that are not associated with running instances incur charges. This check identifies such IPs, allowing you to either associate them with active instances or release them to avoid unnecessary costs.
- **Idle load balancers**: This check identifies Elastic Load Balancers that do not have any registered instances or have very low traffic, suggesting load balancers might be unnecessary and can be removed to save costs.
- **Amazon RDS Idle DB instances**: Similar to EC2 instances, this check detects Amazon RDS instances with very low database connection activity and flags idle databases that may no longer be needed. Organizations can then stop or terminate inactive RDS instances or migrate to a more cost-effective instance type.

Viewing and understanding recommendations

To evaluate a Trusted Advisor check, expand the check to view details related to the check, including its current status and the impacted resources. After expansion, check the alert severity (Red, Yellow, Green), review the recommended action, identify resources, and estimate monthly savings:

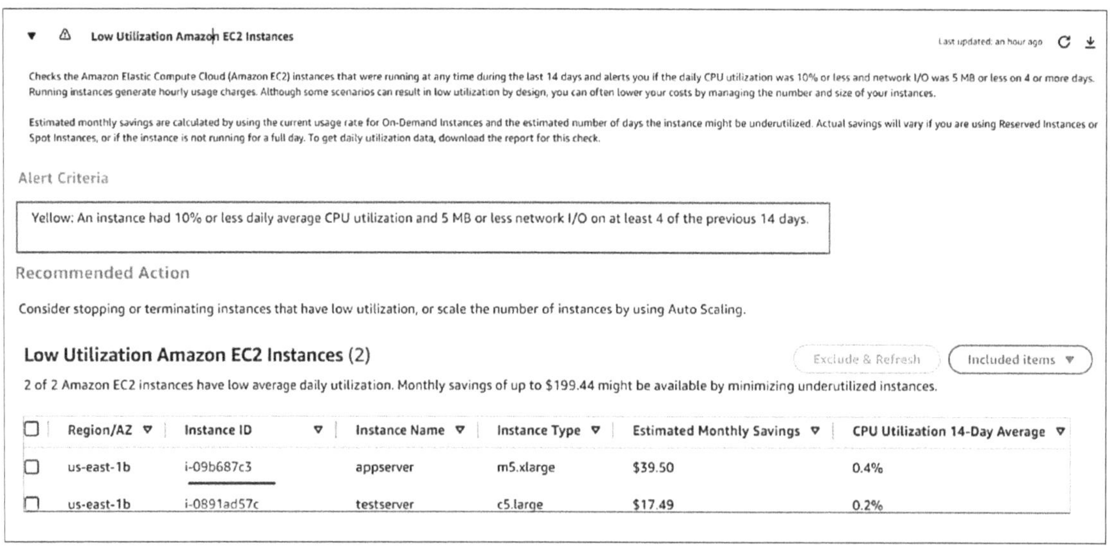

Figure 4.6: Flagging Amazon EC2 Instances having low utilization

There are three categories of alert severity:

- **Red**: Action recommended (critical issues that require immediate attention).
- **Yellow**: Investigation recommended (potential issues that should be investigated).
- **Green**: No problems detected (optimized configuration).

Once you have reviewed the cost optimization check and impacted resources, there are two primary actions you can take:

- **Implement the recommendation**: Some Trusted Advisor checks allow direct execution from the AWS console.
- **Suppressing recommendations**: Not all recommendations need immediate action. If a finding is not relevant, you can suppress it.

For example, take a look at checking low utilization EC2 instances:

1. Click on the **Low Utilization Amazon EC2 Instances check**.
2. Review the list of underutilized instances.
3. Understand the actions you can take to save costs by reviewing **Recommended action** section and the helpful resources provided.
4. Click on an Instance ID to navigate to the EC2 management page.

Choose to stop or terminate the instance.

Alternatively, if you want to suppress the recommendations as instances are deployed as per business requirements, you can follow the given steps:

1. Select the resource you want to suppress.
2. Click **Exclude and Refresh**.

AWS Trusted Advisor is a powerful cost optimization tool that helps organizations reduce unnecessary AWS spending while maintaining performance and security. Businesses can optimize cloud usage and significantly lower their AWS bills by regularly reviewing their recommendations and taking data-driven actions.

Getting started with Cost Optimization Hub

AWS offers a range of tools to help businesses identify, analyze, and optimize their cloud expenses. The AWS Cost Optimization Hub is a feature of AWS Billing and Cost Management and provides a centralized dashboard that consolidates cost-saving recommendations from multiple AWS services, making it easier to track, prioritize, and implement optimizations. It provides a holistic view of cost optimization recommendations, allowing organizations to reduce their AWS spending while maintaining or improving their operational efficiency.

Key features of AWS Cost Optimization Hub

The AWS Cost Optimization Hub offers several capabilities that set it apart from other AWS cost management tools. Let us look at them in detail:

- **Comprehensive cost recommendations**: Unlike standalone tools, the Cost Optimization Hub integrates with other tools like AWS Cost Explorer, Compute Optimizer, and Savings Plan as illustrated in the following figure, to provide more actionable insights:

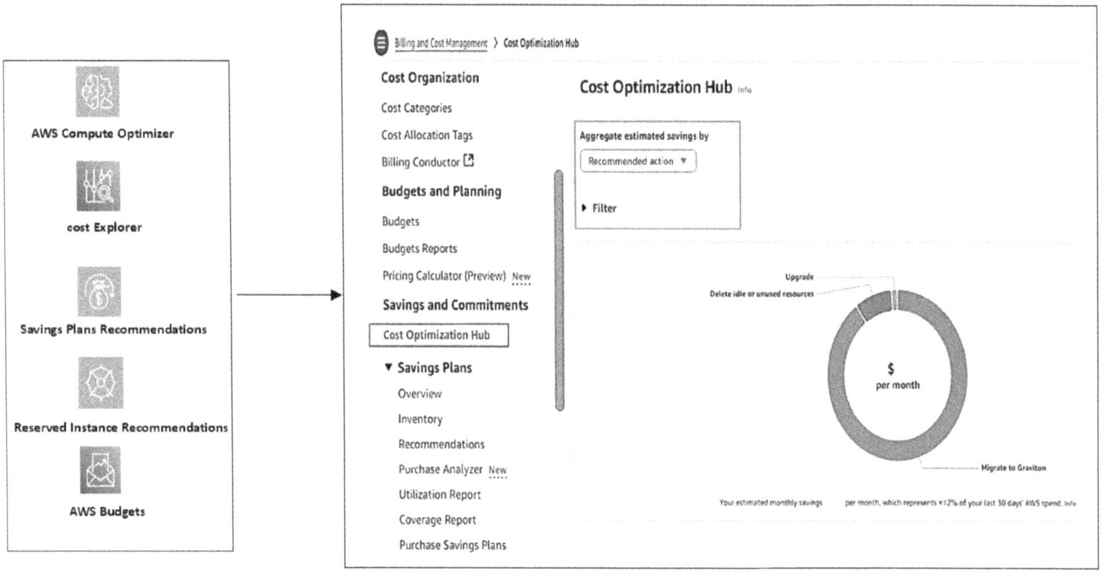

Figure 4.7: Cost Optimization Hub overview

  - Provides a unified view of all potential cost optimizations across AWS accounts and regions.
  - Recommendations are updated daily based on usage and billing data.
  - Recommendations can be exported for detailed analysis and sharing with stakeholders.

- **Prioritization of recommendations**: Users can filter and sort recommendations by AWS account, region, resource type, or implementation effort. Helps organizations focus on high-impact actions that deliver maximum savings.

AWS Cost Optimization Hub versus AWS Trusted Advisor

While both the Cost Optimization Hub and AWS Trusted Advisor aim to help customers optimize their AWS environment, they have distinct focuses and capabilities. Trusted Advisor provides broad best practices, and the Cost Optimization Hub offers detailed, data-driven cost optimization recommendations tailored to an organization's AWS usage. *Table 4.3* summarizes the differences between AWS Cost Optimization Hub and AWS Trusted Advisor:

Feature	AWS Cost Optimization Hub	AWS Trusted Advisor
Focus area	Exclusively on cost optimization. Provides a set of cost optimization recommendations to optimize AWS Spend.	Covers a broader range of areas, including cost optimization, performance, security, fault tolerance, and service limits.
Depth of insights	Provides in-depth cost analysis and tailored recommendations.	General best practices and high-level checks across multiple categories.
Integration	Fully integrated with other AWS cost management tools, such as AWS Cost Explorer and Compute Optimizer.	Standalone tool with limited out-of-the-box integration to other services.
Console access	Billing and Cost Management features	Trusted Advisor family
Example use cases	Underutilized EC2 Instance—Identifies underutilized EC2 instances, suggests specific instance types, and estimates cost savings potential.	Underutilized EC2 instance- Flags low-utilization EC2 instances and provides generic scaling/stopping recommendations.

Table 4.3: *AWS Trusted Advisor and Cost Optimization Hub comparison*

Enabling AWS Cost Optimization Hub

Enabling the Cost Optimization Hub is a simple one-click process from the AWS Billing and Cost Management console. Refer to the following steps:

1. Sign in to the **AWS Management Console**.
2. Navigate to **Billing and Cost Management**.
3. In the left navigation pane, click **Cost Optimization Hub**.
4. If using the tool for the first time, click **Get Started** to enable it.
5. Once enabled, the **Cost Optimization Hub** starts analyzing your AWS environment and generates cost-saving recommendations in about 24 hours:

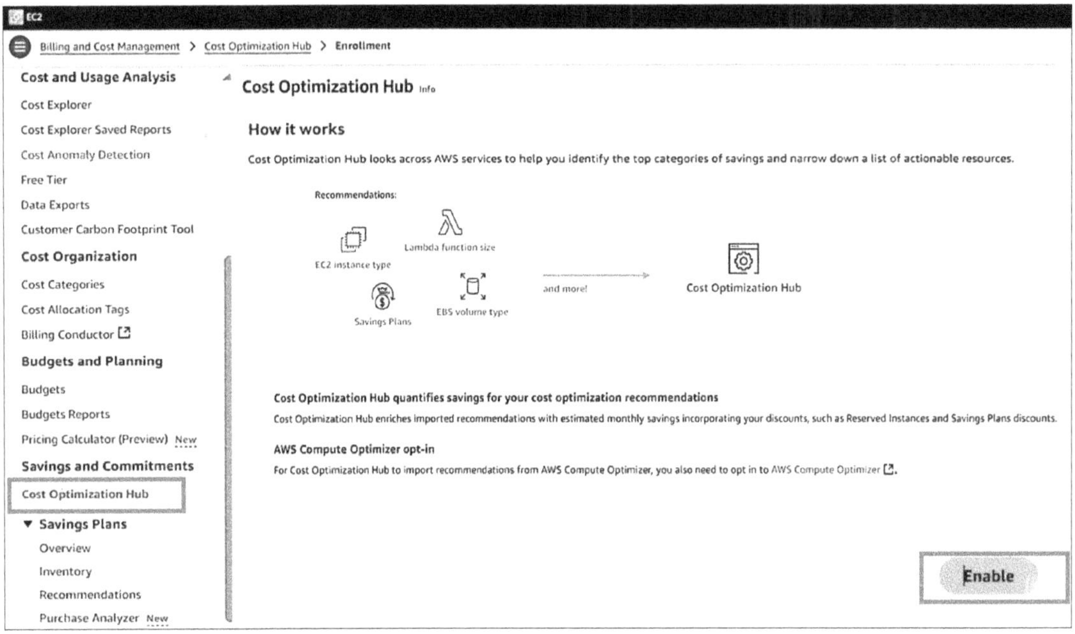

Figure 4.8: Enabling Cost Optimization Hub

Navigating the AWS Cost Optimization Hub

After activation, the Cost Optimization Hub dashboard provides an overview of potential savings:

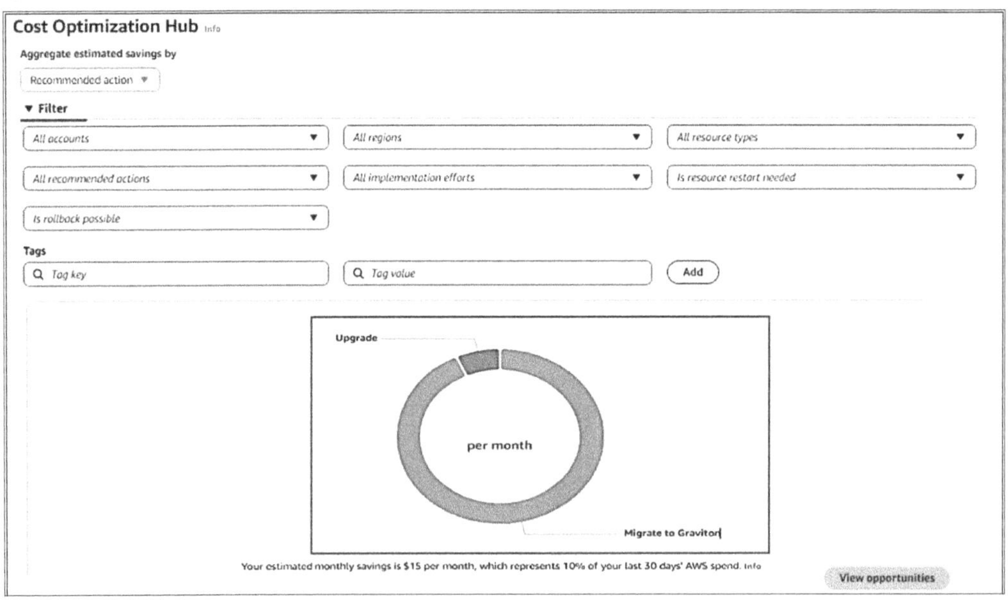

Figure 4.9: Cost Optimization Hub and console

The dashboard consists of the following parts:

- **View mode**: Aggregate estimated savings by AWS Account, AWS Region, Resource type, Tag key, etc.
- **Filtering and prioritizing recommendations**: To focus on high-impact areas, users can filter recommendations based on parameters such as:
    - **AWS account and region**: Optimize cost management across multiple AWS accounts.
    - **Resource type**: Prioritize specific resources such as EC2, RDS, EBS, or Lambda.
    - **Implementation effort**: Identify quick wins vs. long-term optimizations.

For example, if you want to optimize EC2 costs, you can filter by resource type = EC2 instances and view all relevant cost-saving opportunities:

- **Estimated monthly savings**: The total amount you could save by implementing recommended actions. The estimated monthly savings are aligned as per the View mode selected and the filter added. For example, if you select **View mode** as **Aggregate estimated savings by Recommended action**, the estimated monthly savings will show potential savings split by recommended action.

You can click **View Opportunities** to get details of identified resources. The page shows the following details:

- **Resource type and resource ID**: Identifies the specific AWS resources contributing to excess costs.
- **Recommended actions**: Suggestions such as stopping, resizing, upgrading, migrating to Graviton, or purchasing RIs.
- Current and recommended **Resource Summary** based on current usage pattern and optimization potential.
- Estimated monthly savings.
- Implementation effort required to achieve the savings.

Cost Optimization recommendations

AWS Cost Optimization Hub categorizes its recommendations into six key action types. Let us look at them:

- **Stop unused resources**: Identifies idle or unused resources that can be stopped to save costs. Example: Stop EC2 instances running with 0% CPU usage for the last 7 days.
- **Rightsize resources**: Identifies resources with low utilization and suggests downsizing over-provisioned resources to a smaller resource type.

For example, resize an overprovisioned EC2 instance from m5.4xlarge to m5.2xlarge based on utilization data:

- **Upgrade to the latest generation**: Recommends upgrading older resources to newer, more cost-efficient versions.

  Example: Upgrade EBS volumes from gp2 to gp3 for better performance at a lower cost.

- **Migrate to AWS Graviton**: Recommends moving from x86-based instances to AWS Graviton-based instances, which offer better price-performance efficiency.

  Example: Convert an m5 instance to an m6g instance for up to 40% cost savings.

- **Purchase Savings Plan**: Identifies opportunities to switch from on-demand pricing to Savings Plan.

  Example: Recommend Compute Savings Plan to reduce costs for consistently running workloads.

- **Purchase RI**: Recommends Reserved Instances for predictable workloads.

  Example: Purchase 1-year Reserved Instances for RDS databases running 24/7.

The AWS Cost Optimization Hub is a powerful, centralized tool designed to help organizations identify, prioritize, and implement cost-saving opportunities across AWS workloads. By providing actionable recommendations, it helps organizations optimize their AWS spending while ensuring operational efficiency. Unlike AWS Trusted Advisor, which covers a broader range of best practices, the Cost Optimization Hub is exclusively focused on cost savings, offering deeper insights and automated integration with AWS cost management tools. By consistently leveraging the Cost Optimization Hub, businesses can reduce cloud waste, optimize resource usage, and maximize their AWS investment.

Using Azure Advisor to optimize cost

In the preceding section, we explored AWS Trusted Advisor, a tool that provides cloud optimization recommendations for AWS environments, including cost optimization-related recommendations. Azure Advisor serves a similar purpose for Microsoft Azure, offering insights to help organizations optimize their cloud spending, improve security, enhance reliability, and boost performance.

One key difference between the two tools is that Azure Advisor is available to all Azure subscriptions at no additional cost, whereas AWS Trusted Advisor offers tiered access based on support plans. The only limitation with Azure Advisor is that some specific recommendations might require additional paid Azure services or features to be in use. This makes Azure Advisor an accessible and essential tool for anyone managing cloud workloads in Azure.

While AWS Trusted Advisor divides its recommendations into six categories, Azure Advisor focuses on five key areas:

- **Cost**: Optimizing cloud spend.
- **Security**: Identifying security risks.
- **Reliability**: Ensuring high availability.
- **Operational Excellence**: Improving operational best practices.
- **Performance**: Enhancing workload efficiency.

The upcoming section will explore how Azure Advisor's cost recommendations can help optimize Azure cloud spend.

Navigating the Azure Advisor dashboard

To launch Azure Advisor, follow these steps:

1. Log into the Azure portal (**portal.azure.com**).
2. Search for **`Azure Advisor`** in the top search bar.
3. Open the **Advisor** dashboard, where an overview of recommendations for all five categories is displayed:

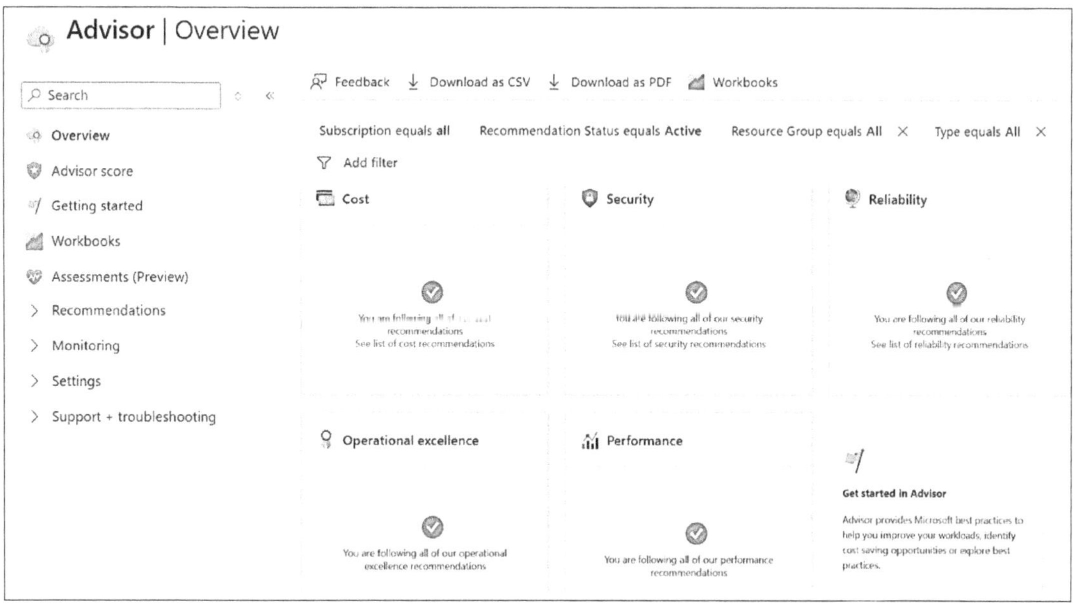

Figure 4.10: Azure Advisor overview

The dashboard is divided into five categories, each representing different areas of optimization. To focus on cost-saving recommendations, navigate to the **Cost** section.

In the **Cost** category, you will find the following:

- The number of cost recommendations applicable to your environment.
- A summary of potential savings.
- Breakdown of impacted resources and their estimated cost-saving potential.

Cost optimization recommendations

Azure Advisor continuously analyzes resource utilization and configuration to provide cost-saving insights.

Here are some cost optimization recommendations that can help lower Azure spend:

- **Right-size or shutdown underutilized VMs**: Similar to AWS Trusted Advisor's low utilization Amazon EC2 Instances check, it identifies Azure VMs that have low CPU utilization over an extended period. The Azure Advisor suggests resizing the VM to a smaller SKU or shutting it down if it is no longer needed.
- **Consider RI for MySQL databases to save over your pay-as-you-go costs**: The check identifies Azure Database for MySQL instances running in the on-demand model and suggests purchasing RI for cost savings.
- **Repurpose or delete idle virtual network gateways**: Similar to AWS Trusted Advisor's Idle Load Balancers check, it identifies unused virtual network gateways with no data transfer for an extended period. The tool suggests either deleting these gateways or resizing them to a lower-cost SKU to reduce costs.
- **Retention policy for classic log data in storage accounts**: The check helps in optimizing Log Data Retention in Storage Accounts by reviewing the retention policy of classic logs and suggesting reducing the retention period to retain less log data. This would reduce unnecessary classic log data and save storage space.

Implementing cost recommendations

To review and apply Azure Advisor's cost recommendations, follow these steps:

1. Navigate to the **Cost** section of the Azure Advisor dashboard.
2. Review recommendations categorized by Impact Level (High, Medium, Low).
3. For each recommendation, review the following:
    a. Potential benefits (Estimated savings).
    b. Impacted resources (List of affected resources).
    c. Description (Detailed recommendation explanation).

4. Click on a specific recommendation to view more details.
5. Click on **Recommended Actions** to open the relevant Azure page or resource page.

Right-size or shutdown of underutilized virtual machines

Follow these instructions to implement the suggested optimization:

1. Open Azure **Advisor** and go to the **Cost** section.
2. Find the rightsize or shutdown underutilized VMs recommendation.
3. Review the list of impacted VMs.
4. Click on a VM to examine detailed utilization metrics.
5. Choose an action suggested by Advisor:
    a. Resize to a lower SKU based on workload needs.
    b. Implement auto-shutdown policies to stop instances when idle.
    c. Delete unused resources.

Alternatively, you can postpone the recommendation for a few weeks if you need more data or dismiss the recommendation if the VM is configured appropriately as per business requirements.

Azure Advisor is an essential tool for optimizing Azure costs. It provides actionable recommendations that help organizations rightsize resources, remove idle workloads, and improve cost efficiency. By integrating Azure Advisor into your cloud management strategy, you can continuously optimize your Azure environment, ensuring cost efficiency while maintaining performance and reliability.

Conclusion

Effective cloud cost optimization requires more than just visibility into usage and spending. While cost observability tools provide valuable insights into usage patterns and cost trends, they do not offer specific recommendations for reducing waste and improving efficiency. This is where cost optimization tools like AWS Trusted Advisor, Azure Advisor, and AWS Cost Optimization Hub become essential. These tools analyze resource consumption and cloud configurations to generate actionable cost-saving recommendations. Each tool has unique capabilities—Trusted Advisor offers broad AWS best practices, Azure Advisor provides Azure-specific recommendations, and Cost Optimization Hub centralizes AWS cost-saving insights with deeper integration across cost management tools.

However, given the large number of recommendations coming from tools and manual analysis, organizations must prioritize optimization efforts based on factors such as potential return on investment, effort required, skill and resource availability, and implementation timelines. This chapter covered how to define priority areas for cost optimization and explored key tools available in AWS and Azure.

In the next chapter, we will focus on compute services, diving deeper into specific strategies to optimize compute costs for workloads running in the cloud.

CHAPTER 5
Optimizing Compute Cost

Introduction

In today's cloud computing landscape, compute services form the core of most organizations' cloud infrastructure. Whether it is **Amazon Elastic Compute Cloud** (**Amazon EC2**), Azure Virtual Machines, or **Google Compute Engine** (**GCE**), these services support essential workloads from web applications to complex databases. As organizations continue their cloud journey, transitioning from traditional data centers, compute services often represent one of the largest elements of cloud spending. This also presents an opportunity for organizations to optimize cloud spending by focusing on compute services.

This chapter explores strategies to maximize the cost-efficiency of your cloud compute resources. We will explore key optimization techniques, including instance rightsizing, workload modernization, elasticity implementation, and leveraging commitment-based savings. Furthermore, you will gain insight into some of the compute specific tools provided by cloud vendors that facilitate cost optimization and learn how to interpret their recommendations.

Structure

In this chapter, we will discuss the following topics:

- Understanding compute services portfolio
- Anatomy of cloud compute pricing
- Tools for analyzing compute usage and spend
- Reviewing cost optimization levers for compute
- Developing a prioritized action plan

Objectives

By the end of this chapter, you will gain essential knowledge and practical skills to optimize your cloud compute costs. You will learn about different cost-saving strategies, including elasticity, rightsizing instances to align with workload requirements, modernizing compute infrastructure for improved efficiency, and leveraging commitment-based savings options. You will gain insight into some of the compute-specific tools provided by cloud vendors that facilitate cost optimization and learn how to interpret their recommendations. Additionally, you will be equipped to develop a prioritized implementation plan that balances estimated savings, the level of effort required, and any potential conflicts among recommendations. While the chapter uses AWS and Azure for illustrative purposes, the principles and strategies discussed can be applied across all major cloud platforms.

Understanding compute portfolio

When selecting compute services for web, application, or database tiers, cloud providers like AWS, Azure, and GCP offer a broad spectrum of instance types and configurations. Understanding your compute portfolio is crucial to defining an effective optimization strategy.

The following figure shows compute services provided by AWS:

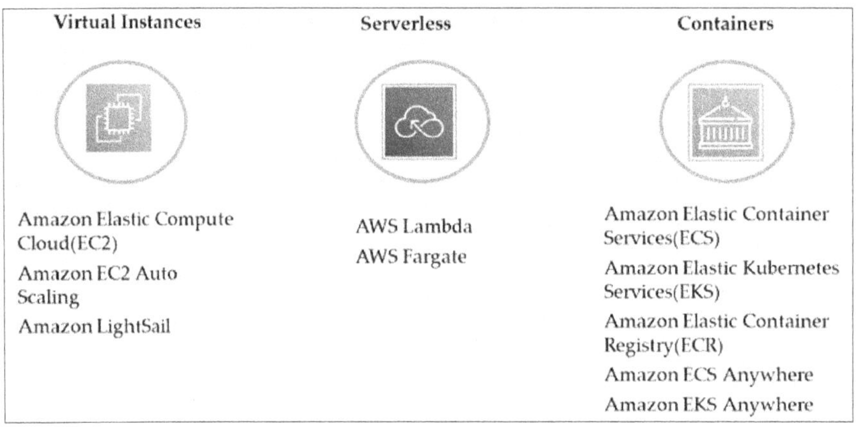

Figure 5.1: AWS compute service

Some commonly used compute services include the following:

- **Virtual machines**: Amazon EC2, Azure Virtual Machines, and Google Compute Engine provide virtual servers in various configurations and are optimized for different use cases. Organizations can select appropriate instances based on vCPU, memory, disk I/O, network throughput, and operating system requirements.
- **Serverless options**: Services like AWS Lambda, AWS Fargate, and Azure Functions enable organizations to run applications without managing underlying virtual instances. These eliminate the need for server provisioning and maintenance, allowing teams to focus on application code development.
- **Container services**: Organizations can host containerized applications using services like Amazon ECS, Amazon EKS, or **Azure Kubernetes Service** (**AKS**), offering flexibility for microservices architectures.

The following figure shows Azure compute portfolio:

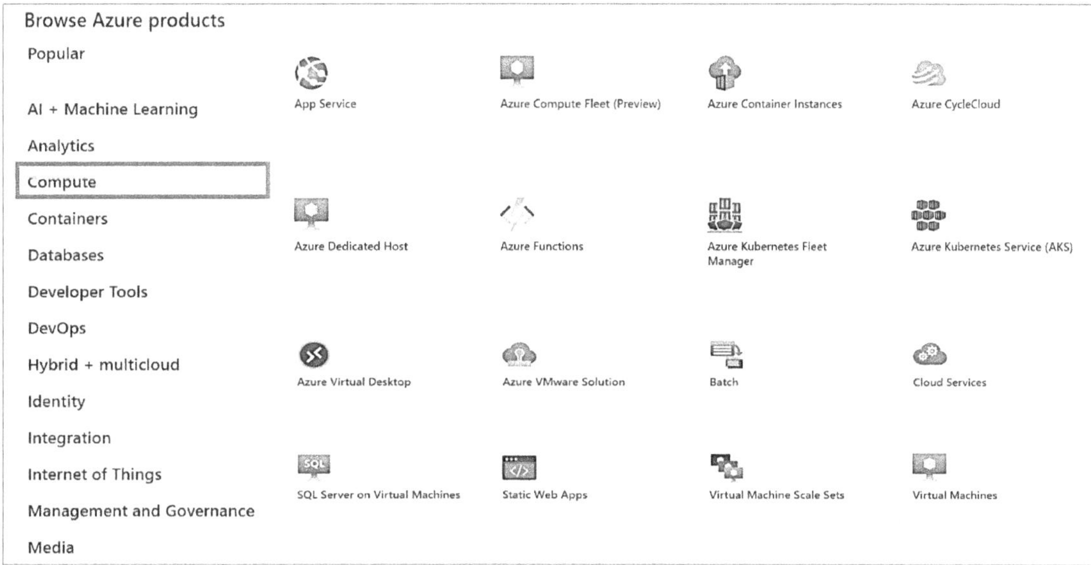

***Figure 5.2**: Azure compute service*

While this chapter will focus primarily on optimizing Amazon EC2 instances, the optimization principles apply to all compute types and cloud providers.

Anatomy of cloud compute pricing

Understanding how compute services are priced is essential when developing your cloud architecture and optimizing compute costs. Let us review some of the key elements that influence compute pricing and explain how they impact your organization's cloud spend:

- **Region**: The price of cloud services, including compute services, varies by region. For instance, the cost of an EC2 instance in Asia Pacific (Mumbai) differs from the same instance type in *US East (N. Virginia)*.
- **Billing units**: Cloud providers use different billing units to charge for compute services, each designed for specific use cases:
    - Per-second billing (e.g., AWS EC2, with a 60-second minimum, Azure virtual machines)
    - Per-hour billing
    - Per-execution (Used primarily for serverless computing e.g., AWS Lambda, Azure Functions)

  Understanding billing units helps estimate costs more accurately, especially when scaling services up or down.

- **Purchase options**: Cloud providers offer flexible purchasing models to meet different budget and usage needs:
  - **On-demand**: Pay as you go model with no commitment.
  - **Reserved Instances/Savings Plan**: Commitment-based savings. Commitment for 1 or three years for a discount of up to 70%.
  - **Spot Instances**: Purchase unused compute capacity at ~90% discounts, but with the risk of interruption.

  Let us take an example to understand how EC2 pricing varies based on the purchase option you choose. Consider an m5a.large instance running in the Ohio (us-east-2) region:
  - **On-demand**: As per the Amazon EC2 public pricing page, running an m5a.large on the on-demand model costs $0.086 per hour. The on-demand model provides the highest flexibility option, and you pay for compute capacity by usage with no long-term commitment.
  - **1-year Reserved Instance/Savings Plan**: If you commit to a 1-year term, the hourly rate drops to $0.063 per hour. This offers a substantial discount in exchange for a commitment.
  - **Spot Instances**: Spot pricing is dynamic and is based on available EC2 capacity. With Spot, you pay as per the current spot price for the time your instance is running. While the price is variable, the historical average discount for m5a.large is around 55%, which can bring the effective hourly cost down significantly compared to on-demand.

  This example demonstrates how choosing the right purchase option—on-demand, Reserved Instances/Savings Plan, or Spot—can provide significant financial benefit.
- **Operating system**: Compute costs vary depending on the OS:
  - Linux-based instances (e.g., Amazon Linux, Ubuntu) are generally cheaper.
  - Windows and **Red Hat Enterprise Linux** (**RHEL**) include additional licensing fees, raising per-hour costs.
- **Processor type**: The type of processor affects both performance and price. Cloud providers offer instances powered by:
  - **Intel**: Widely supported, but generally more expensive.
  - **AMD**: Lower cost (~20% savings compared to Intel).
  - ARM **based**: Some cloud providers offer ARM based instances, such as Graviton (AWS only). These instances are optimized for performance and are cost effective compared to Intel (~40% savings versus Intel).

- **Instance type and size**: Instance families are designed for specific workloads. Examples include the following:
  - o General purpose (e.g., t3, m5)
  - o Compute optimized (e.g., c5)
  - o Memory optimized (e.g., r5)
  - o Accelerated computing (e.g., p4, g4)

  The size of the instance (e.g., large, large, xlarge, 2xlarge) plays a major role, as it determines the number of vCPUs, memory, network bandwidth, and storage IOPS.

The following figure illustrates how the various configuration choices we have discussed directly influence Azure Virtual Machine pricing. You can select parameters like **Region**, **OS/Software**, **Category**, **VM Series**, and pricing model to filter the results. The table then displays specific instance types, detailing their CPU and RAM, along with the corresponding on-demand and Savings Plan prices. This example helps you understand how each input impacts the pricing of a virtual machine on the cloud.

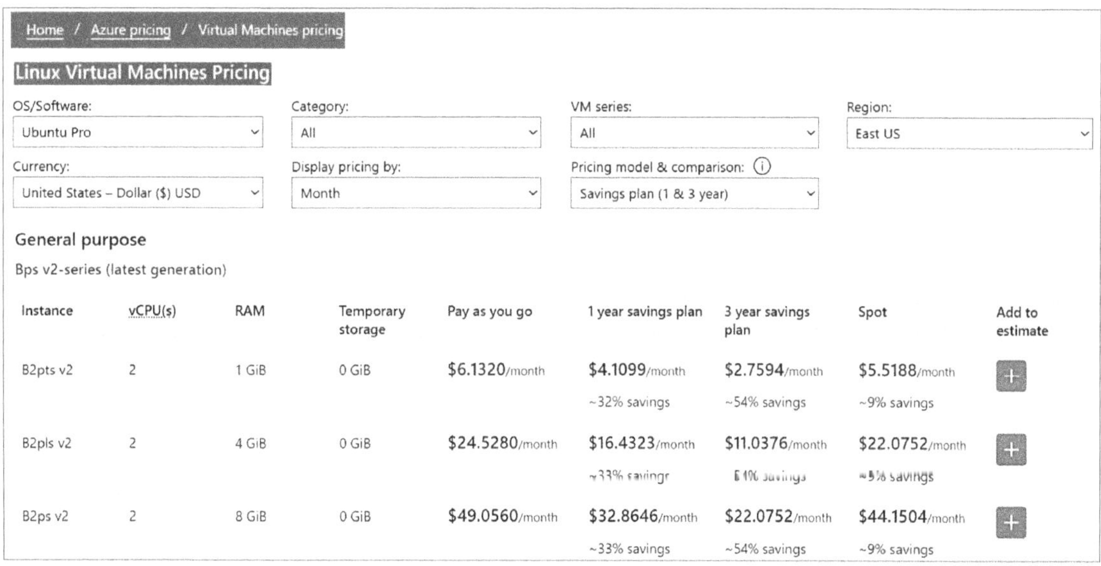

***Figure 5.3**: Azure Virtual Machine pricing snapshot*

Tools for analyzing compute usage and spend

Before looking into optimization techniques for compute, it is essential to gain visibility into how the organization is currently using compute resources and analyze compute spend from different dimensions. We have reviewed tools that can be leveraged for analyzing compute usage and spend in earlier chapters, and they are summarized in the following table. We will start by exploring some of the key tools provided by AWS, and is grouped into three categories.

Category	Tool	Description
Observability	AWS Billing console	View consolidated billing data and invoices.
	AWS Cost Explorer	Visualize usage and cost trends across services and leverage filters to dive deep into compute usage and spend.
	AWS CUR	Provides detailed, resource-level usage and cost data.
	Cost and Usage dashboard	Pre-built dashboards (via QuickSight) such as CID.
Optimization	AWS Trusted Advisor	Checks for underutilized instances and unused resources.
	Compute Optimizer	Rightsizing and modernization guidance based on usage patterns.
	AWS Cost Optimization Hub	Centralized dashboard for providing recommendations based on cost-saving opportunities and has integration points with different tools and services.
Estimation	AWS Pricing Calculator	Estimate the compute cost for deploying the workload. Can also be used for comparing costs for different instance configurations.

Table 5.1: Tools for analyzing compute usage and spend

Similar to AWS, Azure provides a comprehensive set of cost-management tools to help users analyze the pricing of Azure compute services in detail. Under the umbrella of Azure Cost Management + Billing, these native tools offer deep visibility into spending patterns, cost drivers, and usage trends. These integrated tools are essential for monitoring, analyzing, and forecasting costs specific to your Azure compute offerings (such as virtual machines, containers, and functions).

Reviewing compute costs using AWS Cost Explorer

Let us begin by analyzing compute usage, specifically Amazon EC2, which is typically the most significant contributor to compute costs.

These are the steps to use AWS Cost Explorer:

1. Go to the **AWS** console and navigate to **Billing and Cost Management**.
2. Launch **Cost Explorer** from the left-hand menu.
3. Apply the following filters:
    a. **Date range**: Last three months
    b. **Granularity**: Monthly
    c. **Dimension**: Service

4. This will generate a view as shown in the following figure and help you understand how much of your overall cloud spend is attributable to EC2. If EC2 is among the top five contributors to your cloud spend, it indicates a high potential for savings through optimization.

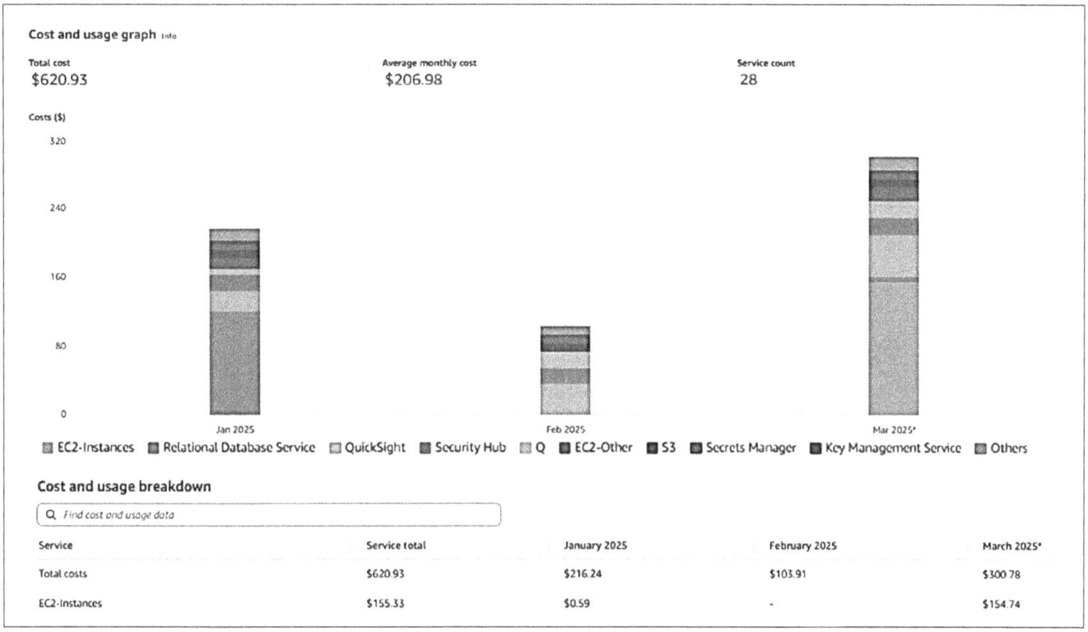

***Figure 5.4:** Spend by service*

5. Once you have compared EC2 spending with overall cloud spending, the next step is to drill down further into instance type and purchase options. This will help us understand the different instance types currently deployed and whether purchase options like Spot and Reserved Instances are leveraged.

    a. In **Cost Explorer**, change the dimension to **Instance Type**.

    b. Set **Service** to **Elastic Compute Cloud-Compute** (**EC2**).

The view illustrated in the following figure will display the cost breakdown by instance families (e.g., m5.large, c5.xlarge):

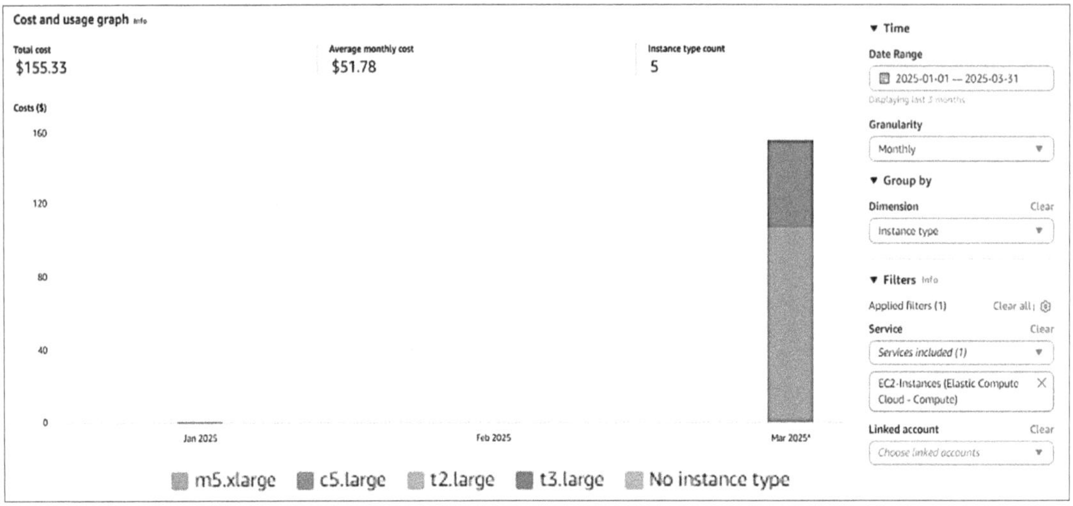

Figure 5.5: EC2 spend by instance type

6. You can change dimensions and filter to analyze compute spend from a different perspective, such as:

    a. **Understand region-wise spend**: Change the dimension to **Region** to evaluate EC2 spend by region and identify the region where workloads are hosted.

    b. **Analyze usage patterns**: Change **Granularity** to **Daily** or **Hourly** to detect 24x7 usage patterns such as spikes during business hours. This will help understand if usage varies by peak and off-peak load or is constant usage.

    c. **Purchase options**: Change dimension to **Purchase type** to view spend by purchase options-on-demand, Spot, or Reserved Instances.

Correlating AWS Cost Explorer findings with Billing console

To validate findings or get an invoice-style breakdown, follow these steps:

1. Go to the AWS **Billing and Cost Management** dashboard and select **Bills**.
2. Select a **Billing period** for analysis.
3. In the tab **Charges by service**, expand **Elastic Compute Cloud,** as shown in *Figure 5.6*.
4. You can explore EC2 spend from different dimensions, such as:

    a. Regional usage and instance type.

b. Total running hours.

c. Billed amount.

d. Purchase options used (on-demand, Spot, Reserved Instances).

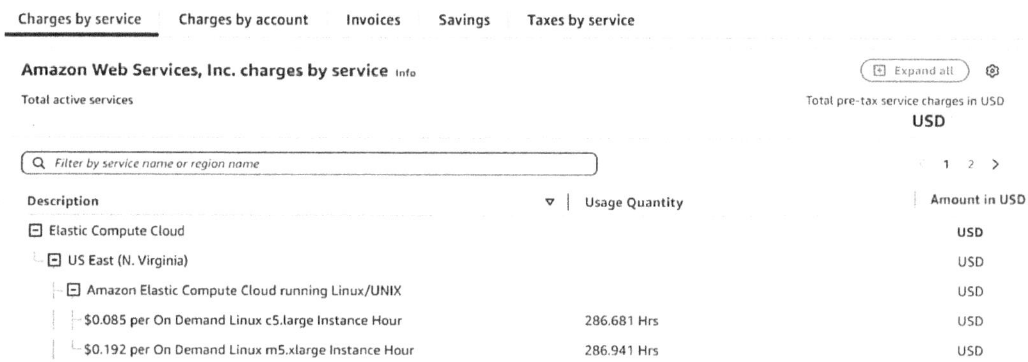

***Figure 5.6**: AWS Billing console - EC2 spend analysis*

Accessing granular data, cost, and usage reports

For detailed analysis down to the Resource ID level, use the **Cost and Usage Reports** (**CUR**) in combination with Amazon Athena (for querying data) and QuickSight dashboards (for visual insights)

Some of the examples where CUR can be useful:

- Find top 10 most expensive EC2 instances by instance ID.
- Group costs by environment tags if applicable (e.g., Prod, Dev).
- Analyze usage trends over time for specific workloads.

AWS Trusted Advisor

AWS Trusted Advisor provides recommendations across multiple categories, including **Cost optimization**. It checks and identifies any underutilized EC2 instances, idle load balancers, and other cost-saving opportunities. Go to the AWS **Trusted Advisor** console and select the **Cost optimization** category to review the EC2 related checks.

AWS Cost Optimization Hub

The Cost Optimization Hub consolidates recommendations from multiple sources, providing a unified view of optimization opportunities across your AWS environment. Go to AWS **Cost Optimization Hub** and filter by Resource type: **EC2 Instance** to review recommendations specific to Amazon EC2.

Leveraging AWS Compute Optimizer

AWS Compute Optimizer uses machine learning models to analyze historical usage data and generate tailored recommendations for cost and performance optimization. It supports and provides recommendations for EC2 instances, EC2 Auto Scaling groups, EBS volumes, Lambda functions, RDS databases, and ECS services on Fargate.

Some key benefits of using AWS Compute Optimizer include the following:

- AWS Compute Optimizer is a complementary service available to all AWS customers.
- Recommendations based on a 14 or 32-day lookback period (93 days with enhanced infrastructure metrics – paid option).
- Customization options to restrict rightsizing and modernization recommendations (e.g., organization can configure to restrict recommendations to Graviton based instances only).
- Visibility into performance metrics and migration effort for implementing the recommendations shared.

Enabling Compute Optimizer

To enable AWS Compute Optimizer, follow:

1. Go to the AWS console and search for `Compute Optimizer`.
2. Click **Get Started** and opt-in.
3. Wait for up to 24 hours for recommendations to populate.

The **AWS Compute Optimizer** dashboard, as shown in the following figure, provides a view into recommendations generated by **Compute Optimizer**:

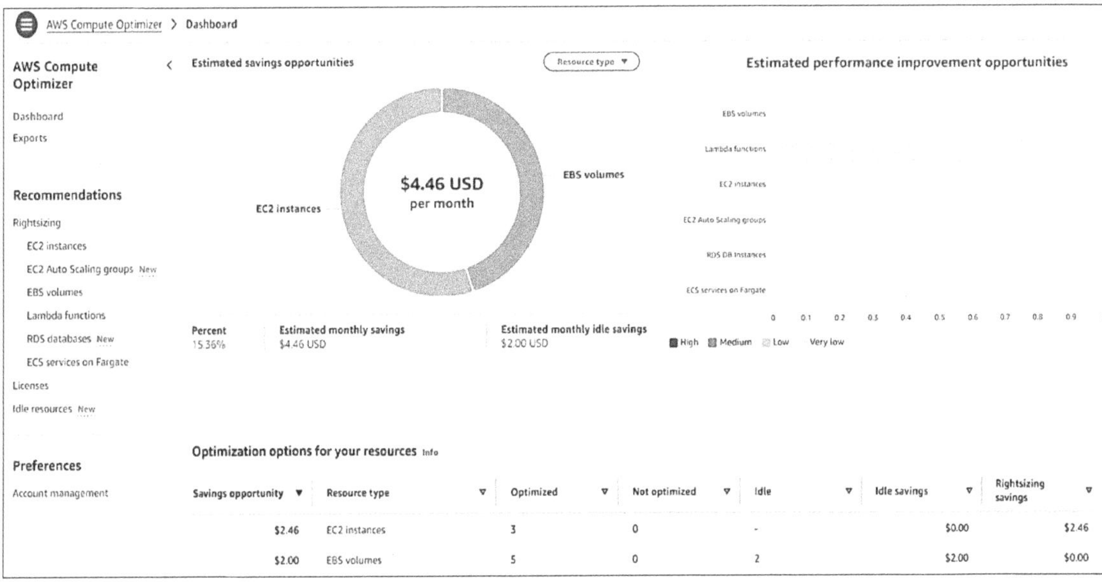

***Figure 5.7**: AWS Compute Optimizer dashboard*

You can customize your recommendation preferences by navigating the **General** and **Rightsizing** link in the left pane

Comparing AWS Compute Optimizer and Cost Optimization Hub

Both AWS Compute Optimizer and Cost Optimization Hub are important tools in your cost optimization journey. However, they serve different purposes, use different data sources, and provide different types of recommendations. Understanding their differences will help in using these tools effectively.

Refer to the following table:

Topic	Compute Optimizer	Cost Optimization Hub
Primary purpose	Provides machine learning-based rightsizing and modernization recommendations for supported AWS resources, but mainly focuses on Compute.	Centralized hub for tracking and reviewing cost-saving opportunities, and has integration with multiple tools and services.
Supported resource	Mainly Compute and Storage resources—EC2, Auto Scaling groups, EBS Volumes, RDS databases, Lambda functions, ECS on Fargate.	Wider coverage across AWS services, such as compute, storage, networking, and databases.

Topic	Compute Optimizer	Cost Optimization Hub
Data source	Utilizes CloudWatch metrics for up to 32 days (93 days with Enhanced Infrastructure metrics).	Has integration points with different tools and services.
Customization features	Customize rightsizing preferences like instance families, CPU headroom, and memory thresholds.	Limited customization options compared to the compute optimizer.
Pricing	Compute Optimizer basic recommendations are free and leverage CloudWatch metrics without any additional service charges. Compute Optimizer also has a paid option - Enhanced Infrastructure Metrics. This feature extends the analysis period, enabling the service to leverage up to 93 days of utilization history for deeper insights and a better understanding of long-term usage patterns.	AWS Cost Optimization Hub is free. It is part of the AWS Cost Management and Billing console, and there are no usage charges for the same.
Comparative analysis	Provide a detailed charts and metrics comparison feature to understand the impact before implementing the changes.	Not available
Use cases	Good for rightsizing and modernization requirements, and before making any Reserved Instance commitments.	Understand cost optimization opportunities available in the account.

***Table 5.2**: Compute Optimizer and Cost Optimization Hub comparison*

Organizations are using these tools to develop their compute optimization implementation plan. Teams can start by looking into AWS Cost Optimization Hub to identify areas with the biggest cost savings potential and then move to AWS Compute Optimizer to validate and develop rightsizing or modernization actions for individual workloads.

Reviewing compute cost using Azure cost analysis

Azure Cost Management + Billing provides detailed visibility into your Azure spending and helps you analyze, optimize, and forecast costs across services. You can use this tool to drill down into Azure Virtual Machine charges and understand cost trends over the required period of time. Steps to analyze Azure Virtual Machine costs:

1. Open the **Azure portal** and navigate to **Cost Management + Billing**.
2. Expand **Cost Management**.

3. Select **Cost Analysis**.
4. **Apply the following filters**:
   - **Scope**: Choose the subscription or resource group you want to analyze.
   - **Time range**: Select **Last 6 months**.
   - **Service name**: Filter to **Virtual Machines** or **Compute,** depending on your setup.
   - **Granularity**: Choose **Monthly** to observe month-over-month trends.
5. **Use Group By options to break down VM costs by**:
   - **Resource**: To identify specific VMs with the highest spend.
   - **Meter category**: Compute hours, disks, bandwidth, etc.
   - **Region**: To compare cost differences across locations.
   - **Pricing model**: On-demand, Reserved Instances, Savings Plan.

The visualization helps you understand virtual machine costs by highlighting key details such as region, resource usage, and pricing model. This insight makes it easier to identify optimization opportunities, such as rightsizing the VM or purchasing a Reserved Instance or Savings Plan, to reduce on-demand spend.

Putting it all together

By combining the tools discussed in this section, organizations can build a comprehensive analysis of the compute environment. These tools can help identify key areas for cost optimization by answering critical questions such as:

- *Where and how are workloads running?*
- *What factors are driving your computational expenses?*
- *Which areas offer the highest potential for optimization?*

This visibility forms the foundation of any cost optimization strategy and ensures that actions such as rightsizing or committing to reservations are based on accurate, contextual data.

Reviewing cost optimization levers for compute

After reviewing compute spend and recommendations from tools like AWS Compute Optimizer and Trusted Advisor, you need to spend time understanding your workload behavior and financial policies approved by the organization. This will help in developing compute optimization strategies aligned with workload requirements and compliant with the financial policies of the organization.

Understanding your workload characteristics

To develop effective optimization strategies, you need to understand your workload characteristics and how compute resources are currently being utilized in your organization. Some of the key questions to answer are listed here:

- **Instance type selection**:
    - *How do you select instance types for your workloads?*
    - *Is the selection based on workload characteristics, such as compute-intensive, memory-intensive, or is it based on policy defined by the organization, such as using general-purpose instances for all workloads?*
- **Instance sizing**:
    - *What processes do you use to determine instance sizes?*
    - *Is there a formal capacity planning process in place to define vCPU, Memory, Storage IOPS, and network throughput requirements?*
- **Processor requirements**:
    - *Are your workloads tied to specific processor types (Intel, AMD, Arm-based), or can they run on any processor architecture?*
- **Peak and off-peak usage handling**:
    - *How do you manage peak usage requirements? Are instances provisioned for peak load, or do they scale dynamically?*
- **Modernization plans**:
    - *Do you have plans to modernize your infrastructure in the coming months?*
    - *What visibility do you have into workload requirements and compute usage growth for the next one to three years?*
- **Environment classification**:
    - *How do you differentiate between business-critical, production, and non-production workloads?*
    - *Do you apply different instance allocation strategies based on environment type?*
- **Operating system requirements:**
    - *Are your applications tied to specific operating systems like Windows, RHEL, or can they run on various Linux distributions like Ubuntu or Amazon Linux?*

- **Purchase options:**
    - *How do you define whether to use on-demand or Reserved Instances?*
    - *Any agreement with the finance team on the criteria for making Reserved Instances and savings plan purchases?*

Understanding these aspects will help you design an effective compute allocation strategy tailored to your organization's needs.

Implementing elasticity to optimize compute cost

One of the advantages of cloud compared to traditional on-premise infrastructure is elasticity—the ability to adjust computing capacity in response to fluctuating demand automatically. This means organizations can dynamically scale resources up when needed and scale down during idle periods, ensuring they only pay for the resources they consume.

Elasticity improves operational efficiency and offers one of the most effective ways to reduce cloud spending, especially for workloads that do not require continuous availability.

Why elasticity matters

Let us consider a scenario where a virtual machine is running uninterrupted for an entire month and would accrue approximately 720 hours of compute usage (30 days x 24 hours). However, many workloads, particularly non-production workloads such as development, UAT, or training environments, may be used only during standard working hours (e.g., 9 AM to 6 PM, Monday to Friday). Keeping these instances running overnight or on weekends leads to a significant waste.

By implementing scheduled shutdowns during weekends alone, organizations can reduce runtime by 192 hours monthly (8 weekends x 24 hours), delivering 27% cost savings. These savings increase substantially when you consider shutting down instances after office hours and during public holidays.

Building elastic workloads

To make the most of elasticity in the cloud, organizations should follow two guiding principles:

- **Scale dynamically based on demand**: Instead of provisioning resources such as compute instances for peak usage at all times, utilize services like EC2 Auto Scaling groups to match compute capacity with real-time demand. This avoids both over-provisioning (waste) and under-provisioning (performance issues).
- **Avoid running idle resources**: Identify resources that are not actively in use, especially during nights, weekends, or holidays, and shut them down. This is particularly effective for non-production workloads or seasonal workloads with predictable idle periods.

Reviewing elasticity in your workload using AWS Cost Explorer

To evaluate whether your workloads are elastic or running 24/7 unnecessarily, you can use AWS Cost Explorer:

1. Open the AWS console and navigate to **Billing and Cost Management**.
2. Launch **Cost Explorer**.
3. Apply the following filters:
    a. **Time Period**: Last 30 days
    b. **Granularity**: Daily
    c. **Group by**: Instance Type
    d. **Filter**: Purchase option includes on-demand (not including instances covered by Reserved Instances or Savings Plan)

Analyze the resulting graph pattern:

- **Flat usage patterns**: If the daily usage graph for a particular instance type is flat across all days and hours, this indicates constant usage, and the instance may benefit from introducing elasticity into workloads. Review the following figure for a sample usage pattern.
- **Variable patterns** suggest elasticity is already being leveraged, though further optimization may be possible.

Figure 5.8: Using Cost Explorer to check elasticity

Note: **The cost benefits of elasticity mainly apply to on-demand resources, where you pay as per usage. For resources covered by Reserved Instances or Savings Plan, you will be charged for the full commitment irrespective of whether the resources are running or not.**

Solutions for elasticity

Cloud providers offer a range of solutions that make it easier to automate scaling and shutdown schedules:

- **AWS Instance scheduler**: The solution automates the start and stop schedules for EC2 and RDS instances. It enables teams to perform the following:
    - Define operational hours for non-production environments.
    - Use tags to target specific instances.
    - Schedule across multiple AWS regions and accounts.

  Example use case: A QA environment used from 9 AM to 6 PM on weekdays is automatically shut down at night and on weekends. Instead of running 168 hours per week, the environment only runs 50 hours, resulting in up to 70% cost savings.

  Azure offers a similar capability through Azure Automation's Start/Stop VMs, which can be used to schedule startup and shutdown aligned with office hours and other availability requirements.

- **Auto Scaling groups**: Auto Scaling helps maintain the ideal number of EC2 instances based on demand. You define scaling policies using metrics such as:
    - CPU utilization
    - Network traffic
    - Custom application metrics

  When demand increases, new instances are launched automatically. When demand drops, excess instances are terminated. This is especially valuable for production workloads that experience traffic fluctuations (e.g., e-commerce websites, share market).

Best practices for Elastic workload design

Elasticity is one of the key levers of cloud cost optimization. By aligning compute resource consumption with actual business needs, especially for variable and non-critical workloads, organizations can significantly reduce their cloud bills without sacrificing performance or availability.

Some of the best practices to be followed when designing workload for Elasticity:

- **Understand usage patterns**: Monitor peak vs. idle usage duration and identify opportunities for scheduling or scaling.
- **Tag everything**: Use consistent tagging (e.g., Environment, Owner, Schedule) to automate shutdowns and reporting.
- **Design for statelessness**: Where possible, architect applications to be stateless so that instances can be safely terminated without data loss.
- Start with simple shutdown schedules, implement auto scaling for production systems, and continuously review usage patterns to refine your elasticity strategy.

Compute modernization

Cloud providers like AWS, Azure, and GCP regularly introduce new instance families, processor types, and performance enhancements to keep up with changing workload demands and industry innovations. For organizations operating in the cloud, it is essential to periodically modernize their compute infrastructure to stay competitive and also to maximize the price-performance ratio.

Compute modernization refers to the process of upgrading or reconfiguring cloud resources to newer, more efficient, and cost-effective alternatives. In the upcoming subsections, we will explore three main aspects of compute modernization:

- Instance modernization
- processor modernization
- **Operating system** (**OS**) optimization

Instance modernization and upgrading to a newer generation

Instance modernization involves moving workloads from older generations of Amazon EC2 instances and Azure Virtual Machines to the latest available instance families. Cloud providers continuously release new instance types that offer improved performance, better hardware efficiency, and lower costs.

Example: Suppose your application currently runs on Amazon EC2 C4 instances, a compute-optimized generation that is now a few years old. AWS has since released C5, C5a, and C6g instances, each offering a better price-performance ratio. Older generation instances may still be supported, but are not optimized for cost.

Migrating to new generation instances, such as C5 or C6g, can provide two distinct cost benefits:

- **Lower hourly cost**: Newer instance families often come with reduced pricing. Use Pricing Calculator to compare the price difference between two generations and understand savings through upgrades.
- **Improved performance**: Better hardware may allow you to downsize (e.g., from c4.xlarge to c5.large) while maintaining or even improving workload performance.

However, migration complexity must be considered. Newer generations may use different processor architectures, networking capabilities, or AMI requirements. Testing, benchmarking, and compatibility validation are essential to ensure a smooth and safe migration.

Processor modernization, choosing the right processor architecture

Modern cloud platforms offer multiple processor options for the same instance family. These include the following:

- Intel-based instances (widely supported and used).
- AMD-based instances (e.g., m5a, c5a).
- ARM based processors offered by cloud providers such as Graviton-based instances from AWS.

Comparing the cost of instances based on different processors will help in choosing the right instance type. For example, AWS offers 20% discounts on AMD-based instances compared to Intel equivalents, while Graviton-based instances (ARM architecture) can deliver up to 40% cost savings and a better price-performance ratio. Switching to a more efficient processor type for organizations with hundreds or thousands of EC2 instances can yield substantial cost reductions.

Some of the considerations when migrating:

- Graviton requires compatibility. Applications must be re-architected and compiled for ARM architecture.
- Some legacy software may not yet be compatible with non-Intel processors.
- Testing and performance benchmarking should be part of any modernization rollout.

Operating system optimization

The choice of OS has a direct impact on computing cost. While cloud platforms support a wide range of OS options, licensing costs for commercial distributions can impact your bill. Some of the commonly used OS distributions include:

- Linux distributions like Amazon Linux or Ubuntu are open-source and free to use.

- Windows Server or RHEL instances can have additional licensing and subscription charges.

For example, an m6g.large instance running Windows may cost double of the same instance running Amazon Linux.

Identifying modernization opportunities

Before launching a modernization effort, it is crucial to understand which instances are being used, how much they cost, and whether they are candidates for an upgrade:

- **Billing console**: Leverage the AWS Billing console to identify legacy instances used by the organization:
    1. Navigate to the AWS **Billing and Cost Management** console and select **Bills**.
    2. Expand the **EC2** section to see usage by region, instance type, and total cost.
    3. You can explore EC2 spend to understand.
        a. Regional usage and instance type - The naming convention highlights instance family, size, and processor used.
        b. Total running hours
        c. Billed amount
        d. Purchase options used (On Demand, Spot, Reserved Instances)
- **AWS Cost Explorer**: You can also use AWS Cost Explorer to identify legacy instances used by the organization:
    1. Go to the AWS console and navigate to **Billing and Cost Management**.
    2. Launch **Cost Explorer** from the left-hand menu.
    3. Apply the following filters:
        a. **Duration**: Last 30 days
        b. **Granularity**: Daily
        c. **Dimension**: Instance Type
        d. **Purchase option**: On-Demand

    The graph will show different instances currently used. The naming convention helps in identifying Instance generation, Processor type, and other specifications, which can be used for analyzing modernization opportunities.
- **Athena with CUR**: Run SQL queries on CUR to analyze spend by instance type over time. Sample SQL query:

```
SELECT
  product_instance_type,
  SUM(line_item_unblended_cost) AS ec2_cost
  FROM your_athena_db.cur-table-name
  WHERE line_item_product_code = 'AmazonEC2'
    AND line_item_line_item_type = 'Usage'
    AND bill_billing_period_start_date >= DATE 'yyyy-mm-dd'
    AND bill_billing_period_start_date < DATE 'yyyy-mm-dd'
  GROUP BY product_instance_type
  ORDER BY ec2_cost DESC;
```

This query will show the spend by EC2 instance type for the date range provided. This will help in understanding the different instance types used, as shown in the following figure:

#	product_instance_type	ec2_cost
1		12.599145772900155
2	t2.large	0.3092044032
3	t3.large	0.2761315648

***Figure 5.9**: CUR query output - spend by instance type*

Tips:

- **Replace `your_athena_db.cur-table-name` with your actual table name.**
- **Modify the date range based on your analysis period.**

Quantifying modernization benefits

Before implementing any changes, it is important to validate expected savings using the AWS Pricing Calculator, which allows you to compare costs across different instance types and purchase options. The sample cost comparison of general-purpose instances in the Asia Pacific (Mumbai) region is shown in the following table and is based on AWS public on-demand pricing, sourced directly from the AWS public pricing pages. You can also perform a similar comparison using the AWS Pricing Calculator to evaluate additional configurations or newer instance generations. Always refer to the AWS public pricing page for the latest pricing information.

Region	Configuration summary	Monthly charges (USD)
Asia Pacific (Mumbai)	Operating system: Linux EC2 instance:m4.large	76.65
Asia Pacific (Mumbai)	Operating system: Linux EC2 instance: m5.large	73.73
Asia Pacific (Mumbai)	Operating system: Linux EC2 instance: m5a.large	40.88
Asia Pacific (Mumbai)	Operating system: Linux EC2 instance: m6a.large	40.5515
Asia Pacific (Mumbai)	Operating system: Linux EC2 instance: m6g.large	36.938
Asia Pacific (Mumbai)	Operating system: Windows Server EC2 instance: m6g.large	140.89

Table 5.3: Comparing instance cost across generations, processor, and OS

Note: **The pricing mentioned in the table is for illustration purposes only and may differ from the official pricing page, as AWS has been optimizing EC2 pricing at regular intervals.**

This comparison illustrates several key insights, such as:

- Newer generations offer incremental savings (m4 to m5).
- AMD instances provide substantial savings (m5 to m5a).
- Graviton instances deliver the greatest savings for Linux workloads.
- Operating system choice significantly impacts costs (Linux versus Windows).

Use AWS tools to accelerate modernization

Leverage AWS Compute Optimizer and Cost Optimization Hub to accelerate the modernization journey. Compute Optimizer provides rightsizing and modernization recommendations based on actual usage data. The tool will recommend newer instance families or Graviton options when beneficial. Cost Optimization Hub aggregates recommendations across services and shares modernization recommendations as available.

Refer to the following figure for the Cost Optimization Hub recommendation:

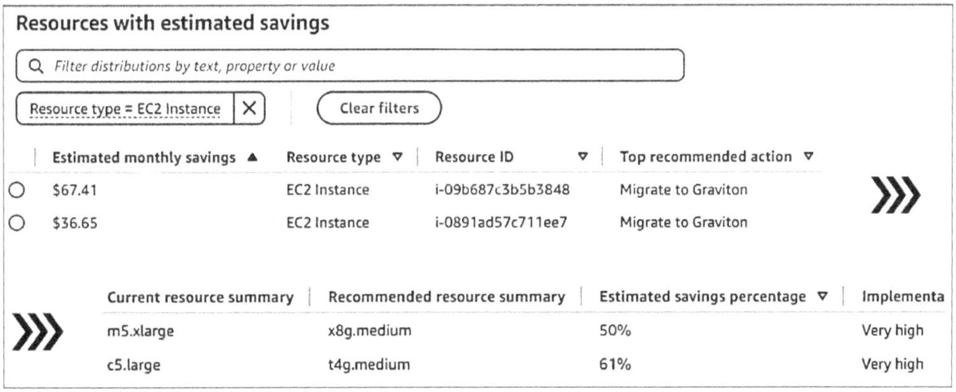

Figure 5.10: Modernization recommendation from Cost Optimization Hub

Planning your modernization journey

Modernization needs significant effort, and the team needs to develop a structured approach to modernize its infrastructure:

1. **Assessment and prioritization**:
   a. Identify modernization opportunities using the tools described in the preceding section.
   b. Leverage AWS Compute Optimizer and Cost Optimization Hub for automated recommendations.
   c. Prioritize based on potential savings, skills availability, and modernization complexity.
2. **Technical evaluation**: Team needs to consider the impact of modernization, such as:
   a. Potential code changes or recompiling requirements, especially for architecture changes (x86 to ARM).
   b. Impact on performance and user experience.
3. **Testing and validation**:
   a. Create a test environment with the target instance types.
   b. Conduct performance testing to ensure workload requirements are met.
   c. Validate functionality across all application components.

Compute modernization represents a significant yet often underutilized cost optimization opportunity. By regularly evaluating and implementing newer instance generations, alternative processor architectures, and appropriate operating systems, organizations can achieve substantial savings while potentially improving performance.

Compute rightsizing

Rightsizing refers to the process of aligning compute resources (such as Amazon EC2 instances) with the actual workload requirements to avoid over-provisioning or under-provisioning. In the cloud, each instance type provides different combinations of vCPU, memory, and network capabilities. Selecting the appropriate instance type based on application demands—CPU, memory, network, and storage throughput ensures workloads run efficiently without paying for unused capacity.

Unlike traditional infrastructure, where resources are fixed, cloud environments enable continuous optimization. Many organizations initially over-provision resources during migration to the cloud to avoid any performance bottlenecks. Similarly, when workloads are initially deployed in the cloud, the choice of instance size is often driven by rough estimations.

These assumptions may not hold true once the application starts running at scale. Over time, actual resource utilization may reveal that certain instances are over-provisioned, leading to wasted costs, or are under-provisioned, causing performance bottlenecks. A rightsizing exercise helps in reviewing and adjusting resources to meet application needs at the lowest effective cost.

Example: Suppose an EC2 c5.2xlarge instance is hosting a web application, but consistently shows only 10% CPU utilization and moderate network throughput. A Rightsizing recommendation might suggest switching to a lower instance type, such as c5.large or m5.large, to save cost. For an environment with 20 such c5.2xlarge instances running 24x7, Rightsizing savings can be substantial.

AWS tools for compute rightsizing

AWS provides robust tools to support rightsizing across multiple services:

- **AWS Trusted Advisor**: Trusted Advisor includes checks for low-utilization EC2 instances. It analyzes usage patterns (primarily CPU and network activity) and flags instances that are underused. You can access this check by navigating to the Trusted Advisor dashboard and selecting cost optimization.

  Example: If an EC2 instance runs with CPU usage below 5% for over 14 days, Trusted Advisor will flag it as a candidate for rightsizing or termination, as shown in the following figure:

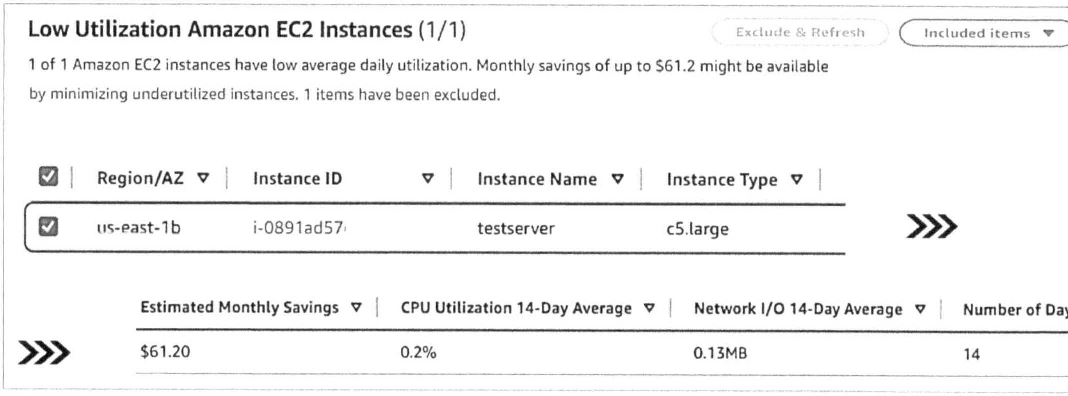

Figure 5.11: Trusted Advisor Checks for EC2 Instance

- **AWS Compute Optimizer**: Compute Optimizer is a comprehensive tool that generates a rightsizing recommendation for compute. It evaluates CloudWatch metrics like CPU utilization, disk IOPS, and network throughput. If memory metrics are required, you must install the CloudWatch Agent on your instances, as memory is not analyzed by default.

  Refer to the following figure for a sample recommendation from AWS Compute Optimizer:

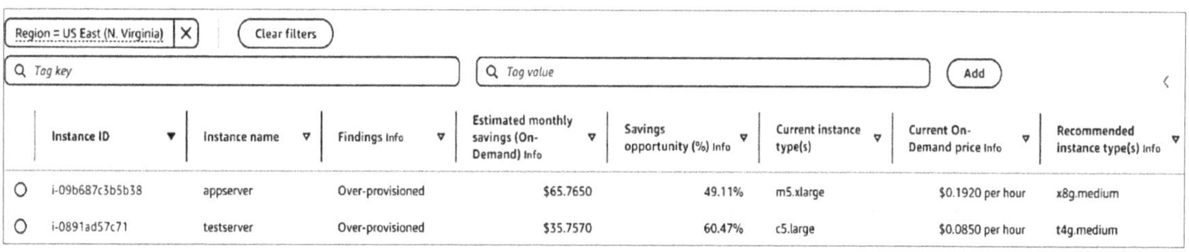

Figure 5.12: Rightsizing recommendation

The recommendation shown by the compute optimizer includes the following:

- Current and recommended instance type and pricing.
- Estimated monthly savings.
- Performance risk assessment.
- Migration effort score.

Select one of the instances to review the recommendation details, including different options available for rightsizing as shown in the following figure:

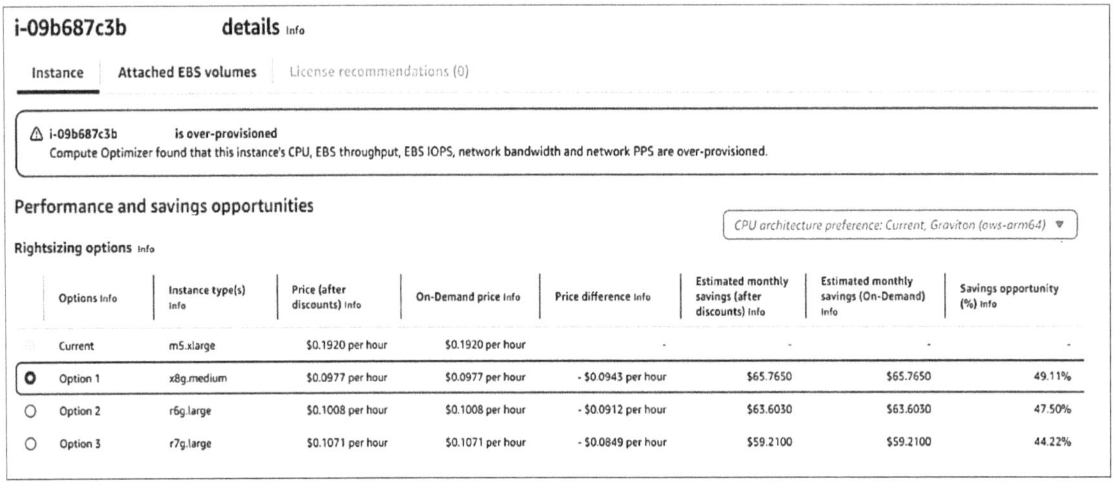

Options Info	Instance type(s) Info	Price (after discounts) Info	On-Demand price Info	Price difference Info	Estimated monthly savings (after discounts) Info	Estimated monthly savings (On-Demand) Info	Savings opportunity (%) Info
Current	m5.xlarge	$0.1920 per hour	$0.1920 per hour	-	-	-	-
Option 1	x8g.medium	$0.0977 per hour	$0.0977 per hour	- $0.0943 per hour	$65.7650	$65.7650	49.11%
Option 2	r6g.large	$0.1008 per hour	$0.1008 per hour	- $0.0912 per hour	$63.6030	$63.6030	47.50%
Option 3	r7g.large	$0.1071 per hour	$0.1071 per hour	- $0.0849 per hour	$59.2100	$59.2100	44.22%

Figure 5.13: Compute Optimizer detailed recommendation page

AWS Compute Optimizer side-by-side metric comparisons

Compute Optimizer also provides an option to compare the performance metrics of the current instance with the recommended instance to understand the impact of rightsizing:

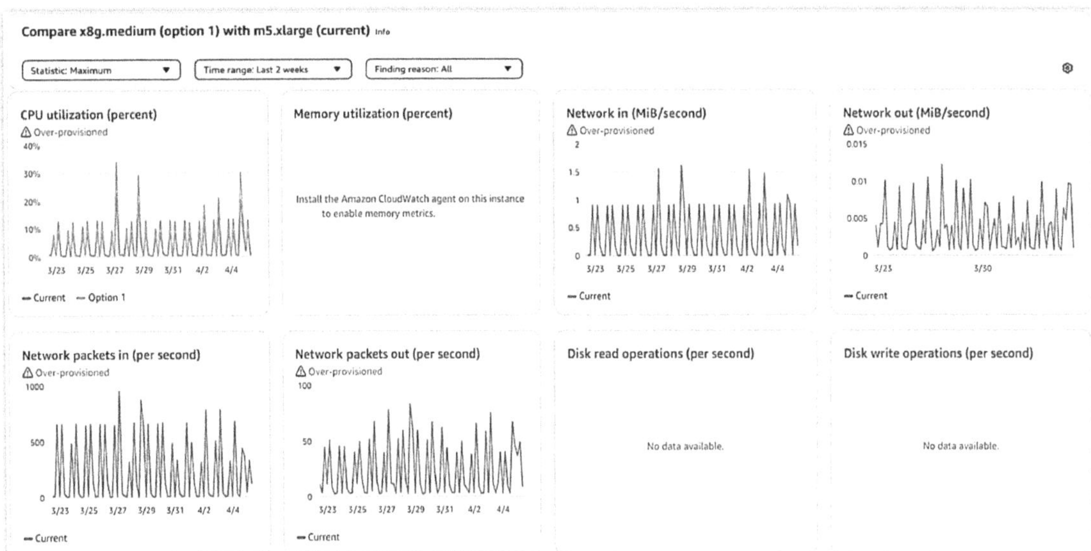

Figure 5.14: Comparing metrics before upgrade

Planning your rightsizing journey

Rightsizing engagement needs to be planned to avoid any impact on workload availability.

Here are some key considerations while planning:

- **Lookback period**: The default lookback period used by tools is 14 days, which may not capture usage variations for workloads with longer cycles. Adjust this window based on your workload profile.
- **Metrics coverage**: Tools use CPU, disk I/O, and network metrics by default. For memory-intensive applications, like in-memory databases or caching layers, configure CloudWatch to track memory usage explicitly.
- **Operational impact**: Rightsizing may require instance restarts or changes to Auto Scaling configuration. Plan changes during maintenance windows or leverage blue/green deployments.
- **Skill and ownership**: As with modernization, successful rightsizing depends on team capabilities, clear ownership of workloads, and proactive governance.

Follow these steps in compute rightsizing:

1. **Monitor actual utilization**: Collect usage metrics such as CPU utilization, disk I/O, network throughput, and (optionally) memory usage over a defined period (e.g., 14–30 days).
2. **Analyze usage patterns**: Identify which instances are underutilized or overloaded based on threshold metrics.
3. **Review recommendations**: Leverage AWS native tools to assess recommended instance types that better match workload demands.
4. **Implement changes**: Migrate or resize instances after performing performance benchmarking and using strategies such as blue-green deployments or launch templates.

Compute rightsizing is one of the most impactful and recurring practices in cloud cost optimization. By continuously evaluating compute usage and aligning resources to actual demand, organizations can achieve significant cost savings. With AWS's sophisticated rightsizing tools and a systematic implementation approach, organizations can confidently optimize their compute resources to achieve maximum value from their cloud investments.

Purchase options for compute cost optimization

One of the most effective ways to reduce cloud compute costs is by selecting the right purchasing option for your workloads. Cloud providers like AWS, Azure, and Google offer a variety of pricing models to accommodate different usage patterns and business needs. Each option is designed to balance flexibility, cost savings, and operational risk. The three primary purchase models available in most public clouds are:

- On-demand Instances
- Spot Instances

- Reserved Instances

Choosing a purchase option

Before committing to a purchasing strategy, consider the following factors:

- **Usage visibility (one–three years)**: Determine whether you have predictable workloads that will remain active over time. If so, Reserved Instances or Savings Plan make sense. If your workload is short-lived or seasonal, on-demand or Spot might be more appropriate.
- **Growth potential**: If you anticipate significant changes in workload volume (scaling up or down), you may want to under-commit slightly (e.g., commit to 70–80% of your average usage) and leave the rest flexible.
- **Workload characteristics**: *Can your application tolerate interruptions?* If yes, Spot Instances can help you save big. For business-critical or stateful applications, consider RIs or Savings Plan.
- **Budgeting and payment preferences**: Potential savings vary by payment model. Let us understand this in brief:
    - **All upfront**: Highest savings
    - **Partial upfront**: Moderate savings
    - **No upfront**: Least savings but improves cash flow

Leveraging Spot Instances

On-demand instances offer maximum flexibility; however, it is also the most expensive option in the long run. Spot Instances allow users to leverage the unused capacity of the cloud provider at a discount of up to 90% compared to on-demand rates.

However, they come with the caveat that the cloud provider may reclaim the capacity with short notice (e.g., a two-minute termination warning in AWS).

Here are some lifecycle differences:

- **On-demand**: On-demand instance lifecycle starts when the instance is launched and ends when the instance is terminated.
- **Spot**: A Spot Instance's lifecycle begins when the cloud provider makes the capacity available and launches your instance. The lifecycle ends in one of two ways: either the cloud provider reclaims the capacity after sending an interruption notice, or you manually terminate the instance yourself.

Spot Instances are well-suited for the following:

- Fault-tolerant workloads (e.g., data processing jobs, batch workloads).

- Stateless applications and containerized environments.
- CI/CD pipelines, testing, and development environments.
- Big data, machine learning, and rendering workloads.

Analyzing spot instance usage

Use AWS Cost Explorer to evaluate Amazon EC2 usage across purchasing models:

1. Navigate to AWS **Billing and Cost Management**.
2. Open **Cost Explorer**.
3. **Filter by**:
    a. **Duration**: Three months
    b. **Granularity**: Monthly
    c. **Dimension**: Purchase option
    d. **Service**: EC2
    e. **Usage type group**: EC2: Running hours

You will be able to see how your compute usage is split across on-demand, Spot, or Reserved Instance purchase options. In the following figure, the organization is only using on-demand instances, and there are no Spot or Reserve Instances currently being used.

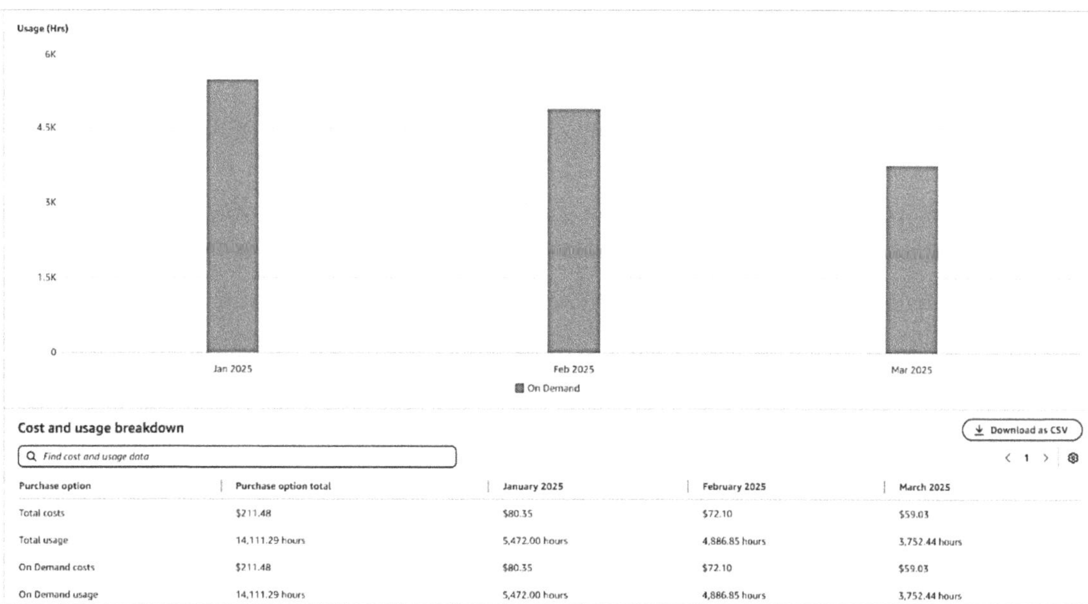

***Figure 5.15**: Amazon EC2 spend by Purchase option*

Here are some best practices for spot instances:

- Diversify across instance types and availability zones to increase allocation chances.
- Use Spot Fleets or EC2 Auto Scaling groups with mixed instance policies.
- Implement fault-tolerant architectures (stateless services, queues, retries) to handle interruptions.
- Use Spot Instance Advisor to assess interruption frequency and select the most reliable instance types per region.

Reserved Instances and Savings Plan

Cloud providers offer commitment-based savings, where organizations can commit to a specific usage pattern for one or three years in exchange for significant cost savings of up to 70% compared to on-demand rates. AWS provides options to purchase Reserved Instances or a Savings Plan for your compute workload.

- **RIs** are tied to a specific instance family, region, and OS.
- **Savings Plan** provide the same benefits as RIs but with greater flexibility. You commit to a certain dollar-per-hour usage, and the discount applies to matching compute usage.

We will limit the scope to the AWS Savings Plan, but the concept applies to RIs as well.

AWS Savings Plan

AWS offers two types of Savings Plan: Compute Savings Plan and EC2 Instance Savings Plan:

- **Compute Savings Plan**: Most flexible, applies to any instance family, size, OS, region, or even Fargate and Lambda.
- **EC2 Instance Savings Plan**: Offers slightly higher discounts but applies only to a specific instance family within a region.

  Example: If an organization commits to $10/hour under a Compute Savings Plan, any EC2, Fargate, or Lambda usage that fits under this spend will receive the applicable Savings Plan's discount. If you exceed $10/hour, the remaining running hours are billed at on-demand rates. Compute Savings Plan provides flexibility as you can change from one instance type to another, such as m5 to c5 instance, and continue to get savings plan benefits. However, the EC2 Instance Savings plan is limited to a particular instance family, such as m5 instances in N. Virginia Region.

Analyze RI/SP coverage and utilization:

In *Figure 5.15*, we have reviewed how to check the purchase options used currently and understand if the organization is using Reserved Instances or Savings Plan.

Review your RI/SP coverage before making any purchase decision:

- Go to AWS **Billing and Cost Management** console.
- Select **Savings Plan (SP)** or **Reserved Instances (RI)** as per organization policy.
- Review the **Coverage Report** to see what percentage of your on-demand spend is covered by RI/SP, as shown in the following figure:

***Figure 5.16:** AWS Savings Plan coverage report*

Figure 5.16 shows that 100% of compute instances are using On-Demand Rates and are not covered by any Savings Plan.

Review savings plan utilization:

- Go to the **AWS Billing and Cost Management** console.
- Select **Savings Plan (SP)** or **Reserved Instances (RI)** as per organization policy.
- Review the **Utilization Report** to see if Savings Plan or Reserved Instances purchased earlier are being fully utilized or if there is wastage. If utilization of the Savings Plan or Reserved Instance is low, the organization needs to investigate.

Organization can use **Recommendations** under the AWS Savings Plan or Reserved Instance section to get RI and SP related recommendations. Provide details such as:

- Savings Plan Type
- Savings Plan Term

- Payment option
- Lookback period - (usually 7, 30, or 60 days)

Once you provide the required details, as shown in the following figure, AWS will generate a recommendation for the Savings Plan to be purchased by the organization:

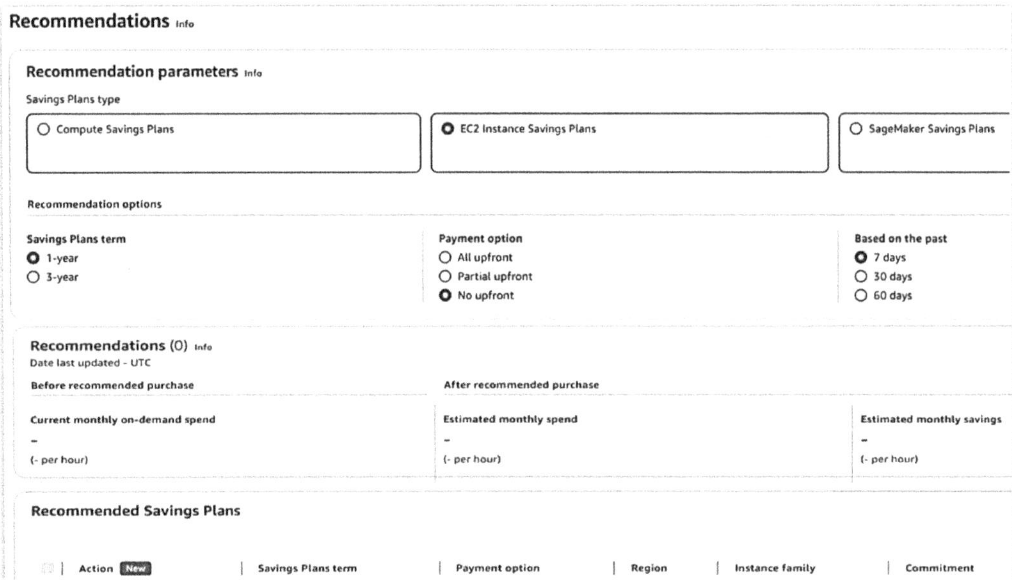

Figure 5.17: Generating Savings Plan recommendation

AWS is launching a new feature called **Purchase Analyzer** to simplify the analysis and purchase of Savings Plan as per organization policies:

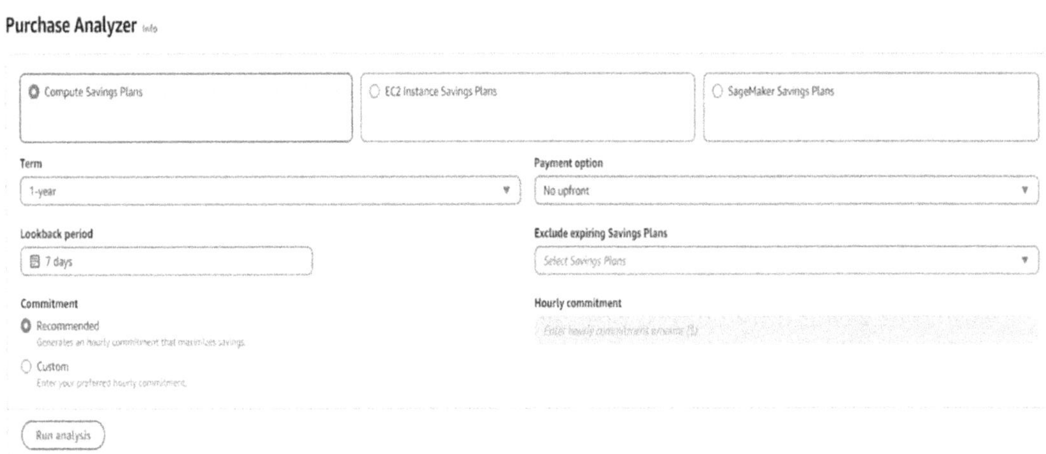

Figure 5.18: Generating Savings Plan recommendation using Purchase Analyzer

Reserved Instances and Savings Plan are like a legal contract, and cloud providers generally do not approve the cancellation of Reserved Instances and Savings Plan. It is essential for an organization to do due diligence before making any long-term commitments. Here are some factors to consider when choosing a **Purchase** option:

- **ROI calculation**: Cloud providers generally offer one- or three-year plans for Reserved Instances. Before purchasing, evaluate the ROI and break-even duration for commitment-based models, as well as ensuring the investment is not wasted due to wrong instance type usage.
- **Commitment quantity**: Review current usage patterns and forecasted growth or scale-down events to estimate how much you should commit (e.g., 80% of your baseline usage). This will require the organization to have visibility into future usage and growth expectations.
- **Payment terms**: Cloud providers have different payment terms, and discounts vary by payment term selected. Payment term examples are full upfront, partial upfront, or monthly recurring payments. The organization needs to decide the right payment term considering the discount and cash flow.
- **Flexibility offered**: Cloud providers have different types of RI/SP for different business needs. The organization needs to review the instance type usage and flexibility requirements and compare them with the discount available. A more restrictive RI/SP may offer a higher discount, but carries a risk of getting wasted if the instance type needs to be changed later.

Choosing the right purchase option is essential for maintaining a cost-efficient cloud environment. By understanding your workload behavior and leveraging Spot Instances for flexibility, Reserved Instances and Savings Plan for predictability, and on-demand for agility, you can tailor your cloud infrastructure to achieve financial and operational efficiency.

Developing a prioritized action plan

Throughout this chapter, we explored different cost optimization levers for compute service. These include increasing elasticity, modernizing instance configurations, eliminating idle resources, rightsizing, adopting Spot Instances, and using commitment-based pricing options like Reserved Instances or Savings Plan.

However, identifying opportunities is not enough. To maximize impact and ensure cost savings are realized, organizations must build a prioritized action plan that balances potential savings, complexity of implementation, skill availability, and interdependencies between actions.

Sample prioritization framework

The following table illustrates how recommendations can be organized and prioritized based on key decision criteria. Follow the steps given in the preceding chapter to assign priority to the recommendation provided.

Recommendation	Estimated monthly savings ($)	Implementation time	Resource requirments	Dependency	Priority
Elasticity (Instance scheduler, Auto Scaling)	$$	Medium	Medium	None	
Instance Modernization (New generation, AMD/ Graviton adoption)	$$	High	High	Code changes Performance testing	
Remove Idle Instances	$$	Low	Low	None	
Rightsizing EC2 instances	$$	Medium	Medium	Performance testing	
Spot Instances	$$	High	High	Architecture redesign to handle interruptions	
Purchase RI/ SP	$$	Low	Low	All other optimizations	

Table 5.4: Developing a priority action plan

The information can be depicted in the impact and complexity graph:

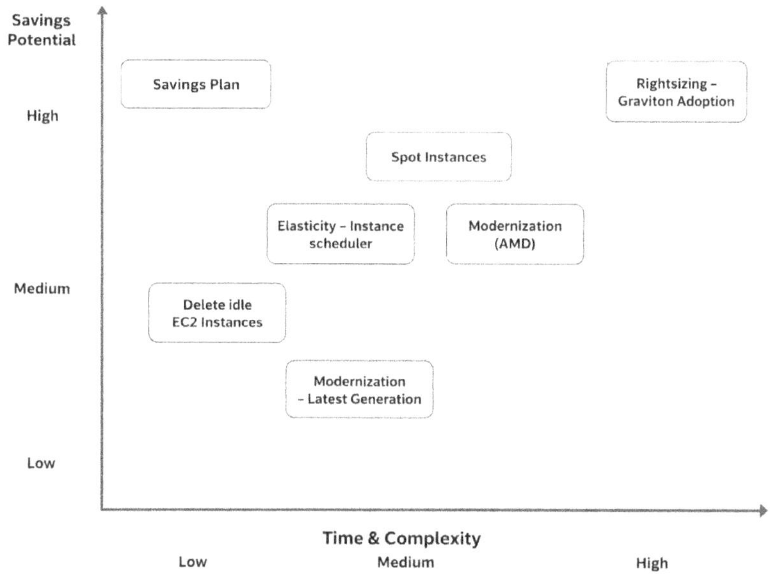

Figure 5.19: Impact and complexity graph

Note: **Commitment-based models like Reserved Instances or Savings Plan may offer the highest savings potential, however, they should be considered only after other recommendations have been implemented. Making commitments prematurely may lead to underutilization of reserved capacity and reduced ROI.**

This chapter has explored key optimization levers that help reduce compute spend:

- **Elasticity**: Minimize runtime for non-critical resources.
- **Modernization**: Leveraging newer, more efficient instance types to improve the price-performance ratio.
- **Rightsizing**: Aligning instance specifications with workload requirements and actual usage.
- **Purchase options**: Optimizing buying strategies for maximum savings.

Conclusion

Compute services are the core services consumed by many organizations and typically represent one of the largest cost elements in cloud deployments, often appearing in organizations' top five cloud expenditures. The key to cost optimization success lies in implementation, following a well-planned sequence that considers dependencies and organizational constraints. By following the compute cost saving strategies discussed in this chapter, organizations can achieve significant cost reductions while maintaining or improving workload performance.

In the next chapter, we will explore optimization strategies for storage services, another major contributor to cloud costs. The principles and methodologies discussed for compute optimization will provide a foundation for approaching storage cost optimization.

CHAPTER 6
Optimizing Storage Cost

Introduction

It is likely that you have heard the phrase, data is the new oil. This statement holds true now more than ever, as the volume of data being generated and stored continues to grow at a rapid pace. According to some studies, the total amount of stored data doubles roughly every four to five years. This data growth is only expected to accelerate with the increasing adoption of analytics, **machine learning** (**ML**), and **generative AI** (**GenAI**) workloads.

For organizations moving workloads to the cloud, storage is another critical service alongside compute. Storage services are usually among the top five services of cloud spending by organizations. As such, optimizing cloud storage costs has become a strategic priority to optimize cloud spend.

This chapter focuses on developing a strategy to optimize storage costs in the cloud. We will explore techniques to reduce the **per-gigabyte** (**per GB**) cost of storing data for an organization without compromising performance, availability, or compliance. You will learn how to choose the right storage class, migrate data to cost-effective storage tiers, optimize API usage, and enhance backup mechanisms to reduce unnecessary costs.

Structure

In this chapter, we will discuss the following topics:

- Cloud storage portfolio and charging mechanism
- Tools for analyzing and optimizing storage usage
- Levers for optimizing cloud storage cost
- Developing a prioritized action plan

Objectives

By the end of this chapter, you will develop a thorough understanding of various cloud storage services offered by major providers such as AWS and Azure. You will gain insight into the key pricing elements that influence overall storage cost and how to assess their impact. The chapter will also introduce tools that help analyze storage usage patterns and provide actionable recommendations to optimize spend. You will learn how to align storage services effectively with your workload requirements and explore various cost optimization strategies, including rightsizing storage, migrating to lower-cost tiers, optimizing data access patterns, and leveraging reserved capacity.

While we use AWS and Azure examples throughout this chapter, the principles and strategies discussed are applicable across all major cloud platforms.

Cloud storage portfolio and charging mechanism

Organizations need reliable and scalable storage for diverse workload requirements such as hosting websites, running applications, analyzing large datasets, or backup needs. Cloud providers such as AWS, Microsoft Azure, and **Google Cloud Platform** (**GCP**) offer a wide variety of storage services, each tailored to different needs and performance requirements for the workload.

In this section, we will understand the different types of storage offerings from cloud providers and then dive deeper into how cloud storage services are charged.

Understanding the cloud storage portfolio

Storage services are classified as block storage, file storage, and object storage to support diverse workload and access requirements. The following *Figure 6.1* shows the AWS storage services portfolio:

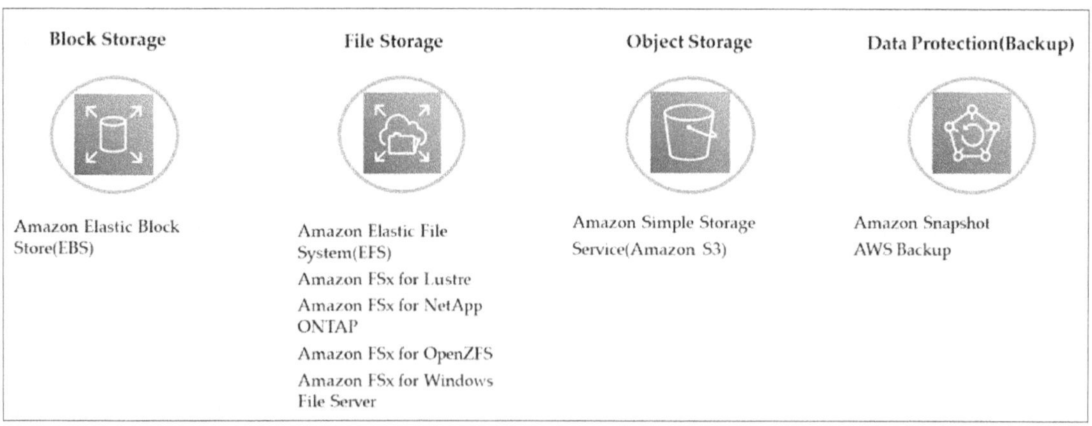

***Figure 6.1**: AWS storage services*

Block storage

Block storage provided by cloud providers works similarly to the traditional disk drives that you find in data centers. Data in block storage is stored in fixed-sized blocks. Block storage is highly efficient and can be directly attached to a compute resource (such as Azure virtual machines and Amazon EC2 instances).

Examples:

- AWS **Elastic Block Store** (**EBS**)
- Azure Managed Disks

These storage volumes provide high performance and are suitable for workloads such as databases and applications that require low-latency access to data. If you are running a Microsoft SQL Server or an Oracle database on an Amazon EC2 instance, you would likely use Amazon EBS to store the database files.

File storage

File storage organizes data in a hierarchical structure of files and folders, much like the file system on computing resources. This type of storage allows mounting of storage from different operating systems and access via industry-standard protocols such as **Network File System** (**NFS**) or **Server Message Block** (**SMB**).

Examples:

- AWS **Elastic File System** (**EFS**)
- Azure Files

File storage is ideal for applications that need shared access across multiple systems. such as content management systems, or legacy applications that were built to use on-premise file servers.

Object storage

Object storage is designed to handle vast amounts of unstructured data like documents, images, videos, and backups. Each object contains the data itself, some metadata, and a unique identifier. Object storage is designed for durability and scalability and can be accessed from across geographies using a specified URL.

Examples:

- AWS **Simple Storage Service** (**S3**)
- Azure Blob Storage

Data protection and backup services

In addition to primary storage, cloud providers offer services to protect your data through features like snapshots, replication, versioning, and backup services.

Examples:

- AWS Backup
- Azure Backup

The following figure shows the Azure storage portfolio:

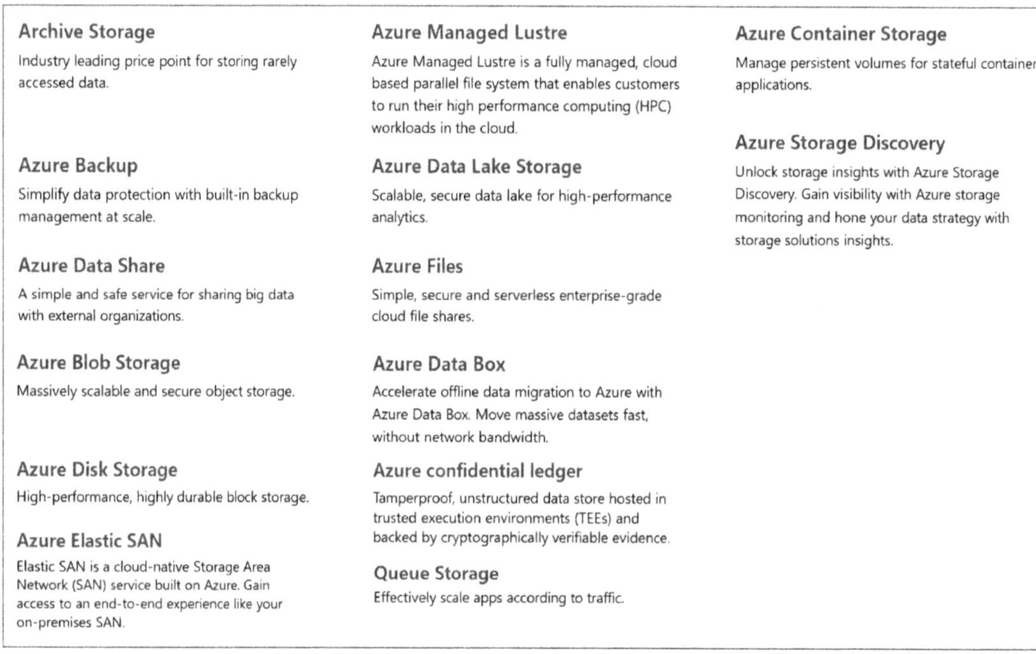

Figure 6.2: *Azure storage service*

Anatomy of cloud storage pricing

Now that we have a basic understanding of different storage types, let us look at how cloud storage costs are calculated. There are different pricing elements that impact how storage usage is charged for an organization. Understanding how storage services are priced is essential when developing your strategies to optimize storage costs.

Provisioned vs. consumed storage

Understanding the difference between provisioned and consumed storage is crucial for assessing the impact of storage allocation:

- **Provisioned storage**: In some cases, organizations are billed based on the amount of storage provided for the workload. The amount is charged irrespective of whether storage is used or not.
- **Consumed storage**: In other cases, you are billed only for the actual amount of storage you use.

Example: If you provision 500GB of Amazon EBS storage but you use only 250GB, you will be charged for the full volume provisioned (500GB) even if usage is only 50%. However, if you store 250GB of data in Amazon S3, you will be charged only for 250GB of the consumed storage.

Refer to the following *Figure 6.3* to understand how Amazon EBS is charged based on provisioned storage:

$0.01375 per GB-Month of snapshot archive data stored - Asia Pacific (Sydney)	GB-Mo	USD
$0.018 per GB-month of Cold HDD (sc1) provisioned storage - Asia Pacific (Sydney)	GB-Mo	USD
$0.048 per provisioned MiBps-month of gp3 - Asia Pacific (Sydney)	GiBps-mo	USD
$0.055 per GB-Month of snapshot data stored - Asia Pacific (Sydney)	GB-Mo	USD
$0.096 per GB-month of General Purpose (gp3) provisioned storage - Asia Pacific (Sydney)	GB-Mo	USD
$0.12 per GB-month of General Purpose SSD (gp2) provisioned storage - Asia Pacific (Sydney)	GB-Mo	USD

***Figure 6.3**: AWS Billing console—EBS charges*

Region-based pricing

Just like other cloud resources, cloud storage pricing also varies from one region to another. For example, storing 1GB of data on an AWS GP3 volume costs $0.0912/GB-month in Asia Pacific (Hyderabad), while if you store the same 1GB data in US East (Ohio), you will be charged $0.08/GB-month. When designing your cloud infrastructure, always factor in regional pricing differences.

Billing units

Different types of storage have different billing metrics. When estimating your cloud costs, an organization must consider all applicable storage charges, which are based on different billing units and not just the cost of storing the data. For example, when storing data in Amazon S3, you may be charged for API calls and tools used apart from storage charges. A team needs to understand that in the cloud, storage charges are not limited to data storage charges, but there are other elements that can impact the overall storage cost. The following table provides a detailed description of billing units:

Storage billing unit	Description
GB-month	Cloud storage charges are typically based on GB-month, a common storage pricing unit. GB-month is defined as the cost of storing 1GB of data for 1 month. Example: • Storing 100GB of data for a full month = 100GB-months. • Storing 100GB for only 15 days (half a month) = 50GB-months. Refer to *Figure 6.3* to understand how Amazon EBS provisioned storage is charged based on GB-month (GB-Mo).
Provisioned IOPS-month	Charges for the **input/output operations** (**IOPS**) provisioned for the storage volume.
Provisioned MB/s-month	Charges for throughput provisioned for storage volume.
API call charges	Cost for making storage-related API calls (Example: API calls for uploading, downloading, listing objects).
Data transfer charges	Cost of transferring data from storage to the internet or for replication.

***Table 6.1**: Storage billing units*

Purchase options, reserved capacity, and commitment-based discounts

Many cloud providers offer savings based on a commitment to a certain level of usage in advance. For example, Azure Blob Storage reserved capacity can offer up to 38% savings compared to pay-as-you-go pricing.

Tiered pricing model

Both AWS and Azure offer tiered pricing for object storage. This means that as your usage grows, the price per GB decreases, helping you save money at scale. Refer to *Figure 6.4* to understand how organizations can utilize the benefits of a pricing tier as they scale data storage on a cloud provider:

Region:

US East (N. Virginia)

	Storage pricing
S3 Standard - General purpose storage for any type of data, typically used for frequently accessed data	
First 50 TB / Month	$0.023 per GB
Next 450 TB / Month	$0.022 per GB
Over 500 TB / Month	$0.021 per GB
S3 Intelligent - Tiering * - Automatic cost savings for data with unknown or changing access patterns	
Monitoring and Automation, All Storage / Month (Objects > 128 KB)	$0.0025 per 1,000 objects
Frequent Access Tier, First 50 TB / Month	$0.023 per GB
Frequent Access Tier, Next 450 TB / Month	$0.022 per GB
Frequent Access Tier, Over 500 TB / Month	$0.021 per GB

Figure 6.4: *Amazon S3 tiered pricing model*

Backup charges

Cloud providers offer native tools like AWS Backup and Amazon snapshots to simplify taking backups of your critical data stored. The charges for backup data, such as snapshot storage, may be different from other storage types. For example, when you take a backup on AWS through a snapshot, you will be charged for snapshot storage charges based on GB-month. You will also be charged retrieval charges when you restore a snapshot, and an additional fee is based on the volume and type of retrieval.

Tools for analyzing and optimizing storage usage

As organizations deploy their workloads on cloud platforms and the usage of storage grows, keeping track of usage patterns and associated costs becomes important. Cloud providers offer tools to help users understand their storage consumption, analyze spending, and find opportunities to optimize costs. In previous chapters, we reviewed cost observability tools. This section explores various tools available to analyze and optimize cloud storage costs, with a particular focus on AWS services. *Table 6.2* provides an overview of tools that offer visibility into storage usage, costs, and potential optimization opportunities:

Category	Tool	Description
Cost Observability: Observability tools help organizations monitor and understand where and how they are spending on storage services. They provide the visibility needed before taking any optimization actions.	AWS Billing console	View consolidated billing data, invoices, and service-wise charges.
	AWS Cost Explorer	Visualize storage and other service costs. Drill down on storage cost using filters like service, API operation, region, or usage type.
	AWS CUR	Provides granular, resource-level data about storage usage and cost. Can be queried using Athena and visualized with QuickSight.
	Cost and Usage Dashboard	Pre-built dashboards (via QuickSight) such as the Cost Intelligence Dashboard.
Cost Optimization: Optimization tools help in finding underutilized resources, identifying savings opportunities, and receiving actionable recommendations.	AWS Trusted Advisor	Checks for underutilized EBS volumes and suggests opportunities to delete or rightsize volumes.
	Compute Optimizer	Provides rightsizing recommendations for EBS volumes, optimizing disk type, storage size, IOPS, and throughput.
	AWS Cost Optimization Hub	A centralized dashboard that consolidates cost-saving recommendations across different AWS services, including storage services.
Forecasting and estimation	AWS Pricing Calculator	Estimate storage cost for deploying the workload. Can also be used for comparing costs for different storage configurations.
Storage-specific analysis tools: AWS provides storage analysis tools for deep insights into Amazon S3.	Amazon S3 Storage Lens	Visibility into S3 usage patterns, with cost optimization and data protection recommendations.
	Amazon S3 Inventory	Provides reports listing objects and metadata for compliance, auditing, and lifecycle management.
	Amazon S3 Storage Class Analysis	Monitors object access patterns and recommends moving infrequently accessed data to lower-cost storage classes.

***Table 6.2**: Tools for analyzing storage usage and expenditure*

Reviewing storage costs with AWS Cost Explorer

As we have seen in the preceding chapters, AWS Cost Explorer is a powerful tool that allows you to analyze different service costs, such as storage costs, identify trends, and key cost drivers.

The following are the steps for using AWS Cost Explorer for analyzing storage usage trends:

1. Go to the AWS console and navigate to **Billing and Cost Management**.
2. From the left menu, launch **Cost Explorer**.
3. In **Cost Explorer**, both EBS volume charges and snapshot charges are bundled under the service called **EC2-Other**. Apply the following filters to analyze Amazon EBS and snapshot charges:
    - **Date range**: Last 3 months
    - **Granularity**: Monthly
    - **Service**: EC2-Other (for EBS and snapshot charges)
    - **Dimension**: API operation

After applying the filters mentioned in the preceding list, you will see a detailed breakdown of your storage-related expenses as shown in *Figure 6.7*. You can identify charges related to Amazon EBS (gp2 volumes, gp3 volumes) and backup-related charges (snapshot):

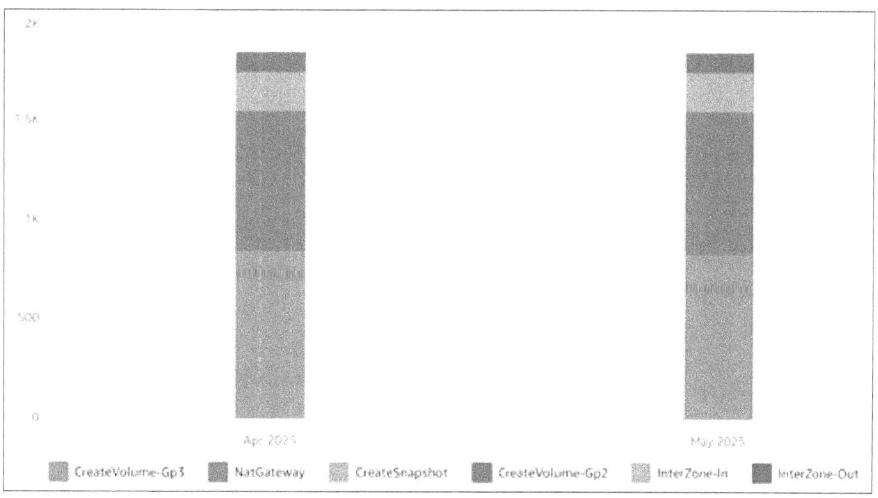

Figure 6.5: *Amazon EBS and snapshot charges*

Similarly, you can analyze:

- Amazon S3 charges by setting the **Service** filter to **Simple Storage Service (S3)**.
- Amazon EFS charges by setting the **Service** filter to **Elastic File System**.

Correlating Cost Explorer findings with Billing console

The AWS Billing console provides an invoice-style view that can validate your Cost Explorer findings. The following are the steps to review storage charges via the Billing console:

1. Navigate to the AWS Billing and Cost Management dashboard.
2. Select **Bills** from the left menu.
3. Choose the relevant billing period.
4. Expand the **Elastic Compute Cloud** under **Charges by service** tab to find detailed charges for compute charges and related Amazon EBS storage charges. Depending on usage, you will find charges related to the following:
    - EBS volumes (gp2, gp3, HDD types)
    - Snapshot storage
    - Provisioned IOPS and throughput

Refer to *Figure 6.3* for more details. For Amazon S3 storage, expand the **Simple Storage Service** section under **Charges by service** tab to locate Amazon S3 related charges such as storage charges, API call charges, data transfer charges, and any additional charges from usage of management tools like S3 Storage Lens and S3 Inventory.

Refer to the following *Figure 6.6* to understand Amazon S3 related charges in Billing console:

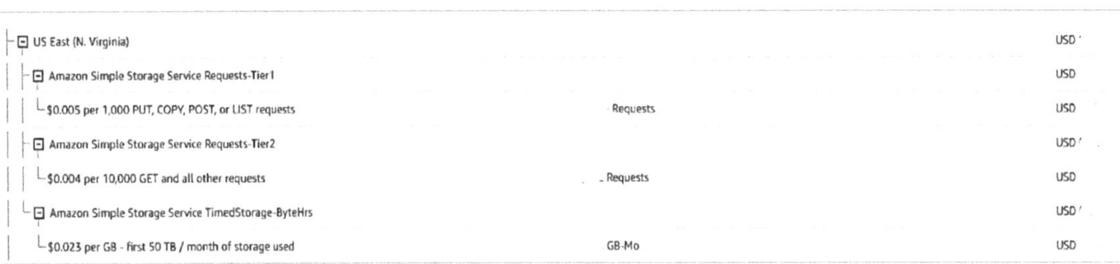

***Figure 6.6**: AWS Bills - Amazon S3 charges*

Accessing detailed data with Cost and Usage Reports

The CUR provide the most granular level of cost data and helps drill down to the resource ID. By analyzing CUR data using tools like Amazon Athena and Amazon QuickSight, you can get information such as the following:

- Identify the Top 10 most expensive S3 buckets.
- Identify the Top 10 largest EBS volumes.
- Split the cost between storage charges and API charges.
- Group costs by environment tags (e.g., production vs. development).

Using AWS Trusted Advisor for EBS optimization

AWS Trusted Advisor provides cost optimization checks, especially for EBS volumes, such as the following:

- **Underutilized Amazon EBS Volumes**: Identifies volumes unattached to any instance or with low IOPS over the past seven days.
- **Amazon EBS over-provisioned volumes**: Suggests resizing of EBS volumes based on usage metrics like throughput and IOPS.

You can get the results of these checks by selecting the **Cost Optimization** category within the AWS Trusted Advisor console.

Rightsizing EBS volumes with AWS Compute Optimizer

In the previous chapter, we used AWS Compute Optimizer for rightsizing compute instances. AWS Compute Optimizer also offers rightsizing suggestions for Amazon EBS volumes based on actual utilization patterns. The following are the steps for using AWS Compute Optimizer:

1. Open the AWS console and launch **AWS Compute Optimizer**.
2. Navigate to **EBS Volumes** under the **Rightsizing** panel.
3. Review volumes categorized as:
    - Optimized
    - Not Optimized
4. For each **Not Optimized** volume, Compute Optimizer suggests up to 3 options to rightsize your EBS Volume based on one of the following options:
    - Disk type (e.g., switching from gp2 to gp3).
    - Optimal storage size.
    - Recommended IOPS and throughput settings.

Compute Optimizer also provides access to performance metrics to help make informed resizing decisions.

AWS Cost Optimization Hub

The AWS Cost Optimization Hub aggregates recommendations across services, providing a unified view of optimization opportunities across your AWS environment. The following are the steps for reviewing recommendations shared by AWS Cost Optimization Hub:

1. Access the **Cost Optimization Hub** via the AWS console.
2. **Filter by Resource type**: EBS volume. This filter will generate a consolidated list of opportunities to save on storage costs as shown in the following *Figure 6.7*:

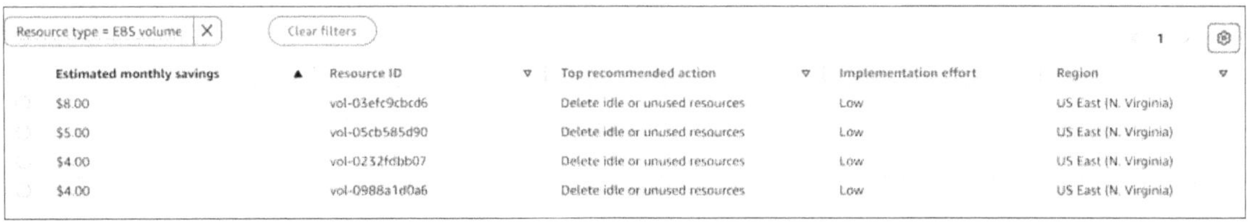

***Figure 6.7**: AWS Cost Optimization Hub—Savings opportunities*

Amazon S3 Storage Lens

S3 Storage Lens provides a high-level and detailed view of S3 storage usage. This provides a good starting point to evaluate usage of Amazon S3 storage from different perspectives, including reviewing cost and data protection-related recommendations.

The following are the steps to use Amazon S3 Storage Lens:

1. Open the AWS console and launch **Amazon S3**.
2. Under the **Storage Lens** section in the left menu, click **Dashboards** and launch the **default-account-dashboard**. You can also choose to create a custom dashboard by selecting **Create Dashboard**.

This will open a form like shown in *Figure 6.8*. You need to provide all the details, including whether you want to use free metrics available with the Storage lens or deploy **Advance metrics and recommendation** which is a paid option.

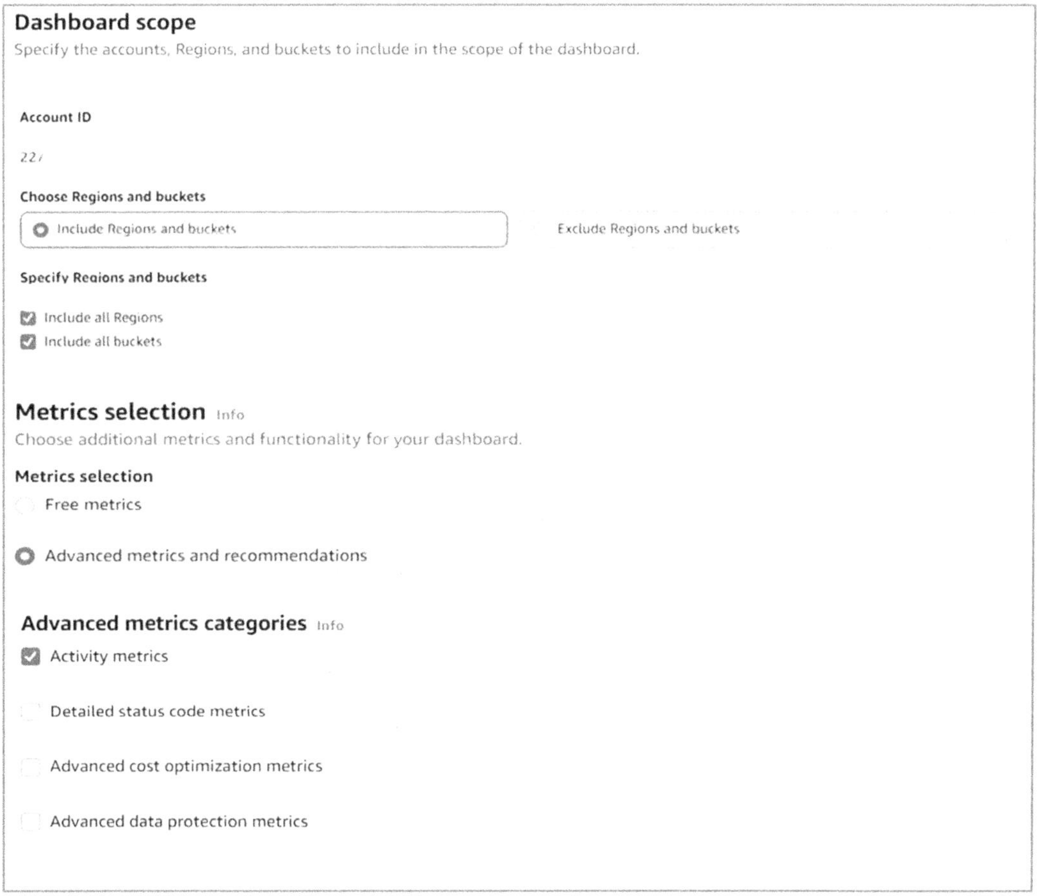

***Figure 6.8**: Create Amazon S3 Storage Lens dashboard*

The S3 Storage Lens dashboard can help you get relevant insights on Amazon S3 usage, such as the following:

- Bucket level details, including top bucket by size, object count, and average object size.
- Usage of different storage classes.
- Cost optimization and data protection recommendations.

Refer to *Figure 6.9* to review the S3 Storage Lens dashboard:

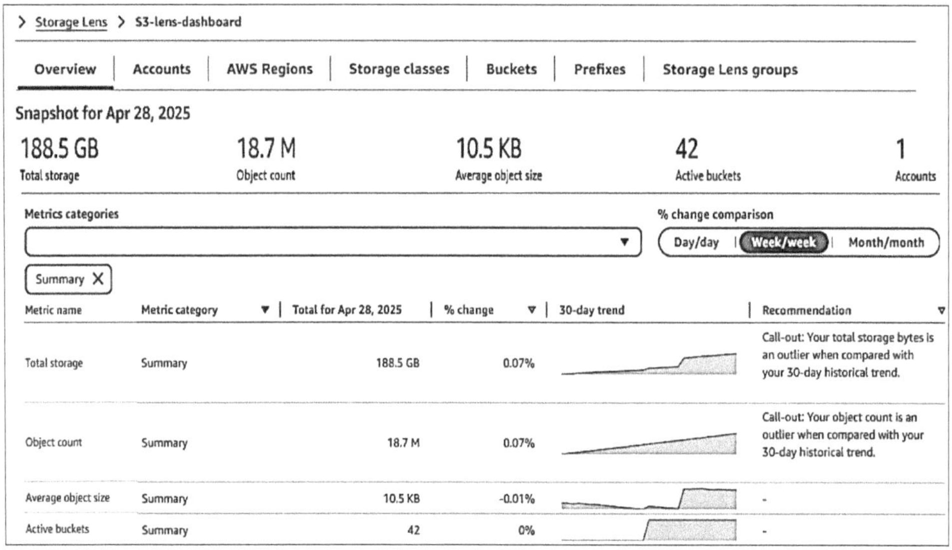

Figure 6.9: Amazon S3 Storage Lens dashboard

Amazon S3 Storage Class Analysis

S3 Storage Class Analysis (**S3 Analytics**) monitors object access patterns of your bucket to determine the right storage class. For example, if objects are infrequently accessed, you can transition them from **Standard to Infrequent Access** (**S3 IA**) or Glacier Archival storage.

Amazon S3 Analytics is a paid feature, charged per million objects monitored. You can use filters like prefix or object tags to reduce Storage Class Analysis charges. To use Storage Class Analysis, perform the following steps:

1. Open the Amazon S3 console.
2. Select a Bucket where you want to configure Storage Class Analysis and navigate to the **Metrics** tab.
3. Click **Create analytics configuration** to create Storage Class Analysis. It can take up to 48 hours to generate initial data. Refer to *Figure 6.10* on creating Storage Class Analysis.
4. 30 days of observations are generally needed for useful recommendations.

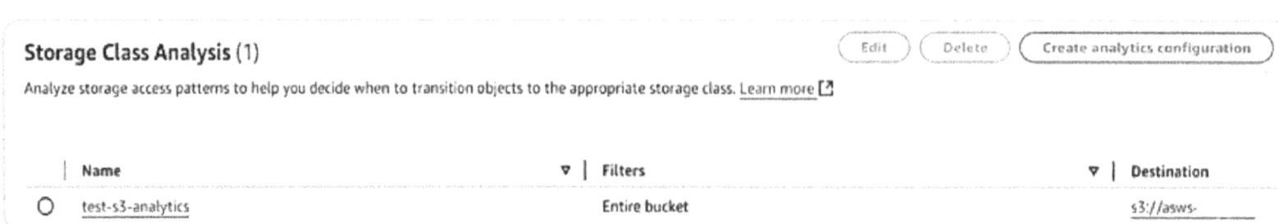

Figure 6.10: Amazon S3 Analytics

Amazon S3 Inventory

S3 Inventory generates reports listing all objects in a bucket along with metadata such as the following:

- Storage class
- Size
- Version id
- Replication status
- Last modified date

S3 Inventory is a paid feature and is charged per million objects listed. The report is useful for compliance audits and validating lifecycle configurations. To configure Amazon S3 inventory, perform the following steps:

1. Open the **Amazon S3** console.
2. Select Bucket where you want to create the Amazon S3 Inventory and go to the **Management** tab.
3. Under **Inventory configurations**, click **Create inventory configuration**.

Putting it all together

By leveraging the tools discussed, organizations can:

- Understand their full storage footprint across Amazon storage, such as EBS, S3, EFS, and other services.
- Identify which storage classes and regions are contributing most towards cloud expenditure.
- Distinguish between storage charges and API call charges.
- Get recommendations on optimization opportunities.
- Make data-driven decisions for rightsizing and cost-saving actions.

Levers for optimizing cloud storage cost

Cloud providers offer scalable storage services, but without proper management, the cost of storage services can spike quickly. To manage and reduce storage charges, it is important to understand the different levers and strategies that can be leveraged to optimize the storage-related charges.

Before implementing any cost-saving measures, it is important to assess your workload patterns, the nature of the data being stored, and how your applications interact with that data. This ensures that any action taken does not impact the performance or availability of critical systems.

Choosing the right type of storage

Cloud providers offer multiple types of storage, such as block, file, and object, with each type optimized for different workloads. With so many options available, organizations need to make smart choices based on their workload requirements, usage patterns, and long-term planning. Selecting the right storage type for your application is the first and most important step in cost optimization. The step should be included in the initial phases of design and development and reviewed before deployment of the workload to the cloud.

Understanding access method and protocol

The type of storage you choose depends on how your application accesses data. The choice between block, file, and object storage depends on your specific application needs and data access patterns:

- **Block storage**: This type of storage is attached directly to virtual machines or compute instances. Ideal for low-latency, high-performance workloads like databases or boot volumes.
- **File storage**: File storage is good for applications requiring shared file systems and standard access protocols like NFS or SMB. Ideal for content management systems, shared drives, and development environments where multiple instances need access to the same data.
- **Object storage**: Object storage provides a feature to access objects via API calls and over the internet. Ideal for storing large volumes of unstructured data like images, media files, analytics data, and backups.

Tip: **The access protocol is often the first factor in determining the right storage for the workload. For example, if your workload requires NFS protocol access, file storage is the most appropriate.**

Frequency of access

How often you access your data has an effect on which storage class is the most cost-effective. Organizations need to classify data based on access patterns and how often they need it. Let us examine access patterns to consider the right storage class:

- **Hot data**: Data that is frequently accessed and requires real-time access should be stored in a high performance storage class.

- **Warm data**: Data that is infrequently accessed but needs fast retrieval when required. Such data can be stored in moderate-cost storage with slightly lower performance compared to hot data for cost benefits.
- **Cold or archival data**: Data that is rarely accessed but is required for regulatory and compliance requirements. Such data can be moved to low-cost archival storage such as Amazon Glacier.

Access pattern

The way your application accesses data (randomly or sequentially) can also impact performance and cost. Here is how random and sequential access patterns impact storage choices:

- **Random access**: Suitable for workloads like databases that access data in a non-linear pattern. Block storage is often ideal here.
- **Sequential access**: Used in scenarios like log analysis or media streaming, where data is read or written in order. Object or file storage may be more appropriate.

Operation type is read or write

Understanding whether your workload is read-heavy, write-heavy, or **write-once-read-many** (**WORM**) helps you select storage with suitable **input/output operations per second** (**IOPS**), throughput, and durability configurations. Let us explore how different read-write patterns influence your choice of storage solutions and their configurations:

- **Read-heavy**: Choose storage types optimized for read throughput, such as block storage or object storage with CDN integration.
- **Write-heavy**: Choose storage that supports high write throughput.
- **WORM**: Useful for logs or compliance data where data is written once and must remain unmodified.

Performance metrics: Latency, IOPS, and throughput

Each application has specific performance needs. **Identify** the following for your workload:

- **Latency**: How quickly the data must be retrieved. These are critical metrics for real-time applications.
- **IOPS**: Useful for workloads like transactional databases.
- **Throughput**: Required for large file transfers or video streaming.

Choosing a storage solution that overperforms can lead to unnecessary costs, while an underperforming storage solution can throttle your application. Rightsizing based on actual metrics prevents overprovisioning and ensures an optimal cost-to-performance ratio.

Availability and durability requirements

When designing your storage architecture, balancing availability requirements against cost considerations is crucial. Understanding your tolerance for data loss and downtime will guide your storage decisions:

- **Availability**: If your data is critical, consider storage classes that replicate across multiple **availability zones** (**AZs**) to ensure high availability and durability. For less sensitive workloads, you may choose single-zone options to reduce cost.
- **Data durability and acceptable loss**: Different storage classes offer varying levels of durability. For instance. Amazon S3 standard storage offers durability of 99.999999999% (eleven nines).

Future growth and scalability

Estimate how your storage needs will grow in the next 6–12 months. Choose a storage that can scale without requiring major architectural changes, manual provisioning, or major disruptions. The following are some other considerations:

- **File size support**: *Are there limits on object or file sizes?*
- **Client compatibility**: *Is your application running on Linux, Windows, or both?* Some storage services are better suited for Windows clients (e.g., SMB protocol) while others support Linux environments (e.g., NFS).
- **Security features**: Verify if security features such as encryption options, access control mechanisms, and compliance certifications offered by the storage service meet the organization's regulatory and compliance requirements.
- **On-premise compatibility**: If you are using hybrid cloud or planning a migration, verify compatibility with on-premises storage solutions.

Removing idle resources

With the ease of deploying resources in the cloud, teams frequently spin up resources such as compute instances and storage volumes for temporary workloads, such as testing, development, or experimentation. If organizations lack proper resource management practices, the associated storage volumes might be lying around unused long after the compute instances are deleted. This results in what is known as **storage sprawl**, which is a slow build-up of unused or orphaned storage resources that continue to incur charges.

Let us take an example to understand this in detail. An organization creates a testing environment in AWS using two EC2 instances, each with four EBS volumes of 50GB, and an S3 bucket to store logs and images. After six months of development, the EC2 instances are terminated, but the eight attached EBS volumes and the S3 bucket remain in the account. These resources continue to incur costs even though they are no longer in use.

To optimize cost, organizations need to identify and remove idle storage.

Unused EBS volumes

AWS provides several tools to detect idle EBS volumes, such as the following:

- **AWS Compute Optimizer**: Navigate to the AWS Compute Optimizer console, and then perform the following steps:
    1. Select the **Idle Resources** section.
    2. Identify EBS volumes with low or no activity over a specific period (typically 30 days).
    3. For any idle volume that is no longer needed, take a backup (snapshot) if required, and then delete the volume to stop incurring costs.

    Refer to *Figure 6.11* for identifying idle resources through AWS Compute Optimizer:

Figure 6.11: AWS Compute Optimizer: Recommendations for idle resources

- **AWS Trusted Advisor**: To utilize AWS Trusted Advisor, open the dashboard and execute the following steps:
    1. Go to the **Cost Optimization** category.
    2. Click on Underutilized Amazon EBS Volumes.
    3. Review the list and verify whether any volume is part of a **disaster recovery** (**DR**) setup or another valid use case. If not, proceed to delete the volume after taking a snapshot.

Refer to *Figure 6.12* to identify idle EBS volumes from AWS Trusted Advisor:

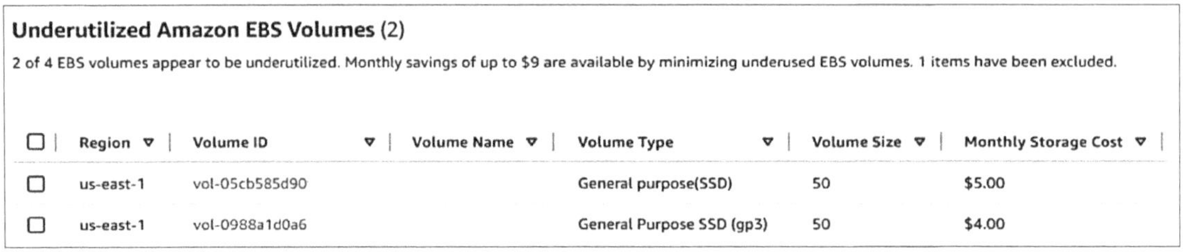
Underutilized Amazon EBS Volumes (2)

2 of 4 EBS volumes appear to be underutilized. Monthly savings of up to $9 are available by minimizing underused EBS volumes. 1 items have been excluded.

Region	Volume ID	Volume Name	Volume Type	Volume Size	Monthly Storage Cost
us-east-1	vol-05cb585d90		General purpose(SSD)	50	$5.00
us-east-1	vol-0988a1d0a6		General Purpose SSD (gp3)	50	$4.00

***Figure 6.12**: AWS Trusted Advisor—Underutilized Amazon EBS Volumes*

You can also get information about idle EBS volumes and potential from AWS Cost Optimization Hub.

Unused S3 buckets

S3 charges are based on the volume of data stored and the storage class. Even if a bucket has not been accessed for months, it will still generate charges if data is stored in it. Organizations need to identify buckets that are no longer required and delete the underlying objects to save S3 costs.

The following are the steps to identify buckets that are no longer required:

1. List and analyze the purpose of each bucket in the following manner:
    - *Was it used for temporary testing or development?*
    - *Does it serve as part of a DR plan?*
    - *Does it store sensitive data that is required to be retained for compliance?*
2. Use CUR along with Amazon Athena. Write SQL queries to identify S3 buckets with zero GET, PUT, or LIST operations over the last 180 days.
3. Analyze the output to create a list of potentially idle buckets. The following are some recommended actions:
    - If the data needs to be stored for reasons such as compliance but is rarely accessed, move it to a lower-cost storage tier such as S3 Glacier or Glacier Deep Archive.
    - If the bucket is no longer needed, delete the objects to stop all associated charges.

Rightsizing storage

Rightsizing involves aligning provisioned storage resources with actual usage. This applies particularly to storage services that charge based on provisioned capacity rather than consumed storage. Block storage, like Amazon EBS and Azure disks, is charged based on provisioned size, while object storage, like Amazon S3 and Azure Blob Storage, is charged based on actual usage.

The following are some key areas of wastage:

- **Over-provisioned storage size**: Volumes sized provisioned are much larger than usage.
- **IOPS over-provisioning**: For performance-optimized volumes (like io1 or io2 EBS volumes), if provisioned IOPS exceed the actual peak usage, costs can increase significantly.
- **Throughput over-provisioning**: Some volumes allow throughput configuration that can exceed usage.

AWS EBS Pricing in *Figure 6.13* illustrates how over-provisioning of resources can increase storage cost:

Region:

Asia Pacific (Singapore)

Amazon EBS Volumes

With Amazon EBS, you pay only for what you provision. The pricing for Amazon EBS volumes is listed below.

Volume Type	Price
General Purpose SSD (gp3) - Storage	$0.096/GB-month
General Purpose SSD (gp3) - IOPS	3,000 IOPS free and $0.006/provisioned IOPS-month over 3,000
General Purpose SSD (gp3) - Throughput	125 MB/s free and $0.048/provisioned MB/s-month over 125
General Purpose SSD (gp2) Volumes	$0.12 per GB-month of provisioned storage
Provisioned IOPS SSD (io2) - Storage	$0.138/GB-month
Provisioned IOPS SSD (io2) - IOPS	$0.072/provisioned IOPS-month up to 32,000 IOPS
	$0.050/provisioned IOPS-month from 32,001 to 64,000 IOPS
	$0.035/provisioned IOPS-month for greater than 64,000 IOPS
Provisioned IOPS SSD (io1) Volumes	$0.138 per GB-month of provisioned storage AND $0.072 per provisioned IOPS-month
Throughput Optimized HDD (st1) Volumes	$0.054 per GB-month of provisioned storage
Cold HDD (sc1) Volumes	$0.018 per GB-month of provisioned storage

***Figure 6.13**: Amazon EBS pricing*

The following are some tools that can help with rightsizing:

- **Amazon CloudWatch**: Use observability tools like Amazon CloudWatch to monitor key metrics such as volume usage (GB), IOPS, and throughput. Analyze trends to determine optimal capacity requirements.
- **AWS Compute Optimizer**: Provides recommendations to rightsize EBS volumes based on actual utilization patterns. Suggests optimized volume size, IOPS, and throughput for better cost-efficiency.

- **AWS Trusted Advisor**: Trusted Advisor has checks, such as Amazon EBS over-provisioned volumes, to help identify underutilized volumes and offers guidance on downsizing.

Let us consider a scenario of storage optimization: An organization has provisioned an io1 EBS volume with 3,000 IOPS, but monitoring shows the workload only utilizes 500 IOPS during peak hours. Cost optimization tools will flag this as a rightsizing opportunity. Once identified, there are two main options to optimize costs. First, the organization can modify the IOPS configuration of the io1 volume to match the actual requirement of 500 IOPS. Alternatively, the organization could migrate to a more cost-effective storage solution, such as switching from io1 to a general-purpose gp3 volume, provided it meets the workload's performance requirement.

Modernization of storage types

Cloud provider focuses on providing new features and storage offerings that offer better price to performance ratios. By adopting newer storage types, organizations can reduce costs without sacrificing performance.

Case study: Transitioning from Amazon EBS gp2 volume to gp3

In 2020, AWS introduced gp3 volumes, which offer enhanced performance and cost benefits compared to gp2 volumes, such as the following:

- **Performance and storage decoupling**: Unlike gp2, where IOPS scales with storage size (3 IOPS per GB), gp3 allows you to configure IOPS and throughput independently of volume size.
- **Cost savings**: gp3 is priced approximately 20% lower per GB compared to gp2. Refer to *Figure 6.13* to compare the price difference between gp2 and gp3 storage.
- **Scalability**: gp3 volumes allow up to 16,000 IOPS and 1000 MB/s of throughput.

Let us say a workload needs 200GB of storage and 3000 IOPS. With gp2 volume type, you would need to provision 1TB of volume (considering3 IOPS per GB), even if only 200GB of storage is required. This leads to over-provisioning and unnecessary costs. With gp3, you can provision a 200GB volume and configure it to deliver 3000 IOPS and 125 MB/s throughput. If your workload requires IOPS or throughput beyond gp3 default baseline, you will need to provision additional IOPS and throughput. This will reduce the overall cost savings, but gp3 is still generally more cost-effective than gp2 for most use cases.

Identifying upgrade candidates

To find gp2 volumes that can be migrated to gp3, perform the following actions:

- Open **AWS Cost Optimization Hub** under the **Billing and Cost Management** dashboard.
- **Filter by resource type**: EBS volume.
- Click on **View opportunities**.
- Look for volumes recommended for upgrade along with estimated savings and implementation effort.

Figure 6.14 shows upgrade recommendations suggested by **AWS Cost Optimization Hub,** including the saving potential and effort requirement. Cloud providers keep on launching new resources and features. Organizations need to track new launches and make use of them to get a better price-performance ratio.

***Figure 6.14**: AWS Cost Optimization Hub - Modernization recommendation*

The following are the steps to upgrade EBS volumes from gp2 to gp3:

- Open the AWS console and go to the **EC2 service** page.
- Select **Volumes** under the **Elastic Block Store** section.
- Select the **gp2** volume to be upgraded.
- Click **Modify Volume**.
- Change the volume type to gp3 and set the desired IOPS and throughput.
- Save changes. In most of the cases, downtime may not be required.

Modernizing I/O-optimized volumes

If your workloads currently use io1 or io2, evaluate whether the performance they provide is truly necessary. These volumes are more expensive but offer higher durability and guaranteed IOPS. If current IOPS requirements are moderate and latency tolerance is acceptable, switching to gp3 can offer significant savings. Alternatively, you may consider switching from io1 to io2, which offers better durability at a lower price point.

Identifying storage tier based on access patterns

After selecting the right storage type, you can further reduce costs by transitioning data between storage tiers as its access patterns evolve. Cloud providers like AWS and Azure offer multiple storage tiers within the same service, especially in object storage like Amazon S3 and Azure Blob Storage. Refer to *Figure 6.15* to understand the different storage tiers offered by Amazon S3:

S3 Standard - General purpose storage for any type of data, typically used for frequently accessed data	
First 50 TB / Month	$0.023 per GB
Next 450 TB / Month	$0.022 per GB
Over 500 TB / Month	$0.021 per GB
S3 Intelligent - Tiering * - Automatic cost savings for data with unknown or changing access patterns	
Monitoring and Automation, All Storage / Month (Objects > 128 KB)	$0.0025 per 1,000 objects
Frequent Access Tier, First 50 TB / Month	$0.023 per GB
Frequent Access Tier, Next 450 TB / Month	$0.022 per GB
Frequent Access Tier, Over 500 TB / Month	$0.021 per GB
Infrequent Access Tier, All Storage / Month	$0.0125 per GB
Archive Instant Access Tier, All Storage / Month	$0.004 per GB
S3 Intelligent - Tiering * - Optional asynchronous Archive Access tiers	
Archive Access Tier, All Storage / Month	$0.0036 per GB
Deep Archive Access Tier, All Storage / Month	$0.00099 per GB
S3 Standard - Infrequent Access ** - For long lived but infrequently accessed data that needs millisecond access	
All Storage / Month	$0.0125 per GB
S3 Express One Zone - High-performance storage for your most frequently accessed data	
All Storage / Month	$0.11 per GB
S3 Glacier Instant Retrieval *** - For long-lived archive data accessed once a quarter with instant retrieval in milliseconds	
All Storage / Month	$0.004 per GB
S3 Glacier Flexible Retrieval *** - For long-term backups and archives with retrieval option from 1 minute to 12 hours	
All Storage / Month	$0.0036 per GB
S3 Glacier Deep Archive *** - For long-term data archiving that is accessed once or twice in a year and can be restored within 12 hours	
All Storage / Month	$0.00099 per GB

***Figure 6.15**: Amazon S3 Storage tiers*

Classifying data by access pattern

Use tools like Amazon S3 Storage Class Analysis to monitor how often data is accessed. You can classify data into the following:

- **Frequently accessed**: Best stored in S3 Standard or S3 Express One Zone.
- **Infrequently accessed**: Move to S3 Standard-IA or S3 One Zone-IA.
- **Archival**: Use Amazon S3 Glacier, Glacier Flexible Retrieval, or Deep Archive.

Transitioning data between storage tiers

Transitioning data between storage classes is managed through lifecycle rules. You can create a lifecycle rule to define the transition of data to a different storage tier based on filters such as prefix, object tag.

The following are some key considerations before defining lifecycle rules for transition:

- **Availability and durability requirements**: Understand what each tier offers to ensure they meet your business requirements.
- **Storage and transition charges**: Transitioning data incurs charges. For example, moving 1 million objects to Glacier can cost around $20 in transition fees. Refer to the section on storage pricing to understand transition charges across storage tiers.
- **Retrieval time and costs**: For example, S3 Glacier Instant Retrieval provides low-cost storage with millisecond access, while Glacier Deep Archive may take hours to retrieve but offers the lowest price per GB.
- **Storage limitations before transitioning**: Some storage tiers may define a minimum object size and storage duration. For Example, Glacier enforces a minimum object size (e.g., 128 KB) and duration (e.g., 90 days). Deleting earlier may trigger early deletion fees, while small files under 128 KB are charged as if they are 128 KB. Knowing such limitations will help in planning and avoiding surprises later.

Reducing costs from API calls

In storage services like S3 and Azure Blob, API calls can become a significant cost component. Even if you reduce storage costs, excessive API usage can still increase your bill. The following sections will discuss some ways to reduce costs from API calls.

Analyzing API charges

Use AWS Cost Explorer or CUR to identify API costs contributing to storage charges, with the following steps and subsequent parameters:

- Launch AWS Cost Explorer from AWS Billing and Cost Management:
    - **Date range**: Last 3 months
    - **Granularity**: Monthly
    - **Filter by service**: S3
    - **View by dimension**: API Operation

Refer to *Figure 6.16* to understand how the API calls can inflate storage charges. You will notice that calls like GET, PUT, and LIST are driving up costs more than storage itself.

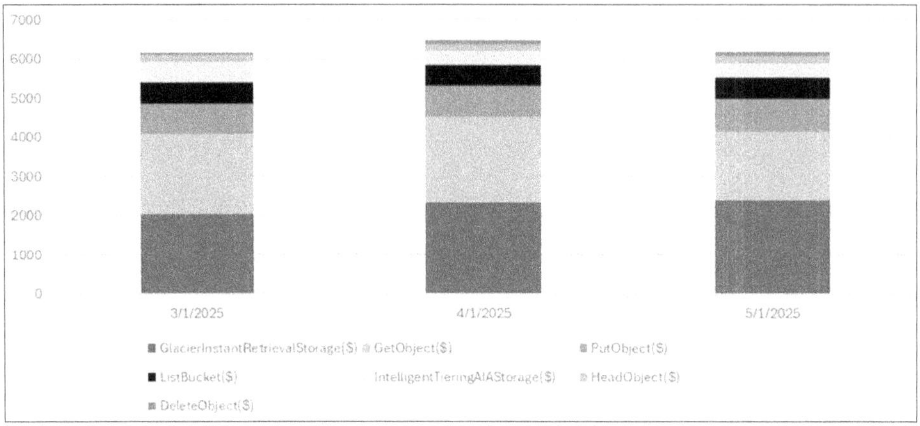

***Figure 6.16**: Analyzing Amazon S3 API charges*

Enable logging and monitoring

Once you have identified the top API calls made to the bucket, the next step will be to understand who is making these calls to the Amazon S3 bucket. To track the trajectory of API calls:

- Enable S3 Server Access Logs.
- Integrate logs with Athena.
- Run queries to identify top users and applications making requests.

Optimize high-cost API calls

Optimizing your expensive S3 API operations can significantly reduce storage costs. Let us examine frequently used S3 API operations:

- **GET object and PUT object calls**: These are common operations for any storage, as users will be putting objects into an Amazon S3 bucket and retrieving objects from an Amazon S3 bucket. Steps like consolidating small files into larger archives (e.g., ZIP) can reduce the number of requests. Also, evaluate alternate solutions such as implementing CloudFront or similar CDNs to cache static files locally, reducing the number of S3 GET requests.
- **LIST operations**: Excessive LIST calls may indicate poor design. Consider the need for excessive LIST calls and redesign how data is accessed.
- **Transition charges**: Instead of transitioning all objects, you can transition select objects based on a filter, such as a prefix or object tags. Develop smart lifecycle policies to transition objects across storage tiers. This ensures only relevant data is transitioned, reducing unnecessary API calls and transition charges.

Optimizing backup-related charges

Backups are critical for data protection, DR, and compliance. However, if not managed properly, backup storage costs can grow significantly over time. Cloud providers offer features like snapshots and managed backup services (such as AWS Backup) to simplify backup operations. Understanding how these are priced and how to manage them efficiently is important for reducing unnecessary costs.

Understanding how snapshots are priced

Refer to *Figure 6.17* to get a summary of EBS snapshot pricing:

EBS Snapshots Storage Pricing	
Standard	$0.05/GB-month
Archive	$0.0125/GB-month
EBS Snapshots Restore Pricing	
Standard	Free
Archive	$0.03 per GB of data retrieved

***Figure 6.17**: Amazon EBS snapshots charges*

Snapshot pricing generally involves the following two main cost components:

- **Snapshot storage cost**: This is the charge for storing the actual data in snapshots. Cloud providers support incremental snapshots, where only the changed data blocks since the last backup are stored. For example, AWS EBS snapshots are incremental by default. Only the first snapshot is a full copy, while subsequent snapshots contain only changed blocks. However, if you are using the EBS snapshot Archive tier, snapshots are treated as full copies, and you are billed for the total data stored, not just the changes.
- **Snapshot retrieval charges**: Cloud providers charge for restoring data from snapshots, especially from archival or cold tiers. Retrieval costs may vary based on how quickly the data needs to be accessed—faster retrievals typically cost more.

Analyze your snapshot-related costs

To manage snapshot costs effectively, it is essential to understand how much you are being charged. In AWS, the charges of snapshots typically appear under the EC2-Other category. Analyze your EBS snapshot costs by following these steps in the AWS Cost Explorer:

1. Launch **AWS Cost Explorer** from the **Billing and Cost Management** dashboard.
2. **Filter by Service**: EC2-Other
3. Set the **Group By** dimension to **API Operation**
4. Look for operations like **CreateSnapshot** to evaluate trends over the last few months.

Compare snapshot costs to volume storage

If your snapshot costs exceed the cost of storing the primary data, it is an indicator to review your backup strategy. For example, if your monthly Amazon EBS storage cost is $500, but snapshots cost $700, it is worth revisiting your backup frequency, retention policies, and data change rate.

The following are some of the key questions to review:

- Backup management (frequency of backup creation).
- Process to clean up old snapshots.
- Right tier being used for storing backups.
- Restoration related charges.

Although there is no standard industry ratio between storage and backup costs, a higher backup-to-storage cost ratio often signals the need to review your backup policies.

Implement regular snapshot clean-up

Cloud snapshots, especially incremental ones, can accumulate and consume storage over time, even if individual changes are small. As a best practice, consider deleting snapshots older than 90 days, unless retention is required for compliance or business needs.

Note: **The actual cost savings depend on how much the data changes between snapshots. If the change rate is low, cleaning up may not result in large savings—but it still promotes better hygiene and governance.**

Use managed backup services

Services like AWS Backup and **data lifecycle manager** (**DLM**) help organizations automate backup schedules, retention periods, and snapshot clean-up policies.

The following are some benefits of such services:

- Centralized backup management across services (e.g., EC2, RDS, DynamoDB).
- Policy-based automation for scheduling and deleting snapshots.
- Simplified compliance and audit tracking.

Using reserved capacity to lower storage costs

Some cloud providers offer options for commitment-based savings where you can reserve storage capacity at a discounted rate. For organizations with predictable storage needs, reserved capacity is a powerful way to save costs. By committing to a fixed amount of storage over a one or three-year term, you can get significant discounts compared to on-demand pricing. Azure Storage reserved capacity is an example of the same.

Azure offers reserved capacity pricing for services like Blob Storage. If you commit to one or three years of usage, you can receive discounts of up to 38% compared to on-demand pricing.

This is ideal for workloads where:

- Storage usage is predictable (e.g., long-term analytics, data lakes).
- Data needs to be retained for compliance reasons.
- Backup archives are stored for years.

Developing a prioritized action plan

Once you have identified potential savings across storage types and snapshot charges, the next step will be to assign priority and develop a sprint plan for implementation. Refer to *Chapter 4, Moving from Cost Observability to Cost Optimization,* to understand the process for developing a priority action plan.

Sample prioritization framework

Table 6.3, given as a template / sample for readers to define priorities based on their organization's needs, illustrates how recommendations can be organized and prioritized based on key decision criteria. Follow the steps provided in *Chapter 4, Moving from Cost Observability to Cost Optimization,* to assign priority to the provided recommendations.

Recommendation	Estimated monthly savings ($)	Implementation time	Resource requirements	Dependency	Priority
Identifying the right storage type	$$	Medium	Medium	None	
Removing idle resources	$$	Low	Low	None	
Rightsizing storage	$$	Medium	Medium	None	

Recommendation	Estimated monthly savings ($)	Implementation time	Resource requirements	Dependency	Priority
Storage modernization	$$	Medium	Medium	Performance testing	
Transitioning to the right storage tier depending on the access pattern	$$	High	High	Need to perform after the right storage type has been identified	
Snapshot charges optimization	$$	Medium	Medium	None	
Reserved capacity	$$	Low	Low	All other optimizations have been completed	

***Table 6.3**: Developing a priority action plan*

The information can be depicted in an impact and complexity graph, as shown in *Figure 6.18*:

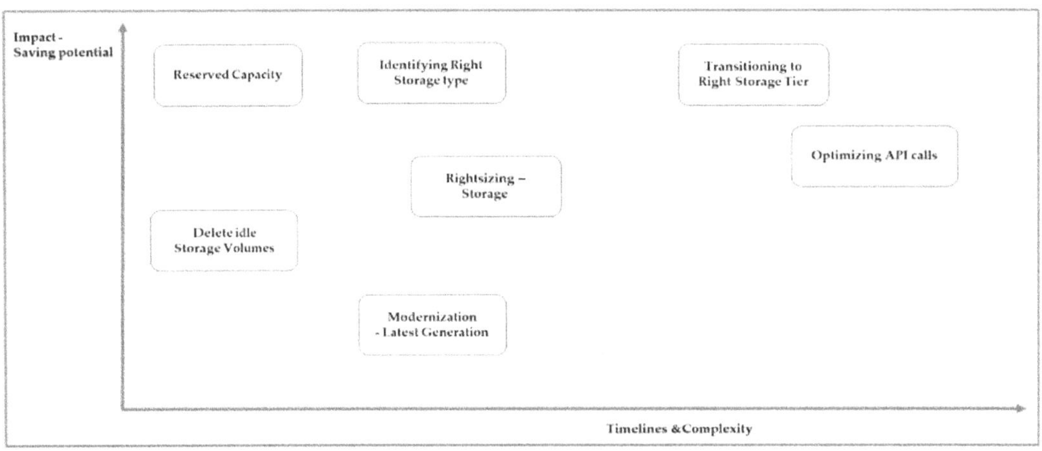

***Figure 6.18**: Impact and complexity graph*

This chapter highlights the following key takeaways and points to remember for storage cost optimization:

- Choose the right storage type to align with workload characteristics.
- Store the data on appropriate storage tiers based on how frequently data is accessed.

- Remove idle and unused storage volumes that contribute to waste.
- Rightsize storage allocations to avoid over-provisioning.
- Modernize storage solutions to take advantage of newer, more cost-effective technologies.
- Manage backup and snapshot costs through retention policies and lifecycle automation.
- Use observability tools like AWS S3 Analytics, Storage Lens, and cost explorer dashboards to monitor usage trends and improve decision-making.

Conclusion

Storage services are core components of any cloud environment and consistently rank among the top five areas of cloud spending for organizations. Cloud providers offer comprehensive storage options for block, file, and object storage, each designed with distinct performance and durability characteristics to support various workloads such as databases, analytics, and AI/ ML applications.

This chapter provided an essential foundation for understanding cloud storage offerings and pricing elements for cloud storage services. While it may seem intuitive to reduce storage spend by choosing a lower-cost storage tier, effective storage cost optimization requires a more comprehensive approach. Organizations must evaluate factors such as data access patterns, application performance requirements, data retention policies, and operational behavior to design an efficient storage strategy.

Once an organization has a clear insight into storage usage and cost drivers, the next step is to create a prioritized action plan for optimizing storage cost. This plan should outline practical steps for implementation, consider interdependencies across teams or workloads, and align with organizational constraints such as compliance, budget cycles, and resource availability.

By consistently applying these strategies, organizations can optimize their storage usage, reduce waste, and significantly cut down on storage-related charges while maintaining the performance expectation from cloud infrastructure.

In the next chapter, we will shift our focus to database services, another major component of cloud infrastructure and a significant contributor to overall cloud costs. We will explore various strategies to optimize database usage and spending while ensuring data availability, performance, and reliability.

CHAPTER 7
Optimizing Database Cost on Cloud

Introduction

In today's digital world, databases serve as the core component of all major workloads, storing critical data that powers everything from customer transactions to business analytics. Whether it is an e-commerce platform processing millions of orders, a healthcare provider maintaining patient records, or a financial institution handling real-time transactions, databases play a pivotal role in supporting core business functions.

Cloud providers offer a broad portfolio of database services, catering to organizational needs through diverse database solutions. These offerings include traditional relational databases such as Amazon RDS or Azure SQL Database, NoSQL databases such as Amazon DynamoDB or Azure Cosmos DB, and specialized databases such as graph databases and time-series databases. While these managed database services eliminate many operational overhead costs, organizations often face challenges in optimizing their database cost on the cloud.

Cloud database services are designed to align with cloud-native principles like elasticity, scalability, and the pay-as-you-go pricing model. As organizations move from traditional on-premises database deployments to cloud-based solutions, it introduces new cost dynamics. Unlike fixed-cost on-premises deployments, cloud databases follow a consumption-based pricing model, where costs can vary significantly based on factors such as instance size, storage allocation, I/O operations, and data transfer. This chapter aims to help you understand how to optimize database costs in the cloud by taking a holistic approach, combining architectural best practices, observability best practices, right-sizing strategies, and leveraging platform-specific tools. While the emphasis will be on cloud-native managed databases, many principles will also apply to self-managed databases running on compute instances.

Structure

In this chapter, we will discuss the following topics:

- Understanding cloud database portfolios
- Anatomy of cloud database pricing

- Tools for analyzing database usage and spend
- Cost Optimization levers for cloud databases
- Developing a prioritized action plan

Objectives

By the end of this chapter, the readers will develop a comprehensive understanding of the different types of database services offered by cloud providers and the cost implications of various deployment options. They will learn how to use native tools to analyze your organization's database usage, identify key cost drivers, and select the most cost-effective deployment models based on workload requirement (self-managed vs. cloud-managed, provisioned vs. serverless). The chapter will also guide them through implementing cost optimization strategies such as rightsizing, modernization, and elasticity, and help them create a prioritized plan to achieve both quick wins and sustainable long-term savings. While AWS services and tools will be used as primary examples, the principles and strategies covered are equally applicable to other major cloud platforms, including Microsoft Azure and **Google Cloud Platform** (**GCP**).

Understanding cloud database portfolios

Cloud service providers such as AWS, Microsoft Azure, and Google Cloud offer a diverse range of database services to cater to various application needs. Cloud database services are primarily offered under two models: **infrastructure as a service** (**IaaS**) and **platform as a service** (**PaaS**). The details are as follows:

- **IaaS model**: In the IaaS model, cloud providers are responsible for deploying and managing the underlying infrastructure components, such as virtual machines, storage, and networking components. Organizations are responsible for installing, configuring, and managing the operating system, database software, and applications. This model offers greater control and flexibility but requires more administrative effort. This model is very similar to an organization deploying database software on top of a virtual machine or a physical server in a data center.
- **PaaS model**: PaaS offerings abstract the underlying infrastructure and database components, allowing organizations to focus on application development and data management. The cloud provider manages the infrastructure, operating system, and database software. Examples include Amazon RDS and Azure SQL Database.

This chapter focuses on PaaS offerings, given their widespread adoption and relevance in cloud-native architectures.

Relational databases

Relational databases are structured to store data in tables with rows and columns, adhering to **atomicity, consistency, isolation, durability** (**ACID**) properties. They are ideal for applications that have structured data and require complex queries and transactions:

- **AWS relational database services**:
  - Amazon RDS (supports MySQL, PostgreSQL, MariaDB, Oracle, SQL Server)
  - Amazon Aurora (MySQL and PostgreSQL compatible)
- **Azure offerings**: Some of the relational database offerings from Azure include:
  - Azure SQL Database
  - Azure SQL Managed Instance
  - **Azure Database for MySQL/PostgreSQL**: Managed services for MySQL and PostgreSQL databases.
  - Oracle Database@Azure

Non-relational databases

Non-relational (**NoSQL**) databases are designed for unstructured or semi-structured data, offering flexibility and scalability. They are categorized based on data models and specialized offerings, and are discussed in the following sections.

Key-value stores

A key-value database stores data as pairs—a unique key and its corresponding value. This database is ideal for storing massive amounts of data and is extremely fast for reading and writing data. Examples include:

- **Amazon DynamoDB**: Offers a fully managed and serverless key-value database.
- **Azure Cosmos DB**: Provides a globally distributed, multi-model database service.

Document database

These databases store information as documents, usually in JSON or similar formats. Each document can have a flexible structure, which means one document does not have to follow the same format as another.

- Amazon DocumentDB is designed for JSON document storage and is compatible with MongoDB.
- Azure Cosmos DB

In-memory database

These databases store data directly in the system's memory (RAM) instead of on a hard disk. Since memory access is much faster than disk access, the performance is lightning-fast. This is good for applications that need instant responses, and common use cases include data caching and session management. The details are as follows:

- **Amazon ElastiCache**: Supports Redis and Memcached for real-time applications.
- **Azure Cache for Redis**: Offers high-throughput and low-latency data access.

Graph databases

These databases are designed to store data and relationships. Instead of rows and columns, they use nodes (data points) and edges (connections between nodes). This is good for applications exploring and analyzing how things are connected. The database allows applications to make fast queries about complex relationships between data. Ideal use cases include fraud detection systems and social networks:

- Amazon Neptune is optimized for storing and querying highly connected data.
- Azure Cosmos DB includes support for graph databases

Time-series databases

Time-series databases are built to handle data that is recorded over time. They store values along with timestamps and are optimized for analyzing patterns or trends over time:

- Amazon Timestream is designed for IoT and operational applications.
- Azure Time Series Insights.

Anatomy of cloud database pricing

Understanding how cloud providers structure their database service pricing is crucial for effective cost management and optimization. Database pricing is complex, involving multiple factors that can significantly impact your cloud spend. These factors include the cloud service model used (IaaS or PaaS), deployment configuration, choice of database engine, licensing model, instance specification, geographic location, and payment option. Each of these elements plays a role in determining your overall cloud database costs. For example, opting for a cloud managed database service (PaaS) might cost more compared to a self-managed option (IaaS) but could save on operational expenses. Similarly, your choice of database engine, such as open-source MySQL versus proprietary options like Oracle, can have substantial licensing cost implications. By gaining insight into these pricing components, organizations can make informed decisions on optimizing database cloud spend while maintaining the required level of database functionality and reliability.

Evaluating self-managed and cloud managed database options

When comparing self-managed (IaaS) databases with cloud managed services (PaaS), it is important to understand what components are included in pricing, as well as to factor in the cost for management and operations in evaluation. The details are as follows:

- **Self-managed (IaaS)**: In the self-managed (IaaS) option, organizations install databases on the compute and other infrastructure components provided by cloud providers. Organizations have full control over the database deployed, but are responsible for the database license, platform management, database maintenance, and updates.
- **Managed services (PaaS)**: Cloud managed database pricing typically encompasses infrastructure components like compute cost as well as database licensing cost in some scenarios. The cloud provider is responsible for the maintenance, scaling, and patching of databases and underlying infrastructure components.

Cost analysis between self-managed databases (IaaS) and cloud managed database solutions (PaaS) requires careful consideration of both direct and indirect costs. While the base pricing of self-managed databases may appear lower, organizations need to account for additional operational costs, including system administration, maintenance, security management, and technical support. In contrast, managed database services typically bundle these operational components into their pricing structure. To determine true **return on investment** (**ROI**), businesses should evaluate hidden costs such as staff training, monitoring tools, backup solutions, and the time spent on routine maintenance tasks. This holistic approach to cost assessment enables organizations to make well-informed decisions on selecting self-managed or cloud-managed databases that align with both their technical requirements and financial objectives.

Understanding database cost components

When choosing the cloud database solution, it is important to understand what components are included in the pricing apart from instance or compute pricing, as well as identifying elements that are excluded. Some of the components require particular attention:

- **Storage**: Database storage is billed separately from compute resources. For example, if your deployment requires 100GB of storage, you will incur charges based on both the storage type selected (such as SSD or standard) and the space allocated. These costs accumulate independently of your database instance fees.
- **Backup and snapshots**: Backup charges may not be included in database instance pricing and in storage costs and need to be factored separately.
- **Data transfer**: Charges apply for data transferred out of the cloud provider's network. Ingress is usually free, while egress rates vary by region and volume. We will discuss more about data transfer charges in the coming chapters.

- **Licensing**: Licensing is a complex topic, and an organization needs to validate if the database instance pricing provided by the cloud provider is inclusive of the database engine license. Generally, cloud providers have both options available for organizations to choose from: **license included** (**LI**) or **bring your own license** (**BYOL**) model. Licensing costs can significantly impact total expenses, especially for commercial databases like Oracle or SQL Server, and need to be reviewed to determine whether the same is included or excluded from cloud database pricing.

Purchase models

Cloud providers offer flexible purchasing models to meet different budget and usage needs:

- **On-demand**: Pay-as-you-go model without long-term commitments. Suitable for unpredictable workloads.
- **Reserved Instances**: Commit to a 1 or 3-year term in exchange for discounted rates, ideal for steady-state workloads.
- **Serverless**: Charges are based on actual usage, measured in **request units** (**RUs**) or similar metrics.

Region-based pricing

Prices vary across regions due to factors like infrastructure costs and demand. For example, running an Amazon RDS instance in Asia Pacific (Mumbai) may differ in cost compared to running an RDS instance in US East (N. Virginia). Identify the region and availability zone based on your application hosting requirements to leverage optimal pricing as well as to avoid any data transfer charges.

Instance types and sizes

Database offerings from cloud providers come in different sizes. Selecting the appropriate instance type (e.g., General Purpose, Memory Optimized) and size (e.g., t3.medium, r5.large) is crucial. Over-provisioning leads to unnecessary costs, while under-provisioning can affect performance.

Processor types

The underlying processor impacts performance and cost. AWS offers instances powered by Intel, AMD, and its custom Graviton (ARM-based) processors, with Graviton instances often providing cost savings.

Billing units

Database services are billed using different units, as demonstrated in the following table:

Billing unit	Description
Per-hour	**On-demand database** (**DB**) instances are charged based on the number of hours your DB instance runs. The price of a database instance varies by the instance type selected.
Gigabyte-month (**GB-month**)	This unit is commonly used for storage pricing. It represents the cost of storing 1 GB of data for one month. Prices differ based on storage type. This unit also applies to backup storage costs, which include both automated and manual backups.
vCore per hour	Some providers base their charges on **virtual CPU cores** (**vCores**) used per hour. This model may also apply to extended support costs charges for the database being used post the end of the support period.
Data transfer charges (GB transferred)	Cost of transferring data from a database for replication or high availability across AZ or regions.
DTU-based pricing	DTU based pricing is Specific to Azure SQL Database, combining CPU, memory, and I/O resources into a single unit.
RU	Used by services like Azure Cosmos DB and Amazon DynamoDB to measure throughput. Billing is based on the number of RUs consumed.
I/O operations	Some services, like Amazon Aurora, charge separately for I/O usage, typically per million requests.

***Table 7.1**: Cloud database billing units*

Navigating the complex landscape of cloud database services requires a thorough understanding of available offerings and their pricing structures. By aligning database choices with workload requirements and implementing strategic cost optimization practices, organizations can achieve both performance and budgetary goals.

Tools for analyzing database usage and spend

Optimizing database costs in the cloud requires both visibility into spend and usage as well as getting actionable insights. Without a clear picture of how much you are spending and where those costs are coming from, it is not possible to optimize cloud costs effectively. In this section, we will explore a suite of tools offered by AWS that can help you analyze, monitor, and optimize database usage and spending. Many of these tools were introduced in earlier chapters for general cost analysis, but here we will focus specifically on how they can be used for database cost optimization. Understanding and properly utilizing these tools enables organizations to:

- Monitor database resource consumption.
- Identify cost trends and patterns.
- Make informed decisions about database resource allocation.
- Implement data-driven optimization strategies.

By focusing on these database-specific applications of AWS cost management tools, organizations can develop more targeted and effective cost optimization strategies, as demonstrated in the following table:

Category	Tool	Description
Cost Observability: The tools help in reviewing database services consumed by the organization, including total usage and spend.	AWS Billing console	View consolidated billing data, invoices, and service-wise charges.
	AWS Cost Explorer	Visualize database usage and cost. The tool can also be used to do trend analysis, understand elasticity, and identify modernization opportunities.
	AWS Cost and Usage Reports	Provides granular, resource-level data about database usage and cost. Can be queried using Athena and visualized with QuickSight.
	Cost and Usage Dashboard	Pre-built dashboards (via QuickSight), such as the cost intelligence dashboard
	AWS CloudWatch	AWS CloudWatch is a monitoring service with a wide range of metrics for providing insights into different services, including databases.
	Amazon RDS Performance Insights	Helps to analyze and tune database performance.
Cost Optimization: Optimization tools help to find underutilized resources, identify savings opportunities, and receive actionable recommendations.	AWS Trusted Advisor	Checks for idle RDS instances and suggests opportunities to optimize RDS.
	Compute Optimizer	Provides rightsizing recommendations for RDS as well as helps in identifying idle resources.
	AWS Cost Optimization Hub	A centralized dashboard that consolidates cost-saving recommendations across different AWS services, including database services.
Estimation	AWS Pricing Calculator	Estimate the cost of consuming database services. Can also be used for comparing costs for different instance types and storage options for databases.

Table 7.2: *Tools for analyzing database usage and spend*

Gaining visibility into database usage and spend

Understanding database usage patterns and associated costs is the foundation of effective cost optimization. This visibility enables decisions about cost optimization strategies such as rightsizing, instance selection, and potential architectural changes. AWS provides several native tools to help organizations achieve this visibility, with AWS Cost Explorer being one of the most commonly used options.

Reviewing database cost using AWS Cost Explorer

As discussed in the preceding chapters, AWS Cost Explorer is a foundational tool for tracking and visualizing cloud spending. It enables you to build a comprehensive understanding of cost trends, analyze usage, and identify the services and components that are driving your bill. When it comes to databases, AWS Cost Explorer helps you isolate and monitor database-specific costs such as compute, storage, and backup.

Steps to use AWS Cost Explorer for database analysis are as follows:

1. Open the AWS console and go to **Billing and Cost Management**.
2. In the left-side menu, select **Cost Explorer** to launch the dashboard.
3. Apply the following filters:
    - **Date range**: Select the last 3 months to capture recent trends.
    - **Granularity**: Set to Monthly for higher-level trend analysis.
    - **Service**: Filter to show only services like Amazon RDS and DynamoDB.
    - **Dimension**: Choose a service for a high-level view.

Once the filters are applied, the dashboard will display your organization's database-related expenditure. For example, the following figure shows that most of your database usage is tied to Amazon RDS (relational databases), with a smaller cost coming from DynamoDB (NoSQL key-value database):

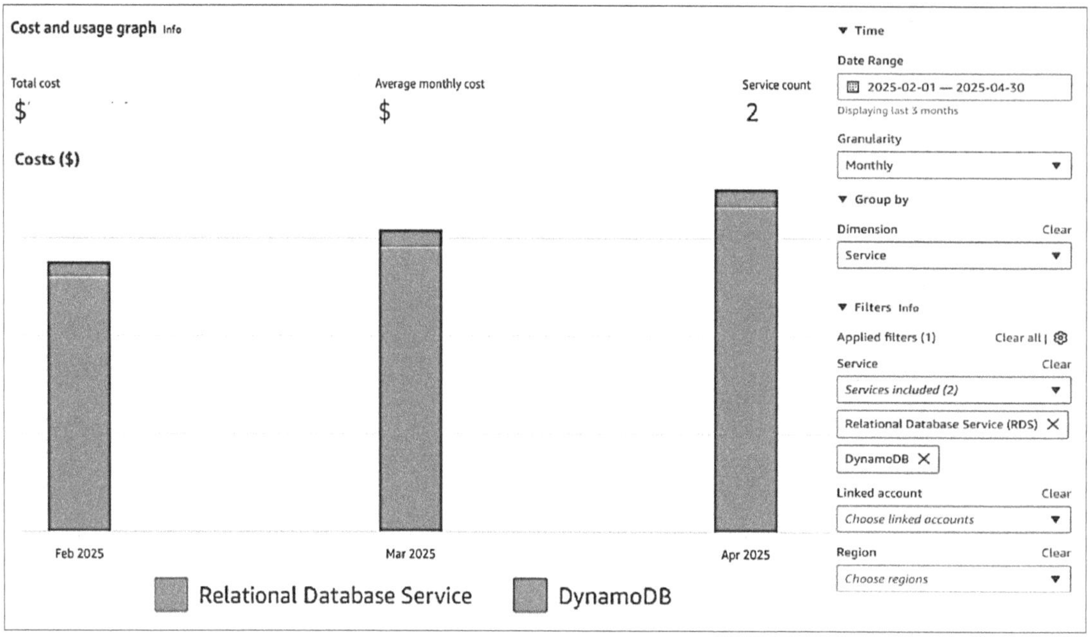

***Figure 7.1**: Cost Explorer for database analysis*

By changing the dimensions from service to usage and to instance type, you can look at database expenditure from a different perspective, such as:

- Amazon RDS charges by instance type
- Segregating Amazon RDS spend into instance spend versus storage and backup spend.

Correlating Cost Explorer findings with Billing console

While Cost Explorer is great for trends and visualizations, the Billing console provides a more detailed, invoice-style breakdown of charges. It can be used to cross-verify findings from Cost Explorer.

Steps to validate database charges are as follows:

1. Go to **Billing and Cost Management** in the AWS console.
2. Select the **Bills** tab.
3. Choose the appropriate billing period (e.g., current or past month).
4. Expand the line items for database-related services, such as:
    - **Relational Database Service** (RDS)
    - DynamoDB

Expanding relational database service will show detailed charges for Amazon RDS, such as:

- Instance types and total hours used.
- Storage-related charges, including provisioned IOPS or throughput.
- Backup-related costs.

Refer to the following figure to analyze relation database (Amazon RDS) charges for the last month:

Description	Unit
Asia Pacific (Sydney)	
Amazon Aurora Storage and I/O	
USD 0.11 per GB-month of consumed storage for Aurora MySQL	GB-Mo
USD 0.22 per 1 million I/O requests for Aurora MySQL	IOs
Amazon Relational Database Service Backup Storage	
$0.095 per additional GB-month of backup storage exceeding free allocation running MySQL	GB-Mo
$0.095 per additional GB-month of backup storage exceeding free allocation running PostgreSQL	GB-Mo
USD 0.095 per GB-month of backup storage exceeding free allocation	GB-Mo
Amazon Relational Database Service for Aurora MySQL	
$0.35 per RDS db.r6i.large Single-AZ instance hour (or partial hour) running Aurora MySQL	Hrs
USD 0.023 per GB-month of backup storage exceeding free allocation for Aurora MySQL	GB-Mo
Amazon Relational Database Service for Aurora MySQL Reserved Instances	
Aurora MySQL, db.r5.large reserved instance applied, db.r5.xl instance used	Hrs
USD 0.0 hourly fee per Aurora MySQL, db.r5.large instance	Hrs
Amazon Relational Database Service for MySQL Community Edition	
USD 0.026 per db.t3.micro Single-AZ instance hour (or partial hour) running MySQL	Hrs
USD 0.052 per db.t3.micro Multi-AZ instance hour (or partial hour) running MySQL	Hrs
USD 0.052 per db.t3.small Single-AZ instance hour (or partial hour) running MySQL	Hrs

Figure 7.2: AWS Billing console - Amazon RDS

Similarly, for DynamoDB, charges are shown in the billing units, such as:

- **Read capacity units** (RCUs)
- **Write capacity units** (WCUs)
- Data storage

Refer to the following figure to understand DynamoDB spend in-depth:

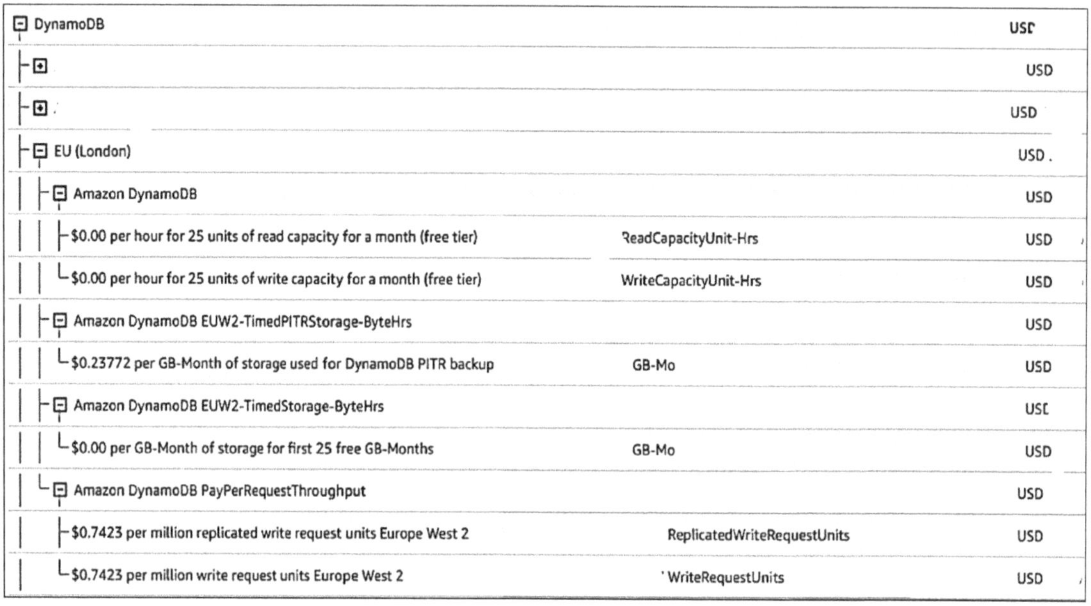

***Figure 7.3**: AWS Billing console - DynamoDB*

Accessing granular data using Cost and Usage Reports

The CUR provides the most granular level of cost data, including resource-level cost and usage data that can be used for in-depth analysis.

Some of the insights you can get from CUR are as follows:

- Identify the top 10 most expensive RDS instances by resource ID.
- Break down total database spend into categories like instance, storage, and backup.
- Use cost allocation tags (e.g., Environment) to compare production vs. development costs.

This level of visibility allows you to pinpoint inefficiencies at the individual resource level and take precise action.

AWS CloudWatch

Amazon CloudWatch is typically used for monitoring different services such as compute, EBS volumes, and databases. It also plays a big role in cost observability and fine-tuning cost optimization recommendations shared by tools like Trusted Advisor by helping you understand how efficiently your databases are being utilized.

Some of the key metrics to watch are as follows:

- CPU utilization
- IOPS consumption
- Freeable memory
- Database connections.

Low usage across these metrics can indicate underutilized or oversized instances, a key opportunity for rightsizing.

Amazon RDS performance insights

RDS performance insights provide deeper visibility into the performance of your relational databases. It helps you analyze queries, wait events, and bottlenecks, which can affect your database performance. High database load due to inefficient queries can lead to the need for more powerful (and expensive) instances. By identifying and tuning problematic queries, you may avoid unnecessary scale-ups and rightsize your database instances.

Getting cost saving insights from tools

Apart from cost observability tools, AWS provides various native tools and services that provide actionable insights for cost optimization.

Optimization with AWS Trusted Advisor

AWS Trusted Advisor helps identify opportunities to reduce waste and improve cost efficiency by running best-practice checks across services. Database-specific checks in the Trusted Advisor include:

- **Amazon RDS idle DB instances**: Detects RDS databases that are underutilized or unused and are great candidates for downsizing or termination.
- **Amazon RDS Reserved Instance optimization**: Suggests switching from on-demand to RIs based on your usage patterns to save 30-70%.

Steps to access Trusted Advisor checks are as follows:

1. Go to the **Trusted Advisor** console.
2. Select the **Cost Optimization** category.
3. Review the database-related checks. Refer to the following figure for some of the database related checks in the **Trusted Advisor** console:

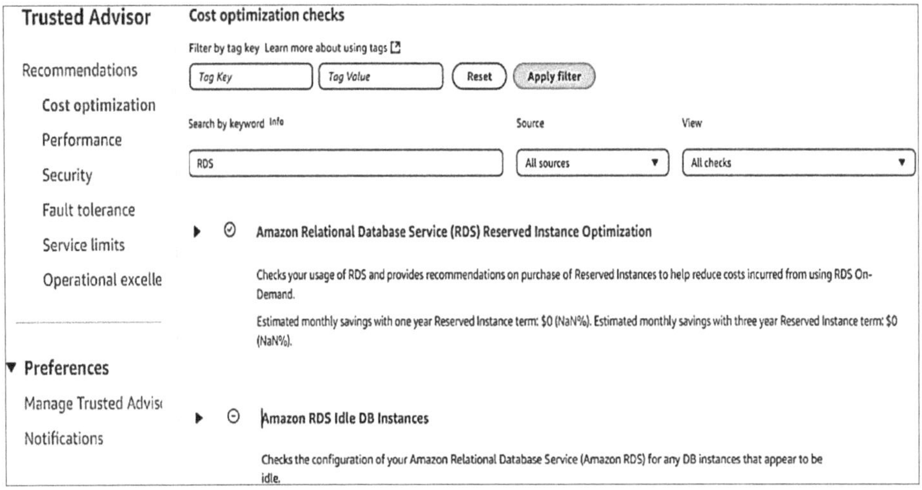

***Figure 7.4**: Trusted Advisor check for database*

Rightsizing recommendations with AWS Compute Optimizer

In the preceding chapter, we used AWS Compute Optimizer for rightsizing compute instances and EBS volumes. AWS Compute Optimizer also offers rightsizing suggestions for RDS instances, based on utilization patterns.

Steps to use AWS Compute Optimizer for RDS are as follows:

1. Open **Compute Optimizer** from the AWS Console.
2. Navigate to **RDS Databases** under the **Rightsizing** panel.
3. Review rightsizing suggestions for RDS as shown in the following figure:

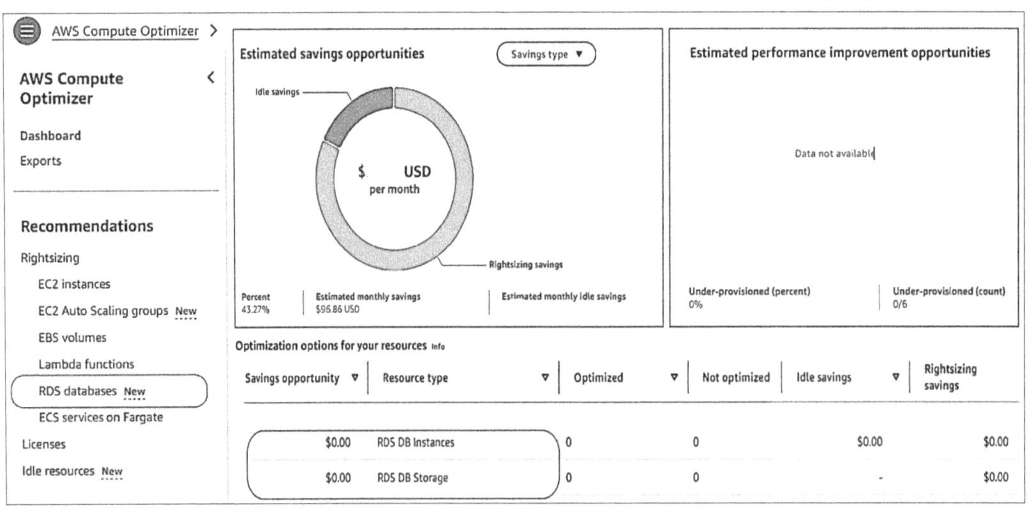

***Figure 7.5**: Compute Optimizer recommendation for RDS*

You can examine recommendations as well as performance metrics of instances to make informed resizing decisions.

Centralized cost actions with AWS Cost Optimization Hub

AWS Cost Optimization Hub is a relatively newer tool that consolidates optimization opportunities across services in one place.

Steps to use Cost Optimization Hub for database services are as follows:

1. Launch the **Cost Optimization Hub** in the AWS console.
2. Use filters to focus on database resources like:
    - RDS DB Instances
    - DynamoDB
    - MemoryDB

This view provides a comprehensive list of cost-saving recommendations across your cloud database workload, helping you prioritize actions based on potential savings. Refer to the following figure for **Cost Optimization Hub** console and applying the resource filter:

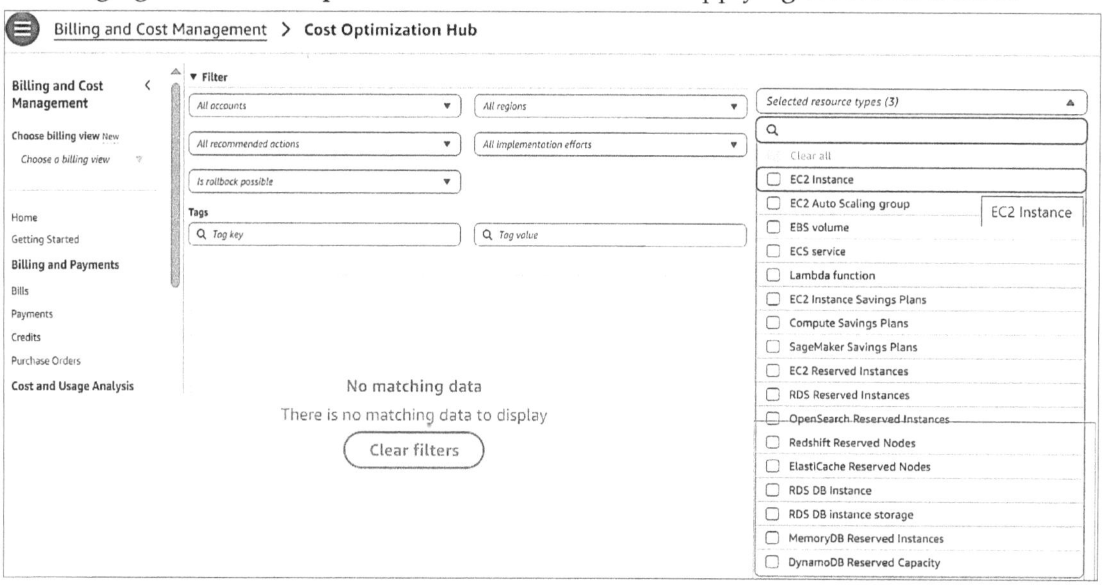

Figure 7.6: *AWS Cost Optimization Hub for database*

Estimating and comparing costs

Forecasting cloud database costs requires an understanding of the pricing models of AWS database services, different deployment options, and your specific workload requirements. AWS provides several tools that help organizations create detailed cost estimates, compare different architectural choices, and make cost efficient decisions.

AWS Pricing Calculator

Before launching a new database or making changes to an existing one, it is important to estimate the impact on cost. The AWS Pricing Calculator helps you:

- Estimate monthly charges for various database services.
- Compare instance types and storage configurations.
- Simulate Reserved Instances vs. on-demand pricing.

Putting it all together

Cloud providers have a set of tools for cost observability, cost optimization, and cost estimation. By leveraging the right tools, teams can uncover hidden inefficiencies, forecast future costs, and build a cost-aware culture. Whether you are running a small web app or managing enterprise-grade databases, tools like AWS Cost Explorer, CUR, CloudWatch, and Trusted Advisor are essential for keeping your database costs under control and aligned with your business goals. To effectively monitor your database costs across your cloud workloads, follow the given approach:

1. **Assess usage patterns**:
    - Use AWS Cost Explorer, Bills, CUR, and CloudWatch to understand where and how you are spending.
    - Identify which databases, such as relational (RDS, Aurora) or non-relational (such as DynamoDB), contribute most to your costs.
2. **Break down the costs**: Use Billing console and Athena queries on CUR to get details such as:
    - Split of database spend into categories such as:
        - o Compute (instances)
        - o Storage (GB stored, IOPS)
        - o Backups and snapshots charges.
    - Mapping Resource IDs to spend.
3. **Identify optimization opportunities**:
    - Use Trusted Advisor to identify idle databases.
    - Use Compute Optimizer for rightsizing recommendations.
    - Use performance insights and CloudWatch for reviewing database metrics and tuning workloads.

4. **Plan for the future**:
   - Use AWS Pricing Calculator to estimate costs before launching new resources.
   - Regularly review recommendations from the Cost Optimization Hub.

Cost Optimization levers for cloud databases

There are different cost optimization strategies for databases deployed on cloud platforms. Optimizing cloud database costs requires careful consideration, as databases are the backbone of most business operations and directly affect user experience. Before implementing any cost-saving measures, an organization should conduct a thorough analysis of its workload patterns, data characteristics, and application-database interactions. This evaluation helps prevent any impact on system performance and availability.

Choosing the right database type

When planning to optimize database costs in the cloud, the first step is selecting the right type of database for your workload. Databases are critical components of any workload, and making the wrong choice can lead not only to overspending but also to performance issues, reduced reliability, and even business disruptions.

When selecting a database type, consider the following:

- The nature of the workload. (transactional, analytical, batch, etc.)
- The data structure and consistency requirements.
- Performance needs, including latency and throughput.
- Scalability patterns—both current and anticipated.
- Operational complexity and skill requirements.

Once this assessment is complete, you can make informed decisions about which database type and deployment model will best balance performance, manageability, and cost-effectiveness.

Choosing between relational and non-relational databases

Cloud providers like AWS, Azure, and Google Cloud offer both relational and non-relational databases, also known as SQL and NoSQL databases, respectively. Selecting the right one is one of the most critical decisions for controlling costs and improving system efficiency.

Relational databases

Relational databases (**RDBMS**) like MySQL, PostgreSQL, Oracle, and SQL Server are well-suited for structured data with defined relationships. They are ACID-compliant, making them ideal for applications that require strong data integrity, such as:

- Banking and finance systems
- E-commerce platforms
- Inventory management tools
- **Customer relationship management** (**CRM**) applications

Cost consideration: Relational databases typically require more compute and storage resources to maintain consistency and support complex queries (joins, aggregations, transactions). They are best suited when business requires strict accuracy and real-time consistency (ACID compliance).

Non-relational databases

Non-relational databases (NoSQL) such as document databases (MongoDB, Amazon DocumentDB), key-value stores (Redis, DynamoDB), and graph databases (Amazon Neptune) are suited for document which are semi-structured or unstructured. These databases are designed for speed, flexibility, and scalability. They are ideal for:

- Applications with unstructured or semi-structured data.
- Use cases where schema changes are frequent.
- Real-time analytics and caching.
- Social media applications and recommendation engines.

Cost advantage: NoSQL databases can help reduce costs through better scalability and dynamic schema support. They are also suitable for workloads where eventual consistency is acceptable, reducing the computational overhead needed for strict data validation.

Commercial vs. open-source databases

Another important consideration is whether to use a commercial database or an open-source alternative. This choice can significantly influence the **total cost of ownership** (**TCO**). Commercial databases often come with licensing fees and support contracts, whereas open-source databases can be deployed for free, although they may require skilled resources for ongoing maintenance and depend on the community for bug fixes. For example, a startup building a new SaaS application might choose PostgreSQL over a commercial database such as MS SQL Server or Oracle to minimize upfront costs.

Commercial databases

Examples include Oracle, Microsoft SQL Server, and IBM Db2. These databases offer:

- Advanced features such as high availability, clustering, and advanced tools for performance insights.
- Dedicated technical support with defined **service-level agreements** (**SLAs**).
- Compliance with industry regulations and robust security features.

Cost considerations:

- Licensing fees can be substantial, especially for large-scale deployments. It may also require expensive support contracts.
- Pricing models may include per-core, per-user, or usage-based fees.
- Long-term vendor lock-in may limit migration and modernization options.

Open-source databases

Some of the commonly used open-source databases include MySQL, PostgreSQL, and MariaDB. These are free to use and supported by a community of developers. Some open-source databases also have enterprise versions with professional support.

Cost advantages:

- No upfront licensing cost.
- Flexibility in deployment and customization.
- Reduced total cost of ownership, especially for non-critical workloads.

Considerations:

- Community support may not meet enterprise SLA requirements.
- Advanced features may be limited or require manual implementation.
- Security patches and compliance configurations need to be handled in-house.

Self-managed vs. cloud-managed databases

We have seen differences between self-managed and cloud-managed databases in the preceding section. Cloud providers offer both self-managed and cloud-managed (database-as-a-service) database options. Choosing the right operational model can significantly impact cloud cost. Many organizations begin their cloud journey with a lift-and-shift approach and start with self-managed databases and later modernize to cloud-managed services as part of a modernization strategy.

Self-managed databases

In this option, the organization deploys and manages the database on virtual machines or physical servers. The organization is responsible for installation, configuration, patching, backups, scaling, and monitoring. The use case for self-managed databases may vary, such as a regulated healthcare company may choose self-managed databases due to compliance requirements around infrastructure control.

Advantages:

- Greater control over the environment.
- Customization based on internal requirements.
- No dependency on vendor-imposed limitations.

Challenges:

- Management overhead.
- Need for skilled **database administrators** (**DBAs**).

Cloud-managed databases

Services like Amazon RDS, Azure SQL Database, and Google Cloud SQL allow organizations to use databases without worrying about infrastructure maintenance. Features include automated backups, patch management, scaling, and monitoring.

Advantages:

- Pay-as-you-go pricing includes compute, storage, and management.
- Reduced need for in-house DBAs lowers operational costs.
- Can be more expensive per unit resource, but saves costs on staffing and downtime.

Note: **Organizations need to understand the shared responsibility model for cloud-managed databases. For example, in cloud-managed databases, cloud providers manage the infrastructure and basic database maintenance, but users are still responsible for data access controls, query optimization, and schema design.**

Provisioned vs. serverless databases

Provisioning refers to allocating a fixed amount of compute and storage to a database, while serverless databases automatically scale based on demand. Some cloud providers offer serverless database options for some of the database engines.

Provisioned databases

These are ideal for steady workloads that need consistent performance. These are typically used in production environments with steady, predictable traffic patterns that require reliable, continuous access. Examples include Amazon RDS instances and Azure Database for PostgreSQL (provisioned).

Pricing is as follows:

- Charged based on the instance type (e.g., db.r6g.large) and the number of hours the instance is running.
- Can take advantage of RI for long-term discounts.

Serverless databases

Serverless databases are ideal for workloads with variable usage patterns. Think of applications that experience busy periods during business hours but minimal activity outside them. Serverless databases have automatic scaling capabilities as they monitor workload patterns and adjust capacity accordingly. This automated scaling makes it a cost-effective solution for applications with fluctuating demands, as you only pay for the resources you actually use. This approach eliminates the need to provide for peak capacity while avoiding the waste of maintaining unused resources during quiet periods. Examples include Amazon Aurora Serverless and Azure SQL Serverless.

Benefits are as follows:

- Pay only for what you use (per second or per request).
- Ideal for unpredictable or infrequent workloads.
- Reduces risk of overprovisioning and idle resources.

Considerations before leveraging a serverless database option:

- Comparatively more expensive than the provisioned option for steady workloads.
- May introduce latency when scaling up after inactivity.
- Not suitable for high-throughput, latency-sensitive applications.
- If you are migrating from provisioned to serverless, keep a close watch on database metrics for any performance impact as well as for any cost impact.
- Use cost alerts or budget controls to avoid unplanned expenses.

Rightsizing and modernization

Two powerful levers to control and reduce your database costs are rightsizing and modernization. These efforts, when executed correctly, can significantly improve your cost-efficiency while maintaining or even improving performance.

Database rightsizing

In a cloud environment, over-provisioning of resources leads to wastage, while under-provisioning can degrade performance and affect user experience. Rightsizing is the process of aligning your infrastructure resources, such as **virtual CPUs** (**vCPUs**), memory, storage, and IOPS, with actual usage patterns. In the context of databases, rightsizing means selecting the appropriate instance size and configuration that aligns with the needs of your application, ensuring sufficient capacity to meet your performance requirements

For example, a fintech organization is running its production MySQL database on an Amazon RDS instance db.r5.4xlarge, but notices that maximum CPU and memory utilization is less than 10% of available capacity. This indicates over-provisioning and wastage of resources. By switching to a smaller size instance, such as db.r5.xlarge, the organization can significantly reduce monthly costs while still meeting peak usage requirements.

Tools providing rightsizing recommendations

AWS provides several native tools to help with identifying and acting on rightsizing opportunities. The details are outlined in the following sections.

AWS Trusted Advisor

Trusted Advisor includes a check called **Amazon RDS idle DB instances**. This helps identify RDS databases that have not had any connections in the last seven days. These databases may be lying around because of older projects, testing environments, or development workloads.

Steps to use AWS Trusted Advisor are as follows:

1. Launch **Trusted Advisor** from the AWS management console.
2. Under **Cost Optimization**, check for idle DB instances.

Once idle instances are identified, you can take action such as taking a snapshot and stopping or terminating the idle database instances. Alternatively, you can also rightsize the database instance to a small instance size to save running costs.

AWS Compute Optimizer

AWS Compute Optimizer analyzes key performance metrics from Amazon CloudWatch, such as:

- CPU utilization
- Database connections
- Disk IOPS
- Network throughput

Based on this data, it provides detailed recommendations for:

- Rightsizing underutilized databases.
- Identifying idle resources.

Refer to *Figure 7.7* for a sample recommendation from AWS Compute Optimizer:

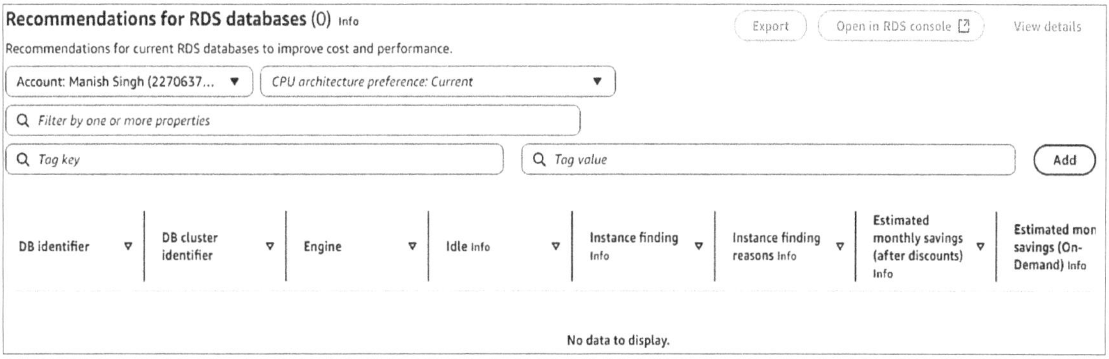

***Figure 7.7**: Compute Optimizer rightsizing recommendation.*

The recommendation shown by Compute Optimizer includes:

- Database identifier and DB engine
- Findings
- Current and recommended instance type and pricing
- Estimated monthly savings
- Performance risk assessment

This allows technical teams to make informed decisions supported by real-time data.

Database modernization

Modernization is a broader initiative compared to rightsizing. It involves upgrading database environments to leverage newer technologies and infrastructure that offer improved cost efficiency, better performance, and long-term support.

Let us explore the three key aspects of database modernization:

- Instance modernization
- processor modernization
- **Upgrade**: End of support version

Instance modernization and upgrading to newer generations

Cloud providers periodically launch new generations of instance families that offer better price-performance ratios. Older instance families often run on outdated hardware and are more expensive compared to newer ones. For example, if you are currently running Amazon Aurora on db.r4.xlarge, migrating to db.r6g.xlarge (Graviton-based) or db.r5.xlarge (Intel-based) can offer a better price-performance ratio due to architectural improvements and better efficiency.

Processor modernization and switching to cost-efficient architectures

AWS offers multiple processor architectures for the same instance family:

- Intel-based instances (widely supported and used).
- ARM based processors offered by cloud providers such as Graviton-based instances from AWS.

Graviton processors, developed by AWS using ARM architecture, offer up to 20–40% cost savings for some workloads, while maintaining comparable or even better performance. While migration of compute workloads from Intel to Graviton might require application compatibility testing, for managed services like Amazon RDS, Graviton-based instances (e.g., db.r6g) are fully supported and migration is seamless.

Refer to the following figure to see the cost comparison between Intel-based database instances and Graviton-based instances (ARM architecture):

Name	Group	Region	Upfront cost	Monthly cost
Amazon Aurora MySQL-Compatible	-	US East (N. Virginia)	0.00 USD	229.95 USD
Status	-			
Description:	-			
Config summary	Aurora MySQL Cluster Configuration Option (Aurora Standard), Change records per statement (0.38), Instance Type (db.r6g.large), Nodes (1), Utilization (100 %Utilized/Month), Instance Family (Memory optimized), Pricing Model (OnDemand)			

Name	Group	Region	Upfront cost	Monthly cost
Amazon Aurora MySQL-Compatible	-	US East (N. Virginia)	0.00 USD	503.70 USD
Status	-			
Description:	-			
Config summary	Aurora MySQL Cluster Configuration Option (Aurora Standard), Change records per statement (0.38), Instance Type (db.r5.xlarge), Nodes (1), Utilization (100 %Utilized/Month), Instance Family (Memory optimized), Pricing Model (OnDemand)			

***Figure 7.8**: Intel and Graviton price comparison*

Upgrading outdated database versions

Using **end-of-support** (**EOS**) database engine versions comes with additional support charges and operational risks. Most cloud providers impose additional charges for EOS database versions. These charges cover extended support requirements but can significantly inflate your database costs. For example, if you are running MySQL 5.6 on RDS (which is past its EOS date), AWS will charge an additional fee. To mitigate end-of-support charges, organizations should upgrade their end-of-support databases to a supported version at the earliest.

Look at *Figure 7.9* to understand the impact of having end-of-support database in your inventory:

***Figure 7.9**: Extended support charges*

Identifying modernization opportunities

Before talking about a database modernization project, it is crucial to understand your current database environment, analyze its associated costs, and evaluate its potential for upgrades. By leveraging available tools, you can make informed decisions about which instances are ideal candidates for rightsizing and modernization.

AWS Billing console

You can enable the AWS Billing console through the following steps:

1. Go to **Billing and Cost Management** in the AWS console.
2. Select the **Bills** section.
3. Expand **Amazon RDS** services to view:

- Instance types
- Region-wise usage
- Total running hours
- Purchase option (on-demand or Reserved)

By analyzing this data, you can identify:

- Old generation instances (e.g., db.r4, db.m4). The naming convention highlights the database instance family, size, and processor used.
- High-cost instances
- Purchase options used (on-demand, Reserved Instances)

The information will help in identifying any end of life or legacy database instances, which can be reviewed for modernization opportunities.

AWS Cost Explorer

AWS Cost Explorer can also be used to review different database instances consumed by the organization and identify legacy or end of support instances for modernization opportunities. Follow the given steps to review the database instance types leveraged by the organization:

1. Go to the AWS console and navigate to **Billing and Cost Management.**
2. Launch **Cost Explorer** from the left-hand menu.
3. Apply the following filters:
    - **Duration**: Last 30 days
    - **Granularity**: Monthly
    - **Dimension**: Instance type
    - **Service**: RDS
    - **Purchase option**: On-demand

Use the resulting graph to identify old-generation or expensive instances. The naming convention helps in identifying instance generation, processor type, and other specifications, which can be used for analyzing modernization opportunities.

AWS Athena with CUR

For advanced users, CUR offers granular billing data that can be queried using Amazon Athena. Using appropriate queries, you can extract the resource ID and other information to take targeted action for modernization.

Planning your rightsizing and modernization journey

Rightsizing and modernization require structured planning and phased execution. The idea is to minimize any impact on database performance and user experience. A sample rightsizing and modernization approach is given as follows:

1. **Assessment and prioritization**:
    - Identify rightsizing and modernization opportunities using tools like Compute Optimizer and Cost Explorer.
    - Identify top candidates based on idle metrics, costs, and EOS status.
    - Prioritize based on potential savings, modernization complexity, and business impact.
2. **Technical evaluation**:
    - Evaluate compatibility between current and target instance types.
    - Determine if application changes are required.
    - Assess downtime implications.
    - Develop rollback plans if the modernization activity fails.
3. **Testing and validation**:
    - Create test environments with target configurations.
    - Perform performance benchmarking.
    - Monitor key metrics (CPU, memory, storage IOPS, latency).
    - Validate full application functionality.
4. **Execution and monitoring**:
    - Modernize non-critical environments first (e.g., dev/test).
    - Gradually implement in production.
    - Monitor post-modernization performance.
    - Compare projected vs. actual cost savings.

Rightsizing and modernization are among the most effective strategies to optimize database costs in the cloud. By aligning resources with actual usage and continuously evolving your infrastructure to leverage new-generation hardware and processors, organizations can achieve a balance between cost efficiency and high performance. Use tools provided by cloud providers to regularly review instance utilization, eliminate idle databases, upgrade legacy environments, and embrace cost-efficient processor architectures like Graviton. These efforts will ensure your cloud database architecture remains lean, modern, and cost-effective.

Implementing elasticity

One of the biggest advantages of running workload in the cloud is the ability to scale dynamically and pay only for what you consume. In traditional on-premises or self-managed databases, once you have bought a database license or provisioned hardware, you need to pay for it irrespective of whether the database is in use or not. But with cloud-managed databases, you are billed for actual usage.

Imagine an organization having a test environment where the database is used only during business hours, Monday through Friday. If the database runs continuously 24x7, the organization is paying for many hours of unused resources, including weekend usage when no one is using it. By shutting down database instances outside business hours, the company could save roughly 30% of the total cost.

Evaluating elasticity with AWS Cost Explorer

To understand whether your database workloads are elastic or consistently running 24/7, use AWS Cost Explorer. Follow the steps provided:

1. Open the AWS console and navigate to **Billing and Cost Management**.
2. Launch **Cost Explorer**.
3. Apply the following filters:
    - **Time period**: Last 30 days
    - **Granularity**: Daily
    - **Dimension**: Instance Type
    - **Filter**: Purchase Option: On-demand (not including instances covered by Reserved Instances)
    - **Service**: RDS
4. Analyze the resulting graph pattern:
    - **Flat usage patterns**: If the daily usage graph for a particular instance type is flat across all days and hours, this indicates constant usage, and the instance may benefit from bringing elasticity into workloads. *Figure 7.10* illustrates a sample usage pattern.
    - **Variable patterns**: Suggest that elasticity is already being leveraged, though further optimization may be possible.

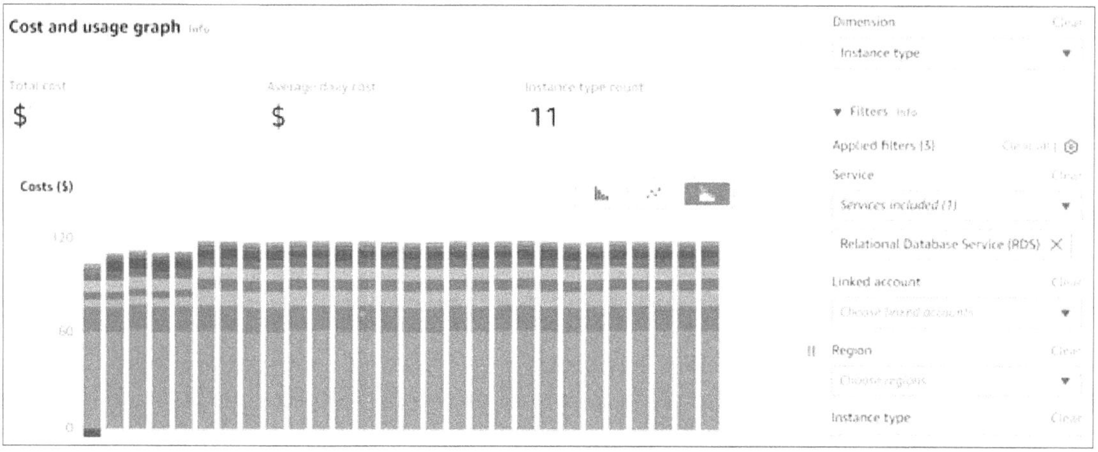

Figure 7.10: Using Cost Explorer to check elasticity

Note: **Elasticity primarily benefits from on-demand pricing. If your instance is covered by an RI, you will be charged regardless of whether the database is running or not. Also, consider if you are using BYOL models, which may not benefit from shutdowns if license costs are fixed.**

Solutions to achieve elasticity in workload

Cloud providers offer multiple ways to automate start/stop schedules and resource scaling:

AWS Instance Scheduler

The solution discussed in the compute section also applies to Amazon RDS. AWS Instance Scheduler automates the start and stop schedules for RDS instances. It enables teams to:

- Define working hours for non-production databases (e.g., 9 AM to 6 PM, Mon–Fri).
- Use tags to target specific instances.
- Manage schedules across multiple AWS accounts and regions.

Serverless databases

Some managed databases offer serverless deployment options, such as Amazon Aurora Serverless and Azure SQL Database Serverless.

Serverless databases automatically scale database resources based on actual traffic. If your workload has sporadic or unpredictable usage, serverless options let you pay per request, rather than keeping instances running all the time.

Autoscaling options for NoSQL databases

For NoSQL databases such as Amazon DynamoDB or Azure Cosmos DB, you pay based on RCUs/WCUs. To avoid over-provisioning of capacity units, you can leverage autoscaling features provided by cloud providers. Enable autoscaling, which automatically adjusts capacity units in response to traffic patterns. This ensures you are not paying for unused capacity during low-traffic periods and still meet demand during peaks.

Optimizing storage and backup costs

When analyzing database costs, it is important to go beyond compute resources. Often, a significant portion of your bill may come from storage and backup charges. As such, focusing only on the instance cost of the database may not yield desired cost-saving results.

Components of cloud database pricing

Most cloud managed database services have three main cost elements:

- Compute and licensing
- Storage
- Backup and snapshots

To analyze where you are spending the most:

1. Go to AWS **Billing and Cost Management**.
2. Select **Bills** from the left-hand panel.
3. Explore the **RDS** section under your bill.
4. Review cost breakdowns for compute, storage, and backup.

Alternatively, you can also leverage AWS Cost Explorer to segregate database charges into compute, storage, and backup costs. Consider an organization where the majority of its database-related cloud expenses are attributed to backup costs. Refer to the following figure to understand the segregation of database charges into compute, storage, and backup using AWS Cost Explorer. In such cases, the organization's database infrastructure may be efficiently sized for compute and storage needs, but the backup strategy may need to be reviewed.

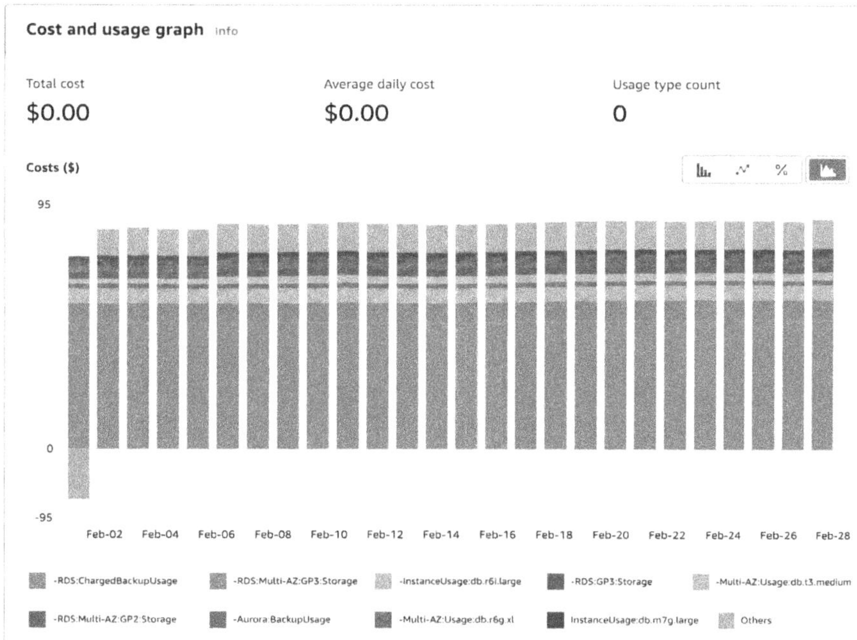

***Figure 7.11**: Segregating database charges*

Optimizing storage costs

Drawing from our earlier chapter on storage optimization strategies, similar principles can be effectively applied to database storage management, particularly for services like cloud-managed databases. Follow the following steps to optimize your database storage costs:

1. **Choose the right storage type**: Cloud providers like AWS offer multiple storage types:
    - gp2 (General Purpose SSD)
    - gp3 (Next-gen SSD, cost-effective)
    - Provisioned IOPS (high-performance, more expensive)

    When workloads are first launched, they often use higher-performing storage options. Periodic reviews help ensure storage is appropriate for actual needs. Review database performance metrics to identify the right storage type for your workload. For example, migrating from gp2 to gp3 can reduce storage costs by up to 20%. Similarly, if you are using provisioned IOPS and performance metrics can be met by General Purpose SSD, consider downgrading to gp3 to save cost.

2. **Rightsize allocated storage**: Avoid over-provisioning by:
    - Monitoring storage usage using Amazon CloudWatch metrics.
    - Reviewing performance insights to understand IOPS and throughput requirements.

3. **Use storage auto-scaling**: Some cloud providers offer automatic storage scaling. For example, RDS storage auto scaling can increase storage size when nearing limits. This reduces the need to provision large amounts up front.

Optimizing backup costs

Backups are essential for business, but they can also become expensive if not managed properly.

Understanding backup pricing

The first step is to understand how the cloud provider is charging for backups, including manual and automatic backups. Let us try to understand the same using AWS as an example:

- Automated backups are free up to the allocated database size. Any backup storage beyond that is chargeable.
- Snapshots are incremental but still contribute to total backup storage.

If your RDS instance has 100GB of allocated storage, backup storage up to 100GB is free. Beyond that, you pay per GB per month as per applicable pricing for the region.

Best practices for reducing backup costs

Some of the approaches to save backup costs are as follows:

- **Implement regular snapshot cleanup**:
    - Old snapshots accumulate and use space.
    - Set policies to delete snapshots older than 90 days (or based on your compliance needs).
- **Use centralized backup services**: Tools like AWS Backup allow:
    - Policy-driven automation for snapshot creation and deletion.
    - Centralized management across services (EC2, RDS, DynamoDB, etc.).
    - Audit and compliance reports.

Commitment-based savings

Cloud providers offer commitment-based pricing to encourage long-term usage. The most common model is RIs, where you can reserve database capacity for 1 to 3 years in exchange for significant discounts compared to on-demand pricing.

Checking RI coverage in AWS

To evaluate how much of your database usage is covered by RIs, follow the given steps:

1. Open **Billing and Cost Management** in the AWS console.
2. Launch **Cost Explorer**.
3. Under the **Reservations** section, check the **Coverage report**.
4. Apply appropriate filter:
    - **Service**: RDS
    - **Time range**: Last 3 months

Refer to the following figure to understand RI coverage for an organization:

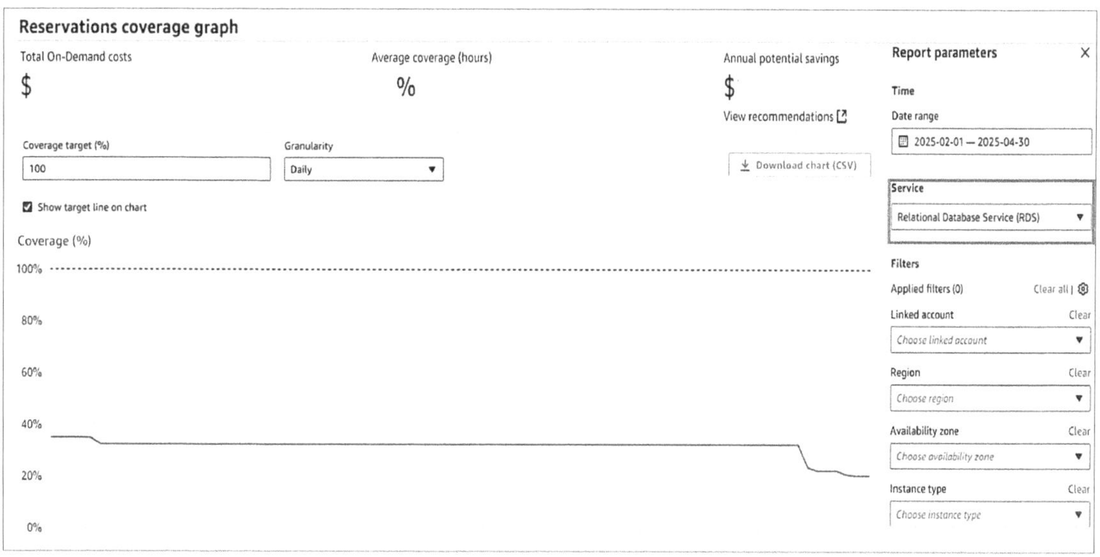

Figure 7.12: RDS RI coverage report

The graph will show:

- **RI coverage percentage**: Lower values indicate you are using expensive on-demand pricing and have potential to save cost through RI commitments.
- **Potential savings**: Helps you evaluate cost-saving opportunities.

Getting RI recommendations

To get a recommendation on what Reservation to purchase, you can make use of the recommendations provided by AWS. The steps are as follows:

1. Open the AWS console and navigate to **Billing and Cost Management**.
2. Launch **Cost Explorer**.
3. Under **Reservations** section, check **Recommendation**.
4. Apply applicable filter:
    - **Service**: RDS
    - **Term (commitment term)**: 1 year or 3 years
    - **Loopback period of recommendation**: 60 days
    - **Payment option**: All upfront/partial upfront or no upfront.

Refer to the following figure for generating the RI recommendation from the AWS Cost Explorer console:

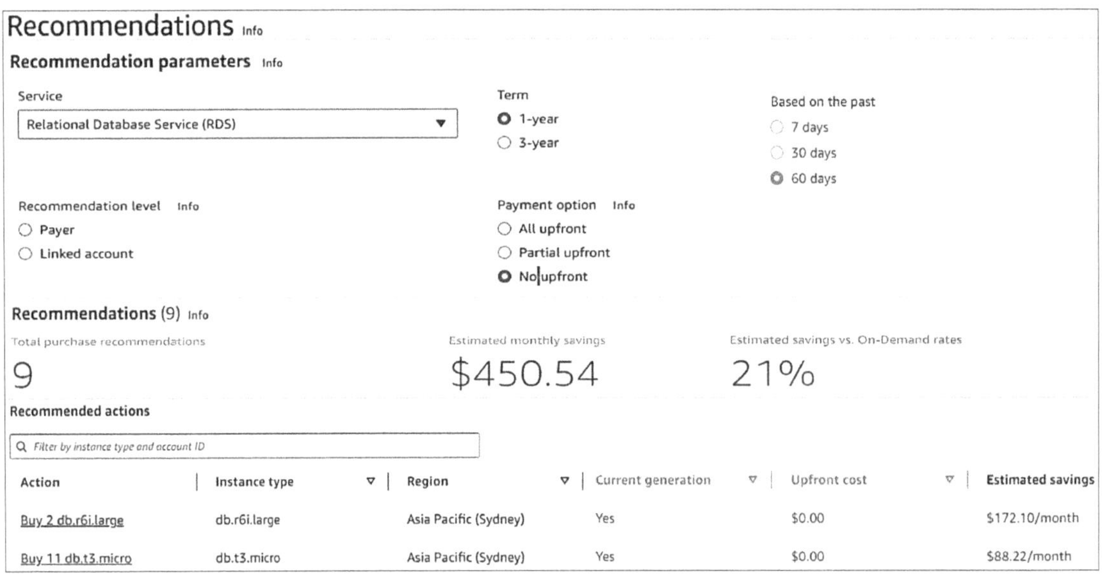

***Figure 7.13**: RDS RI recommendation*

Considerations before purchasing the database RI are as follows:

- **Flexibility**: Check for family and size flexibility provided by RIs. The team needs to be aware of restrictions imposed by RI purchases to avoid any wastage.
- **Forecasting**: RI purchase should account for future database requirements and should consider events and projects that can lead to downsizing of instances, migrating to newer instance families, or modernizing architecture.
- **Risk vs. reward**: Organizations need to balance between cost savings and flexibility. Longer commitments offer better discounts but bind you for the duration of the RI purchase.

Avoiding wastage from past RI purchases

Organizations need to identify any wastages from RI purchases made in the past and should develop a plan to leverage the investment already made. To check for wastages:

1. Open the AWS console and navigate to **Billing and Cost Management**.
2. Launch **Cost Explorer**.
3. Under the **Reservations** section, check the utilization report.
4. Apply applicable filter:
    - **Service**: RDS
    - **Date range**: Specify data range to review.

    Refer to the following figure:

Figure 7.14: RDS RI utilization report

Reviewing database architecture for cost optimization

The design and deployment of your database architecture have a direct influence on costs. While it is important to ensure availability, performance, and resiliency, it is equally critical to avoid over-provisioning or choosing unnecessarily expensive configurations. In the following sections, let us look at a few architectural aspects that can affect cost.

Availability requirements

Availability refers to how accessible your database remains during failures, updates, or system maintenance. In cloud environments, you can configure high availability through options such as multi-AZ deployments, but such deployments can be expensive for non-critical workloads. For example, deploying a multi-AZ RDS instance can cost almost twice as much as a single-AZ instance.

For mission-critical workloads, such as production databases for customer-facing applications, multi-AZ setups (available in services like Amazon RDS or Azure SQL Database) are recommended. These configurations replicate the database across multiple availability zones to provide automatic failover. However, for development, testing, or internal applications where occasional downtime is acceptable, you might opt for single-AZ deployments, which are significantly more cost-effective.

Resiliency requirements

Resiliency ensures that your database can recover from unexpected disruptions. Before choosing a resiliency strategy, assess how much downtime your application can tolerate and whether backup and restore mechanisms are sufficient or if you need a continuously running standby instance. Choosing the right level of resiliency solution based on business needs prevents you from overpaying for highly resilient architectures that may not be necessary.

Implementing caching layers

Frequent access to the same set of data can lead to higher database loads and larger instance sizing. One design to optimize database load is to use in-memory caching solutions, such as Amazon ElastiCache (Redis or Memcached) or Azure Cache for Redis. Caching offloads repetitive reads from the database, reduces latency, and lowers the compute requirements for your database engine.

For example, in a high-traffic e-commerce application with thousands of users querying product catalogs or user sessions, caching can significantly reduce the load on the database, allowing you to use smaller and cheaper instance types.

Query optimization

One of the most overlooked but highly impactful areas of database cost optimization is query performance tuning. Many organizations scale up their database instances simply to process inefficient or long-running queries. Poorly written SQL queries or missing indexes increase the load on the database, leading to high CPU, memory, and I/O consumption. As data grows, these inefficient queries begin to have a compounding effect, requiring larger instance types and more expensive storage to maintain performance.

Instead of immediately upgrading to a larger database instance to address Query performance, start by identifying and improving inefficient queries. Optimizing high-impact queries can allow you to downgrade to smaller instance types, delay the need to upgrade to a large instance, while maintaining overall performance.

Developing a prioritized action plan

Once you have identified potential cost optimization opportunities for your database services, the next crucial step is developing a structured implementation strategy. Begin by evaluating which cost optimization levers apply to your specific design and deployment scenario, then calculate the potential savings each option could deliver. With these opportunities identified, you will need to prioritize them based on key decision criteria such as implementation effort, expected cost savings, technical risk level, business impact, and resource availability. These evaluated options can then be organized into a prioritized action plan with defined implementation timelines. For a detailed understanding of how to develop and execute your priority action plan, including the recommended prioritization framework and methodology, refer to *Chapter 4, Moving from Cost Observability to Cost Optimization*. This framework will help you systematically assess and rank each recommendation according to your organization's specific requirements and constraints, ensuring the most effective path to optimization.

Sample prioritization framework

The following table illustrates how recommendations can be organized and prioritized based on key decision criteria:

Recommendation	Estimated monthly savings ($)	Implementation time	Resource requirement	Dependency	Priority
Identifying the right database for your workload	$$	Medium	Medium	Top priority	P1
Removing idle resources	$$	Low	Low	None	
Rightsizing and modernization	$$	Medium	Medium	Performance testing	
End of support: Upgrading to a supported version	$$	High	High	Performance testing	
Implementing elasticity	$$	Low	Low	None	

Recommendation	Estimated monthly savings ($)	Implementation time	Resource requirement	Dependency	Priority
Backup charges optimization	$$	Medium	Medium	None	
Reserved capacity	$$	Low	Low	All other optimizations	
Query optimization	$$	High	High	None	
Reviewing database deployment architecture: Availability, scalability, resiliency	$$	Medium	Low	Should be combined with identifying the right database for your workload.	P1

Table 7.3: Developing a priority action plan

This information can be depicted in the impact and complexity graph as shown in the follwing figure:

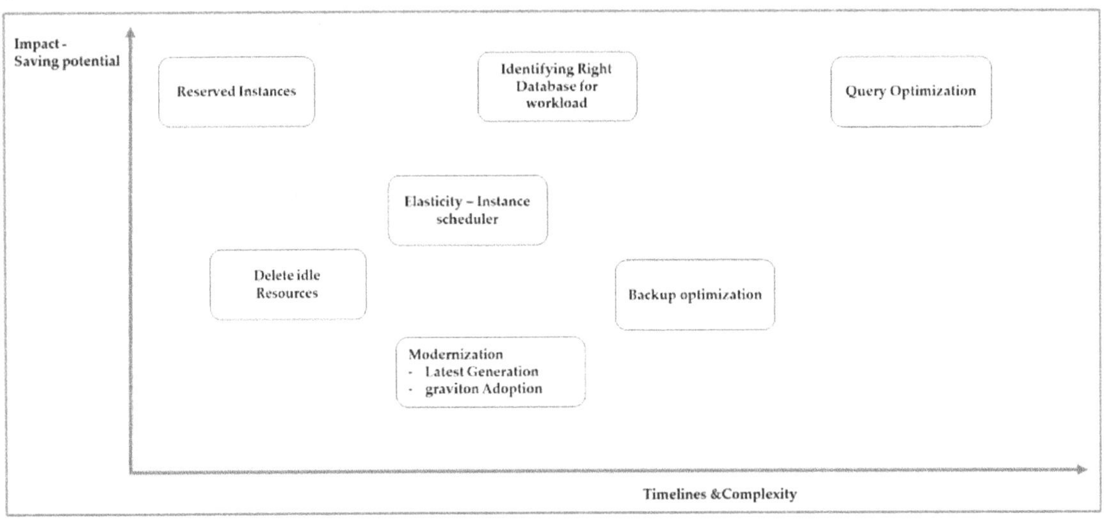

Figure 7.15: Impact and complexity graph

Note: **Commitment-based models like RIs or Savings Plan may offer the highest savings potential; however, they should be considered only after other recommendations have been implemented. Making commitments prematurely may lead to underutilization of reserved capacity and reduced ROI.**

Conclusion

Databases are central to nearly every organization's IT ecosystem, whether running in data centers or in the cloud. From processing transactions like banking and e-commerce orders to managing internal functions such as payroll, HR, and analytics, database services are essential for daily operations. Cloud providers have a broad portfolio of services offering relational databases, key-value stores, document databases, and graph databases to meet diverse workload requirements. This wide range of choices supports faster and more flexible application development. However, it also introduces complexity and can lead to rising cloud costs, especially when database services are provisioned without visibility or governance. Many organizations face the challenge of tracking and managing database expenditure effectively.

This chapter focused on providing a structured approach to understanding and optimizing cloud database costs. We reviewed the key pricing components that contribute to overall database spend, such as compute charges, storage costs, IOPS provisioning, backup retention, and licensing. We also explored the tools offered by cloud providers such as AWS to improve visibility, such as AWS Cost Explorer, Billing console, and CUR.

Beyond visibility, we discussed optimization levers such as rightsizing, modernization, using reserved capacity, and adjusting backup configurations. Tools like AWS Trusted Advisor, Compute Optimizer, and the Cost Optimization Hub help streamline the cost optimization journey by offering data-driven recommendations based on actual usage patterns. Once insights are gathered, teams should develop a targeted and prioritized action plan to implement changes in a structured and low-risk manner.

In the next chapter, we will shift our focus to monitoring and logging services, another often-overlooked contributor to cloud costs, and examine how to manage them effectively without compromising visibility or operational performance.

CHAPTER 8
Optimizing Cloud Observability Cost

Introduction

As businesses move their workloads to the cloud, being able to monitor and understand what is happening in their systems and applications becomes essential. Observability is the term used to describe the tools and practices that provide this visibility. Observability includes monitoring, which tracks system activity in real-time, and logging, which records events and actions that have occurred over time. Together, these capabilities help organizations to detect problems quickly, ensure that systems are working properly, and meet security and compliance requirements.

While observability is crucial for smooth operations, it can also become a major contributor to cloud costs. Cloud providers offer native observability tools such as Amazon CloudWatch, AWS CloudTrail, AWS Config, Azure Monitor, and Google Cloud Operations Suite. In addition, many organizations use third-party platforms such as Datadog (**https://www.datadoghq.com**) and New Relic (**https://www.newrelic.com**) for observability and performance tracking. Both cloud-native tools and 3rd party observability tools offer a pay-as-you-go pricing model for cloud workloads. Charges depend on pricing elements such as the number of resources being monitored, the number of metrics being collected, the volume of logs generated, and how long this data is stored. As the cloud footprint grows, so does the volume of observability data, often resulting in unexpectedly high bills if not monitored and optimized properly.

This chapter aims to help you understand the pricing of observability services and guide you in managing these costs effectively. You will learn strategies to balance system visibility with cost efficiency, such as choosing the right metrics, managing log retention, and reviewing usage patterns. While we use AWS and Azure services and tools to illustrate these ideas, the techniques discussed here can be applied to any major cloud platform and monitoring solutions.

Structure

In this chapter, we will discuss the following topics:

- Understanding cloud observability portfolio

- Tools for analyzing observability usage
- Levers for optimizing cloud observability cost
- Developing a prioritized action plan

Objectives

By the end of this chapter, the readers will have a clear understanding of cloud-native monitoring and logging services, as well as the key pricing components that contribute to observability costs. They will also explore tools and techniques to analyze usage patterns and identify cost drivers, helping them make informed decisions about what to monitor and how long to retain logs. Through real-world examples and practical guidance, the readers will develop the skills needed to make informed decisions about their observability setup, balancing crucial system oversight with cost efficiency. They will also learn best practices for setting up cost-effective observability frameworks, including strategies to optimize services such as Amazon CloudWatch, AWS CloudTrail, AWS Config, and Azure Monitor. This knowledge will be particularly valuable as organizations continue to scale their cloud infrastructure and face rising monitoring and logging costs. Finally, they will be able to create a prioritized implementation plan that can serve as the foundation for a focused cost optimization sprint or project.

While AWS and Azure services are used for illustration, the strategies presented can be applied across all major cloud platforms' monitoring solutions.

Understanding the cloud observability portfolio

Observability is a crucial part of cloud operations that helps organizations monitor the health, performance, and security of their applications and infrastructure. Whether workloads run in a traditional data center or in a public cloud, monitoring and logging are essential to ensure systems run smoothly, problems are identified quickly, and performance is optimized.

In the cloud, observability goes beyond basic monitoring. It includes metrics, logs, events, and traces, helping teams understand not just what went wrong, but also why it happened. Cloud service providers offer built-in observability tools that integrate seamlessly with other services. In addition, organizations may also use third-party solutions for more advanced or cross-platform visibility.

This section focuses on the native observability services offered by the major cloud providers such as **Amazon Web Services** (**AWS**), **Microsoft Azure**, and **Google Cloud Platform** (**GCP**). We will explore observability services offered by cloud providers, how these services are priced, and how you can make cost-effective decisions while maintaining operational visibility.

Observability tools from major cloud providers

Cloud platforms include built-in observability services that help organizations monitor performance, troubleshoot issues, and optimize costs across applications and infrastructure. These tools collect and correlate metrics, logs, and traces to provide deep visibility into resource utilization, system health, performance, reliability, and security. The following sections provide an overview of observability offerings from major cloud providers.

Amazon Web Services

AWS provides a wide range of observability services to monitor and manage cloud workloads. These services are tightly integrated with AWS resources and provide insights into infrastructure, application, and user activity. Key AWS observability services are as follows:

- **Amazon CloudWatch**: CloudWatch is the primary monitoring service in AWS. It collects and tracks metrics, logs, sets alarms, and can trigger automated actions. It supports monitoring for a wide variety of AWS resources, including EC2 instances, Lambda functions, RDS instances, containers, and custom applications.

  Features include:

  - Metrics and dashboards
  - Alarms and notifications
  - Container insights
  - CloudWatch Logs and Log Insights
  - **Application performance monitoring** (APM)
- **AWS CloudTrail**: AWS CloudTrail records API calls and activity performed by users, services, or applications across the AWS environment. It provides governance, compliance auditing, and operational insight. You can track management events (example, IAM changes) and data events (example, S3 object access).
- **AWS Config**: AWS Config provides a detailed view of the configuration of AWS resources in your account, including how resources are related to one another and how they were configured in the past. This service monitors configuration changes to AWS resources and checks for compliance with organizational policies. It maintains a history of changes and supports automated rule evaluations. For example, if someone changes the configuration of an S3 bucket to make it public, AWS Config can detect it, log the change, and alert administrators. Some of the AWS Config functionalities include:
  - Maintaining a resource inventory and configuration history.
  - Tracking configuration changes over time.
  - Monitoring compliance against defined policies.

- **AWS Systems Manager**: AWS Systems Manager is a comprehensive operations management service that helps organizations manage and automate tasks across AWS resources. It enhances visibility through automated inventory collection and patch compliance reporting, ensuring resources remain secure and up-to-date. It provides a centralized operational hub allowing teams to view and resolve issues across their entire infrastructure from a single interface.

Microsoft Azure

Azure offers a comprehensive observability solution through Azure Monitor, which integrates metrics, logs, and distributed tracing across applications and infrastructure into a single platform. It supports nearly all Azure services and can also monitor hybrid or multi-cloud environments. Key components of Azure's observability services portfolio include:

- **Azure Monitor**: Azure Monitor collects and analyzes telemetry data from Azure resources and applications to track performance, availability, and reliability. It includes:
    - Metrics and dashboards
    - Alerts and automation
    - Application Insights (APM)
    - Container Insights and VM Insights
- **Logs Analytics Workspace**: Azure Monitor uses Log Analytics workspaces, which allow users to run powerful queries on log data for diagnostics, insights, and troubleshooting.
- **Azure Activity Log**: This service records subscription-level events such as resource changes and deployment activities. It helps track who did what and when across the Azure environment.
- **Azure Policy**: While not a monitoring tool directly, Azure Policy ensures that resources comply with defined rules and standards. It integrates with Azure Monitor and Azure Security Center to support governance and compliance.

Google Cloud Platform

Google Cloud Platform (**GCP**) focuses on providing unified observability through the Google Cloud Operations Suite, formerly known as Stackdriver. It combines monitoring, logging, tracing, and error reporting into a single platform. Key GCP observability services include the following:

- **Cloud Monitoring**: Enables real-time monitoring of GCP resources, custom workloads, and third-party cloud services. Dashboards, metrics, and alerting rules help in keeping services performant and stable.

- **Cloud Logging**: A scalable logging service that ingests logs from GCP services and applications and supports querying, alerting, and exporting logs to BigQuery, Cloud Storage, or external systems for long-term analysis.
- **Cloud Trace**: Offers distributed tracing for applications running on GCP or hybrid environments. It visualizes request paths and latency between services, making it easier to identify performance bottlenecks.
- **Cloud Error Reporting**: Automatically aggregates and analyzes application errors to show patterns and frequency.
- **Cloud Profiler**: Helps developers understand the runtime behavior and performance of their applications using low-overhead profiling.

Pricing models for cloud observability services

Understanding the pricing structure of observability services is crucial for cost optimization. Unlike compute services that are charged based on instance size and running hours, observability services have more complex pricing models.

Free Tier inclusions

Most cloud providers offer a free usage tier to help teams get started. Let us look into Amazon Web Services' Free Tier for Amazon CloudWatch, as shown in the following figure:

Free tier

You can get started with Amazon CloudWatch for free. Most AWS Services (EC2, S3, Kinesis, etc.) send metrics automatically for free to CloudWatch. You can learn more about AWS Free Tier here.

Logs	5 GB Data (ingestion, archive storage, and data scanned by Logs Insights queries) 1,800 minutes of Live Tail usage per month (approximately an hour per day)
Metrics	Basic Monitoring Metrics (Metrics sent from AWS Services by default) 10 Metrics (of Custom Metrics and Detailed Monitoring Metrics) 1 Million API requests (not including GetMetricData, GetInsightRuleReport and GetMetricWidgetImage: these 3 operations are always charged)
X-Ray traces	The first 100,000 traces recorded each month are free. The first 1,000,000 traces retrieved or scanned each month are free
Dashboard	3 Custom Dashboards referencing up to 50 metrics each per month. Additionally, all Automatic Dashboards are free.
Alarms	10 Alarm metrics (only applicable to Standard resolution alarms that list metrics directly and don't use a Metrics Insights query)
Contributor Insights for CloudWatch Logs	1 Contributor Insights rule per month The first 1 million log events that match the rule per month

***Figure 8.1**: Amazon CloudWatch Free Tier inclusions*

Many observability services provide Free Tier options that allow organizations to begin monitoring without immediate cost. While these limits vary across cloud providers, they enable basic visibility into applications and infrastructure. The following are examples of Free Tier allowances offered by AWS, Azure, and GCP:

- **AWS Free Tier examples**:
  - **CloudWatch**: 10 custom metrics and 10 alarms.
  - **CloudTrail**: First copy of management events in each region.
  - **Config**: Limited configuration items and rules evaluations.
- **Azure Free Tier examples**:
  - **Azure Monitor**: 5 GB of data ingestion per month.
  - **Log Analytics**: Limited data retention and query capabilities.
  - **Activity Log**: Basic activity logging.
- **GCP Free Tier examples**:
  - **Cloud Monitoring**: First 150 MB of ingested data.
  - **Cloud Logging**: First 50 GB of logs per month.
  - **Error Reporting**: First 1,000 error events.

Always refer to the public pricing of cloud service providers to get the latest details on Free Tier inclusions.

Component-based pricing

Each observability service has multiple components with distinct billing models. Let us understand the different components and billing units of key AWS observability services.

- **Amazon CloudWatch**: The following table illustrates some of the components of Amazon CloudWatch and their respective billing units:

Component	Billing unit
Metrics	Per metric per month
Logs	This has two pricing elements: Ingestion charges are based on per GB of logs ingested. Storage charges: log storage is charged separately based on per GB of logs stored.
Alarms	Per alarm evaluation

Component	Billing unit
Dashboards	Per dashboard, per month
Container Insights	Charged based on the number of metrics collected (or observations) by Container Insights.

***Table 8.1**: Amazon CloudWatch component and billing unit*

- **AWS CloudTrail** and **AWS Config**: It has different billing units for components compared to Amazon CloudWatch, and are shown in the following table:

Component	Billing Unit
AWS CloudTrail—Management event	Per 100,000 management events delivered. (Note: First copy is delivered free of charge)
AWS CloudTrail – Data event	Per 100,000 data events delivered.
AWS CloudTrail – Insight events	Events analyzed per Insight type.
Config Recording	Per configuration item delivered per AWS account per AWS Region.
AWS Config rules	Per rule evaluation per region.

***Table 8.2**: Amazon CloudTrail and config billing unit*

Once you have analyzed the different components of observability services and their related billing units, the next step is to understand the pricing structure by referring to the cloud provider's public pricing page.

For example, the pricing tier of Amazon CloudWatch metrics, which is billed per metric per month, is shown in the following figure:

Tiers	Cost (metric/month)
First 10,000 metrics	$0.30
Next 240,000 metrics	$0.10
Next 750,000 metrics	$0.05
Over 1,000,000 metrics	$0.02

***Figure 8.2**: CloudWatch metrics pricing tier*

We have also reviewed the billing unit of Amazon CloudWatch alarms earlier. The pricing structure of Amazon CloudWatch alarm is shown as follows:

Region:

US East (Ohio)

Standard Resolution Metrics Alarm

Cost for metrics listed directly(/alarm/month)	$0.10 per alarm metric
Cost for PromQL queries	$0.10 per alarm + $0.01 per million samples scanned per evaluation
Cost for Metrics Insights queries(/alarms/month)	$0.10 per metrics analyzed

High Resolution Metrics Alarm

Cost for metrics listed directly(/alarm/month)	$0.30 per alarm metric

Aggregated Alarms

Alarm Type	Cost(/alarms/month)
Composite Alarm	$0.50 per composite alarm

Figure 8.3: *CloudWatch alarm pricing*

Similar to AWS observability services, Azure Monitor and GCP operations suite have different components, with each having a different billing unit. The following figure shows the Azure Monitor pricing page for **Metrics** pricing:

Logs | **Metrics** | Alerts | Notifications | Web Tests | SCOM managed instance

Native Metrics

Native metrics include platform and customised metrics.

Costs for customised metrics are based on the number of samples ingested and the number of API calls made for query.

Platform and customised metrics are retained for 90 days. Billing is not yet enabled for customised metrics.

Feature	Free units included	Price
Platform Metrics Ingestion[1]	Unlimited	Free
Customised metrics ingestion (preview)[1]	None	$0.16 / 10 million samples ingested
Platform and customised metric queries (preview)	First 10,00,000 API calls per month	$0.01 / 1,000 API calls

Figure 8.4: *Azure Monitor Metrics pricing*

Google Cloud Monitoring pricing is based on specific usage metrics and billing units. The following figure presents a summarized view of the key pricing elements and their corresponding billing units:

Feature	Price	Free allotment per month	Effective date
All Monitoring data except data ingested by using Google Cloud Managed Service for Prometheus	\$0.2580/MiB[1]: first 150–100,000 MiB \$0.1510/MiB: next 100,000–250,000 MiB \$0.0610/MiB: >250,000 MiB	All non-chargeable Google Cloud metrics First 150 MiB per billing account for metrics charged by bytes ingested	July 1, 2018
Metrics ingested by using Google Cloud Managed Service for Prometheus, including GKE control plane metrics	\$0.06/million samples[†]: first 0-50 billion samples ingested[#] \$0.048/million samples: next 50-250 billion samples ingested \$0.036/million samples: next 250-500 billion samples ingested \$0.024/million samples: >500 billion samples ingested	Not applicable	August 8, 2023
Monitoring API calls	\$0.01/1,000 Read API calls (Write API calls are free)	First 1 million Read API calls included per billing account	July 1, 2018 through October 1, 2025
Monitoring API calls	No charge for write API calls Read API calls: \$0.50/million time series returned[♥]	Write API calls: Not applicable Read API calls: First 1 million time series returned per billing account	October 2, 2025
Execution of Monitoring uptime checks	\$0.30/1,000 executions[‡]	1 million executions per Google Cloud project	October 1, 2022
Execution of Monitoring Synthetic Monitors	\$1.20/1,000 executions[*]	100 executions per billing account	November 1, 2023

Figure 8.5: *Google Cloud Monitoring pricing*

When planning your cloud observability strategy, carefully examine which services and components you will implement. Each component uses different billing units and pricing structures that can significantly impact your overall costs.

Storage and retention costs

Storage of observability data like logs and traces can become expensive over time. Here is what you need to know:

- Logs and metrics storage is charged based on GB of data stored and retention periods.
- Longer retention = higher costs

For example, retaining logs for 1 year in Amazon CloudWatch Logs vs. retaining them for 30 days has a significantly different cost. Retain detailed logs for short periods (e.g., 7–30 days), and archive summaries or logs of critical events to cheaper storage (like Amazon S3).

Analytics and insights charges

Some observability tools offer integrated analytics capabilities, and these are charged based on:

- Data scanned per query.
- Processing time or output size.

For example, A team investigating a production issue using CloudWatch Logs Insights might run multiple queries that scan tens or even hundreds of gigabytes of data. Each scan is charged per GB and can impact overall cloud cost. In some cases, querying logs and metrics directly within native observability services such as CloudWatch Logs Insights can become costly at scale. Full-featured analytics services like Amazon Athena or Google BigQuery may offer a more cost-efficient option for large query workloads. Organizations should evaluate the most economical querying approach based on data volume and usage patterns.

Rule evaluation

Services like AWS Config or Azure Policy evaluate resource configurations against defined rules. These are priced by the number of evaluations done per month.

Regional pricing variation

Like other cloud services, cloud observability services pricing often varies by region. For example, CloudWatch log ingestion in Asia Pacific (Mumbai) may cost more than US East (N. Virginia). Organizations with multi-region deployments should factor these variations into their cost planning.

Commitment-based savings

Some providers offer discounts for committed usage. For example, you can commit to a specific data ingestion rate (GB) per day and get a discount on on-demand pricing for log ingestion. However, you need to check with the cloud provider for the availability of commitment-based savings for observability services.

Understanding observability services and their cost structures is key to building a sustainable cloud strategy. While these tools are essential for operational visibility, misconfigurations or unnecessary data retention can lead to bloated bills. In the following section, we will explore how to leverage cloud-native tools to gain comprehensive insights into your observability services related costs and usage patterns.

Tools for analyzing observability usage

Cloud observability solutions provide critical insights into your infrastructure's health and performance, but their costs can quickly escalate without proper management. This section explores the tools for reviewing observability services usage and costs across cloud providers like AWS and Azure.

AWS cost management tools

AWS provides a set of tools that allow you to track, analyze, and optimize the usage and cost of services like Amazon CloudWatch, AWS CloudTrail, and AWS Config. In the preceding chapters, we have leveraged cloud native cost management tools to get insights into service usage and optimize costs. The following table lists some of the commonly used tools for cost and usage analysis:

Category	Tool	Description
Cost Observability: The tools help in reviewing cloud observability services consumed by the organization, including total usage and spend	AWS Billing console	View consolidated billing data, invoices, and service-wise charges.
	AWS Cost Explorer	Visualize observability services usage and cost, such as understanding CloudWatch, CloudTrail, and Config charges. The tool can also be used to do trend analysis, understand the impact of scaling, and identify optimization opportunities.
	AWS Cost and Usage Report	Provides granular, resource-level data about observability services usage and cost. Can be queried using Athena and visualized with QuickSight.
	Cost and Usage Dashboard	Pre-built dashboards (via QuickSight) such as the Cost Intelligence Dashboard.
Estimation	AWS Pricing Calculator	Estimate the cost of consuming different observability services. It can also be used for understanding the costs of different components.

***Table 8.3**: Tools for analyzing usage and spend*

Reviewing observability costs with AWS Cost Explorer

AWS Cost Explorer offers visualization capabilities that help identify cost trends and optimization opportunities for observability services. You can use filters to isolate observability services related data and drill down into details. Follow the given steps to use AWS Cost Explorer for CloudWatch, CloudTrail, and Config:

1. Go to the AWS console and open **Billing and Cost Management**.
2. From the left panel, click on **Cost Explorer**.
3. Apply filters to analyze observability costs:

- **Date Range**: Select your desired timeframe (e.g., last 3 months)
- **Granularity**: Monthly
- **Dimension**: Service
- **Service**: Select CloudWatch, CloudTrail, Config

As shown in the following figure, after applying the required filters, Cost Explorer will show which observability service—CloudWatch, CloudTrail, or Config is adding the most to your monthly AWS spend:

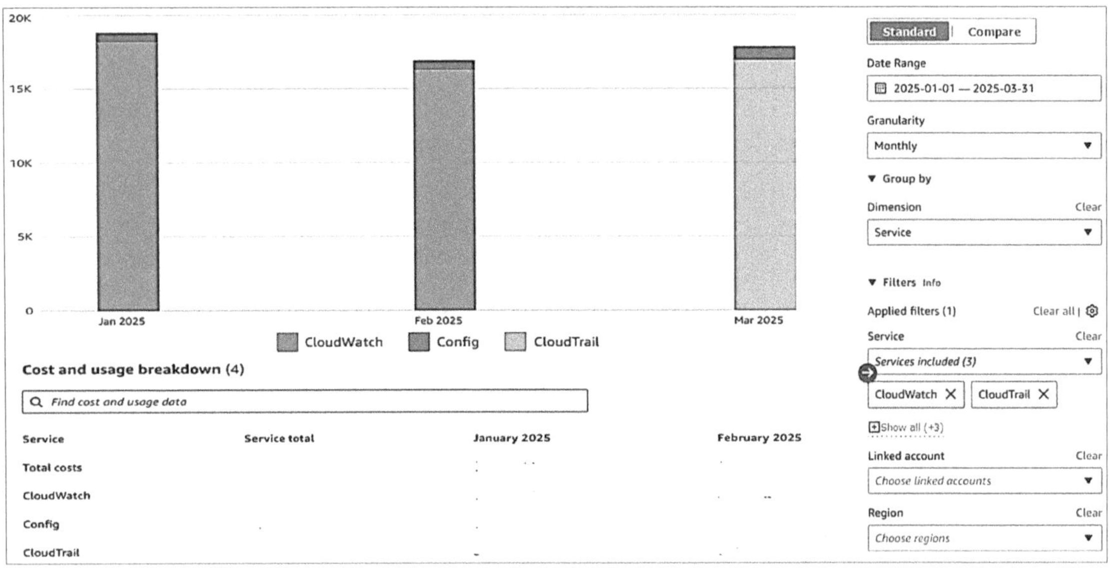

Figure 8.6: *Cost Explorer to analyze observability cost*

You can explore the filters to analyze the cost from different perspectives. For example, by changing the **Dimension** to **`API operations`** or **`Usage type`**, you can isolate which component of the observability service, such as metrics ingestion, log storage, or rule evaluations, is contributing most to cloud costs. In the following figure, you can see that an organization is incurring more than 70% of its observability-related charges due to **PutLogEvents**. This can help direct our focus toward reviewing log ingestion mechanisms and retention settings to optimize cost.

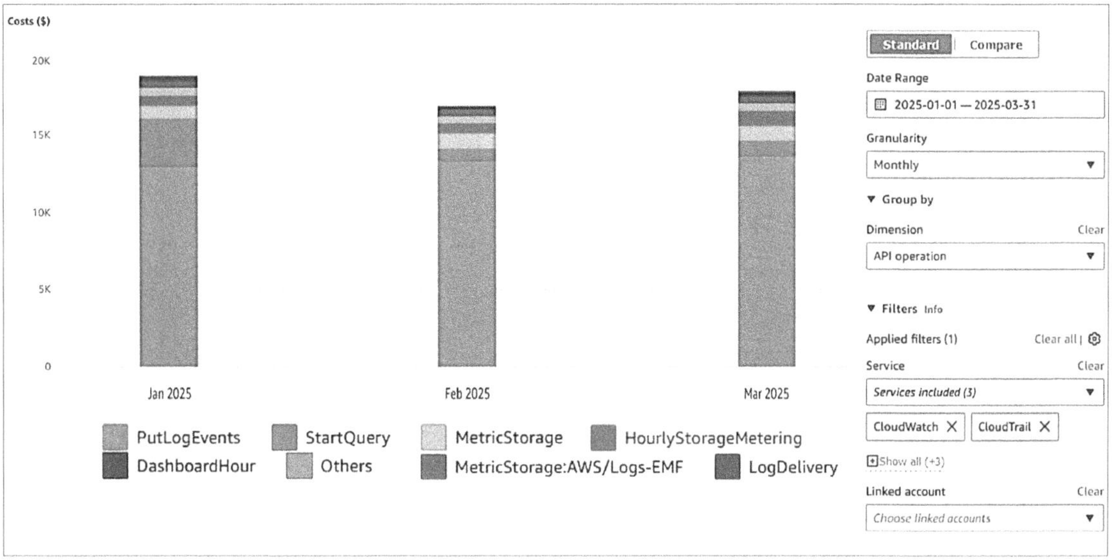

Figure 8.7: Isolating into component-level charges

Correlating Cost Explorer findings with Billing console

The AWS Billing console provides an invoice-style view that can validate your Cost Explorer findings. The following are the steps to review charges of observability services such as Amazon CloudWatch, CloudTrail, or Config via the Billing console:

1. Navigate to the AWS **Billing and Cost Management** dashboard and select **Bills**.
2. Choose the relevant billing period.
3. Under **Charges by Service**, expand CloudWatch, CloudTrail, or Config.

Refer to the following figure to use the Billing console to explore observability-related charges:

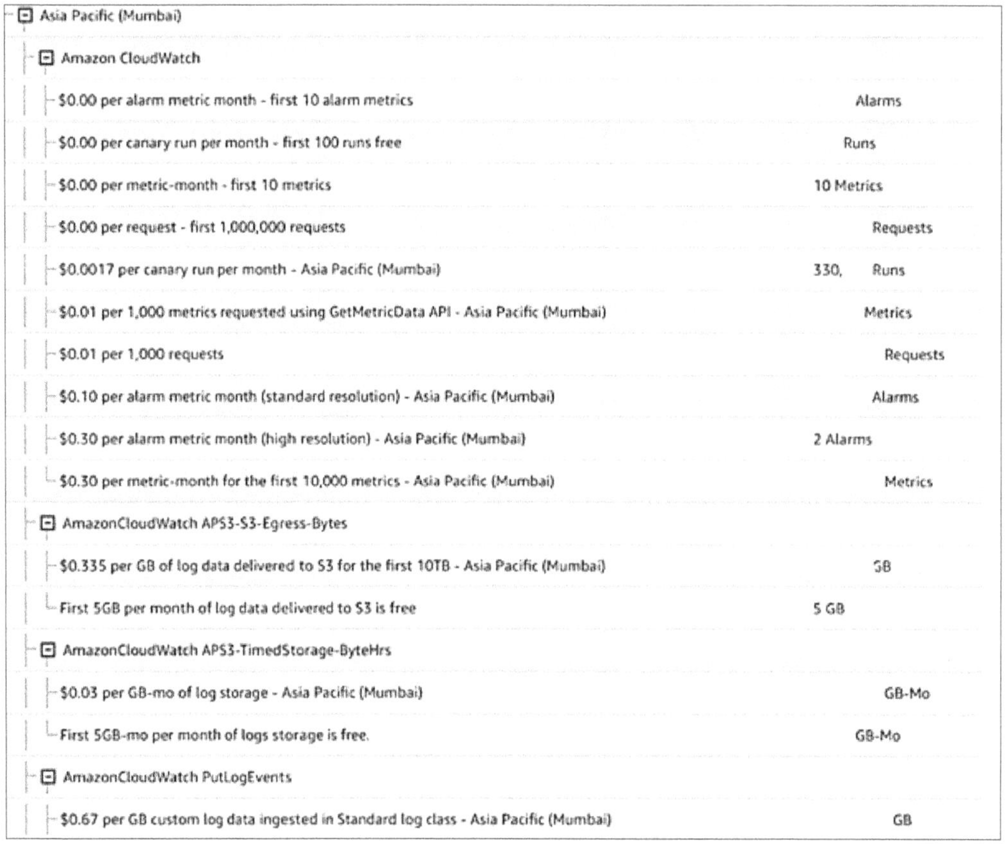

***Figure 8.8**: Using Billing console for observability services*

The information from Bills will help you analyze:

- Overall cost of different observability services.
- Regions that are incurring the charges.
- Charges per feature (e.g., Logs Ingestion, Alarms).
- Billing unit and volumes consumed.

For example, expanding AWS Config might show high charges for custom rule evaluations, which will prompt engineers to reduce evaluation frequency or optimize rules for fewer runs.

Accessing detailed data with Cost and Usage Reports

The **Cost and Usage Reports** (**CUR**) provide the most granular level of cost data and help drill down to the resource ID. By analyzing CUR data using tools like Amazon Athena and Amazon QuickSight, you can get information such as the following:

- *Which EC2 instances generate the most log volume?*
- *Which CloudWatch dashboards (beyond the Free Tier) are incurring the per-dashboard charges?*

For example, CUR Query can help you find which lambda or application log is adding the most to CloudWatch costs. CUR also helps trace log volumes back to specific resource IDs and check any misconfigured log settings.

Azure tools for observability cost Analysis

Microsoft Azure provides a powerful set of observability services, such as Azure Monitor and Log Analytics, along with cost management tools, such as **Cost Management + Billing**. These tools are tightly integrated and help users keep track of costs associated with metrics, logs, and diagnostic settings.

Azure Cost Management + Billing

This tool helps track and forecast spending across Azure services and can also be used to explore charges related to Azure Monitor and Log Analytics. Steps to analyze monitoring costs in Azure are as follows:

1. Open the Azure portal and launch **Cost Management + Billing**.
2. Go to **Cost Analysis**.
3. Filter by:
    - **Service Name**: Choose Azure Monitor and/or Log Analytics.
    - **Group By**: Group by resource or meter category (e.g., *Log Ingestion*).

For example, if you discover that Diagnostic Logs from Storage Accounts are generating high log ingestion costs, you can then disable unnecessary categories like *Read Operations*.

Log Analytics usage and costs

Azure Monitor stores and analyzes log data in a Log Analytics Workspace, and charges are primarily based on:

1. Volume of data ingested.
2. Retention period.
3. Optional features such as data export.

To analyze usage and cost, go to Azure Monitor and select **Logs**:

1. Click **Usage and estimated costs.**
2. Review ingestion-related charges.

For example, consider a hypothetical scenario in which a real estate company notices unexpectedly high cloud bills. Using Azure Cost Management + Billing, the team identifies that a significant portion of the charges is related to Azure Monitor. They then use Log Analytics to drill into log ingestion and retention costs, discovering that 40% of their log expenses come from verbose application logs. By implementing log filtering at the source, the company could significantly reduce its observability costs.

Putting it all together

Cloud service providers have different services to meet an organization's observability requirements. Each service consists of multiple components and follows a distinct charging mechanism, as discussed in the previous section. Organizations can follow a three-step approach to optimize observability costs using native tools across cloud platforms:

- **Identify observability services in use**: An organization may be using only a specific observability service provided by a cloud service provider. For example, an organization running workload on AWS may be using only CloudWatch for their monitoring requirements and have no use case for CloudTrail and AWS Config. Tools such as AWS Cost Explorer or Billing console can be used to list all observability services in use, such as CloudWatch, CloudTrail, or AWS Config.
- **Identify top cost contributors**: After identifying the services in use, the next step is to identify which components leveraged by the organization for their observability requirements are driving the charges. To identify these components:
    a. Drill down into components (e.g., API calls, dashboards, ingestion volume) by applying appropriate filters in AWS Cost Explorer or by expanding the relevant service in the AWS Billing console.
    b. Identify which service components (such as Metrics, Logs) generate the highest cost.
    c. Use CUR to identify resource level details.
- **Take optimization actions**: Once you have identified the service and components that are contributing the most to your cloud monthly spend, you can focus on optimizing the charges incurred. In the next section, we will discuss different levers available for organizations to optimize their observability charges.

Levers for optimizing cloud observability cost

Cloud observability is critical for maintaining the reliability, security, and performance of your workload. However, these monitoring and logging capabilities can become expensive if not configured correctly. Cloud service providers offer several native services for observability—such as CloudWatch, CloudTrail, AWS Config (AWS), and Azure Monitor and Log Analytics

(Azure). While these services offer flexibility and robust features, the pay-as-you-go pricing model can lead to unexpected costs without proper governance.

This section presents practical levers and best practices to reduce and control observability costs across AWS and Azure. We will start with general optimization principles, then get into service-specific strategies for cloud providers, mainly AWS and Azure.

General optimization principles

Before optimizing individual services, organizations should adopt a strategic approach to review their observability services deployment. Let us start by reviewing some of the key strategic levers for cost optimization.

Right-size observability architecture

The first step in a cost-efficient observability setup is designing a solution that aligns with the visibility needs of your workloads. This requires clearly defining what must be monitored and why. Asking the right questions, as given in the following list, helps determine the appropriate level of metrics, logs, and traces to collect:

- *Does your observability requirement vary by environment type—Production vs non-production workloads?*
- *Any regulatory-related observability requirement?*
- *What you need to monitor—Services, Resources, Metrics, and how you would use the information collected?*
- *What alerting thresholds are critical?*
- *Do you review metrics that are configured but not used for any decision-making?*
- *Which logs need to be collected, and where should logs be sent?* For example, if there is a need to collect logs for applications running on EC2, organizations need to decide if all logs should be sent directly to AWS CloudWatch or if alternate solutions like Amazon S3 should be evaluated. Sending logs to native observability services such as AWS CloudWatch might be convenient but expensive.
- *How long do you need to retain the data?*

Environment-based configuration

Different environments (dev, test, UAT, production) have varying monitoring needs. Production systems may need detailed observability data, while dev/test environments may work well with minimal metrics and logs. Avoid applying production-level monitoring to every environment.

Example:

- For dev environments, enable only basic monitoring features of observability services. On AWS, use basic CloudWatch monitoring and avoid detailed monitoring. On Azure, apply minimal diagnostic settings to reduce unnecessary data collection.
- Use default free-tier metrics and restrict log generation for temporary test resources. Refer to the cloud provider's public pricing page to validate free-tier limits by services.

Refer to the following steps to implement the solution:

1. Create an environment classification matrix and define monitoring requirements for each environment type.
2. Document metric collection frequency by environment type.
3. Set log retention periods appropriate to each tier.
4. Configure monitoring tools with environment-specific settings.

Selecting cloud-native or third party observability tools

Organizations often face the choice of continuing with commercial tools (such as Datadog, New Relic), leveraging open-source monitoring tools, or shifting to cloud-native observability tools post-migration to the cloud. Cloud-native tools like Amazon CloudWatch or Azure Monitor integrate better and may cost less over time, but may not meet all the monitoring requirements of your workload.

There are various factors to consider when finalizing the right tool for your workload, such as:

- **User experience and skills gap**: Evaluate your team's familiarity with existing tools versus learning new platforms.
- **Integration dependencies**: Review how observability data connects with your existing solutions and technologies used.
- **Investment maximization**: Consider existing license commitments before switching tools.
- **Support requirements**: Assess differences between commercial support, cloud provider support, and community support for open-source alternatives. Support for deployed tools can be a major factor in your decision
- **Multi-cloud compatibility**: For hybrid or multi-cloud environments, platform-agnostic tools may provide better consistency.
- **Regulatory compliance**: Ensure your chosen observability solution meets industry-specific regulatory and compliance requirements.
- **Workload coverage**: Confirm the tool can monitor your full technology stack (containers, serverless, traditional VMs).

Commitment-based savings

Some cloud providers may offer commitment plans for observability workloads. For example, Azure offers commitment tiers for log ingestion. If you commit to ingesting a specific volume (e.g., 100GB/day), you get a discounted rate compared to on-demand pricing. Check with your cloud providers for the availability of commitment-based savings for observability services.

Steps to implement commitment-based savings:

1. Analyze historical usage patterns over 3-6 months.
2. Identify stable baseline consumption.
3. Commit to 70-80% of baseline for optimal savings.
4. Review utilization quarterly and adjust as needed.

Review storage strategies

Logs and metrics can generate significant storage costs, especially with long retention periods. Consider the following:

- Storing logs in cheaper storage options, such as Amazon S3 or Azure Archive Storage, for long-term compliance.
- Using lifecycle policies to move older logs to cheaper tiers.
- Deleting unused logs from observability services, such as Amazon CloudWatch or Azure Log Analytics, after a retention threshold.

Service-specific cost optimization strategies

We have seen how different observability solutions work and how their pricing elements vary across cloud platforms. Service-specific strategies help organizations control costs by optimizing data collection, storage, and analysis based on the nature and usage of each observability service. The following sections provide practical cost optimization techniques for key monitoring and logging services across AWS and Azure.

Amazon CloudWatch optimization

CloudWatch provides metrics, dashboards, alarms, logs, and application insights. Costs can escalate if not managed well. Follow the given steps to optimize Amazon CloudWatch costs:

1. **Metrics cost optimization**:
   - **Select the right metric resolution for each resource**: In *Figure 8.1* and *Figure 8.2*, we have seen metrics pricing for CloudWatch, and it is summarized as follows for the Ohio region:

- Basic metrics (5-min intervals) are free for EC2 and can be appropriate for most non-production workloads.
- Detailed metrics (1-min intervals) cost $0.30 per metric/month and are ideal for production workloads.
- High-resolution (1-sec intervals) are charged per metric per hour and are recommended only for critical workloads requiring fine-grained monitoring.
- Choose metric granularity based on the criticality and performance sensitivity of the workload:
  - **Non-production EC2 environments (Dev/Test)**: Use basic monitoring with 5-minute metrics. This provides sufficient visibility while keeping costs low.
  - **Production systems with normal performance needs**: Enable detailed monitoring (1-minute metrics) for faster alerting and better scaling decisions (e.g., autoscaling).
  - **Latency-sensitive or mission-critical workloads**: Use high-resolution custom metrics only when you require near real-time troubleshooting or rapid scaling. Costs increase significantly, so apply selectively.

- **Implement selective monitoring**: Focus on monitoring only actionable metrics and remove irrelevant ones. When defining metrics to be monitored for EC2, prioritize essential metrics such as CPU, memory, disk, and network usage rather than enabling advanced metrics that do not serve a clear purpose.

  For example, if 20 EC2 instances are sending 10 detailed metrics each, the Metric cost will be $60/month (20 x 10 x $0.30). Switching some of the EC2 instances depending on criteria such as non-production server to basic monitoring could save the metric related cost.

- **Custom metrics**: Avoid sending excessive custom metrics. Instead, combine related data points into a single API call and batch metrics wherever possible to avoid multiple charges. If you are using any 3rd party tools, review third-party tool configurations to check for excessive API calls.

  In addition to metric storage and retention charges, CloudWatch also bills for API usage when querying or publishing monitoring data. The charges for Amazon CloudWatch API requests vary based on the specific operation being performed and are typically billed per thousand requests. The following figure shows the pricing structure for CloudWatch API operations in the Ohio region:

Region:

US East (Ohio)

API name	Cost
GetMetricData, GetInsightRuleReport	$0.01 per 1,000 metrics requested
GetMetricWidgetImage	$0.02 per 1,000 metrics requested
GetMetricStatistics, ListMetrics	$0.01 per 1,000 requests

API name	Cost
GetDashboard, ListDashboards, PutDashboard and DeleteDashboards requests	$0.01 per 1,000 requests

***Figure 8.9**: CloudWatch API charges*

2. **Alarm management**:
    - Use **composite alarms** to reduce the number of individual alarms.
    - Disable alarms for deleted resources (INSUFFICIENT_DATA state).
    - Limit high-resolution alarms to mission-critical metrics only.

    For example, replacing multiple standard alarms with fewer composite alarms can lead to substantial savings, especially at a large scale.

3. **Amazon CloudWatch Logs**: To optimize charges related to Amazon CloudWatch, follow the steps:
    - **Log filtering**: Filter at source and send only necessary logs. You can start by looking into CUR Queries or the Amazon CloudWatch console to identify resources that are ingesting logs to Amazon CloudWatch.

      The following figure shows log groups from the CloudWatch console:

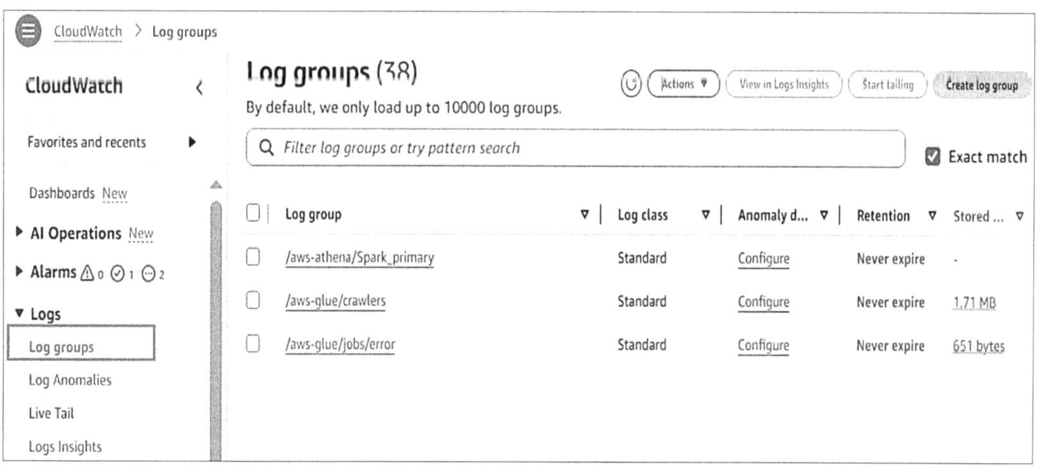

***Figure 8.10**: CloudWatch console—Log groups*

- **Log volume management**: Avoid excessive logging, especially debug/info logs in production. For example, reducing log ingestion from 50GB/day to 20GB saves over 30GB worth of ingestion + storage costs.
- **S3 for long-term storage**: Use S3 for cheaper storage instead of retaining logs in CloudWatch Logs.
- **Retention policies**: Adjust log group retention based on compliance and troubleshooting needs. For example, an organization may define a log retention policy as follows to save cost:
    - 1–7 days for dev/test
    - 30–90 days for production
    - Archive to S3 for anything longer

AWS CloudTrail Optimization

CloudTrail logs both management and data events. The first copy of management events is free; additional copies and data events are billed. Refer to the following figure to understand AWS CloudTrail charges for the Ohio region:

Feature	Pricing
Management events delivered to Amazon S3	$2.00 per 100,000 management events delivered (after first free copy, see AWS Free Tier for details)
Data events delivered to Amazon S3	$0.10 per 100,000 data events delivered
Network activity events delivered to Amazon S3	$0.10 per 100,000 network activity events delivered

Figure 8.11: AWS CloudTrail pricing

To check what is adding to CloudTrail cost, use AWS Cost Explorer and Billing console as per the following steps:

1. Go to AWS **Billing and Cost Management** and launch AWS **Cost Explorer**.
2. Apply the required filter as follows:
    - **Date Range**: Last 3 months

- **Granularity**: Monthly
- **Dimension**: Usage type
- **Service**: CloudTrail

Depending on the filters applied, the output will look as shown in the following figure:

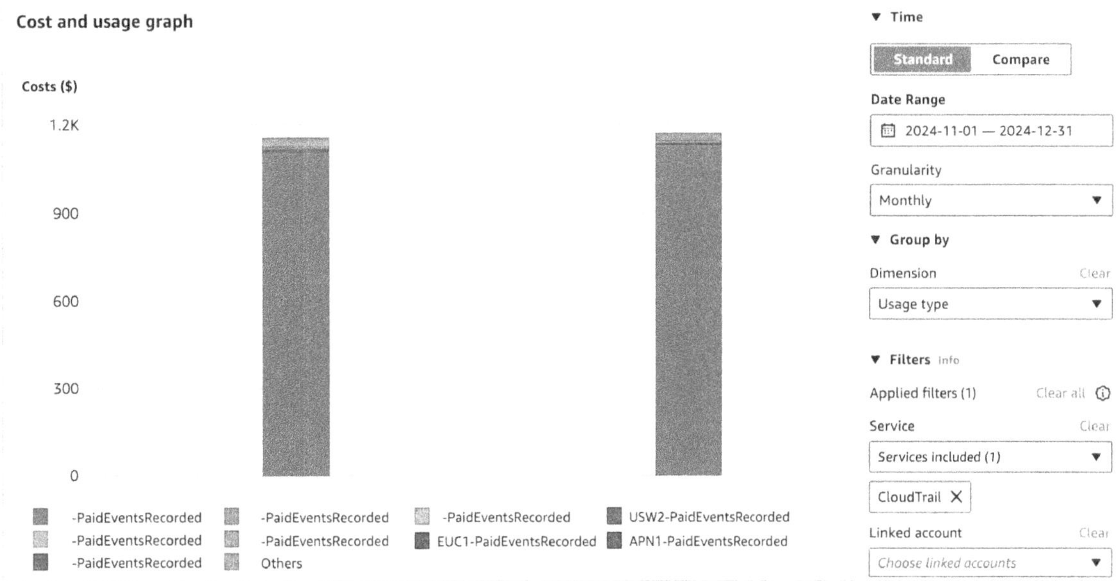

***Figure 8.12**: CloudTrail charges by usage type*

Follow the action item highlighted as follows for optimizing CloudTrail cost:

1. **Avoid duplicate trails**:
   a. Use **Organization Trails** instead of multiple account-specific trails.
   b. One free management event trial can meet most of the organization's requirements.
   c. Consolidate logging across accounts into a central S3 bucket.
2. **Be selective with data events**: Data events (like S3 object-level access or Lambda execution) are more expensive. Enable them only for critical resources such as S3, DynamoDB, Lambda, and Amazon Data Firehose.
3. **Restrict to specific resources**: For example, instead of enabling data events for all S3 buckets, apply it only to the HR-data bucket where audit compliance is required. Refer to the following figure on the options available while enabling data events from the CloudTrail console to scale down data event recording for a specific resource:

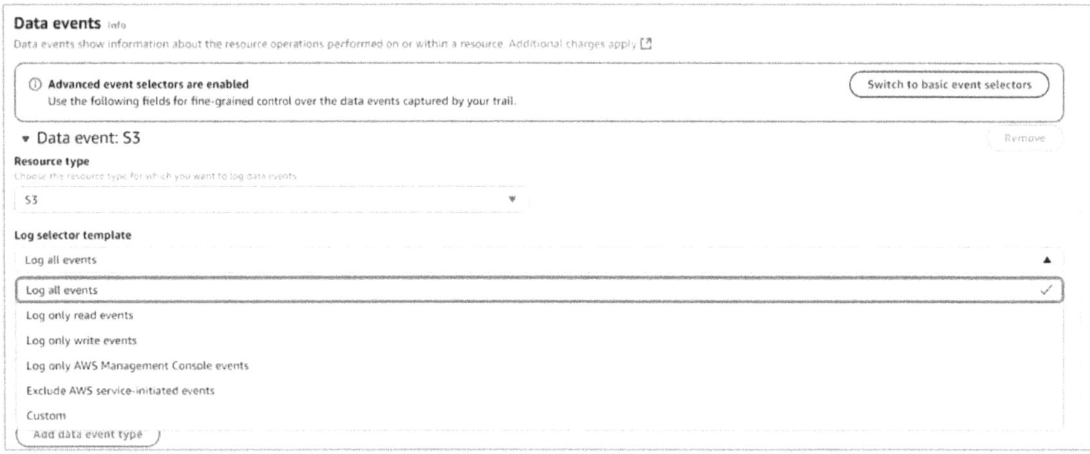

***Figure 8.13**: Selecting the events to be recorded*

4. **Filter API actions**: Apply fine-grained filters to capture only the required actions. Use read, write, or resource-specific filters. The following figure shows the options available when creating a data event from the CloudTrail console:

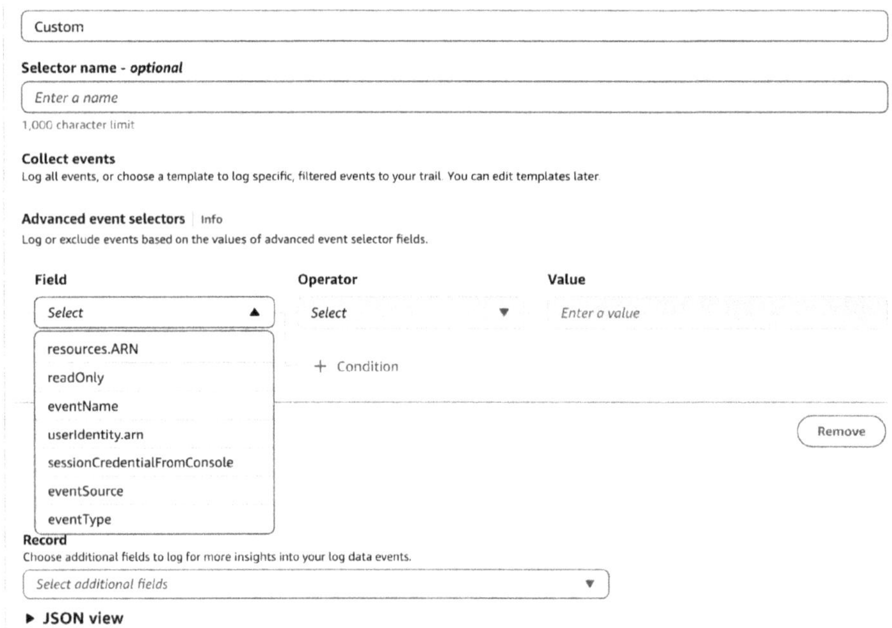

***Figure 8.14**: Configuring granular level event recording*

AWS Config optimization

Config records configuration changes and evaluates compliance using rules. AWS Config has different billing units and pricing models for recording configuration items and for rules evaluation. Refer to the following figure to understand the pricing mechanism for CI recording and for rules evaluation:

	Cost per configuration item delivered per AWS account per AWS Region
Continuous Recording	$0.003
Periodic Recording	$0.012

AWS Config rules evaluations	Price
First 100,000 rule evaluations	$0.001 per rule evaluation per region
Next 400,000 rule evaluations (100,001-500,000)	$0.0008 per rule evaluation per region
500,001 and more rule evaluations	$0.0005 per rule evaluation per region

***Figure 8.15**: AWS Config pricing*

To optimize AWS Config charges:

1. **Optimize resource recording**:
   - Record only critical resource types (e.g., IAM, S3, Security Groups).
   - Exclude high-churn resources like temporary EC2 instances.
   - Use periodic mode instead of continuous recording where possible.

   For example, recording only 20 essential resource types instead of 100+ resource types can reduce costs by 70–80%. Refer to the following figure on enabling Config recording and selecting the appropriate setting to optimize cost:

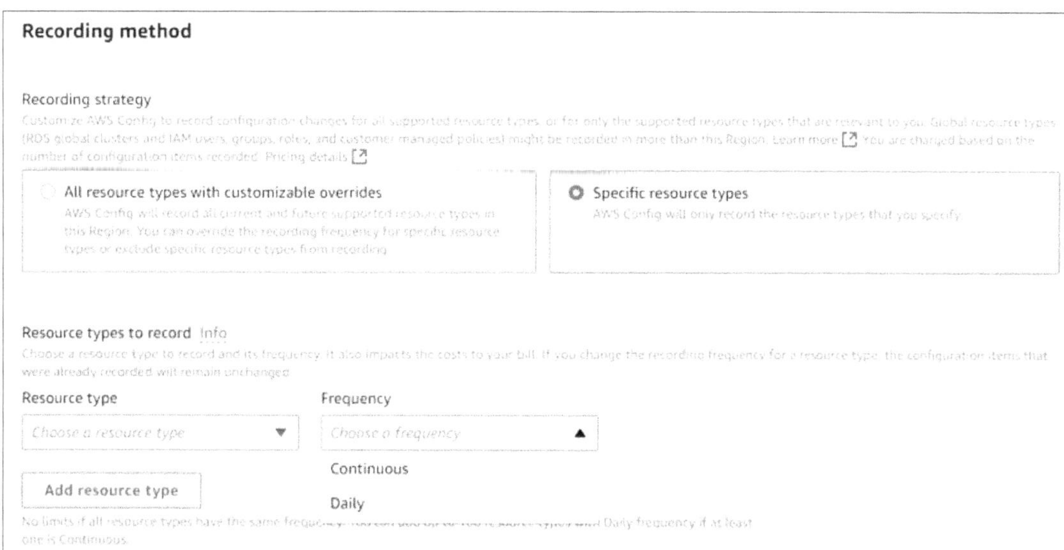

***Figure 8.16**: AWS Config recording configuration*

2. **Optimizing Config rule evaluation**:
   - Reduce frequency of evaluations for stable environments.
   - Combine checks into consolidated rules.

   For example, a rule set to evaluate every 6 hours instead of every hour reduces costs and still maintains compliance assurance.

Azure Monitor and Log Analytics optimization

Azure's observability solution centers around Azure Monitor and Log Analytics to collect and analyze telemetry, logs, metrics, and traces across resources. Since costs scale with ingestion volume, retention duration, and alerting frequency, organizations should fine-tune their monitoring configuration to balance visibility and spend. The following are key strategies to optimize Azure observability costs:

1. **Data collection configuration**: Use **Diagnostic Settings** to define what data to collect from which resources:
   - Only collect logs for essential categories.
   - Avoid verbose and high frequency logging unless required.
   - Review default settings to avoid unwanted charges.
2. **Log retention management**: Set custom retention policies as follows:
   - Keep logs for 30–90 days in Log Analytics.
   - Move older logs to Azure Blob Storage with Archive tier.
3. **Azure alerts and metrics optimization**:
   - **Metric frequency**:
     - Set 1-minute metrics only for critical resources.
     - Use 5-minute intervals for non-critical workloads.
   - **Alert consolidation**:
     - Use dynamic thresholds and smart alerting to avoid over-alerting.
     - Group similar conditions into one alert rule. For example, instead of creating separate alerts for CPU, memory, and disk, use a single alert with conditions for all three.

Optimizing observability costs for a food tech company

Let us consider a hypothetical food tech company to recap the optimization levers for observability services in detail. The company uses Amazon CloudWatch for all logs and metrics, with a unified setup across production, test, and dev environments. Its log ingestion exceeds 100 GB/day, and detailed metrics were applied uniformly across all environments. The DevOps team has been tasked to optimize Amazon CloudWatch cost and other observability-related expenses.

Based on the levers discussed, the DevOps team can take the following actions:

1. Switch dev/test to basic monitoring and have only production servers configured for detailed monitoring. This will reduce metric charges incurred by dev and test servers while ensuring adequate observability for production workloads.
2. Instead of sending logs to Amazon CloudWatch, evaluate moving logs to S3 and using Athena for querying. If stored in Amazon CloudWatch, set a 7-day retention period for logs.
3. Consolidated CloudTrail into a single organization trail. This will minimize charges related to the delivery of management events.
4. If data event has been configured, apply selective data event logging only to critical buckets such as payment and HR related S3 buckets.

Together, these measures significantly reduce observability costs while maintaining the right level of visibility and compliance for critical workloads.

Developing a prioritized action plan

After identifying the key cost drivers and exploring various levers to optimize observability costs, the next logical step is to create a structured approach and time bound plan to implement these changes. This plan will serve as a guide for your teams to systematically implement cost-saving measures while ensuring monitoring and logging requirements are still met. A well-developed action plan ensures that optimization efforts are focused on high-impact areas first, minimizing risk while maximizing cost savings. Refer to *Chapter 4, Moving from Cost Observability to Cost Optimization*, to understand the process for developing a priority action plan.

Sample prioritization framework

Now that you have a list of potential optimization actions, evaluate and prioritize them based on the following criteria:

- **Cost-saving potential**: *How much money can you save by taking optimization action?*
- **Implementation effort**: *Is it a quick configuration change or a full system redesign?*
- **Technical risk**: *Could the change impact operations or compliance?*
- **Business impact**: *Does the optimization affect production monitoring or audit readiness?*
- **Resource availability**: *Do you have the team and tools needed?*

Using a scoring system as discussed in *Chapter 4, Moving from Cost Observability to Cost Optimization,* prioritize the actions. Start with low-effort, high-impact items to generate early wins. Assign clear ownership for each action item and define timelines. Use a sprint-based approach and integrate changes into your regular cloud governance review cycles.

Conclusion

Observability plays a vital role in maintaining workload health, performance, availability, and compliance in cloud environments. However, as workloads scale and environments become more complex, monitoring and logging services can become a significant contributor to overall cloud costs.

This chapter has provided a framework for identifying optimization opportunities across major cloud observability services and developing a prioritized action plan for implementation. From right-sizing metrics and adjusting retention settings to consolidating alarms and applying data filters, each lever contributes to a more cost-efficient monitoring solution. The key to successful observability cost optimization lies in understanding that different workloads have different monitoring requirements, and not all monitoring data carries equal value. By differentiating between critical metrics that drive business decisions and less important data that is rarely used, organizations can implement targeted optimizations that preserve monitoring quality while eliminating waste.

In the next chapter, we will shift our focus to cloud security cost optimization. Just like observability, the costs of security services can quickly add up if not managed properly. We will explore how organizations can balance robust security controls with their cost objectives.

CHAPTER 9
Designing Cost Effective Cloud Security Architecture

Introduction

Security is no longer just a technical requirement but has now become a fundamental business priority. With the rise in cyber threats and data breaches, organizations cannot afford to treat security as a non-functional requirement or an afterthought. Whether workloads are hosted on-premise or in the cloud, strong security controls are essential to protect customer data, ensure compliance, and maintain brand reputation.

As organizations migrate workloads to the cloud, they need to design and deploy security solutions that meet internal security policies and industry regulations. Cloud providers like AWS, Azure, and GCP offer a comprehensive portfolio of native security services, while organizations also have the option to leverage third-party security solutions such as those from Palo Alto Networks, F5, or CrowdStrike. Cloud security services, like any other cloud service, follow a pay-as-you-go pricing model. However, the billing units vary, with some cloud security services getting charged based on hourly usage, while others may follow a monthly subscription plan. As more security controls are enabled to safeguard workloads, the associated costs can quickly add up.

This chapter aims to help organizations optimize the cost of cloud security services without compromising their workload security posture. The goal is not to downgrade the security posture, but to find the right balance between effective security controls and financial sustainability. Readers will gain insights into aligning their security configurations with organizational security and compliance requirements, monitoring security services usage, and identifying opportunities for cost savings. While AWS and Azure security services are used for illustrative purposes, the concepts discussed in this chapter are applicable across other major cloud platforms as well.

Structure

In this chapter, we will discuss the following topics:

- Understanding cloud security services portfolio
- Tools for analyzing security services usage
- Levers for optimizing cloud security services cost
- Developing a prioritized action plan

Objectives

By the end of this chapter, you will have a foundational understanding of the security services offered by cloud providers such as AWS and Azure. You will learn how these services are priced, including the differences in billing units like hourly or monthly charges under the pay-as-you-go model. The chapter will guide you through the tools available to analyze security services usage and identify opportunities to optimize costs without compromising your workload security posture. You will also understand how to align your security configurations with your organization's compliance and operational requirements to ensure both protection and cost-efficiency. Finally, you will be able to develop a prioritized implementation plan that can support sprint cycles aimed at reducing security services related costs. While we use AWS and Azure for illustrative purposes throughout this chapter, the principles and strategies discussed can be effectively applied across all major cloud platforms.

The goal of this chapter is to ensure your workload is secure while remaining financially sustainable for your organization.

Understanding cloud security services portfolio

As organizations migrate workloads to cloud, security on cloud has become a key focus area. While cloud adoption offers significant benefits such as scalability, agility, and cost-efficiency, it also introduces new security challenges. The traditional model of protecting on-premises infrastructure using physical firewalls, **intrusion detection systems** (**IDS**), and antivirus software needs to evolve. In the cloud, infrastructure is abstracted, dynamic, and shared. This demands a new approach to securing workloads, one that is cloud aware, is scalable, and is aligned with the shared responsibility model.

The shared responsibility model

In a traditional data center, the organization is responsible for end-to-end security, from the physical access controls at the data center entrance to server patching, network security, and application configurations. However, in the cloud model, the cloud provider owns and manages the underlying physical infrastructure, networking, and foundational services, while the organization is responsible for securing the resources and data they create or upload to the cloud. This principle is known as the shared responsibility model. The following figure shows the shared responsibility model for the **infrastructure as a service** (**IaaS**) cloud model:

Responsibility	On-Premise	Cloud
Identity and Access Management	●	●
Network controls	●	●
Data	●	●
Application	●	●
Guest OS	●	●
Hypervisors	●	○
Physical Network	●	○
Host Infrastructure – server	●	○
Edge Locations	●	○
Datacenter security	●	○

● Organization ○ Cloud Service provider

***Figure 9.1**: Shared responsibility model*

Cloud provider responsibilities for cloud security

Cloud providers are responsible for securing the underlying infrastructure that hosts their cloud services. This includes:

- **Physical security**: Managing access to data centers, surveillance, and environmental controls.
- **Network infrastructure**: Securing physical network devices, internal network routing, firewalls, and switches.
- **Host infrastructure**: Securing the server hardware, storage, and the hypervisor.
- **Patching for managed services**: For services like managed databases or serverless functions, cloud providers ensure that the platform is up to date and secure, with required bug fixes applied.
- **Compliance controls**: Ensuring cloud infrastructure complies with regulatory standards such as ISO 27001, SOC 2, and PCI-DSS.

Organization responsibilities for security in the cloud

Organizations are responsible for everything they deploy or configure in their cloud environment. These include:

- **Identity and access management (IAM):** Controlling who can access which cloud services and resources using cloud-provided IAM tools.
- **Data protection**: Classifying data, encrypting sensitive information, and managing encryption keys.
- **Network security**: Defining network segmentation, configuring firewall rules, and monitoring traffic.
- **Application and OS security**: Applying patches, configuring permissions, and securing endpoints.
- **Monitoring and incident response**: Setting up alerting, auditing logs, and responding to security events.

For example, if you are using Amazon EC2 (AWS) or Azure Virtual Machines, the cloud provider is responsible for the security of physical servers, hypervisors, and all underlying infrastructure, including network routers and switches. You are responsible for securing the guest operating system, configuring software firewalls, managing user access, protecting hosted data, and keeping the guest operating system patched.

Understanding the shared responsibility model is essential for all organizations. Without clarity, organizations may wrongly assume that security is entirely handled by the cloud provider, which can lead to gaps and vulnerabilities.

Third-party security services

Organizations migrating to the cloud often need to decide whether to adopt cloud-native security services or continue using third-party security solutions. Cloud providers offer a comprehensive portfolio of built-in security services and offer deep integration with cloud resources, simplified deployment, and consumption-based pricing. However, many organizations may already have security tools for areas such as SIEM, vulnerability management, **cloud security posture management** (**CSPM**), endpoint protection, and threat detection. Some of the examples of third-party security solutions include:

- **IAM**: Tools like Okta or Ping Identity offer advanced **single sign-on** (**SSO**) and lifecycle management that works across multiple cloud providers and on-premises applications.
- **Infrastructure and workload protection**: Platforms such as Palo Alto Prisma Cloud, CrowdStrike Falcon, and Splunk provide deep visibility into containers, serverless functions, and virtual machines across AWS, Azure, and GCP.

Organizations should evaluate several factors when selecting between cloud-native and third-party security services, including:

- **Existing security investments**: Consider current licenses and any long-term contracts with security vendors before finalizing the tools to be used after migrating to the cloud.

- **Multi-cloud and hybrid support**: Third-party tools may provide a unified security policy, monitoring, and reporting interface across on-premises, hybrid, and multi-cloud environments.
- **Integration requirements**: Evaluate how the finalized security solution integrates with cloud services, identity platforms, CI/CD pipelines, and existing SOC tools.
- **Feature depth and maturity**: Compare detection capabilities, automation features, reporting, and threat intelligence coverage between third-party and cloud native security services.
- **Operational familiarity**: Assess team expertise with existing tools versus the learning curve for new cloud-native services.
- **Compliance and audit needs**: Ensure the solution meets industry regulations and supports required reporting and evidence collection.
- **Scalability and performance**: Confirm the tool can handle cloud-scale workloads and dynamic environments.
- **Cost considerations**: Evaluate the total cost of ownership, including licensing, data ingestion, storage costs, and operational overhead.

Core categories of cloud security services

Security services offered by cloud providers can be categorized into six broad categories. Understanding each category and the related services available helps in building a secure, compliant, and cost-effective security architecture. Some of the products may offer features that span across categories. Let us look at some of the services offered by cloud providers, such as AWS and Azure, across different categories, which are explained in the following sections.

Identity and access management

IAM is the backbone of cloud security and helps define who has access to which resources and under what conditions. Organizations need to follow the principle of least privilege to protect their resources and data. Some of the key services in the IAM category from AWS and Azure are:

- **AWS IAM**: Help set up access control, policy definitions, and MFA enforcement.
- **AWS organizations**: Provides multi-account management and governance using **service control policies** (**SCPs**).
- **Amazon Cognito**: Adds user authentication, authorization, and user management to web and mobile apps.
- **Azure Active Directory (Azure AD)**: Identity and access management service that supports SSO, conditional access, multi-factor authentication, and identity protection.

- **Microsoft Entra permissions management**: Manages permissions across multi-cloud environments.

Detective controls

These services help in identifying potential security threats by monitoring resource configurations, access patterns, and network activity, and generating alarms and notifications:

- **AWS CloudTrail**: Records API calls made in an AWS account and helps perform security audits and investigations.
- **Amazon GuardDuty**: A threat detection service that uses machine learning to detect anomalies such as brute force attacks or access from unusual locations.
- **AWS Config**: Tracks configuration changes and compliance violations across AWS services.
- **Azure Monitor**: Collects and analyzes metrics and logs from applications and resources.
- **Azure Activity Logs**: Helps track operations performed on Azure resources.
- **Microsoft Defender for Cloud**: Provides threat detection, security recommendations, and compliance insights for hybrid and multi-cloud environments.

Infrastructure protection

These services help protect compute, networks, and edge components from common attacks like DDoS, port scanning, and traffic sniffing:

- **AWS shield (standard and advanced)**: Provides DDoS protection at the network and transport layers.
- **AWS web application firewall (WAF)**: Blocks malicious traffic based on custom rules or managed rule groups.
- **AWS security groups and NACLs**: Provide instance-level and subnet-level network access control.
- **Network firewall**: A managed stateful firewall that filters traffic between virtual networks.
- **Azure DDoS protection**: Automatically mitigates large-scale attacks with telemetry and analytics.
- **Azure network security groups (NSGs)**: Define rules for traffic flow in and out of Azure resources.

Data protection

This category focuses on ensuring the confidentiality, integrity, and availability of data:

- **AWS Key Management Service (KMS)**: Allows centralized creation and management of encryption keys.
- **AWS Secrets Manager**: Securely stores and rotates API keys, database credentials, and secrets.
- **Amazon Macie**: Uses ML to discover and classify sensitive data like PII in S3 buckets.
- **Azure Key Vault**: Helps safeguard cryptographic keys and secrets used by cloud applications.
- **Azure Disk Encryption**: Uses BitLocker or DM-Crypt to encrypt virtual machine disks.

Application security

Application-level security helps developers and DevOps teams build secure apps from the start. Some of the key services for application security from AWS and Azure are:

- **Amazon Cognito**: Adds user sign-in and access control capabilities to web and mobile apps.
- **AWS Inspector**: Scan for vulnerabilities in code and deployed applications.
- **AWS CodeGuru**: Offers security and performance feedback in pull requests.
- **Azure app service authentication**: Enables built-in authentication using identity providers like Azure AD, Google, or Facebook.
- **Web application firewall**: Protects against OWASP Top 10 attacks.

Incident detection and response

These services are designed to detect, manage, and respond to security incidents:

- **AWS Security Hub**: Aggregates findings from AWS and third-party tools for centralized visibility.
- **AWS Systems Manager Incident Manager**: Automates incident response playbooks.
- **Amazon Detective**: Helps investigate and analyze root causes of suspicious activities.
- **Microsoft Sentinel**: Azure's cloud-native SIEM solution that collects data from across environments for threat detection and incident response.
- **Azure Logic Apps**: Automate workflows to respond to alerts or compliance violations.
- **Azure Automation Runbooks**: Execute predefined steps for remediation actions.

The portfolio of security services demonstrates the comprehensive solution provided by major cloud providers to address organizations' security needs. Organizations need to evaluate their security and compliance requirements and choose services that align with their security strategy while maintaining cost efficiency. Organizations should regularly review the latest offerings and updates from their cloud providers as security services and features are continuously evolving.

Pricing models for cloud security services

When organizations rely on cloud-native security services to protect their infrastructure, understanding the pricing models of these services becomes essential. Unlike compute or storage resources, where pricing is often straightforward and charged per hour of a running instance or per GB of data stored, security services tend to have more complex pricing structures. The pricing structure of cloud security services varies significantly depending on the security service used, the protection features enabled, and how the security service is integrated with other cloud services in the environment.

Optimizing costs without compromising security posture requires a clear understanding of how each security service is billed, which components are charged, and where savings opportunities may exist. This section provides an overview of security service pricing for **Amazon Web Services** (**AWS**) and Microsoft Azure, with examples across key categories.

Free Tier inclusions

Many security services come with a Free Tier, allowing customers to start using the service without incurring immediate charges. Leveraging free-tier limits is an effective cost optimization approach, especially for small to mid-sized environments and during **proof-of-concept** (**PoC**) deployments. The Free Tier helps organizations understand usage and calculate the pricing impact of using a particular security service once the Free Tier limit is exhausted.

The following are examples from AWS highlighting the Free Tier limits of security services:

- IAM and IAM Identity Center are available at no additional cost.
- Amazon Cognito, which provides user authentication and identity management, offers three pricing tiers—lite, essentials, and plus, classified depending on enhanced features and performance levels. The Amazon Cognito public pricing page provides details on the differences between these tiers. Amazon Cognito offers a Free Tier of up to 10,000 **monthly active users** (**MAUs**) for the first 12 months under its lite plan.
- AWS Shield Standard (basic DDoS protection) is available by default at no additional cost for all AWS customers.
- When you subscribe to AWS Shield Advanced (the paid option of AWS Shield), you get limited access to AWS WAF features at no extra charge.

- AWS Security Hub provides 10,000 free ingested security findings per month per account.

The following are some Azure examples showing Free Tier limits available for security services:

- Azure Active Directory Free Tier provides user authentication, SSO, and limited security reporting.
- Microsoft Defender for Cloud offers free vulnerability assessments and basic threat detection for selected services.
- Azure Key Vault includes limited free transactions per month (up to 10,000 standard operations).

Teams should check the cloud providers' public pricing page to verify which services are free and under what conditions, as cloud providers regularly update service pricing and Free Tier limits. Combining multiple Free Tier offerings can deliver baseline protection at minimal cost.

Component-based pricing

Security services often include multiple features or modules, with each feature having a different pricing structure. This modular pricing helps customers scale usage based on their resource protection requirements and pay only for the components they use. However, it can also result in unexpected costs if components are enabled without reviewing their alignment with the organization's security requirements. Let us look at some of the security services to illustrate component-based pricing and how the billing unit varies by components used:

- **AWS WAF**: AWS WAF includes standard WAF rules and is charged as per the following:
    - **Web ACLs**: Charged per month per ACL.
    - **Rules**: Charged per month per rule.
    - **Request volume**: Charged per million requests processed.
    - **Add-ons**: Like bot control and fraud control are billed separately and have different billing units

When deploying AWS WAF, it is important to finalize which components the team will use as charges vary depending on WAF components configured. Refer to the following figure to understand AWS WAF pricing structure:

AWS WAF Bot Control Fraud Control DDoS Protection

You will be charged for each web ACL that you create and each rule that you create per web ACL. In addition, you will be charged for the number of web requests processed by the web ACL. Pricing may vary across AWS Regions. Monthly fees are prorated hourly. Pricing for AWS WAF Classic is the same as shown in the table below.

Region:

Asia Pacific (Singapore)

Resource Type	Price
Web ACL	$5.00 per month (prorated hourly)
Rule	$1.00 per month (prorated hourly)
Request	$0.60 per 1 million requests
Bot Control and Fraud Control	Additional cost as per tabs above

Figure 9.2: AWS WAF component and pricing

- **Microsoft Defender for Cloud**: As per the Microsoft Azure pricing page, Microsoft Defender for Cloud is free for the first 30 days. Any usage beyond 30 days will be automatically charged as per usage. Microsoft Defender includes plans for compute, storage, databases, containers, and more. Each plan has a per-resource or per-instance fee, such as per Azure VM or per instance for databases. Refer to the Azure public pricing page, as shown in the following figure, to understand the Microsoft Defender pricing plan:

Resource Type	Resource	Price
Servers	Microsoft Defender for Servers Plan 1	**$4.906**/server/month
	Microsoft Defender for Servers Plan 2	**$14.60**/server/month
Containers	Microsoft Defender for Containers	**$6.8693**/vCore/month[4]
Databases	Microsoft Defender for SQL on Azure-connected databases and Microsoft Defender for SQL Servers on machines (in Azure, or Arc-enabled)	**$15**/Instance/month[2]
	Microsoft Defender for SQL Servers on machines (outside Azure and not Arc-enabled)	**$10.95**/Instance/vCore/month[3]
	Microsoft Defender for MySQL	**$15**/Instance/month
	Microsoft Defender for PostgreSQL	**$15**/Instance/month
	Microsoft Defender for MariaDB	**$15**/Instance/month
	Microsoft Defender for Azure Cosmos DB[5]	**$0.8760** per 100 RU/S/hour
Storage	Microsoft Defender for Storage[1]	**$10** per storage account/month[6]

Figure 9.3: Microsoft Defender for Cloud pricing by component

Billing units

Billing units for cloud security services vary by service and by the components used, and understanding these billing units is critical in the cost optimization journey. In the previous section, we explored the billing units for AWS WAF and Microsoft Defender. Refer to the following table to learn about the billing units of some commonly used security services:

Service	Billing unit
AWS Shield Advanced	Monthly subscription cost per organization.
AWS WAF	Component-based billing units, such as per ACL, per rule, or per million requests.
Amazon GuardDuty	Per GB of log data analyzed. The price varies depending on the log type ingested.
AWS Security Hub	Per security check and per ingested finding(event/month).
Azure Firewall	Per deployment hour and per GB of data processed.
Azure DDoS Protection	Monthly subscription cost per public IP with additional charges for data usage.

***Table 9.1**: Cloud security services billing units*

Regional price variations

Pricing for cloud services, including security services, often varies by region due to infrastructure costs, local compliance requirements, and demand patterns. For example, Amazon GuardDuty may cost more per GB in the Asia Pacific (Mumbai) region than in US East (N. Virginia). Refer to the following figure for pricing variation across regions:

US East (N. Virginia)

AWS CloudTrail Management Event Analysis	
Per one million events / month	$4.00 per one million events

VPC Flow Logs and DNS Query Log Analysis	
First 500 GB / month	$1.00 per GB
Next 2,000 GB / month	$0.50 per GB
Next 7,500 GB / month	$0.25 per GB
Over 10,000 GB / month	$0.15 per GB

Asia Pacific (Mumbai)

AWS CloudTrail Management Event Analysis	
Per one million events / month	$4.40 per one million events

VPC Flow Logs and DNS Query Log Analysis	
First 500 GB / month	$1.10 per GB
Next 2,000 GB / month	$0.55 per GB
Next 7,500 GB / month	$0.28 per GB
Over 10,000 GB / month	$0.17 per GB

***Figure 9.4**: Amazon GuardDuty pricing variation across region*

Commitment-based savings

Some cloud providers offer discounts for committed usage of security services. For example, AWS Shield Advanced has a one-year minimum subscription term. Similarly, Azure may offer a discounted rate for committed usage for the term. Estimate your long-term security usage and evaluate whether volume or commitment-based discounts apply. Reach out to your cloud provider for private pricing tiers or enterprise agreements.

Exploring pricing of AWS security services

Let us explore some of the services from AWS to understand the concepts learned in precedng section, such as component-based pricing, billing unit, and how usage is charged based on different factors:

Amazon Cognito

Amazon Cognito enables secure user authentication for applications. Pricing for Amazon Cognito is based on features used, such as:

- **Identity management**: Charged per MAU.
  - **Plans available**: Lite, essentials, and plus, classified depending on enhanced features and performance tiers.
  - MAU is counted if any user interaction (e.g., login, password reset) occurs.
  - Only one charge per MAU per month.
- **Data synchronization**: Optional and is charged based on the data transferred.
- **Add-ons** such as API call, **machine-to-machine** (**M2M**) auth.

Refer to the following figure to understand Amazon Cognito billing units and charges varying by region and components used:

Pricing table for Amazon Cognito tiers

Essentials Plus Lite

Region:

US East (Ohio)

MAUs	Price per MAU
First 10,000 (Free-tier)	$0.00
Greater than 10,000	$0.015

Pricing table for Amazon Cognito add-ons

API quotas M2M authorization Cognito Sync

Region:

US East (Ohio)

API Category	Continuous use for full month	Use for partial month
User authentication	$20.00	$45.00
User creation	$20.00	$45.00
User federation	$20.00	$45.00
User read	$20.00	$45.00
User resource read	$20.00	$45.00
User token	$20.00	$45.00
User resource update	$20.00	$45.00
User update	$20.00	$45.00
User account recovery	$20.00	$45.00

***Figure 9.5**: Amazon Cognito tiers and add-ons*

Reviewing the Amazon Cognito pricing page, you can identify:

- Pricing plan based on different tiers.
- Billing unit and charges (such as per MAU or API calls).
- **Component-based pricing**: Billing unit and charges for different components such as API calls, M2M authorization, and Cognito Sync.

Amazon GuardDuty

GuardDuty is a fully managed threat detection service. Pricing dimensions vary by components used and are detailed as follows:

- **Foundational threat detection (per GB)**: Includes analysis of the following logs and is charged per GB of data analyzed:
    - CloudTrail logs
    - VPC flow logs
    - DNS query logs
- **Optional protection plan**s: Pricing varies by plan, based on event count, log volume, EBS size, vCPU usage, or network activity. Some of the plans available are:
    - **S3 Protection**: Charged per million data events.
    - **EKS Runtime Monitoring**: Charged per million audit logs.
    - **Malware Protection**: Charged per GB of EBS volume scanned.
    - **RDS Protection**: Charged per **virtual CPU** (**vCPU**).
    - **Lambda Protection**: Cost increases with network activity volume.

Refer to the following figure to explore Amazon GuardDuty pricing for its components and available add-on protection plans:

Foundational threat detection pricing

Region:
US East (Ohio)

AWS CloudTrail Management Event Analysis	
Per one million events / month	$4.00 per one million events

VPC Flow Logs and DNS Query Log Analysis	
First 500 GB / month	$1.00 per GB
Next 2,000 GB / month	$0.50 per GB
Next 7,500 GB / month	$0.25 per GB
Over 10,000 GB / month	$0.15 per GB

GuardDuty protection plans

S3 Protection | EKS Protection | Runtime Monitoring | Malware Protection | RDS Protection | Lambda Protection

AWS CloudTrail S3 Data Event Analysis	
First 500 million events / month	$0.80 per one million events
Next 4,500 million events / month	$0.40 per one million events
Over 5,000 million events / month	$0.20 per one million events

Figure 9.6: *Amazon GuardDuty pricing plan*

AWS Security Hub

Security Hub consolidates findings from AWS services and third-party tools to provide a unified view of your security posture.

- **Security Checks**: Charged per check (e.g., checking EC2 against CIS standards).
- **Finding Ingestion Events**: Charged per ingested event beyond the Free Tier.

Refer to the following figure to explore the various AWS Security Hub components and how pricing varies by region and component:

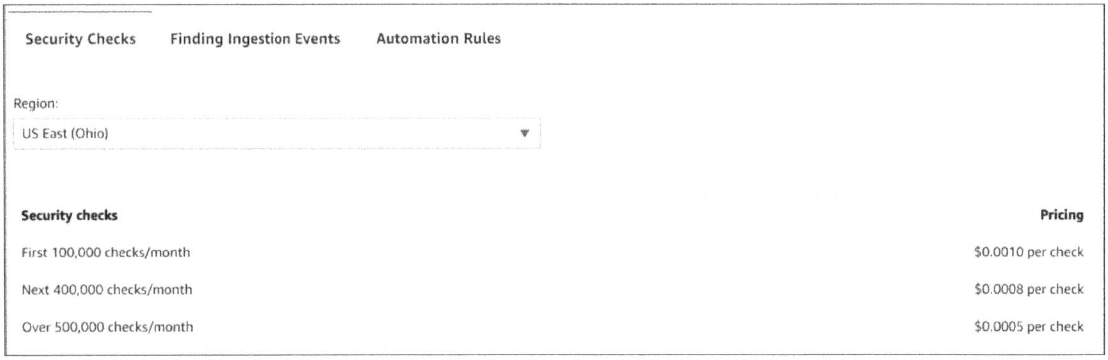

***Figure 9.7**: Security Hub pricing*

AWS Shield Advanced

This security service provides advanced DDoS protection. Pricing is $3,000/month flat fee per organization (covers multiple accounts). Data transfer out is charged separately by GB.

Exploring pricing of Azure Security Services

Microsoft Azure offers a broad portfolio of cloud-native security services across identity management, threat detection, infrastructure protection, data protection, and incident response. Similar to AWS, Azure security services follow diverse pricing models based on service type, features enabled, data volume processed, and usage frequency. Understanding these pricing structures is essential to accurately estimate costs, avoid unexpected charges, and design cost-efficient security architectures on Azure.

Azure security services are typically billed based on metrics such as the number of protected resources, data ingestion volume, analysis frequency, API calls, or enabled protection plans. Some services also offer Free Tiers, trial periods, or bundled pricing options that can reduce initial adoption costs. However, as workloads scale and additional security features are enabled, costs can grow quickly if usage is not actively monitored.

Before deploying or expanding Azure security controls, organizations should review the pricing model of each service, identify the key billing units, and understand how features affect monthly costs. Azure's public pricing pages and the Azure Pricing Calculator provide detailed cost breakdowns and can be used to estimate expenses based on expected usage patterns. Let us explore some of the services to understand the concepts learned in the previous section, such as component-based pricing, billing unit, and how usage is charged based on different factors:

- **Microsoft Defender for Cloud**: Microsoft Defender for Cloud is Azure's cloud-native security management and threat protection service that helps organizations secure their workloads across Azure, hybrid, and multi-cloud environments. It combines security posture management, workload protection, and threat detection into a single platform. It is charged based on enabled protection plans (for example, servers, containers, databases, or storage accounts) and the number of protected resources. Refer to *Figure 9.3* for more details on pricing.

- **Microsoft Sentinel**: Microsoft's cloud-native **Security Information and Event Management** (**SIEM**) and **Security Orchestration, Automation, and Response** (**SOAR**) platform. It helps organizations collect, analyze, and correlate security data from across their cloud, on-premises, and multi-cloud environments to detect threats, investigate incidents, and automate response actions. As a cloud-native SIEM, Sentinel is billed based on the volume of data ingested for analysis and data retention. Refer to the following figure to understand the pricing of Microsoft Sentinel in US EAST.

SKU	Meter type	Price
Pay-as-you-go	Analysis (GB)	$4.3 USD
100 GB Commitment Tier	Commitment Tier/Day	$296 USD
200 GB Commitment Tier	Commitment Tier/Day	$548 USD
300 GB Commitment Tier	Commitment Tier/Day	$800 USD
400 GB Commitment Tier	Commitment Tier/Day	$1037.33 USD
500 GB Commitment Tier	Commitment Tier/Day	$1265 USD
1000 GB Commitment Tier	Commitment Tier/Day	$2480 USD
2000 GB Commitment Tier	Commitment Tier/Day	$4800 USD

***Figure 9.8**: Microsoft Sentinel pricing*

- **Azure Firewall**: It is offered in three SKUs (tiers)—Basic, Standard, and Premium, designed to meet different performance, feature, and cost needs. The pricing for Azure Firewall is a combination of a fixed hourly rate (per deployment hour) and a variable data processing fee. Refer to the following figure for Azure Firewall pricing:

Azure Firewall			
	Basic	Standard	Premium
Deployment	$0.395 per deployment hour	$1.25 per deployment hour	$1.75 per deployment hour
Data Processing	$0.065 per GB processed	$0.016 per GB processed	$0.016 per GB processed
Capacity Unit	N/A	$0.07 per Capacity Unit Hour	$0.11 per Capacity Unit Hour

***Figure 9.9**: Azure Firewall pricing*

- **Azure DDoS Protection**: Unlike other services, Azure's network protection plan is a flat-fee model designed for enterprise-wide coverage. It has two components:
  - **Fixed Monthly Fee**: Approx. $2,944 per month for up to 100 resources.
  - **Overages**: If you protect more than 100 resources, an additional monthly fee per resource applies.
- **Azure Key Vault**: Charged based on the number of operations and key or secret storage.

In this section, we explored pricing models for cloud security services and how various factors can impact security services costs. Before deploying security controls, it is important for an organization to understand:

- Which security service to use.
- Which components and features to deploy for each security control.
- Billing units for services and components used.
- Free Tier inclusions, volume discounts, or bundle offerings.

By leveraging Free Tiers, choosing only the necessary security services and components, and understanding billing units for services and components deployed, organizations can maintain a strong security posture while optimizing costs. In the next section, we will explore tools to continuously monitor cloud security spending.

Tools for analyzing security services usage

As organizations adopt cloud-native security solutions to protect their workloads, it is easy for security related costs to go unnoticed as security services are spread across multiple pillars, such as identity, detection, data protection, infrastructure protection, and incident detection and response. While ensuring a strong security posture is essential, it is equally important to monitor and manage the associated costs. Without proper visibility, organizations risk overspending, often paying for unused features, duplicate security tools, and excessive protection measures. This section explores how to monitor the cost of cloud security services using native tools from cloud providers such as AWS and Azure. By leveraging cost monitoring tools from AWS and Azure, teams can answer key questions such as:

- *Which security services are contributing most to the cloud bill?*
- *What components within each service are driving up costs?*
- *Are we utilizing the security services deployed effectively or paying for unused capabilities?*

AWS cost management tools

AWS provides a suite of native tools to monitor usage and costs for all services, including security services. The cost management tools used for managing compute, storage, database, and observability costs can be extended to security services, with minor adjustments to filters and reporting. Let us explore some of the key tools provided by AWS for monitoring and forecasting security services cost:

Category	Tool	Description
Cost Observability: The tools help in reviewing the cost of security services consumed by the organization, including total usage and spend	AWS Billing console	View consolidated billing data, invoices, and service-wise charges. Since cloud providers may not bundle security related products under a common category, such as security and compliance, you will need to explore individual security services to get insight into usage and cost.
	AWS Cost Explorer	Visualize security services related usage and cost data. The tool can also be used to do trend analysis, forecasting, and dive deep into specific components that are adding to the security services cost.
	AWS CUR	Provides granular, resource-level data about security services usage and cost. Can be queried using Athena and visualized with QuickSight.
	Cost and Usage Dashboard	Pre-built dashboards (via QuickSight), such as the cost intelligence dashboard, to visualize the granular level of cost and usage data.
Estimation	AWS Pricing Calculator	Estimate the cost of consuming security services. The AWS Pricing Calculator can also be used for estimating the cost of enabling a particular security feature.

***Table 9.2**: Tools for analyzing usage and spend*

Identify security services in use

As organizations may deploy different security services over time, teams should start by listing all the security services being used in their account. These typically fall under six major pillars:

- **Identity and access management**: IAM, Cognito
- **Detection**: AWS Config, CloudTrail, GuardDuty, Security Hub
- **Infrastructure protection**: AWS WAF, inspector, shield advanced
- **Data protection**: KMS, Secrets Manager

- **Application security**: AWS CodeGuru
- **Incident detection and response**: Amazon Detective

Once you have prepared this inventory, you can begin monitoring using the tools mentioned in *Table 9.2*.

Reviewing security services costs with AWS Cost Explorer

AWS Cost Explorer offers visualization capabilities that help in identifying cost trends and optimization opportunities for AWS services. Follow the steps given to use *AWS Cost Explorer* for Security Services:

1. Go to the AWS console and open **Billing and Cost Management**.
2. From the left panel, click on **Cost Explorer**.
3. Apply filters to analyze observability costs:
    - **Date Range**: Last 3 months
    - **Granularity**: Monthly
    - **Dimension**: Service
    - **Service**: Select security services deployed, such as Cognito, GuardDuty, Security Hub, WAF, and Inspector.

This will generate a view as shown in the following figure to highlight which security services are costing the most each month:

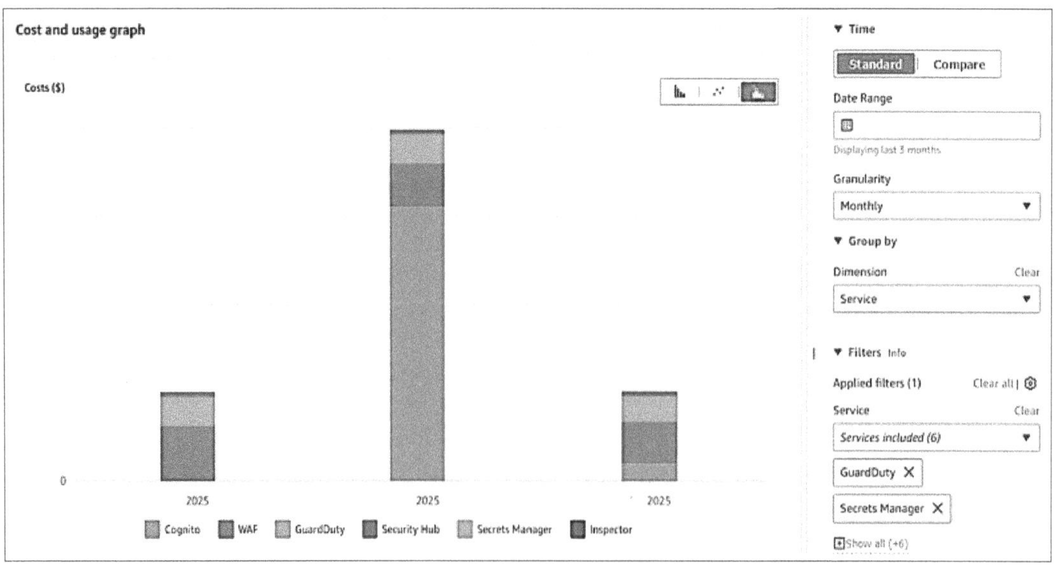

Figure 9.10: Cost Explorer to analyze security services cost

Once you have identified the top security services by spend, you can then dive deep into specific service to get insights into cost incurred. For example, to get insight into GuardDuty charges, change the **Dimension** filter to **`Usage type`** and restrict **Service** filter to **GuardDuty**. This will show whether GuardDuty charges are coming from foundational data source analysis or add-on protections plan like EKS Runtime Monitoring or S3 data event scanning, as shown in the following figure:

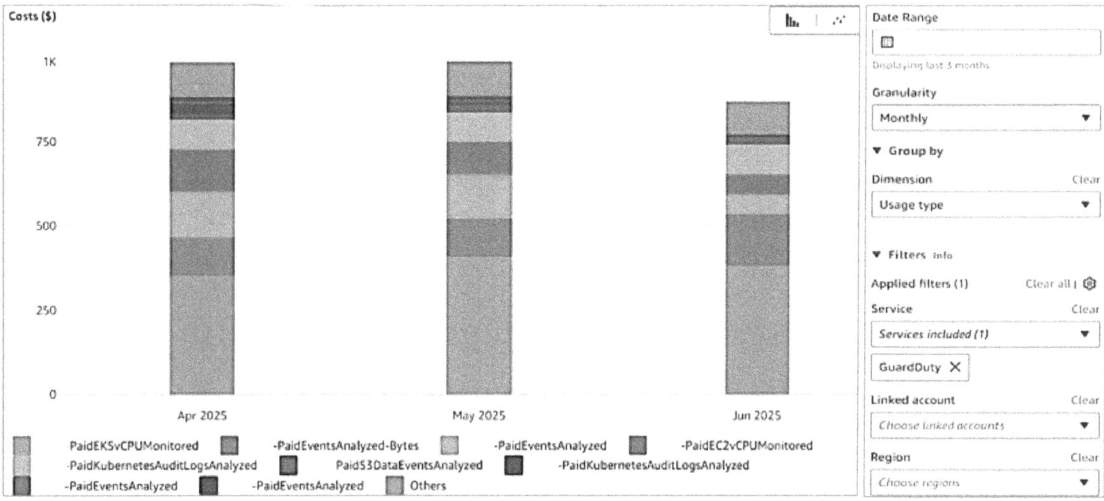

Figure 9.11: Isolating GuardDuty component level charges

Correlating Cost Explorer findings with Billing console

We have seen in previous chapters how the Billing console gives an invoice-like view of your monthly charges. To analyze security services costs using the Billing console:

1. Navigate to the AWS **Billing and Cost Management** dashboard and select **Bills.**
2. Choose the relevant billing period.
3. Under **Charges by Service**, expand each security service, such as **GuardDuty**, **WAF**, and **Config**. The following figure shows charges related to GuardDuty:

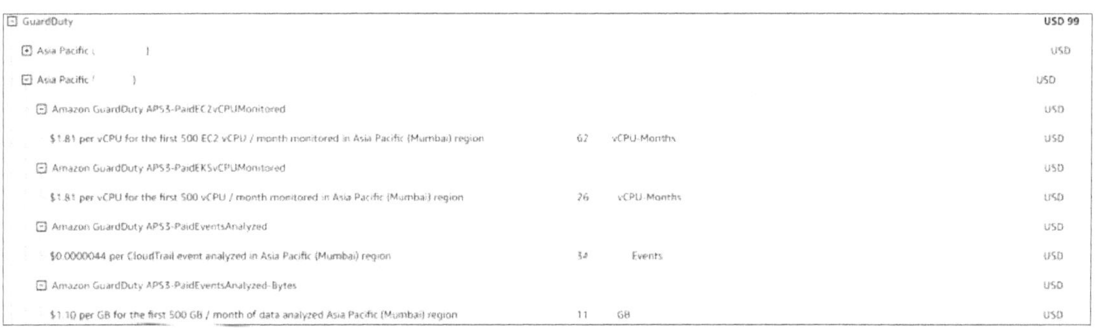

Figure 9.12: Using Billing console for security services

The information from **Bills** will help you analyze:

- Overall cost of different security services.
- Regions that are incurring the charges.
- Feature-specific charges (e.g., foundation logs vs. protection services).
- Billing unit and volumes consumed.

Accessing detailed data with Cost and Usage Reports

CUR is AWS's most detailed cost-tracking tool. It provides usage data at the resource, API, or even tag level and can be analyzed using Amazon Athena or visualized in QuickSight. You can write CUR queries to analyze security services-related charges, including resourcing incurring the charges.

Azure tools for security services Cost Analysis

Azure provides its own set of native tools for cost tracking under the umbrella of Azure **Cost Management + Billing**. These tools are integrated with other Azure services and are useful for analyzing and forecasting costs related to Azure security offerings.

Identify Azure security services in use

Similar to the steps shown in the AWS section, start by identifying Azure security services deployed by the organization, such as:

- **Identity management**: Azure Active Directory
- **Detection and monitoring**: Microsoft Defender for Cloud, Sentinel, Azure Monitor
- **Data protection**: Azure Key Vault, Azure Information Protection
- **Infrastructure protection**: Azure Firewall, Azure DDoS Protection
- **Incident detection and response**: Microsoft Sentinel, Logic Apps for automated response

Once you have identified the security services deployed, use the given steps to analyze related costs.

Azure Cost Management + Billing

Azure **Cost Management + Billing** tool helps you visualize, analyze, and manage your Azure spending. It can be customized to track security-related charges. Steps to analyze security costs:

1. Open the Azure portal and launch **Cost Management + Billing**.
2. Go to **Cost Analysis**.
3. Configure the view using the following settings:
   - **Scope**: Choose subscription or resource group.
   - **Granularity**: Monthly
   - **Service Name**: Filter for security services used, such as Microsoft Defender for Cloud, Azure Firewall.

   Refer to the following figure for Azure Cost Analysis:

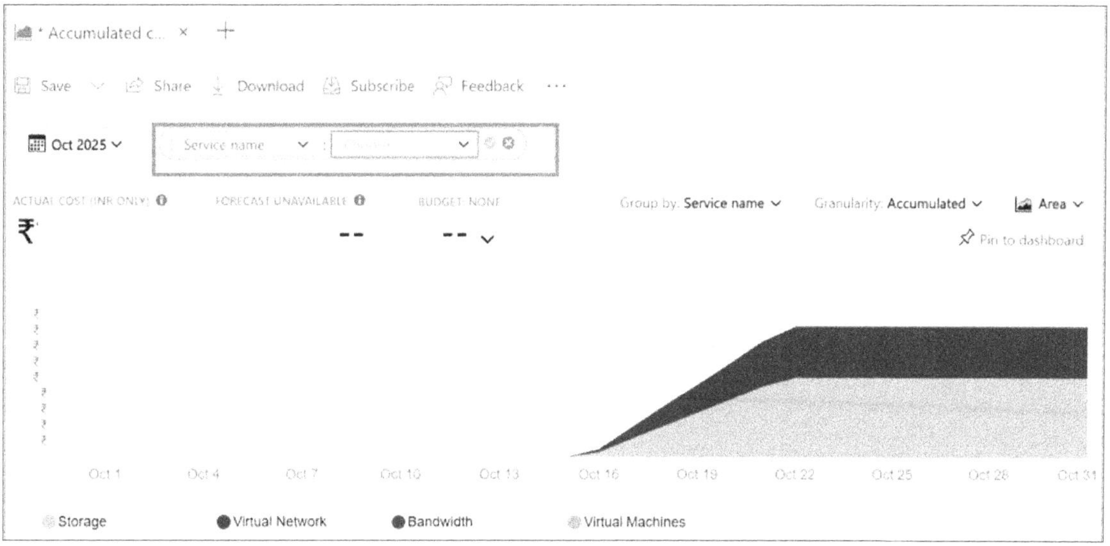

***Figure 9.13**: Using Azure Cost Analysis for security services*

Azure's Cost Analysis tools also support custom views and dashboards, allowing security teams to create tailored reports focusing on their specific areas of responsibility.

Putting it all together

Cloud-native security services are essential for protecting workloads deployed in the cloud, meeting compliance requirements, and maintaining operational integrity. However, their costs can add up quickly as new services and features are enabled over time.

Both AWS and Azure offer powerful tools for visualizing, analyzing, and forecasting security-related spending. By regularly using tools such as AWS Cost Explorer, the Billing Console, AWS Cost and Usage Reports, and Azure Cost Analysis, organizations can gain clear visibility into their cloud security related costs, identify savings opportunities, and ensure cost-effective protection.

Here is a simple framework to help you regularly monitor and manage cloud security service costs across AWS and Azure:

1. **Inventory of security services in use**: Start by identifying the security services deployed in your cloud accounts. These may include services activated during past security assessments, penetration tests, or compliance projects. It is common for organizations to lose track of services enabled earlier or trial features that continue to incur charges.
2. **Identify top cost contributors**: Use tools like AWS Cost Explorer or Azure Cost Analysis to identify which security services or features are responsible for most of your security spend. Prioritize investigation of services that are rapidly increasing in cost or are consistently incurring high monthly charges.
3. **Take optimization actions**: Once you have identified the services and components that are contributing the most to your cloud monthly spend, you can focus on optimizing the charges incurred. In the next section, we will discuss different levers available for organizations to optimize security related charges.

Levers for optimizing cloud security services cost

In the previous section, we explored how to monitor the cost of cloud security services using native tools. Now, we will shift focus to optimization levers that organizations can use to reduce and control cloud security costs without compromising their security posture. Remember that any cost optimization-related changes must align with your organization's security policies and compliance requirements. Regular security audits and penetration testing remain essential to identify any security gaps after implementing cost optimization measures.

This section is divided into two parts:

- **General optimization principles**: Broad strategies that apply across all security tools and environments.
- **Service-specific recommendations**: Targeted actions for reducing the cost of specific services from AWS.

General optimization principles

These are foundational recommendations that apply across all cloud environments and security tools. The generic optimization recommendations discussed in this section will help organizations align security needs with business objectives, reduce redundancy, and control unnecessary spending.

Right-size security architecture

Before choosing security tools, organizations should evaluate their threat landscape and compliance needs. There is no theoretical limit to the number of security controls an organization can implement. The key is to develop a clear understanding of the workload's exposure and identify the actual attack surface. This approach enables the implementation of minimal yet effective security controls that meet security and compliance requirements while remaining cost-effective.

Several factors must be considered when designing the right security solution:

- **Threat vectors**: Identify the potential sources of threats. These could be external attacks (e.g., DDoS, phishing), internal threats (e.g., insider misuse), or unintentional errors.
- **Understanding security solutions**: There are different security products available addressing the security needs of an organization. A clear understanding of each security solution's features and the layer it protects helps ensure you select the right products for your specific security requirements while avoiding costly duplications. In the section, *Understanding cloud security services portfolio*, we have seen how security services can be categorized into six broad categories. Each of these categories can be further classified. For example, infrastructure and data protection services can be further divided into:
    - **Perimeter security solutions**: These protect your cloud accounts and underlying workloads by creating a secure boundary around your cloud environment. Examples include AWS Shield, Azure DDoS Protection, and cloud-based firewalls.
    - **Network security solutions**: These focus on protecting against network-related threats through tools like AWS Network Firewall, Azure Firewall, VPC/VNET security groups, and network access controls.
    - **Host security solutions**: These protect individual hosts against threats through endpoint protection platforms, host-based intrusion detection and prevention systems, and vulnerability management tools.
    - **Application security solutions**: Tools like **Static Application Security Testing** (**SAST**) and **Dynamic Application Security Testing** (**DAST**) help find vulnerabilities in applications before they can be exploited.
    - **Data security solution**: This includes data encryption, tokenization, and access controls, which can help protect confidential data.

It is common for organizations to enable multiple security services that perform similar functions, especially during the initial phases of cloud adoption. The organization needs to ensure there are no duplicate security controls, as these can inflate security costs without adding value. Also, look for standardizing security controls across the organization instead of deploying multiple and diverse security services for different workloads, as it can increase integration and management costs.

Environment-based security configuration

Bad actors typically look for entry points with minimal security controls to gain access to an environment. These entry points can be application endpoints, servers, or end-user devices, regardless of how environments are classified (development, testing, production). While some security solutions, such as perimeter security, network security, and detective controls, should be applied across all environments, other security solutions may be necessary only for production workloads. For example, comprehensive log ingestion and analysis for non-production workload, or malware scanning for non-critical storage buckets, may not be required, whereas these controls are typically essential for production environments. Organization should review their workloads and apply appropriate security controls to internal development or test environments.

Recommended approach:

- **Classify environments:** Environments such as development, testing, staging, and production.
- **Define security controls**: Define security controls that need to be applied at the organization level and the security controls that need to be applied at the workload layer.
- **Apply controls selectively**: Organizations need to apply stricter controls to production and internet-facing systems, but can re-evaluate security controls for non-production environments. However, the organization should document such exceptions for audit requirements.
- **Ensure segmentation between environments**: Maintain strict isolation between different environments to ensure that a compromise in a non-production environment should not impact production workloads.

Evaluating cloud-native and third party security tools

Many organizations are using security solutions such as firewalls, antivirus, and intrusion detection systems for their on-premise environment. However, when workloads are migrated to the cloud, organizations need to re-evaluate security solutions, as many of the hardware-based security products, like traditional firewalls, IDS, and IPS, may become less relevant after cloud migration.

The choice between commercial security tools and cloud-native options depends on several considerations, such as:

- **Service integration**: Cloud native security solutions integrate tightly with cloud services you already use and can provide a better price-performance ratio. For example, if your organization uses AWS CloudFront for a content delivery network, you may benefit more from AWS Shield Advanced and AWS WAF for DDoS protection than from third-party alternatives. Similarly, Azure-native security services often integrate more seamlessly with Azure resources than third-party tools.

- **Application support**: Your workloads may use the latest technologies that security solutions might not support. For Example, when deploying SAST or DAST, ensure the security solution leveraged supports the programming languages your applications use. Similarly, when deploying endpoint security, verify that all your endpoint types are supported by the security solution deployed.
- **Compliance fit**: Security and compliance requirements may necessitate specific controls, and the security products you deploy should meet these compliance requirements. Create a detailed matrix that maps your compliance requirements to the required security controls and ensure your chosen solutions provide complete coverage.
- **Skills availability**: Your organization should have the skills to manage the deployed security products, including any reconfiguration requirements. Cloud-native tools often have a lower learning curve for teams already familiar with the cloud platform, while commercial tools may require specialized expertise.
- **Investment maximization**: Consider consuming existing license commitments before switching tools. If you have invested in commercial security tools and have active licenses, it may be more cost-effective to continue using them until the licenses expire, especially if they meet your security requirements adequately.
- **Multi-cloud compatibility**: For hybrid or multi-cloud environments, platform-agnostic tools may provide better consistency and simplified management. Using different native security tools for each cloud platform increases complexity and may create security gaps at the boundaries between environments.

Leverage Free Tier inclusions

Cloud providers offer Free Tiers for many security services. Understanding these limits can help you design solutions that remain within free usage thresholds or minimize costs once those thresholds are exceeded. For example, in AWS, several security services are available at no additional cost:

- AWS IAM
- AWS Shield Standard
- AWS Security Hub (first 30 days)
- Amazon Inspector (first 15 days)
- GuardDuty (30-day trial for foundational threat detection)

Creating a comprehensive inventory of free security features across your cloud providers helps identify opportunities to leverage Free Tier limits before incurring charges for paid options.

Use commitment-based savings where available

Just like compute and storage services, some security tools offer discounted pricing for long-term or volume-based commitments. For example, AWS may offer discounted rates on Shield Advanced monthly subscriptions and data transfer charges if you commit to specific terms and usage levels. Consult your cloud provider or partner to check eligibility for commitment based pricing or volume discounts. These savings can significantly reduce costs for large environments.

Pre-empt cost impact using free trials and simulations

Many security services offer a trial period to evaluate both their features and pricing impact. Organizations should use this opportunity to simulate workloads and estimate real-world costs. This will help avoid unexpected bills when adopting new security services.

For example, enabling GuardDuty for a large S3 bucket with billions of objects could significantly increase the overall bill. Before implementing such controls, conduct a thorough cost analysis using available estimation features to make informed decisions.

Automate and archive logs efficiently

Logging is critical, but storing security logs for long periods can become expensive. For low-risk workloads or internal workloads, consider reducing log retention duration (For example, from 90 to 30 days) if allowed by compliance requirements, or explore cost-effective storage solutions for long-term log retention.

Recommendations for log management:

- Use storage lifecycle policies to move logs to cold and cheaper storage tiers (e.g., AWS S3 Glacier or Azure Archive).
- Compress logs before storing them to reduce storage costs.
- Retain logs only as long as required by your audit policy.

Service-specific cost optimization strategies

Now, let us explore strategies for optimizing specific cloud-native security services. While these strategies are illustrated using AWS and Azure security services, the underlying concepts are broadly applicable to other cloud platforms, such as Google Cloud, especially when using comparable services. The aim is to help reduce unnecessary security costs while maintaining a strong security posture.

Identity and access management

Most IAM services in AWS, such as IAM roles, policies, and groups, are free to use. However, some services in the IAM portfolio have paid features, such as AWS IAM Access Analyzer and Amazon Cognito. The following section provides recommendations to optimize Amazon Cognito charges.

Amazon Cognito optimization strategies

Amazon Cognito provides authentication and authorization services and is priced based on MAUs and add-on features such as data synchronization. Refer to *Figure 9.5* for more details on the Amazon Cognito pricing model.

Strategies to reduce Cognito costs:

- **Minimize MAUs**: A user is counted as an MAU when your application generates an identity operation for that user within a calendar month, such as sign-up, sign-in, token refresh, password change, or attribute updates. Try to minimize operations that can trigger MAU charges unnecessarily (e.g., **`AdminGetUser`** calls and frequent token refreshes).
- **Efficient user management**: When managing users, doing audits, and generating user reports, consider using the **`ListUsers`** API, which does not activate users and therefore doesn't count toward MAU charges.
- **Optimize MFA usage**:
  - o SMS-based **multi-factor authentication** (**MFA**) incurs additional charges and can become expensive. Bad actors can also inflate SMS usage through bots.
  - o Consider **time-based one-time passwords** (**TOTP**) as a more cost-effective alternative.
  - o If SMS is mandatory, filter suspicious requests by checking IP addresses or phone numbers before triggering SMS messages.
- **Disable advanced security for federated users**: Advanced security features, like compromised credentials check, incur extra charges. Enable them only for local Cognito users, not federated identities that authenticate via third party identity providers (e.g., Google or Facebook sign-ins).
- **Audit unused user pools**: Remove any inactive or experimental pools that might still be generating charges.

Detective controls

AWS offers several detection-oriented services, such as Amazon GuardDuty, Security Hub, and Amazon Inspector. These services monitor environments for misconfigurations, threats, and vulnerabilities, but costs can scale quickly with increases in data volume and evaluation frequency. Let us explore strategies to optimize the cost of detection-oriented services.

Amazon GuardDuty

GuardDuty analyzes logs such as CloudTrail events, DNS queries, and VPC flow logs for suspicious activity. It is charged based on the volume of data analyzed and the protection plans enabled (e.g., S3, EKS, RDS, Lambda). Refer to *Figure 9.6* for details on GuardDuty pricing.

To optimize GuardDuty, follow the following steps:

1. **Disable in unused regions**: If you restrict regions using control tower or SCPs and have no resources deployed in those regions, consider disabling or suspending GuardDuty in those regions. GuardDuty processes global CloudTrail events in each region, resulting in costs even in inactive regions.
2. **Filter malware scans**: GuardDuty malware protection provides options to include or exclude specific Amazon EC2 instances and other resources. Use inclusion or exclusion tags to limit scans to critical EC2 instances and EBS volumes instead of wide scanning of EC2 and EBS volumes.
3. **Evaluate protection plans and applicability**:
    - Enable S3 protection only for sensitive buckets.
    - Use EKS protection for high-risk clusters.
    - Consider whether RDS and Lambda protection are necessary for all environments or can be limited to specific resources.
4. **Monitor API usage**: Third-party CSPM tools often make frequent API calls to AWS services (e.g., every 5 minutes). This can cause increased CloudTrail volume and lead to increased GuardDuty charges. Analyze the CSPM settings and reduce polling frequency.

Amazon Inspector

Amazon Inspector automatically scans EC2 instances, Lambda functions, and container images for vulnerabilities. To optimize Amazon Inspector charges:

- **Use the 15-day free trial**: Understand potential cost impact before enabling at scale.
- **Limit scope of scans**:
    - Scan only production workloads and critical images.
    - Set exclusion rules for temporary or non-critical resources.
- **Remove unused and idle resources**:
    - Remove stale images from ECR, as scanning old and unused images adds no security value but increases cost.

  - Terminate idle EC2 instances and Lambdas, as scanning is not required for such instances.

- **Shift scanning left**: Perform vulnerability scanning during CI/CD stages to reduce runtime inspection costs. Leverage the concept of immutable infrastructure to avoid scanning during runtime.
- **Implement auto scaling**: Use auto scaling and CloudWatch to ensure only active resources are scanned.
- **Immutable infrastructure**: Adopt containerized, immutable architectures to reduce unnecessary scan events on transient workloads.

AWS Security Hub

AWS Security Hub aggregates findings from AWS services and third-party tools and evaluates resources against security standards like CIS or PCI. Refer to *Figure 9.7* for the Security Hub pricing model. To optimize AWS Security Hub charges:

- **Use free trial**: Start with the 30-day free trial to monitor your expected monthly costs.
- **Disable checks for global resources (like IAM) in all but one region**: IAM-related checks are global. If enabled in every region, they are evaluated multiple times, generating duplicate costs. Keep these controls active in only one region (usually the home region).
- **Limit use in non-active regions**: Use SCPs to restrict service deployments in inactive regions. This minimizes duplicate findings and config checks.
- **Avoid redundant Config rules**: Avoid duplicating checks across AWS Config and Security Hub. Teams should spend time evaluating Config rules and conformance packs to reduce the overlap with Security Hub.
- **Disable redundant checks**: Disable controls that do not apply to your workloads or compliance frameworks.

Infrastructure protection

This category includes services like AWS Shield (Standard and Advanced) and AWS WAF.

AWS Shield Advanced

AWS Shield Advanced costs $3,000/month per organization, with additional charges for **data transfer out** (**DTO**). However, it also provides credits for AWS WAF usage, which can offset some of the costs related to WAF deployments. To optimize Shield Advanced charges:

- **Consolidate billing**: If you have multiple payer accounts, coordinate with your AWS account team to consolidate Shield Advanced billing across the organization.

- **Leverage WAF bundling**: Enable AWS Shield Advanced for workloads currently using AWS WAF to benefit from the inclusion of the WAF service in Shield Advanced pricing as per the defined limit.
- **Enable only for critical workloads**: Deploy Shield Advanced only on externally facing business-critical workloads, especially those prone to volumetric attacks.

Azure DDoS protection

Similar to AWS, follow the given steps to optimize Azure DDoS protection related charges:

- **Tenant-wide protection**: A single Azure DDoS protection plan (approximately $2,944/month) covers up to 100 public IPs across your entire tenant. To optimize costs, avoid purchasing separate plans for different subscriptions when one tenant-wide plan can sufficiently protect all required resources.
- **IP protection tier**: If you only have a few public-facing resources (for example, less than 15 public IPs), use the DDoS IP protection tier, which is billed per individual IP (approximately $199/month) rather than a flat monthly fee.

AWS WAF

WAF pricing is based on the number of web ACLs, the number of rules per ACL, request volume, and additional features like bot control and fraud control. Refer to *Figure 9.2* to understand AWS WAF charges.

To optimize WAF charges:

- **Prioritize free managed rule sets**: Use core rule sets or IP reputation lists, which are free. Add paid rules (e.g., bot control) selectively and only if required.
- **Use scope-down statements**: Apply WAF rules only to critical endpoints, reducing the number of rule evaluations.
- **Log filtering**: Log only essential requests. Use log filters to avoid logging benign or known traffic, which can lower destination logging costs.
- **Use edge services**: Route requests through CloudFront before WAF to reduce unnecessary traffic reaching backend services.

Azure Firewall

Azure Firewall pricing depends on deployment hours and the volume of data processed. To optimize Azure Firewall–related charges:

- Use Azure Firewall Basic for low-throughput or non-production workloads.
- Right-size firewall deployments based on actual traffic patterns.

- Avoid routing non-essential traffic through the firewall.
- Consolidate firewall instances where possible to reduce deployment-hour charges.
- Use Azure Firewall Policy Analytics to identify and remove unused or redundant rules that increase processing overhead.

Data protection services

Data security services such as AWS KMS and Secrets Manager are essential, but can become expensive if not managed carefully.

AWS Key Management Service

Key Management Service (**KMS**) charges for active keys and API calls (e.g., encrypt, decrypt). Some of the steps for optimizing KMS include:

1. **Delete unused keys**: Remove old or inactive **customer-managed keys** (**CMKs**) after confirming that keys are no longer needed. However, ensure the keys are not being used to encrypt any data, as deleting a key makes encrypted data unrecoverable.
2. **Limit key rotation**: Rotating keys increases costs, as each rotation creates a new version. Organizations need to define an appropriate key rotation frequency considering both security and cost considerations.
3. **Use S3 bucket keys**: When using SSE-KMS with Amazon S3, enable S3 bucket keys to reduce API calls. This generates a temporary intermediate key per bucket, reducing the number of calls to KMS.
4. **Data key caching**: For applications with high encryption demands, use data key caching to reduce redundant KMS calls. Teams should balance performance and security by tuning cache size and **time-to-live** (**TTL**) settings.
5. **Avoid duplicate logging**: Disable KMS event logging in CloudTrail across multiple trails unless needed for compliance. Logging encrypt/decrypt operations in multiple trails can inflate CloudTrail and KMS costs. Alternatively, use Cloud Trail event selectors to limit what gets logged.

AWS Secrets Manager

AWS Secrets Manager helps store, rotate, and manage application credentials securely. Pricing is based on the number of secrets stored and the number of API requests. To optimize AWS Secrets Manager charges:

- **Remove unused secrets**: Regularly audit and delete secrets that are no longer used.
- **Use parameter store for basic needs**: For environment variables or static values, the systems manager parameter store may be more cost-effective.

- **Implement client-side caching**: Use client-side caching libraries to reduce the number of API calls by serving secrets from a local cache. These libraries update the cache hourly, ensuring applications use the most current secret values.
- **Leverage service integrations**: Use extensions for services like AWS Lambda and Kubernetes (Secrets Store CSI) to enable caching of secrets in serverless, container, and event-driven architectures.
- **Monitor replicated secrets**: Each replica is billed separately. Only replicate secrets across regions if necessary for availability or compliance.

Azure Key Vault

Azure Key Vault pricing is based on the number of operations (approximately $0.03 per 10,000 transactions) and the storage of keys and secrets. Optimizing Azure Key Vault charges is primarily about managing transaction volume. Some optimization strategies organizations can follow include:

- **Implement client-side caching**: A common cause of high Azure Key Vault charges is applications fetching secrets or keys on every web request. Instead, retrieve keys during the first request and cache them in memory where appropriate.
- **Remove unused keys, secrets, and certificates**: Periodically review and delete unused objects to reduce storage and management overhead.
- **Use Azure Managed Identities (system-assigned or user-assigned)**: Managed Identities are a free feature of Microsoft Entra ID and eliminate the need to store credentials in Key Vault, reducing secret management operations.

By applying these targeted optimization levers for each service, organizations can significantly reduce the cost of cloud security services while maintaining the protection your organization needs. These strategies should be revisited regularly as workloads evolve and security services expand.

In the final section of this chapter, we will explore how to build a prioritized action plan that combines general principles with service-specific recommendations, so your team can take practical, phased steps toward a cost-efficient, secure cloud.

Developing a prioritized action plan

Cloud security is a broad and complex area, and making changes for cost savings purposes requires a thoughtful and well-structured approach. Organizations must develop a clear action plan that balances risk management with cost efficiency. Any changes made to optimize costs must not compromise your security posture and regulatory compliance. The following step-by-step approach will help you develop a structured action plan that focuses on high-impact areas first, minimizing risk while maximizing cost savings. Refer to *Chapter 4, Moving from Cost Observability to Cost Optimization,* to understand the process for developing a priority action plan.

Sample prioritization framework

After understanding different security services, cost management tools for monitoring usage and spend, and the key levers for optimizing security services cost, follow the given steps to develop an implementation plan for security services cost optimization:

1. **Document security and compliance requirements**: Start by capturing all the security and compliance requirements specific to your workloads. This may include industry standards (like PCI DSS, HIPAA, or ISO 27001), regulatory obligations, or internal policies. Create a comprehensive mapping that shows which security services address each requirement. This helps prevent accidentally removing controls that are required for critical compliance requirements.
2. **Identify high-cost security services**: Use cloud billing and cost visualization dashboards to identify which security services contribute most to your monthly cloud bills. For AWS, tools like Cost Explorer, the Billing console, and CUR can help identify top cost contributing security services (for example, GuardDuty, AWS Config, or Security Hub), depending on your environment and usage patterns. This helps narrow the scope and focus your optimization efforts on services that will have the greatest impact.
3. **Break down the cost drivers**: Once you have identified the services that incur the highest charges, analyze which specific components or features are driving these charges. For example, if GuardDuty is responsible for high costs, analyze which specific GuardDuty components (e.g., VPC flow logs, DNS logs, or malware scans) are contributing the most. This breakdown provides clarity on which specific features or usage patterns are responsible for the charges.
4. **Understand the pricing models**: Each cloud service has its own billing unit and pricing structure. Understanding this is crucial for identifying opportunities to optimize cost. Some services charge per API call, others by the volume of data scanned or stored. For example, AWS KMS is charged based on the number of encryption requests, while AWS Secrets Manager is charged per stored secret and API call made. Knowing exactly how services are billed helps identify which metrics to optimize.
5. **Prioritize optimization actions**: Once you have identified potential optimization opportunities, evaluate and prioritize them using a consistent set of criteria:
   - **Cost-saving potential**: Estimate the monthly or annual savings for each action.
   - **Implementation effort**: *Is it a quick configuration change or a complex redesign?*
   - **Risk to operations or compliance**: *Evaluate potential impacts on security effectiveness or audit readiness?*
   - **Business impact**: *Does it impact production systems or sensitive environments?*
   - **Resource availability**: Determine if you have the necessary team expertise and tools available to implement the changes.

Create a simple scoring matrix (High/Medium/Low) for each criterion, then rank actions accordingly. Begin with low-effort, high-impact opportunities to gain early wins and build momentum for broader optimization efforts.

6. **Audit and assess the impact**: After implementing changes, conduct audits to ensure that your security posture has not been weakened. Confirm that all regulatory and compliance obligations are still being met. Document all changes along with their security impact assessment to maintain an audit trail for compliance purposes.

Conclusion

Security remains a top priority for organizations moving to the cloud, consistently ranking among the top five areas of concern for cloud-first strategies. Enterprises are not only focused on strengthening security postures but are also increasingly aware of the need to optimize costs while maintaining compliance and protection.

In this chapter, we examined how cloud-native security services spanning different pillars, such as identity and access management, detective controls, infrastructure protection, and data protection, can be aligned with cost optimization efforts. We discussed how to gain visibility into cloud security related costs using billing and other cost observability tools and explored both generic cost optimization approaches and service-specific strategies to reduce costs across services such as Amazon GuardDuty, Inspector, Security Hub, WAF, KMS, and Secrets Manager.

We also outlined a structured framework to create a prioritized action plan that focuses on identifying cost drivers, understanding pricing models, and implementing changes without compromising on risk or compliance. The goal is not just to save costs, but to do so in a responsible and strategic manner that maintains the integrity of workloads deployed on the cloud.

In the next chapter, we will focus on data transfer optimization. In traditional on-premises environments, network costs are generally fixed due to upfront investments in infrastructure such as LANs, WANs, or MPLS circuits. However, in cloud environments, data transfer costs, especially outbound traffic, can quickly become a significant line item in the cloud bill if left unchecked. We will explore the different types of cloud data transfers and strategies that can help you manage and reduce those expenses.

CHAPTER 10
Optimizing Data Transfer Charges on Cloud

Introduction

In traditional on-premises environments, organizations typically estimate bandwidth needs based on user activity and data traffic. They invest in **local area networks** (**LANs**), **wide area networks** (**WANs**), purchase **multiprotocol label switching** (**MPLS**) circuits, and secure internet lines from **internet service providers** (**ISPs**) based on bandwidth requirements. This typically involves fixed costs with upfront payments and monthly subscriptions, regardless of actual data usage. Additionally, most of the internal network setup, such as LANs, is already provisioned and does not need to be factored in for new deployments.

However, in the cloud world, data transfer costs are based on actual usage and can vary from month to month. Cloud providers charge for data transfers between regions, between **availability zones** (**AZs**), or for data transfer out to the internet, and the cost depends on the routing mechanism and volume of data transferred. Many organizations migrating workloads to the cloud or developing cloud-native applications often overlook data transfer considerations during the design phase. As a result, they may encounter unexpected increases in cloud bills compared to initial estimates, leading to budget overruns and leadership questioning the **return on investment** (**ROI**) of their cloud initiatives.

Among all cloud service costs, **data transfer** (**DTO**) is one of the most challenging areas to optimize. Teams often find it difficult to gain insights into application data transfer patterns and identify which specific resources contribute most to these costs. This chapter examines various types of data transfer charges based on source and target resources and routing mechanisms. We will explore the charges associated with data transfer and identify key optimization strategies. Although the examples in this chapter use AWS and Azure, the core principles and optimization strategies discussed can be applied across all major cloud platforms, including Google Cloud.

Structure

In this chapter, we will discuss the following topics:

- Understanding cloud data transfer charges

- Monitoring data transfer cost using native tools
- Levers for optimizing cloud data transfer charges
- Developing a prioritized action plan

Objectives

By the end of this chapter, the readers will have a clear understanding of different data transfer types and their associated networking services charges. They will learn how data transfer between regions, availability zones, and the internet impacts your cloud costs. We will explore tools that can help you analyze data transfer usage and identify which workloads and services incur the highest data transfer charges. They will also review best practices for optimizing data transfer charges without compromising application performance, scalability, and resiliency requirements. Finally, they will be able to create a prioritized optimization plan that aligns with your organization's sprint or release cycles, helping teams systematically reduce unnecessary data transfer charges without disrupting operations. While AWS and Azure are used for illustrations throughout this chapter, the insights and techniques shared here are broadly applicable to other cloud platforms as well.

Understanding cloud data transfer charges

Cloud providers such as AWS, Azure, and Google Cloud have built global infrastructures consisting of regions, AZs, and edge locations. These global infrastructures help organizations meet data residency, high availability, and resiliency requirements. However, when data moves across these boundaries—whether between availability zones, between regions, or out to the internet, data transfer charges may be applicable.

When organizations migrate workloads to the cloud or deploy new applications in the cloud, their primary focus is often on services such as compute, storage, and databases. Organizations also deploy security and observability services to manage their workloads in the cloud. However, data transfer charges, which can significantly impact the monthly cloud bill, are often neglected. Data transfer charges can account for a large part of the total cloud bill, especially for:

- Applications serving global users.
- Non-functional requirements, such as achieving multiple nines of availability (e.g., 99.99% uptime).
- Multi-region architectures for disaster recovery and resiliency.
- Data-intensive workloads with large volumes of data movement.

A well-designed architecture that considers data transfer patterns can help reduce data transfer costs by 30-50%. This section explains the categories of data transfer, common data transfer methods, and the key factors that influence data transfer related charges, so that organizations can design workloads that are highly available and resilient while remaining cost efficient. However, not all data transfer is charged, and the charging policy varies greatly by cloud provider. For example, one cloud provider may have charges for intra availability zone data transfers while another cloud provider may not charge for the same. It is important to understand data transfer patterns and validate the charging policies of your cloud provider.

In the following section, we will explore the different types of data transfer and examine whether each type is subject to charges or free of cost. You will also discover many commonalities in how data transfer is priced across different cloud providers, as the underlying principles governing data transfer charges are largely similar.

Categories of data transfer

Data transfer charges vary depending on the network boundaries traversed by data traffic. It is important for organizations to understand their network architecture and the flow of data across network boundaries defined by the cloud provider. Let us look into network boundaries on AWS and how it impacts data transfer cost, as shown in *Figure 10.1*:

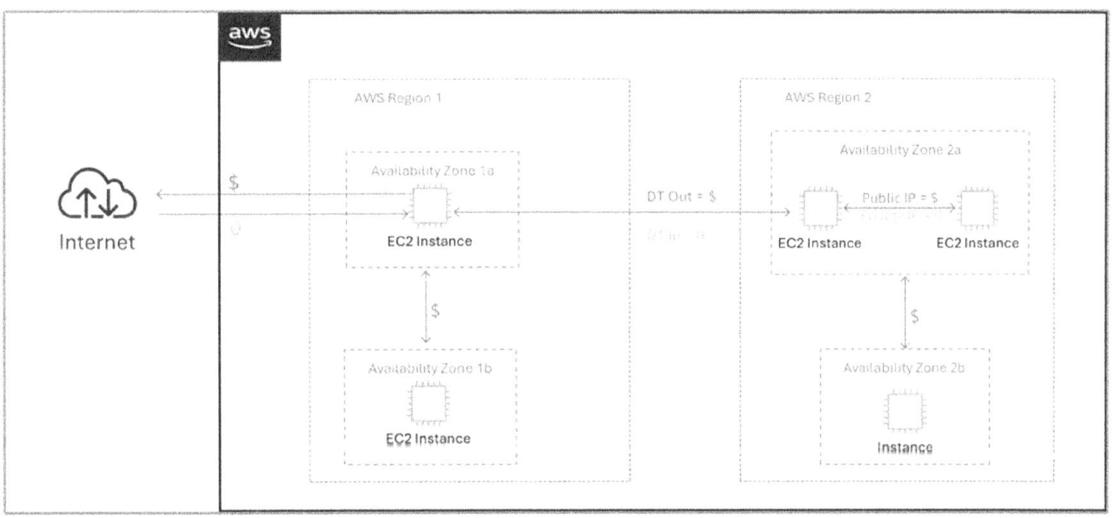

***Figure 10.1**: AWS global infrastructure*

Data transfer between the cloud and the Internet

Data transfer between cloud and Internet, as shown in *Figure 10.2*, is one of the most common and visible forms of data transfer. This occurs whenever users access cloud-hosted applications, download content, upload files, or when IoT devices send data to cloud platforms.

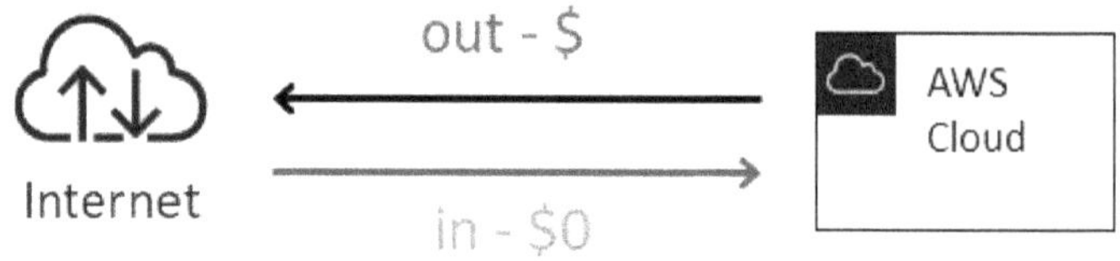

***Figure 10.2**: AWS cloud to Internet data transfer*

This can be further categorized into:

- **Inbound traffic (Internet to Cloud)**: Typically free across AWS, Azure, and GCP. This applies whether a user is uploading files to a web application or sending telemetry data from IoT devices.
- **Outbound traffic (Cloud to Internet)**: Usually charged per GB and varies by region from where traffic is sent to the Internet. *Figure 10.3* shows the pricing of sending data from the Ohio region to the Internet in AWS:

	Pricing
Data Transfer IN To Amazon EC2 From Internet	
All data transfer in	$0.00 per GB
Data Transfer OUT From Amazon EC2 To Internet	
AWS customers receive 100GB of data transfer out to the internet free each month, aggregated across all AWS Services and Regions (except China and GovCloud). The 100 GB free tier for data transfer out to the internet is global and does not apply separately or individually to AWS Regions.	
First 10 TB / Month	$0.09 per GB
Next 40 TB / Month	$0.085 per GB
Next 100 TB / Month	$0.07 per GB
Greater than 150 TB / Month	$0.05 per GB

***Figure 10.3**: DTO pricing to the Internet*

The pricing of data transfer from the AWS region to the Internet shows that:

- Inbound data traffic is free.
- Outbound data transfer is charged as per the tiering mentioned. An organization can leverage the benefits of aggregate pricing to reduce the cost per GB of data transfer.

Azure data transfer to the Internet, a comparable scenario

In Microsoft Azure, data transfer between Azure services and the Internet follows a similar principle:

- **Inbound data transfer (Internet to Azure)**: Free of cost across all Azure regions. This includes users uploading documents to an Azure Blob Storage account, developers pushing code to an Azure VM, or IoT devices sending telemetry data to Azure IoT Hub.
- **Outbound data transfer (Azure to Internet)**: Outbound data transfer occurs when data leaves the Azure network to go to the Internet and is charged per GB of data transferred. Pricing varies by region (e.g., Asia, Europe, North America). Azure follows a tiered pricing model, where higher monthly data transfer volumes reduce per-GB costs.

Data transfer between regions

An organization may need to replicate data between regions for disaster recovery, compliance, or latency reasons. The data transfer between two regions incurs cross-region data transfer charges, as shown in *Figure 10.4*:

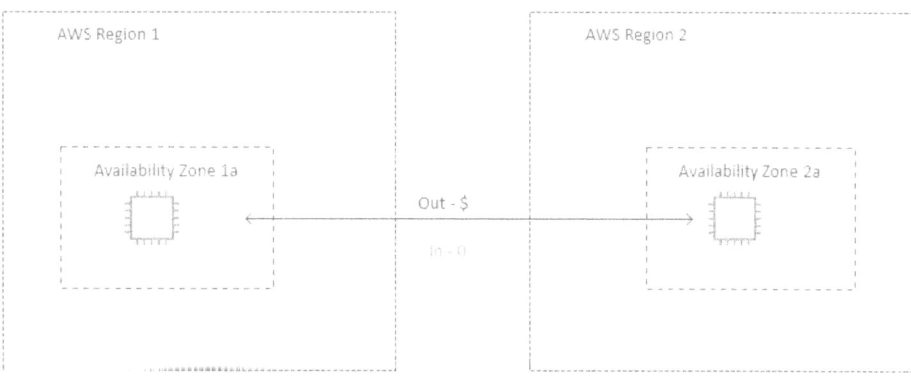

***Figure 10.4**: Inter-region data transfer*

Let us examine how different cloud providers apply charges for inter-region data transfers:

- **AWS deployment**: Outbound traffic from region 1 to region 2 is charged, while inbound traffic at region 2 is free. Pricing varies depending on the destination region. Refer to *Figure 10.5* for inter-region data transfer charges from the Ohio region:

Data Transfer OUT From Amazon EC2 To	
Amazon CloudFront	$0.00 per GB
AWS GovCloud (US-West)	$0.02 per GB
AWS GovCloud (US-East)	$0.02 per GB
Africa (Cape Town)	$0.02 per GB
Asia Pacific (Hong Kong)	$0.02 per GB
Asia Pacific (Hyderabad)	$0.02 per GB
Asia Pacific (Jakarta)	$0.02 per GB
Asia Pacific (Malaysia)	$0.02 per GB
Asia Pacific (Melbourne)	$0.02 per GB
Asia Pacific (Mumbai)	$0.02 per GB

***Figure 10.5**: Inter-region data transfer pricing for AWS*

- **Azure deployment**: Similar to AWS, Outbound transfer from one region to another region incurs inter-region data transfer charges, while inbound is free. Azure has pricing based on geographic grouping, as shown in *Figure 10.6*:

Inter Region

Intra-continental Data Transfer	Price
Between regions within North America Between regions within Europe	$0.02 per GB
Between regions within Asia Between regions within Oceania Between regions within Middle East and Africa	$0.08 per GB
Between regions within South America	$0.16 per GB

Inter-continental Data Transfer	Price
From North America to other continents From Europe to other continents	$0.05 per GB
From Asia to other continents From Oceania to other continents From Africa to other continents	$0.08 per GB
From South America to other continents	$0.16 per GB

***Figure 10.6**: Inter-region data transfer pricing for Azure*

Data transfer between availability zones in the same region

For high availability requirements, workloads are deployed across multiple AZs. For example, an app cluster may have one node in AZ-1a and another in AZ-1b, as shown in *Figure 10.7*. Every replication or data transfer between two availability zones is charged as inter-AZ data transfer.

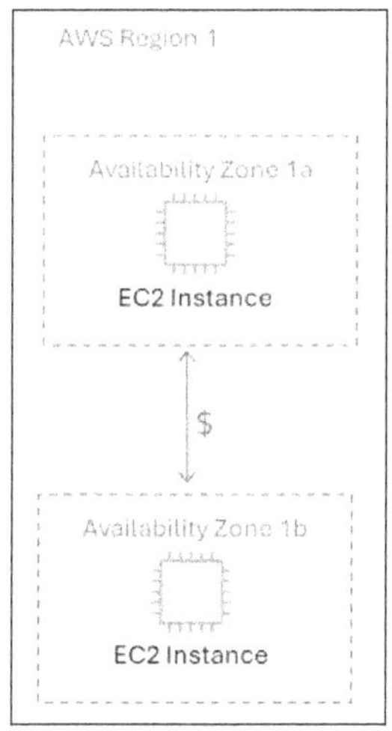

***Figure 10.7**: Inter-AZ data transfer*

Let us examine how cloud providers charge for inter-AZ data transfers:

- **AWS deployments**: In AWS, both inbound and outbound data transfer are charged at $0.01 per GB.
- **Azure deployments**: Azure does not charge for data transfer between availability zones in the same region, regardless of private or public IP usage.

Data transfer within the same availability zone

Data transfer within the same AZ is often free, but there are exceptions depending on the cloud providers. Let us use AWS as an example to understand these exceptions:

- Data between EC2 instances in the same AZ is free if using private IP addresses.
- Using public or Elastic IP addresses—even within the same AZ—incurs $0.01/GB each way.

Data transfer within the same availability zone in Azure is free. For example, when data is exchanged between resources located in the same AZ (such as two virtual machines in the same AZ), no data transfer charges apply, regardless of whether private or public IP addresses are used.

Data transfer between services

Apart from the data transfer category based on network boundaries traversed, it is also important to understand the services engaged in data transfer. Data transfer charges may vary depending on both the network boundaries traversed and the services involved. Refer to *Figure 10.8* to understand how AWS data transfer charges depend on the services involved in data transfer:

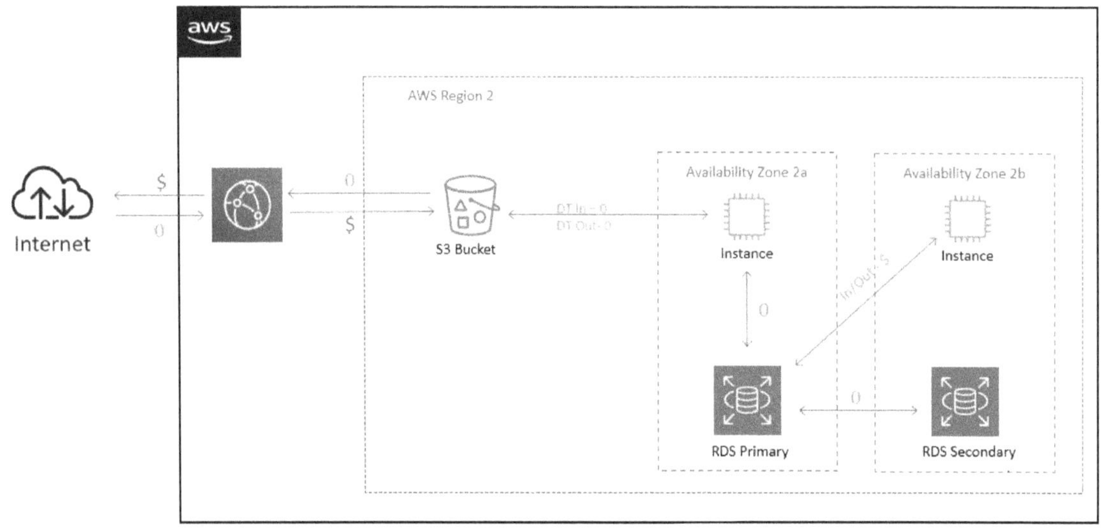

***Figure 10.8**: Data transfer between services*

Figure 10.8 illustrates the impact of AWS services engaged in data transfer. For example:

- Data transfer between EC2 and RDS in the same AZ is free, while data transfer between EC2 and RDS across availability zones is charged as per Inter-AZ transfer pricing.
- Data transfer between S3 and EC2 Instance in the same region is Free.
- Data transferred from origin services like S3 and EC2 to CloudFront is complementary, but data transfer from CloudFront to the origin server is charged.

The team should review service specific data transfer pricing to understand the charges and any exceptions.

Data transfer methods and their cost impact

The networking services associated with data transfer may impact data transfer charges, especially when traffic passes through managed network services. An organization may be using different network services for security, reliability, and latency requirements, such as NAT Gateways, AWS Direct Connect, Azure ExpressRoute, or Site-to-Site VPN. If any network services are in the path of your data transfer, you will incur additional costs for those services, such as network service runtime charges and data processing charges, in addition to standard data transfer charges. For example, if an Amazon EC2 instance in a private subnet accesses the internet through a NAT Gateway hosted in a public subnet, you will incur charges for NAT Gateway runtime hours, data processing, and Inter-AZ data transfer for communication between the EC2 instance and the NAT Gateway.

Common AWS and Azure data transfer methods:

- **NAT Gateway**: NAT Gateway provides internet access to instances hosted in private subnets within a Virtual Private Cloud. Charges include a per-hour running charge for NAT Gateway provisioned and a per-GB data processing fee for data transferred via NAT Gateway.
- **PrivateLink**: Charges include a per endpoint-hour fee and a per-GB data processing fee for data transferred through the endpoint.
- **Transit gateway**: Charges include a per attachment-hour fee and a per-GB data processing charge for data routed through the transit gateway.
- **Site-to-Site VPN**: Charges include a per-hour fee for each VPN connection, in addition to standard data transfer charges.
- **AWS Direct Connect**: Charges include port-hour fees based on connection capacity, along with data transfer charges for outbound traffic from AWS to on-premises networks.
- **Azure ExpressRoute**: Charges include circuit-hour fees based on bandwidth tier, along with data transfer charges depending on the selected billing model.

Free Tier inclusions

Both AWS and Azure provide free inclusions for data transfer, which can be leveraged by organizations. For example, AWS Free Tier includes:

- All inbound data transfer is free.
- 100 GB outbound to the internet per month (across all services, excluding CloudFront).
- 1 TB outbound from CloudFront to the internet per month.

Azure Free Tier includes:

- All inbound data transfer to Azure services is free.
- A limited monthly outbound data transfer allowance to the Internet is included, as shown in *Figure 10.9*.
- Certain Azure services (such as Azure CDN) provide promotional free outbound data transfer quotas during trial periods.

Data Transfer	Price
Data Transfer In	Free
Data transfer within same Availability Zone	Free
Data transfer from Azure origin to Azure CDN'	Free
Data transfer from Azure origin to Azure Front Door Standard/Premium	Free

Internet Egress (routed via Microsoft Premium Global Network)

Source Continent	First 100 GB/Month	Next 10 TB/Month	Next 40 TB/Month	Next 100 TB/Month	Next 350 TB/Month
From North America, Europe to any destination	Free	$0.087 per GB	$0.083 per GB	$0.07 per GB	$0.05 per GB
From Asia (China excluded), Australia, MEA to any destination	Free	$0.12 per GB	$0.085 per GB	$0.082 per GB	$0.08 per GB
From South America to any destination	Free	$0.181 per GB	$0.175 per GB	$0.17 per GB	$0.16 per GB

***Figure 10.9**: Azure Free Tier inclusions*

Regional pricing variation

Data transfer pricing can vary significantly between regions, as shown in *Figure 10.4*. It is important to understand regional data transfer pricing variation when designing your disaster recovery architecture.

Commitment-based savings

If your organization is consistently transferring large volumes of data, you can reach out to a cloud provider and negotiate discounted rates in exchange for committing to a certain monthly data transfer volume. For example, if you have a sustained data transfer requirement exceeding several hundred terabytes per month, you can reach out to a cloud provider for custom pricing agreements.

Key factors influencing data transfer charges

Here is a recap of the key cost drivers of data transfer charges:

- **Network boundaries traversed**: Whether data moves within the same AZ, across AZs, between regions, or to the Internet.
- **Direction of transfer**: Inbound vs. outbound data transfer.
- **Services involved**: Pricing policies and per-GB charges may vary depending on the services engaged in data transfer.

- **Transfer methods**: Networking services such as NAT Gateway, Transit Gateway, VPN, Direct Connect, or ExpressRoute can introduce additional data processing and service-hour costs.
- **Tiered pricing**: Data transfer has a tiered pricing model and provides an advantage of lower per-GB charges as data transfer volume increases.
- **Region**: Data transfer charges may vary by region.
- **Free Tier allowances**: Limited amounts of data transfer may be free and can be useful for initial deployments and testing.

Monitoring data transfer cost using native tools

Data transfer charges can become a significant component of your cloud bill, especially when running workloads such as streaming services, cross-region backups, or multi-region applications. Data transfer charges are incurred when data moves across network boundaries, such as outbound to the Internet, between regions, or between AZs. Teams working on optimizing data transfer charges should consider questions such as:

- *Which data transfer category is costing the most? Is it data going out to the Internet, data moving between regions, or data moving between availability zones within the same region?*
- *Which service and specific resource is responsible for the data transfer? Is it an EC2 instance, an S3 bucket, a load balancer, or something else?*
- *What are the source and destination endpoints of data transfer? It is not enough to know the source doing the data transfer, but it is also important to identify the destination endpoint of the data transfer.*
- *What type of data is being transferred? Is it database queries, web traffic, file uploads, or backups?*

The answers to these questions are not always straightforward. Teams would need to combine information from multiple tools to get the information about the data transfer. This section explains how to use native tools from cloud providers such as AWS and Azure to monitor data transfer usage and costs, and how to correlate data with network monitoring tools like CloudWatch, VPC Flow Logs, and Azure Monitor.

Data transfer analysis in AWS

AWS provides several tools for monitoring service usage and associated charges, including data transfer costs. We have seen in the previous section how these tools can give deep insights into the usage and costs of different services. We will leverage these cost observability tools to get insights into data transfer usage and costs. Let us explore some of the key tools provided by AWS for monitoring and forecasting costs related to data transfer:

Category	Tool	Description
Cost Observability	AWS Billing console	View consolidated billing data, invoices and service wise charges. Cloud providers may not bundle data transfer charges under a common category, and the team will need to explore individual services to get insight into data transfer usage and cost.
	AWS Cost Explorer	Visualize data transfer cost and identify the services incurring these charges. Also, get insights into different data transfer categories and associate network service costs.
	AWS Cost and Usage Report	Provides granular, resource-level data about data transfer charges, which can be queried using Athena and visualized with QuickSight.
	Cost and Usage dashboard	Pre-built dashboards (via QuickSight), such as the cost intelligence dashboard, provide a simplified view of data transfer cost, including data transfer categories, network service charges, and top resources engaged in data transfer.
Cloud Observability services	AWS CloudWatch	AWS CloudWatch is a monitoring service that provides a wide range of metrics to deliver insights into various AWS services, including data transfer metrics that help measure the amount of data transferred by different services.
	VPC Flow Log	AWS VPC Flow Logs captures information about traffic flowing in and out of network interfaces within a VPC. Insights from VPC flow logs help in understanding traffic patterns and the type of data transferred between resources.

***Table 10.1**: Tools for analyzing usage and spend*

Reviewing data transfer costs with AWS Cost Explorer

AWS Cost Explorer is a visualization tool that helps you analyze data transfer usage and charges. With Cost Explorer, you can identify data transfer categories incurring the charges, the services involved in data transfer, as well as charges for network services like NAT Gateway, Site-to-Site VPN, or Direct Connect.

Let us look into the steps to understand charges by data transfer category:

1. Go to the AWS console and open **Billing and Cost Management**.
2. From the left panel, click on **Cost Explorer**.

3. Apply filters to analyze data transfer charges:
   - **Date Range**: Last 3 months
   - **Granularity**: Monthly
   - **Dimension**: Usage type
   - **Filter**: Usage type: Use the search filters depending on the data transfer category you want to analyze:
     - **Internet data transfer**: Search for **`DataTransfer-Out-Bytes`** and **`DataTransfer-In-Bytes`**.
     - **Inter-region transfer**: For AWS region-to-region transfer, AWS reports separate line items:
       - **`SourceRegion-DestinationRegion-AWS-Out-Bytes`** (outbound from source region).
       - **`SourceRegion-DestinationRegion-AWS-In-Bytes`** (inbound to destination region).
       - Search for **`%AWS-Out-Bytes%`** and **`%AWS-In-Bytes%`** to get charges related to Inter-region data transfer.
     - **Inter-AZ transfer**: Search for **`%DataTransfer-Regional-Bytes%`**

This analysis will show which regions generate the most data transfer and which categories incur the highest costs, as shown in *Figure 10.10*:

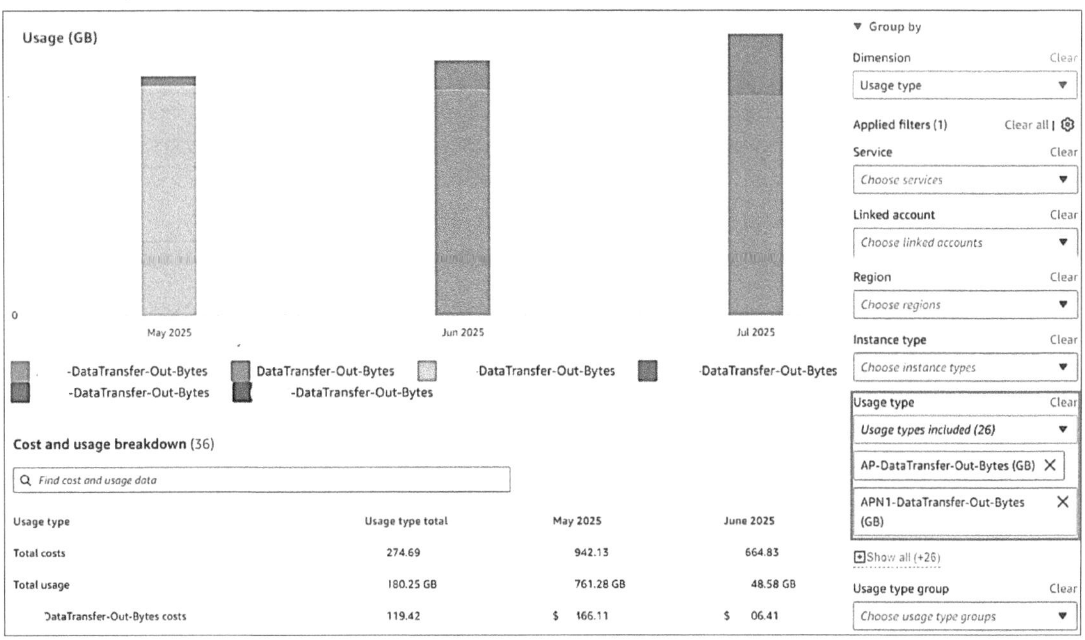

Figure 10.10: Analyzing data transfer category

You can then change the dimension to **Service** or **Linked Account** to identify specific services or accounts responsible for these transfers. *Figure 10.11* shows how applying the **Service** dimension helps in identifying services performing the data transfer:

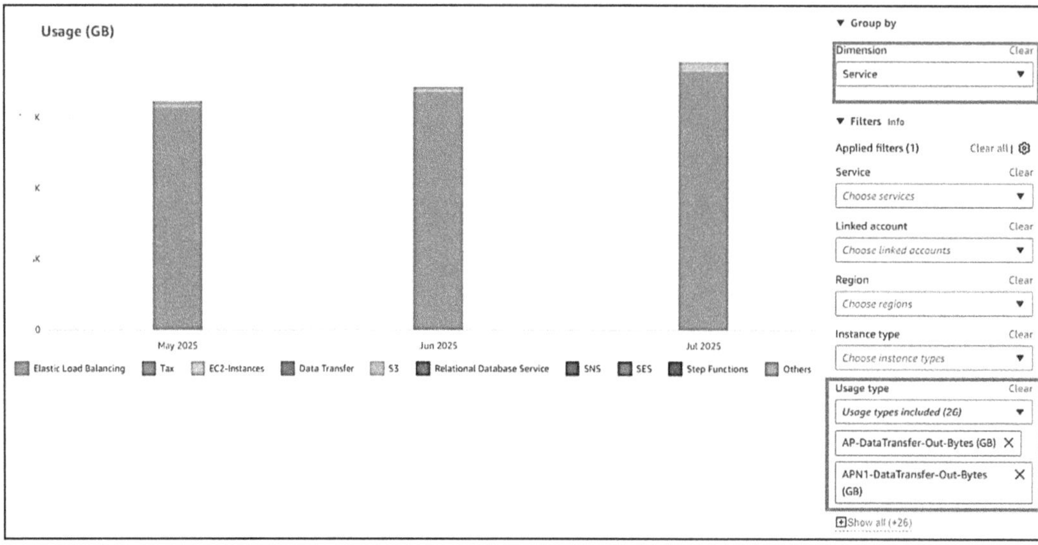

***Figure 10.11**: Data transfer by service*

Correlating Cost Explorer findings with Billing console

The AWS Billing console provides an invoice-style breakdown of your monthly charges. In the AWS Cost Explorer example from the previous section, we identified the services and region incurring the data transfer charges. Using this information, we can further investigate costs in the Billing console. Cloud providers like AWS do not always group all data transfer charges under one service or category, and you can drill down into individual services to identify network-related costs.

Steps to analyze data transfer charges:

1. Navigate to the AWS **Billing and Cost Management** console.
2. Click **Bills** under the **Billing** section.
3. Choose your billing period (e.g., current or last month).
4. Expand **Data Transfer** under **Charges by Service** to view costs for Internet DTO, inter-region data transfer, and inter-AZ data transfer. You will find information like shown in *Figure 10.12*.
5. Also expand other services (e.g., EC2, CloudFront, VPC) to see charges for related network services such as NAT Gateway, VPC Peering, or CloudFront data transfer.

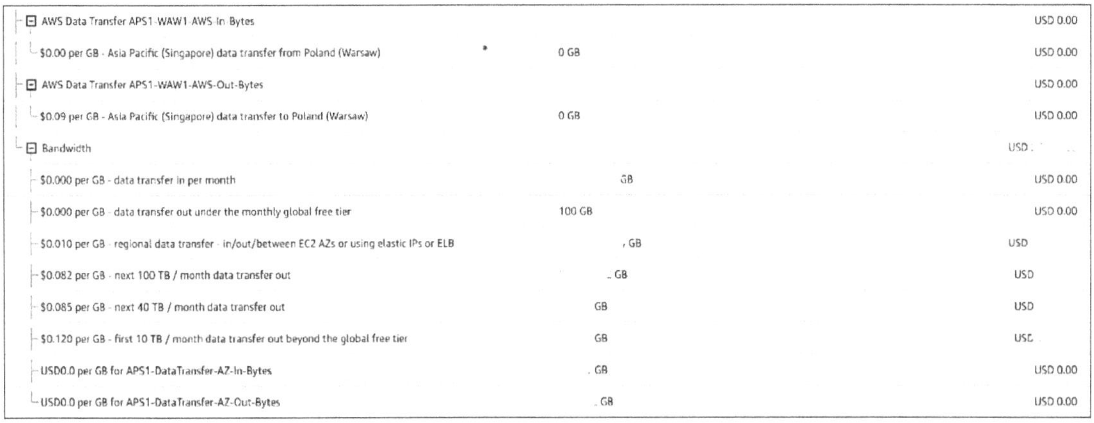

***Figure 10.12**: Using the Billing console for data transfer charges*

The information from the Billing console helps in validating findings from Cost Explorer as well as in understanding billing units and the price per billing unit for different data transfer categories.

Accessing cost and usage data with CUR

The AWS **Cost and Usage Reports** (**CUR**) provide access to a detailed billing dataset, containing per-resource, per-hour usage and cost records. The data from CUR queries helps in identifying resources performing the data transfer.

Some of the useful information that can be extracted from the CUR query includes:

- The AWS account and specific resource generating data transfer traffic.
- The source and destination locations of the data transfer (FromLocation and ToLocation fields).
- Data transfer category.
- Charges broken down by data transfer category, service, or individual resource ID.

SQL query

Resources by data transfer cost over a chosen time frame.

The following query highlights the top resources driving data transfer costs, including accounts, services, and source/destination details over a given time period of time:

```
SELECT
      line_item_product_code AS service,
      line_item_usage_account_id AS account_id,
      DATE_FORMAT(line_item_usage_start_date,'%Y-%m-%d') AS date,
      line_item_usage_type AS usage_type,
      product_from_location AS from_location,
      product_to_location AS to_location,
      product_product_family,
      line_item_resource_id AS resource_id,
      SUM(CAST(line_item_usage_amount AS DOUBLE)) AS sum_line_item_usage_
amount,
      SUM(CAST(line_item_unblended_cost AS DECIMAL(16,8))) AS sum_line_item_
unblended_cost
FROM  {your_cur_database.your_cur_table}
WHERE
    line_item_usage_start_date >= CAST('YYYY-MM-DD 00:00:00' AS TIMESTAMP)
    AND line_item_usage_start_date < CAST('YYYY-MM-DD 00:00:00' AS TIMESTAMP)
    AND product_product_family IN ('Data Transfer', 'DT-Data Transfer')
    AND line_item_line_item_type = 'Usage'
GROUP BY
    line_item_product_code,
    line_item_usage_account_id,
    DATE_FORMAT(line_item_usage_start_date, '%Y-%m-%d'),
    line_item_resource_id,
    line_item_usage_type,
    product_from_location,
    product_to_location,
    product_product_family
ORDER BY
    sum_line_item_unblended_cost DESC
```

Tips:

- Replace `your_cur_database.your_cur_table` with your actual table name.
- Modify the date range based on your analysis period.

Reviewing operational metrics with AWS CloudWatch

Cost observability tools such as AWS Cost Explorer, Billing console, and CUR help in getting insights into data transfer charges. After identifying resources with high data transfer costs, AWS CloudWatch can be used to examine operational metrics and understand usage patterns and anomalies. CloudWatch provides metrics such as:

- **EC2**: NetworkIn/NetworkOut (bytes), NetworkPacketsIn/NetworkPacketsOut
- **S3**: BytesDownloaded, BytesUploaded, NumberOfRequests
- **ELB/ALB**: ProcessedBytes, ConsumedLCUs
- **Log analysis**: CloudWatch Logs Insights for analyzing traffic and request patterns.

AWS VPC Flow Logs

VPC Flow Logs capture detailed information about network traffic flowing through your VPC, helping you understand exactly what type of data is being transferred between resources, as well as source and destination resource IDs. Steps for using VPC Flow logs are as follows:

1. Identify the services and resources driving high data transfer costs using AWS **Cost Explorer** or by using CUR queries.
2. In the EC2 console, select network interface(s) associated with the identified resources.
3. Enable VPC Flow Logs at the network interface, subnet, or VPC level. For the EC2 network interface, go to the **Flow logs** tab, click **Create flow log**.
4. Refer to *Figure 10.13* for enabling VPC Flow Logs
5. Configure the Flow Logs to deliver log data to CloudWatch or S3.
6. Once logs are available in CloudWatch Logs or S3, use **CloudWatch Logs Insights** (for CloudWatch Logs) or **Amazon Athena** (for S3) to query and analyze traffic details such as:
    - Source and destination IP addresses.
    - Bytes transferred.
    - Protocol and port numbers.

Refer to the following figure:

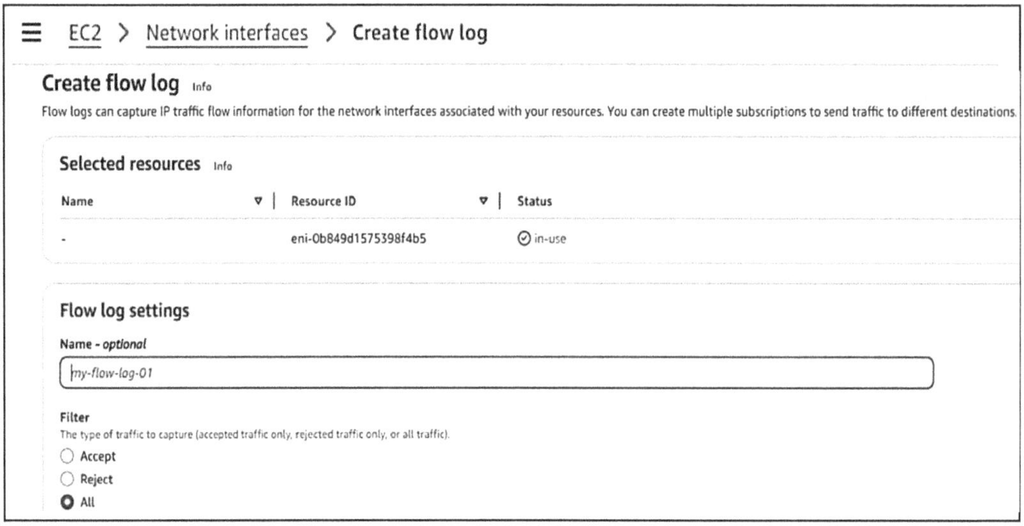

Figure 10.13: *Enabling VPC Flow Log*

Data transfer analysis in Azure

Azure provides a comprehensive suite of cost observability and monitoring tools that help analyze data transfer usage, identify high cost resources, and gain operational insights into traffic patterns. To get data transfer related insights in Azure, leverage the tools as discussed in the following sections.

Reviewing data transfer costs with Azure Cost Analysis

The Azure Cost Analysis tool allows you to identify data transfer charges on the Azure cloud. Steps to identify data transfer costs:

1. Go to **Cost Management + Billing** in the Azure portal.
2. Launch **Cost Analysis**.
3. Configure the following filters:
   a. **Date Range**: Last 3 months
   b. **Granularity**: Monthly
   c. **Group By**: Service Name or Resource
   d. **Filter by** meter category or meter name keywords such as:
      - Bandwidth (for outbound internet transfer)
      - Inter-Region Bandwidth
      - Zone Bandwidth

This analysis helps identify which services, resources, and regions generate the highest data transfer costs.

Corelating charges in the Azure Billing console

The **Azure Billing** section provides invoice-level details of bandwidth charges:

1. In **Cost Management + Billing**, open **Invoices**.
2. Review invoice line items for **Bandwidth**, **Inter-Region Bandwidth**, or **ExpressRoute**.
3. Drill down into service-level details to validate findings from **Cost Analysis**.

This step confirms billing units and price per GB applied to different data transfer categories.

Reviewing operational metrics with Azure Monitor

After identifying resources incurring high data transfer costs, use Azure Monitor to understand traffic patterns and gain insights into usage. Azure Monitor provides operational metrics to analyze traffic behavior. Collect and review the required operational metrics for pattern analysis:

- **Virtual Machines**: Network In, Network Out
- **Storage Accounts**: Ingress, Egress
- **Load Balancers/Application Gateway**: Bytes Processed
- **Azure CDN**: Egress Bytes

These metrics help understand usage patterns and detect anomalies.

Putting it all together

Monitoring data transfer costs requires a multi-faceted approach using both cost management and cloud observability tools. By combining insights from AWS Cost Explorer, CUR, CloudWatch, VPC Flow Logs, and their Azure equivalents, you can gain comprehensive visibility into your data transfer usage and costs. To effectively monitor your data transfer costs across your cloud infrastructure, follow this three-step approach:

1. **Identify data transfer categories and services involved**: Use cost management tools such as AWS Cost Explorer, Azure Cost Management, or billing consoles to determine:
    - *Which data transfer categories (outbound to the internet, inter-region, intra-region) are most expensive?*
    - *Which services generate the most data transfer charges?*
    - *Which regions or availability zones incur the highest data transfer costs?*

This high-level analysis helps focus optimization efforts on areas with the greatest potential savings.

2. **Identify specific resources and patterns**: Drill down to resource-level details using AWS Cost and Usage Reports or pre-built dashboards like the AWS cost intelligence dashboard.
3. **Analyze traffic patterns and data types**: Once you have identified resources incurring the highest data transfer charges, use operational monitoring tools such as CloudWatch, VPC flow logs, and Azure Monitor to understand the nature of the traffic:
    - Use network logging mechanisms such as VPC Flow Logs or Azure NSG Flow Logs to identify source/destination pairs and protocols.
    - Analyze CloudWatch or Azure Monitor metrics to correlate traffic with application events.
    - Set up packet captures for deeper analysis of specific traffic types.

    This detailed analysis helps you understand what data is being transferred, enabling targeted optimization strategies.

Levers for optimizing cloud data transfer charges

Once you have identified cloud data transfer categories and the resources generating these charges, the next step is to focus on optimizing the charges. This section outlines the levers you can use to reduce and control data transfer charges on cloud platforms such as AWS and Azure.

We will begin with general principles of data transfer cost optimization that apply across cloud platforms, and then move on to service-specific strategies. Before implementing any changes, organizations must thoroughly analyze their workload requirements and distinguish between necessary data transfers and misconfigurations. Any optimization should align with the workload's availability, resiliency, and compliance requirements. The objective is to find the right balance between the availability and reliability of your application and the cost optimization expectations of the business.

General optimization principles

These are foundational recommendations that apply across all cloud environments.

Right-size application architecture

Your workload architecture and network design directly impact data transfer charges. The data traversing network boundaries defined by cloud providers, such as regions, availability zones, or the internet, may incur data transfer charges. Organizations should document application availability, resiliency, and compliance requirements to design cost-effective architectures. For example, running EC2 instances in multiple AZs can improve application uptime. However, if instances in one AZ frequently query a database in another AZ, inter-AZ data transfer charges will be applicable in AWS. Refer to *Figure 10.8* for inter-AZ charges.

Some of the key questions to ask before designing an application and network architecture on the cloud:

- *Does your workload require high availability?*
- *If yes, does application architecture need to support AZ failures or a full regional disaster?*
- *Are instances spread across AZs unnecessarily? If you are using a multi-AZ architecture for availability, do your resources need to be distributed across 2 or more availability zones?*
- *What are your disaster recovery requirements? Does data need to be replicated across regions?*
- *Where are your users located, and is the application deployed in the same region?*

Some of the recommendations that can help in optimizing data transfer charges:

- Document availability and resiliency requirements for each workload. A revenue generating workload may have different availability and resiliency requirements compared to internal facing production workload. Not every application will require a multi-AZ or multi-region setup.
- Place dependent components (VMs, databases, storage) in the same availability zone where possible. The team needs to have guardrails for deploying resources across regions and AZs. For example, development and test environments can have all their resources deployed within the same availability zone.
- Consolidate resources regionally if cross-region traffic is not required. Only a limited application and underlying resource may need cross-region data transfer.
- Understand the data transfer pricing policy of different services. For example, AWS does not charge separately for RDS multi-AZ replication traffic. Similarly, data transfer between S3 and EC2 in the same region can be free when using private connectivity through an S3 VPC endpoint. Understanding service-specific charging policies helps in optimizing architecture for cost efficiency.

Match the right data transfer mechanism

As discussed in the previous section, Organizations may be leveraging cloud managed network services for resiliency, security, and latency requirements. Different network services follow distinct charging mechanisms and should be carefully evaluated before deployment:

- **VPC peering/VNet peering**: Provide low latency private connectivity between VPCs, but cross-region peering incurs data transfer charges.

- **Transit Gateway**: Enables centralized routing but includes per-attachment and data processing fees.
- **Direct Connect/ExpressRoute**: Offers a dedicated private link to on-premises, and pricing is dependent on bandwidth capacity and outbound data transfer charges. Organizations should evaluate the long-term costs of Direct Connect or ExpressRoute versus transferring data over the public Internet.
- **NAT Gateway**: Managed NAT Gateway service is charged by hourly usage and per GB of data processed. NAT Gateway can become expensive at scale and needs to be carefully evaluated before usage.

Optimizing networking service costs

Many networking components charge based on running hours and the amount of data processed. Teams should regularly review the usage of networking services and optimize configurations to save costs.

Identify and terminate Idle resources

Idle resources can incur running charges, and these must be identified and terminated. You can leverage different tools to identify idle networking resources:

- **Trusted Advisor**: Leverage **AWS Trusted Advisor** to check for **Inactive NAT Gateways**, **Inactive VPC interface endpoints**, and terminate idle resources. Refer to the following figure for inactive AWS resources checks performed by AWS Trusted Advisor:

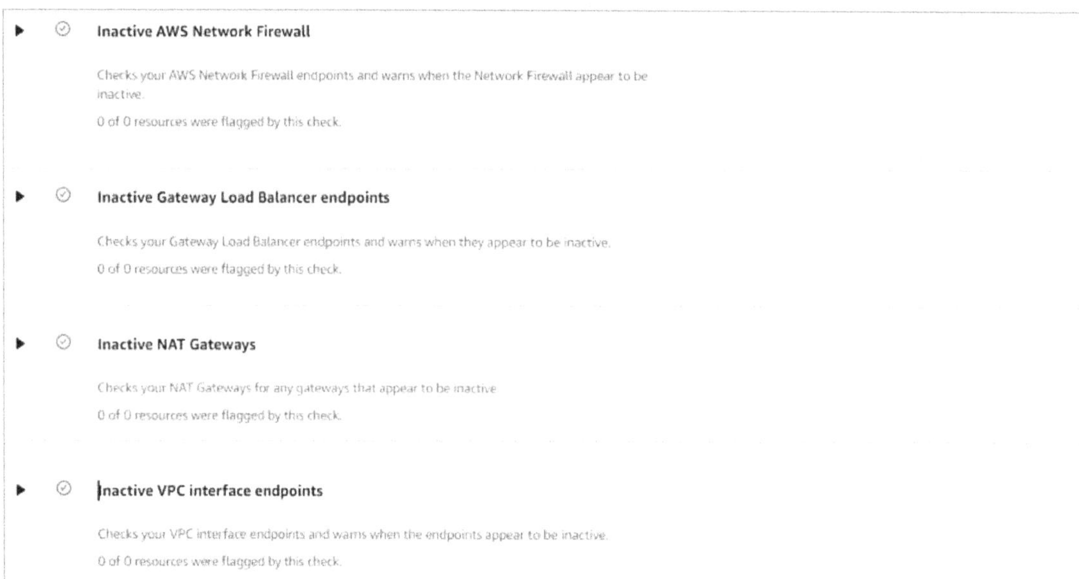

***Figure 10.14**: Identifying Idle resources using TA*

- **VPN Connections**: AWS Site-to-Site VPNs and Azure VPN Gateways are charged for hourly usage. Delete VPN connections with no associated tunnels (unless needed for disaster recovery).
- **Interconnect Links**: If Direct Connect (AWS) or ExpressRoute (Azure) circuits are under-utilized, consider downgrading the bandwidth.

Monitor data processing performed by networking services

Teams should identify opportunities to reduce data processing performed by networking services such as NAT Gateways. The following are some recommendations for optimizing data processing charges:

- Consolidate outbound internet traffic through a smaller set of gateways.
- For frequent downloads (patches, container images), consider:
  - A local cache (e.g., AWS S3 bucket, Azure Blob Storage) to avoid repeated internet downloads and data processing.
  - Using content delivery networks (CloudFront, Azure CDN) for external assets.

Leverage Free Tier

Both AWS and Azure provide Free Tier data transfer allowances as discussed in the previous section. Teams should look to leverage Free Tier limits provided by cloud providers to save data transfer charges.

Consider commitment-based savings

Some cloud providers offer volume-based discounts for large, predictable data transfers. For Example, if your data transfer is constantly above thresholds, such as more than 500 TB per month, you can reach out to the cloud provider for a discounted rate per GB of data transfer.

Service-specific cost optimization strategies

Now, let us explore strategies for optimizing service specific data transfer charges. While these strategies are based on AWS and Azure services, the concepts are broadly applicable to other cloud platforms.

Optimizing data transfer for EC2 and Azure VMs

Let us explore some recommendations to reduce data transfer charges incurred by VM instances:

- Use private IPs for intra-region communication. In AWS, Data transferred over public IPs incurs charges even within the same availability zone.
- Place NAT Gateways in the same availability zone as backend instances to avoid additional inter-AZ data transfer charges.
- Review cross-AZ load balancing configurations to optimize inter-AZ data transfer costs.
- Evaluate the minimum number of replication copies required for redundancy. This will help reduce the number of AZs involved in data transfer.
- Remove unassigned IPs to avoid idle costs. Tools such as AWS Trusted Advisor provide checks to identify unassigned Elastic IPs.

Optimizing data transfer for S3 and Azure Blob Storage

If you are incurring data transfer charges related to storage services, such as Amazon S3 or Azure Blob Storage, consider the following recommendations:

- Keep storage and compute resources in the same region.
- Avoid cross-region replication unless required for DR or compliance.
- Use VPC Endpoints (AWS) or Private Endpoints (Azure) for accessing S3 and Azure Blob Storage to avoid NAT Gateway and public internet data transfer charges.
- Compress large datasets before transfer to reduce the amount of GB getting transferred.
- For large data export jobs, consider alternative solutions such as Snowball (AWS).
- Use a CDN (CloudFront / Azure CDN) to cache static content closer to users, reducing direct storage egress traffic.

Elastic Load Balancing/Azure Load Balancer

For applications with high availability and resiliency setups, load balancers may incur significant data transfer charges and should be reviewed for optimization using the recommendations given as follows:

- **Remove idle load balancers**: Both AWS **Elastic Load Balancers** (**ELB**) and Azure Standard Load Balancer have per-hour and data processing fees. You can use tools such as AWS Trusted Advisor and Azure Advisor to identify idle load balancers. Refer to *Figure 10.15* for **Idle Load Balancer** check performed by AWS Trusted Advisor:

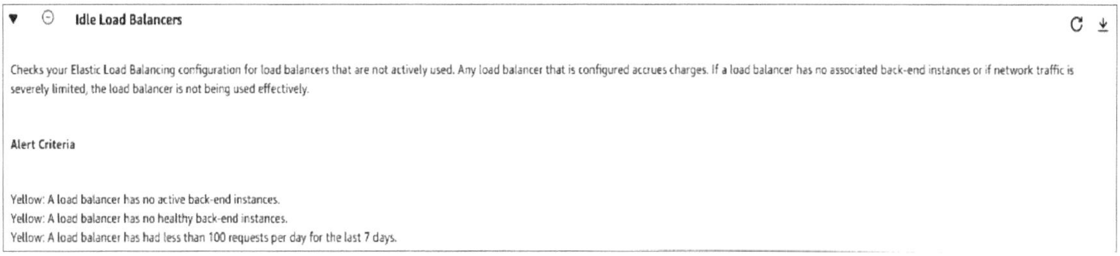

***Figure 10.15**: Idle ELB check with AWS TA*

- Align load balancer deployment with backend resource location to avoid cross-zone data transfer charges.
- If you are incurring high internet egress charges from a load balancer, place a CDN such as CloudFront to reduce data transfer volume.

By implementing these optimization strategies, organizations can reduce their data transfer charges while aligning with required performance, availability, and compliance requirements for their cloud workloads.

Developing a prioritized action plan

Optimizing data transfer charges in the cloud is complex and requires a structured approach that maintains your application's availability, resiliency, and compliance requirements while achieving cost savings. The goal is to identify high-impact changes, sequence them effectively, and implement changes without disrupting critical services. Refer to *Chapter 4, Moving from Cost Observability to Cost Optimization,* to understand the process for developing a priority action plan.

Sample prioritization framework

The following step by step approach will help you develop a structured action plan:

1. **Document availability, resiliency, and compliance requirements**: Before making any changes, define the **non-functional requirements** (**NFRs**) for each workload. Teams can start by categorizing applications based on business impact and aligning architecture accordingly:
    - **Business-critical applications**: May require high availability across three or more AZs with disaster recovery setup across regions.
    - **Standard production workloads**: May only need a multi-AZ setup across 2 AZs.
    - **Non-production and internal facing workloads**: May function with single-AZ deployments.

The sample approach given prevents overprovisioning of infrastructure and unnecessary data transfer charges. Create detailed architecture diagrams and traffic flow maps to identify network boundaries traversed by data.

2. **Isolate data transfer charges by category**: Use cloud billing and cost visualization tools to identify which data transfer categories are contributing the most to cloud charges:

    - Transfer to the Internet.
    - Inter-region data transfer.
    - Data transfer between AZs or within the same Availability Zone.

    For AWS, leverage Cost Explorer, the Billing Console, and CUR to pinpoint data transfer categories and identify the regions and linked accounts incurring these charges. For Azure, use cost management to analyze data transfer costs and Azure Advisor to obtain optimization recommendations. Additionally, identify the networking services involved in data transfer, such as NAT Gateways, VPC Peering, or Direct Connect (AWS), and Virtual Network Peering or ExpressRoute (Azure).

3. **Break down the cost drivers**: After identifying data transfer categories, determine which specific resources are performing these transfers and analyze their traffic patterns. Use tools such as:

    - AWS CloudWatch and VPC Flow Logs
    - Azure Monitor and Network Watcher

    These tools provide insights into traffic flow and help capture information such as source and destination IDs, traffic volume, and the protocol used for data transfers. Look for patterns such as frequent cross-AZ database queries, replication traffic between regions, or large downloads from the internet (Patches, Docker images) that could be optimized. This breakdown helps determine which specific data transfer optimization actions to take.

4. **Identify applicable cost optimization levers**: Based on data transfer category and other information gathered, you can leverage different cost levers available to optimize charges. Identify cost levers that are most applicable to your specific scenario.

5. **Prioritize optimization actions**: Once you have identified potential optimization opportunities, evaluate and prioritize them using a defined set of criteria, such as:

    - **Cost-saving potential**: Estimated monthly or annual savings.
    - **Implementation effort**: Simple configuration change versus major redesign.
    - **Operational risk**: Any impact on the availability, resiliency, or compliance requirement of the application.

- **Business impact**: Whether the changes affect production systems or critical business applications.
- **Skill and bandwidth availability**: Whether you have the necessary team expertise and tools available to implement the changes.

Create a simple scoring matrix (High/Medium/Low) for each criterion, then rank actions accordingly. Begin with low-effort, high-impact opportunities to get early wins and build momentum for broader optimization efforts.

Conclusion

Data transfer charges are one of the most frequently overlooked aspects of cloud architecture. During the design phase, teams are often focused on achieving high availability, scalability, and resiliency. While these goals are critical, the financial impact of replicating data across regions, AZs, or transferring data to the internet is underestimated. By understanding the categories of data transfer, data transfer pricing mechanisms, and the factors that drive these charges, teams can design systems that meet the required performance and availability requirements while remaining cost-efficient.

In this chapter, we explored the fundamentals of data transfer, breaking down data transfer charges into different categories and explaining how data transfer is priced. We explored how to gain visibility into data transfer usage and costs using native cost management tools such as AWS Cost Explorer, the AWS Billing console, and CUR, as well as monitoring services such as Amazon CloudWatch and VPC Flow Logs. We also reviewed several cost optimization strategies that can help in optimizing data transfer charges. To make the process actionable, we outlined a structured framework for cost optimization. Approaching data transfer optimization in a structured way ensures that changes are targeted, measurable, and aligned with the organization's technical and business objectives.

In the next chapter, we will shift from cost optimization to cost governance. While optimization helps bring costs under control, governance ensures that the organization follows the cost optimization principles. By establishing guardrails, enforcing policies, and setting up monitoring processes, organizations can prevent bill shock and maintain financial predictability in their cloud operations. As mentioned earlier, cost optimization is not just a one-time exercise but a continuous practice that becomes far more effective when supported by a robust governance framework.

CHAPTER 11 Establishing Cost Governance and Guardrails

Introduction

Organizations are steadily increasing their IT spend on the cloud as they migrate workloads to take advantage of the flexibility, scalability, and ease of use offered by cloud services. Cloud providers such as AWS, Azure, and GCP enable businesses to accelerate time-to-market and enhance operational agility. However, this rapid cloud adoption also brings challenges in maintaining financial control in an environment where resources can be provisioned with just a few clicks. As a result, many organizations are experiencing cloud costs spiraling out of control and facing unexpected bill shocks. Finance and procurement teams often struggle to align actual cloud usage with planned budgets, resulting in IT spending that exceeds their budget forecasts.

One of the common mistakes organizations make is to equate cost optimization with simply reducing the monthly bill. Organizations should not consider cost optimization as a one-off activity and a reactive exercise, but rather as a continuous practice of **cloud financial management** (**CFM**). CFM integrates three essential pillars: cost observability, which focuses on gaining visibility into cloud usage and spending across workloads, accounts, and teams; cost optimization, which involves leveraging strategies such as rightsizing, eliminating inefficiencies and wastage, and adopting commitment-based savings model to maximize the value of cloud investments; and cost governance, which ensures accountability through policies and processes that guide how resources are provisioned, consumed and managed. Together, these pillars provide a structured and sustainable way to control and optimize cloud costs.

In this chapter, we will explore how organizations can design and implement a cost governance framework and guardrails that help them find the right balance between agility and financial accountability. The goal is not to slow down cloud adoption, innovation, or go-to-market timelines, but to consume cloud resources responsibly.

Structure

In this chapter, we will discuss the following topics:

- Cost governance overview
- Driving accountability through cost allocation
- Setting up cost guardrails
- Handling cost spikes
- Creating a cost-aware culture

Objectives

By the end of this chapter, you will understand the importance of cost governance as part of the cost optimization journey. You will discover methods for establishing financial accountability through a well-defined organization structure and effective cost allocation models. You will explore tagging strategies to drive transparency and accountability in cloud consumption.

This chapter provides practical techniques to prevent cost overruns through proactive guardrails such as budget alerts, anomaly detection, and service control policies, without sacrificing the agility provided by the cloud. Most importantly, you will learn how to create a cost-conscious culture where financial responsibility becomes an integral part of your organization's cloud operations. While examples from AWS and Azure are used for illustration purposes, the concepts and techniques described in the chapter can be applied to all major cloud platforms.

Cost governance overview

Cost governance in the cloud refers to the people, processes, and technologies that govern how organizations procure, consume, and manage cloud resources. Cost governance ensures that cloud spends are predictable, managed responsibly, and cloud usage aligns with business goals. Without proper cost governance, organizations often face challenges such as budget overruns, a lack of accountability, and a lack of transparency in cloud spending. Effective cost governance enables organizations to find the right balance between accelerating innovation and reducing time-to-market while maintaining financial responsibility and control.

Objectives of cost governance

The main purpose of cost governance is not to slow down cloud adoption or restrict innovation, but to provide clear guidelines and to define guardrails for decision-making. Some of the key objectives include:

- **Alignment with business priorities**: Ensuring that cloud usage directly supports organizational goals and priorities.

- **Accountability for spending**: Assigning ownership of costs incurred to the right departments, business units, or teams to ensure accountability for budget adherence and effective cost control.
- **Transparency**: Making cloud costs transparent to stakeholders who incur the charges, as well as to finance and business leaders, is essential. This visibility allows finance teams and other departments to forecast accurately and effectively budget, manage, and track cloud spend.
- **Informed business decisions**: Evaluating **return on investment** (**ROI**) for cloud projects and ensuring that resources are deployed in areas that drive measurable business value.
- **Controlling unexpected costs**: Putting mechanisms in place to identify and mitigate unexpected cost spikes and budget overruns.
- **Creating a culture of cost awareness**: Encouraging every team from business to IT to proactively consider cost implications in all cloud related decisions.

By implementing a strong cost governance framework, organizations gain predictability, accountability, and control of their cloud spend. This not only reduces inefficiencies and wastage in the cloud but also ensures that the cloud spending delivers measurable business outcomes.

Factors influencing cost governance models

The implementation of cost governance models varies depending on the following factors:

- **Cloud maturity**: Whether the organization is new to the cloud or already running multiple or large-scale workloads on the cloud.
- **Customer profile**: Startups may require flexible, lightweight governance models, while enterprises often need stricter governance controls aligned with regulatory requirements.
- **Existing governance models**: Organizations moving from on-premises to cloud often need to update their policies and processes to account for cloud operating models.
- **Regulatory and compliance needs**: Industries with strict compliance requirements may need additional monitoring and automated controls embedded in governance models.

Key pillars of cost governance

Most cost governance frameworks are built around four fundamental pillars, as shown in the figure as follows:

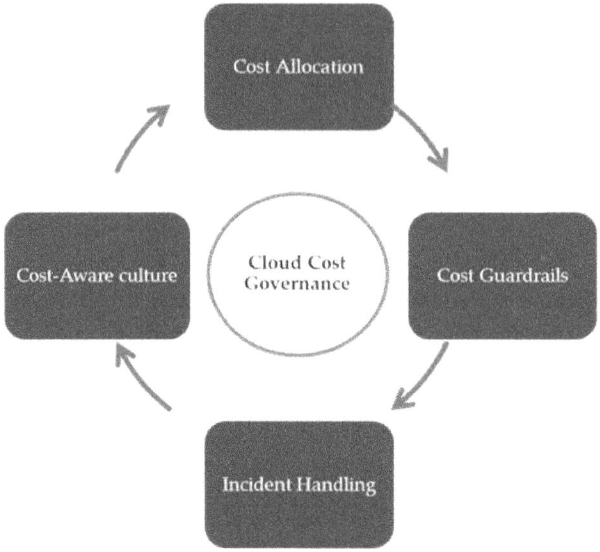

***Figure 11.1**: Cloud cost governance pillars*

An effective cost governance model is typically structured around the following four foundational pillars:

1. **Cost allocation**: Assigning costs incurred to the right business units or projects to ensure accountability. This includes mechanisms, such as showback, chargeback, and tagging strategies.
2. **Cost control and guardrails**: Using budgets, resource policies, anomaly detection, and automated alerts to setup guardrails and define automated actions on budget overruns.
3. **Incident handling**: Establishing processes to quickly address unexpected cost spikes or billing anomalies.
4. **Cost-aware culture**: Incorporating cost conscious behaviour into everyday decision-making so that teams treat the management of cloud related cost as a shared responsibility rather than limiting it to a specific team or group.

Together, these pillars form the foundation for effective cost governance, helping organizations to stay financially disciplined while continuing to innovate and scale on the cloud.

Driving accountability through cost allocation

In organizations, different stakeholders view cloud spending from different perspectives. The finance team needs a breakdown of cloud costs by business unit or department to ensure spending is not exceeding the budget allocated. Business leaders, on the other hand, want to identify which projects or product launches are profitable and deliver measurable returns.

This is where cost allocation plays a critical role. Cost allocation is the practice of distributing overall cloud costs to the organizational units, departments, or projects that incur them. Instead of looking at cloud spend as one consolidated bill, cost allocation breaks it down into meaningful categories that reflect business structures and objectives. In simple terms, cost allocation helps answer questions like: *Who is responsible for each part of the organization's cloud bill?*

Importance of cost allocation

Cost allocation enables organizations to manage cloud spend effectively and serves several purposes:

- **Creating accountability**: As multiple teams consume cloud resources, including shared services and resources, it becomes essential to attribute costs to the right departments or business units incurring the charges. This ensures that the teams driving cloud spend are held accountable for their cloud spending.
- **Enabling ROI analysis**: By mapping costs to specific projects, applications, or business initiatives, organizations gain the ability to evaluate return on investment. This makes it easier to identify which projects or product launches are generating value and which may require re-evaluation. For example, consider a SaaS start-up running multiple customer-facing applications on AWS. By allocating costs per application, the start-up can determine which features or services are expensive to run and decide whether to optimize, re-architect, or adjust pricing for customers consuming the application.
- **Support business planning**: Accurate cost data helps with budgeting and resource allocation for future projects.
- **Enhancing financial transparency**: When teams have visibility into their actual cloud expenditures, it creates a culture of ownership. Understanding what they are spending, and why, reduces surprises and drives more responsible resource usage.

In summary, cost allocation transforms cloud billing data into meaningful insights that drive accountability, informed decision-making, and sustainable growth.

Organization and resource hierarchy

A good cost allocation strategy begins with a well-defined organization and resource hierarchy. Cloud providers such as AWS and Azure offer tools to create logical structures that reflect how a resource hierarchy should be structured in the cloud for purposes such as cost allocation, operations, and security management.

AWS Organizations

AWS Organizations is a governance service that enables centralized management and governance of multiple AWS accounts. Some of the key terms in AWS Organizations include:

- **Management account or payer account**: Responsible for paying the consolidated bill for all accounts within the AWS Organization.
- **Organizational units (OUs)**: Containers for grouping member accounts, often aligned to departments (e.g., Payment, Sales, HR, IT).
- **Member accounts**: Individual accounts that host the resources and are organized under OUs (e.g., prod-sales-account, dev-hr-account).

The AWS Organization design varies by organization, and a sample organization structure is shown as follows for reference:

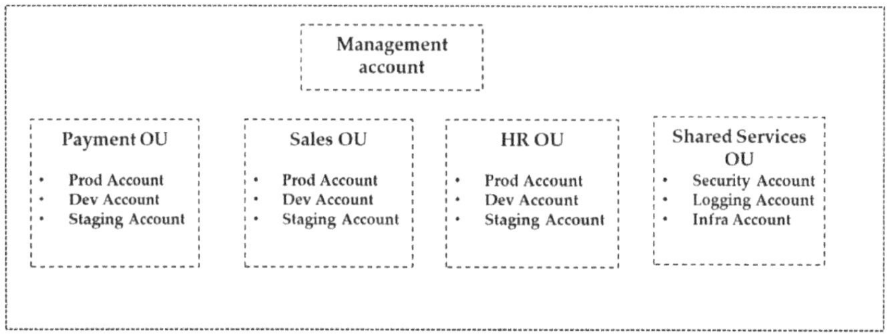

***Figure 11.2**: AWS Organization structure*

Key benefits of AWS Organizations

AWS Organizations offers several benefits that help enterprises manage multiple AWS accounts efficiently and enforce security and compliance across the cloud environment:

- **Consolidated billing**: Combine usage from multiple accounts to benefit from AWS's tiered and aggregated pricing discounts. In Consolidated billing, organizations will receive a single invoice for all their member accounts.
- **Security and compliance**: Apply **service control policies** (**SCPs**) across accounts and centrally manage the security policies from the management account.
- **Cross-account resource sharing**: Share **Reserved Instances** (**RIs**), **Savings Plan**, and other commitments across member accounts.

AWS Organizations simplifies both governance and cost allocation across accounts.

Azure resource hierarchy

Azure provides a slightly different hierarchical structure compared to AWS:

- **Management groups**: Top-level containers holding multiple subscriptions.
- **Subscriptions**: Logical containers for billing and access control.

- **Resource groups**: Collections of resources that share a common purpose, such as an application, project, or staging environment.
- **Resources**: Individual services like virtual machines, databases, or storage accounts.

This hierarchy enables organizations to apply policies, budgets, and tags at different levels, helping track and allocate costs as per requirement. For example, a multi-national company may structure Azure management groups by region (North America, Europe, APJC). Within each region, subscriptions may map to departments, while resource groups may represent individual applications or workload.

Building a cost allocation model

A cost allocation model defines how cloud charges will be mapped back to the business. Designing a good cost allocation model requires collaboration across finance, IT, and business teams. A good model should be transparent, simple to follow, easy to implement, and agreed upon by all stakeholders.

Types of cloud costs

When designing a cost allocation model, organizations need to consider two types of cloud costs:

- **Directly attributable costs**: Charges tied to specific resources or services that belong to a single project, team, or department. For example, consider an HR application for new employee onboarding deployed on AWS, using EC2 instances for web and middleware servers, Amazon RDS databases, and storage services. The costs of the cloud resources consumed by this HR application can be directly attributed to the HR department.
- **Shared costs**: Charges incurred by shared resources and services that are leveraged by the entire organization and cannot be attributed to any specific project or team. For example.
    - o Network infrastructure (AWS Direct Connect, Azure ExpressRoute).
    - o Security infrastructure, such as centralized firewalls and identity services.
    - o Support subscriptions.

Both direct and shared costs need to be considered when designing a cost allocation model. In the following section, we will explore different approaches to attributing shared costs to departments and business units, since directly attributable costs are already mapped to the teams incurring those charges.

Approaches to allocating shared costs

Directly attributable costs can be aligned to the project, team, or department incurring the charges as per the organization and resource hierarchy discussed earlier. However, shared costs are often the most difficult to allocate. Different organizations have different policies for distributing shared costs. Some of the commonly followed cost allocation policies for shared costs are:

- **Equal distribution model**: Costs are split evenly across all departments, regardless of usage. The model is simple to implement but may not accurately reflect actual consumption by different teams and departments.
- **Fixed ratio allocation**: Costs are divided according to a pre-agreed ratio between business units. For example, in a fintech company, the payments division may be assigned a larger share of the shared costs, while Sales, HR, and IT departments distribute the remaining portion based on an agreed allocation formula.
- **Consumption-based allocation**: Shared costs are distributed in proportion to each department's actual usage. For instance, if a business unit accounts for a higher share of total directly attributable costs or resource consumption, it may be assigned a correspondingly higher proportion of the shared costs.

The preceding methods of shared cost distribution can also be adapted for credit distribution or for refunds received from cloud providers, ensuring fair treatment across business units.

Showback and chargeback

Once the cost allocation model is finalized, the organization needs a mechanism to communicate and apply these costs. There are two important concepts for driving and implementing cost allocation:

- **Showback**: It provides visibility into spending without actually charging a specific project, team, or department. Business units and teams can see the costs incurred by them, broken down by service and resource. The key benefits of showback are:
  - Brings transparency into cloud spending.
  - Helps create awareness and accountability.
  - Encourages teams to optimize resource usage.

  A good showback model should include a user-friendly dashboard and support regular reporting on a daily, weekly, or monthly basis. The dashboard should be accessible to team members to explore spend and usage of resources and services consumed by their applications and projects. Tools such as AWS Cost Explorer, AWS Billing console, Azure Cost Analysis, AWS Cost Categories, and AWS Billing Conductor support showback implementation.

- **Chargeback**: Helps bill business units and departments for their cloud spend, including both direct and shared costs. Actual costs are applied against departmental budgets, which helps in building accountability. It will encourage business units and departments to be more prudent with their cloud spend as well as focus on cost optimization exercises. Finance teams can track how individual department spending compares against their budget allocations and use this spend data for future planning. A good chargeback mechanism has transparent policies outlining how costs are calculated and distributed. Chargeback tools are often integrated with financial systems and support the reconciliation process.

Together, showback and chargeback make cloud costs more transparent, fair, and accountable.

Tagging strategies for granular cost allocation

While organizational and resource hierarchies provide a broad structure, tags give the fine-grained details needed for accurate cost allocation. Tags can help in more granular cost allocation than what is supported by the organization hierarchy alone.

Understanding tags

A tag is a key–value pair attached to a resource. For example, if you are looking to do cost allocation based on Department or Project, you can define tags as following and attached to resources:

Key: Department | **Value**: Payment

Key: Department | **Value**: Sales

Key: Department | **Value**: HR

Key: Department | **Value**: IT

Key: Project | **Value**: CustomerPortal

Key: Project | **Value**: CRMNext

Tags serve multiple purposes apart from cost allocation. For example, you can use tags to perform administrative tasks such as developing automated start and stop schedules based on tags or applying security policies to resources based on tags.

Building a tagging model

When developing a tagging strategy, organizations should consider:

- **Purpose of tags**: Define whether tags are being assigned to resources for purposes such as cost allocation, automation, or compliance. For example:

Purpose	Sample tags
Cost allocation	Department, cost center, project
Technical	Environment, application name
Security	Data classification
Automation	Backup schedules, start/stop times

Table 11.1: Developing a tag based on purpose

- **Mandatory vs. optional tags**: Certain tags (example, cost center, owner) can be defined to be mandatory for all resources, and resources should not be allowed to be created till mandatory tags are attached. When designing a tagging strategy, classify tags as mandatory or optional:
  - **Mandatory**: Required on all resources and enforced through policies.
  - **Optional**: Recommended but not enforced.
- **Tag hierarchy**: Align tags with organizational and resource hierarchical structures for consistency.
- **Tag volume**: Decide how many tags to attach to avoid management complexities.
- **Tag lifecycle management**: Ensure tags remain accurate when resources are promoted (e.g., from test to production). The organization needs to define how the tag will be applied during the lifecycle of resources. For example:
  - Adding tags to new resources deployed, updating CloudFormation and Terraform scripts.
  - Updating tags when resources change purpose, for example, from development to production.
  - Removing tags from decommissioned resources.

Implementing tags in AWS

AWS supports two types of tags:

- **User-defined tags**: Created by users
- **AWS-generated tags**: System-generated (like aws:createdBy)

Before tags can be used for cost allocation purposes, the team needs to enable tags for cost allocation. Once enabled in the Billing console, these tags become visible in AWS Cost Explorer, AWS Budgets, and the CUR. Steps to enable cost allocation tags in AWS are as follows:

1. Open the AWS **Billing and Cost Management** console.
2. From the left panel, navigate to **Cost Allocation Tags**.
3. Select the tags you want to activate for cost tracking.

4. Click **Activate** (takes ~24 hours to reflect in reports). Refer to the following figure for reference:

***Figure 11.3**: AWS cost allocation tags*

AWS Cost Categories can further organize tagged resources into meaningful groups for cost reporting. Refer to the next section to know more about AWS Cost Categories.

AWS Cost Categories

AWS Cost Categories allows users to create custom rules for organizing costs across multiple billing dimensions, including AWS accounts, services, and organizational tags. By mapping cost and usage information according to internal business structures, organizations gain better financial visibility and control. For example, businesses can associate specific accounts and tags with projects to track related expenses more effectively. Steps to configure AWS Cost Categories are given as follows:

1. Launch the AWS **Billing and Cost Management** console.
2. From the left panel, click on **Cost Categories**.
3. In the **Cost Categories** console, click **Create cost category** as shown in *Figure 11.4*.
    a. Provide a descriptive name.
    b. Add rules that determine how costs are grouped. Rules can be based on:
        - AWS accounts
        - Services
        - Linked organizational units
        - Resource tags
    c. Add default value for costs not matching any rules.

4. Verify your rules and click **Create**. AWS will start categorizing charges according to the defined rules.

5. You can now use **Cost Categories** in different tools, such as AWS Cost Explorer, Budgets, or AWS CUR, to filter and analyze costs.

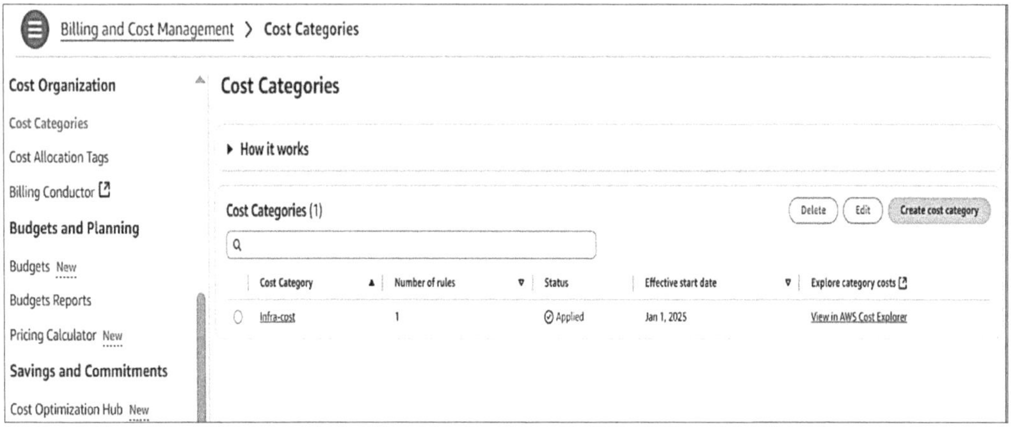

Figure 11.4: AWS Cost Categories

Implementing tags in Azure

Azure supports resource tagging as a foundational capability for cost allocation, governance, automation, and operational management. Tags in Azure are key-value pairs that can be applied to cloud resources to classify and organize them based on business context such as department, project, environment, or cost center. Effective tagging enables organizations to track spending accurately and align cloud costs with business ownership.

Tags can be applied at multiple hierarchy levels, including individual resources, resource groups, and subscriptions. This flexibility allows organizations to design tagging strategies aligned with their organizational structure. Azure also supports tag inheritance through governance controls, ensuring that resources deployed under tagged scopes automatically receive relevant metadata.

Azure provides built-in governance mechanisms to standardize tagging practices:

- **Inheritance policies**: Tags applied at higher levels (e.g., subscription) can be automatically inherited by resources.
- **Policy enforcement**: Using Azure Policy, the organizations can enforce mandatory tagging. For example, if a VM is created without a CostCenter tag, a policy can automatically add it or prevent deployment until tagging is completed.
- **Compliance monitoring**: Policies also help audit untagged or incorrectly tagged resources.

These controls ensure consistency in cost allocation and reporting.

Steps to implement tags in Azure

Follow the given steps to tag a resource with appropriate Tags:

1. Sign in to the Azure portal.
2. Navigate to the resource, resource group, or subscription you want to tag.
3. In the left menu, select **Tags**.
4. Add keyvalue pairs (example, *Department* = *Finance*).
5. Select **Save**.

Viewing costs using tags

Once tags are applied, they can be used in Cost Management + Billing to analyze and allocate costs. To view tagged costs, perform the following steps:

1. Navigate to **Cost Management + Billing**.
2. Select the appropriate scope.
3. Select **Cost Analysis**.
4. In the **Group by** dropdown, choose **Tag**.
5. Choose the required tag key (e.g., Department, Project) to view costs broken down by tag values.

This allows you to see how much each department, project, or environment is spending, making it easier to track budgets, optimize usage, and ensure accountability. Teams can also apply the required tag filter to view costs for a selected tag. Tagged cost views can also be saved as custom reports for recurring analysis. Refer to the following figure to view tagged costs:

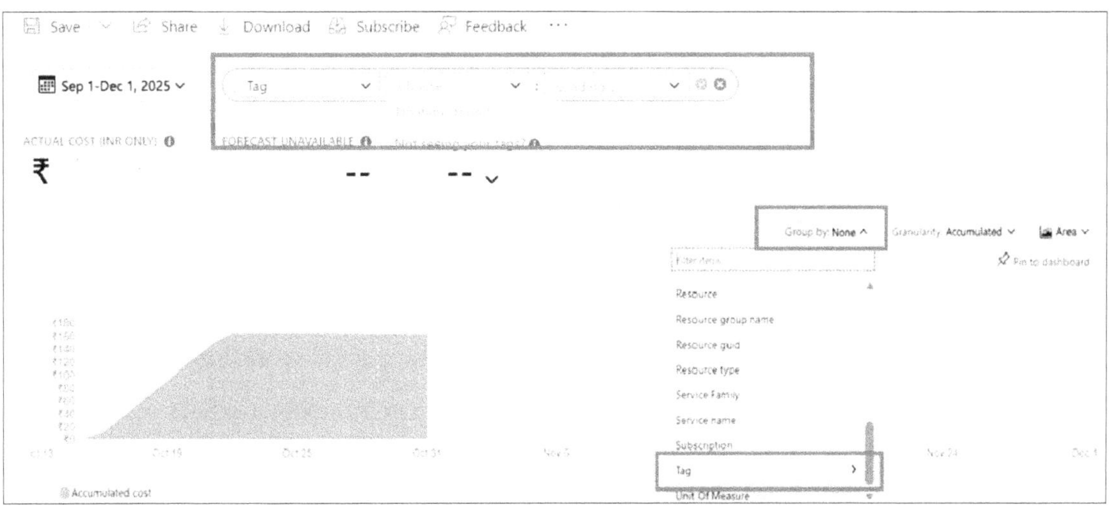

Figure 11.5: Viewing tagged costs in Azure

Tools for cost allocation

Cloud providers offer multiple tools to support cost allocation, both for showback and chargeback, and we have explored many of these tools in the previous chapter. Some of the tools are listed as follows for reference:

- **AWS cost management tools**: Such as AWS Cost Explorer, AWS CUR, which are integrated with tagging and cost categories.
- **AWS billing conductor**: Customizes billing to match your organizational structure.
- **AWS cost categories**: Creates rule-based groupings of costs.
- **Azure cost management**: Provides allocation rules and custom reporting.

Setting up cost guardrails

Cloud platforms provide agility and scalability, and teams can quickly provision resources without the long lead times and procurement processes associated with traditional data centers. The agility has helped fuel innovation and faster go-to-market, but has also introduced financial risks. Without appropriate oversight, cloud resources can spiral out of control, leading to budget overruns. Organizations running workloads on the cloud need cost control mechanisms that balance innovation with financial responsibility. Cost guardrails are preventive controls that help organizations maintain their cloud spending within acceptable limits while allowing teams to innovate and scale efficiently. The cost guardrails are not meant to restrict innovation but to serve as protective boundaries, ensuring that technology decisions remain aligned with financial and business priorities.

In this section, we will explore how to set up effective cost guardrails using cloud-native tools.

Tracking spend against budgets

In a traditional on-premises environment, IT spending is largely predictable. Hardware and software, including servers, storage devices, and networking equipment, are purchased through a well-defined procurement model, with approval processes in place to control spending. Finance teams typically have visibility into these purchases and can ensure that budgets are respected. In the cloud model, the finance team faces difficulties in managing the IT budget as:

- Teams may provision resources bypassing finance approval workflows.
- Misconfigurations or under-optimized resources may inflate cloud bills.
- Finance teams lack visibility into whether cloud spending aligns with allocated budgets.

To address these challenges, cloud providers such as AWS, Azure, and GCP offer budgeting tools that allow organizations to define spending thresholds, monitor consumption, and receive alerts when costs approach or exceed defined thresholds.

AWS budgets and alerts

AWS budgets are one of the mechanisms to track and control spending in AWS. It allows you to set custom cost and usage budgets, monitor spend against defined budgets, and trigger alerts and automated actions when thresholds are breached.

AWS budgets pricing

AWS budgets pricing depends on the features used and is discussed for illustration purposes. Refer to the AWS public pricing page for the latest pricing information:

- **Monitoring and alerts**: Basic AWS budgets features, such as setting budget rules and receiving notifications, are free.
- **Budget actions**: Up to two automated actions are free; any additional actions incur a charge of $0.10 per day.
- **Budget reports**: Delivered reports are charged at $0.01 per report delivery.

Defining budget rules

When setting up a budget, organizations should consider the following:

- **Budget type**: AWS supports setting up different budget types, such as:
  - **Cost budget**: Monitor spend by service or aggregate spend.
  - **Usage budget**: Track resource consumption. For example, GB of storage consumed or compute running hours.
  - **Savings plan budget**: Track utilization of committed Savings Plan.
  - **Reservation budget**: Track Reserved Instance coverage and utilization.
- **Duration**: Budgets can be defined on a monthly, quarterly, or annual basis, depending on the financial planning cycle.
- **Budget amount**: Decide whether the budget is fixed (e.g., $50K per month) or variable, adjusting based on historical usage patterns.
- **Scope**: Apply filters to track usage and spending at different levels, such as:
  - Entire organization
  - Linked accounts

- Specific services
- Regions
- Specific tags (e.g., Project=CRMNXT)

- **Thresholds and notifications**: Define multiple thresholds and escalation paths. For example:
  - **Spend reaching 70% of the budget**: Notify the project lead.
  - **Spend reaching 80% of the budget**: Escalate to the IT manager.
  - **Spend reaching 100% of the budget**: Notify senior leadership.
- **Automated actions**: Budgets can also enforce controls, such as:
  - Stopping or terminating instances when limits are exceeded.
  - Restricting new resource launches using IAM or SCP policies.

Steps to create a budget in AWS

Follow these steps to create budget rules and define alerts that send notifications when the specified budgets are breached:

1. Navigate to the AWS **Billing and Cost Management** console.
2. Under the **Budgets and Planning** section, select **Budgets**.
3. Click **Create budget**. Refer to the following figure for reference:

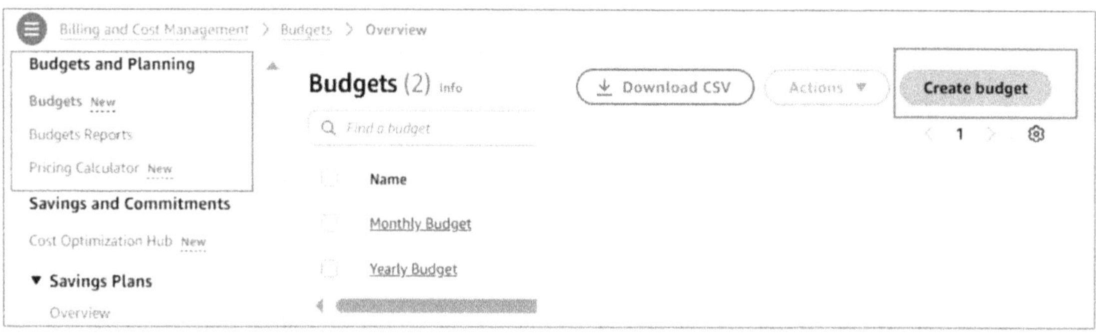

Figure 11.6: AWS budgets

4. Choose **Customized budget** option for flexibility.
5. Select the budget type (Cost, Usage, Savings Plan, or Reservation). For this exercise, choose **Cost** as shown in the following figure:

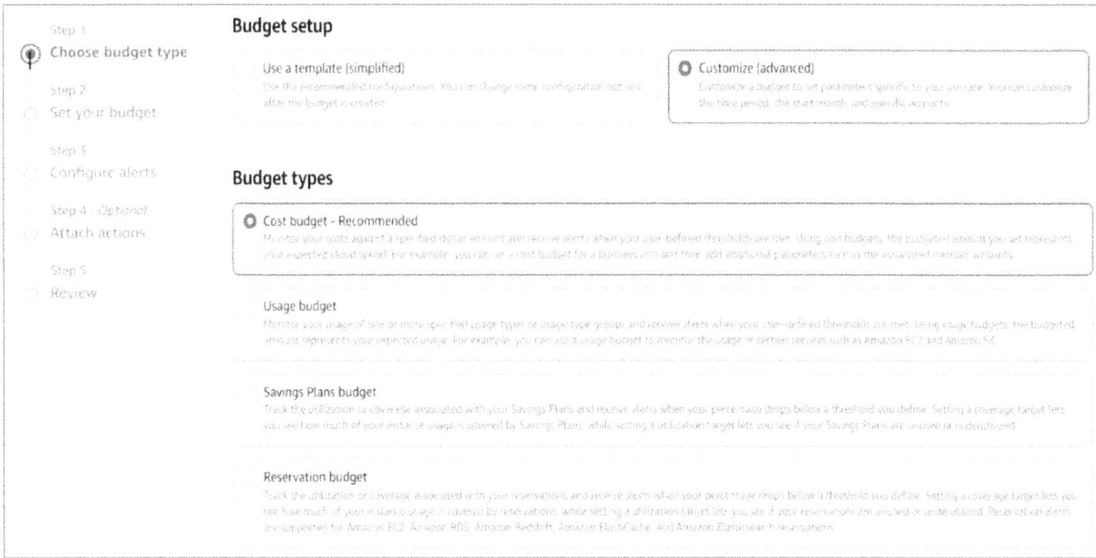

Figure 11.7: AWS budge setup

6. Enter details as discussed in the **Defining Budget Rules** section—duration, budgeting type, and amount.
7. Define the scope using filters like linked account, service, region, or tags.
8. Set up to five notification rules with escalation mechanisms as shown in the following figure:

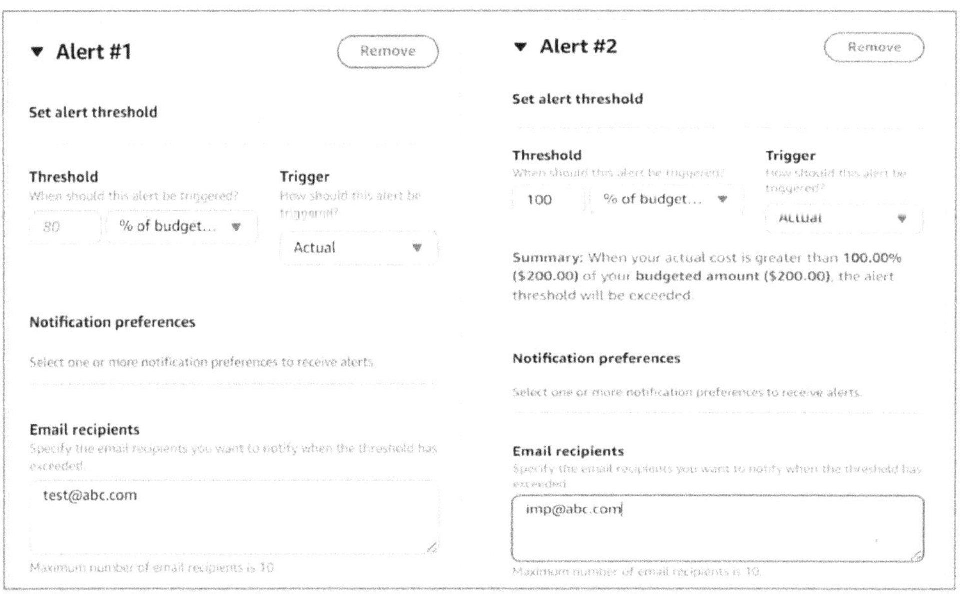

Figure 11.8: Setting alert for budget threshold

9. Add automated actions, such as:
   - Restricting launches via IAM policies.
   - Enforcing SCPs.
   - Stopping instances when thresholds are breached.

   Once configured, budgets appear in the budgets dashboard, where you can track:
     - Current vs. forecasted spend
     - Threshold breaches
     - Usage patterns

This proactive mechanism ensures that spending is continuously aligned with IT and business budgets.

Implementing budgets in Azure

Azure offers similar functionality through Azure budgets in the Cost Management + Billing service. Azure budgets enable organizations to set spending limits across cloud scopes such as subscriptions, resource groups, or management groups. By defining a budget threshold for a specific time period, such as monthly, quarterly, or annually, teams can proactively monitor spending and take action before costs exceed planned allocations. Budgets form a foundational component of cloud financial governance by linking consumption monitoring with automated alerting.

Azure budgets operate by continuously tracking actual and forecasted costs against defined thresholds. When spending reaches configured percentage levels such as 50%, 75%, 90%, or 100%, the system triggers alerts. Notifications can be sent via email or routed through action groups, which allow alerts to reach multiple stakeholders or integrated systems. These notifications can also initiate automated responses, including webhooks, Logic Apps, or Azure Functions, enabling rapid remediation. Beyond alerting, budgets help organizations analyze consumption trends and refine cost optimization strategies over time.

Steps to set up Azure budgets and alerts

To set up budget rules and alerts in Azure, follow the given steps:

1. Go to **Cost Management + Billing**.
2. Select **Budget** under **Cost Management** section.
3. Click **+Add** to create a new budget as shown in the following figure:

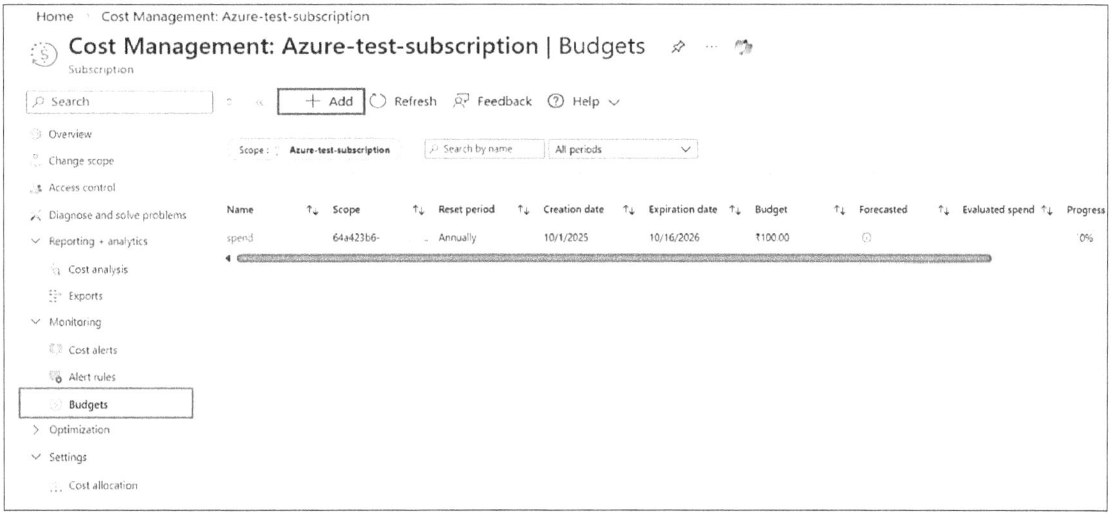

***Figure 11.9**: Creating budget rules in Azure*

4. Define the scope (example subscription, resource group).
5. Apply filters such as tags or services.
6. Enter budget details:
   - Reset period (monthly, quarterly, yearly)
   - Duration
   - Budget amount
7. Configure alerts based on actual or forecasted spending.
8. Define action groups to specify actions, such as stopping a virtual machine. The following figure illustrates the steps to create Azure budget alert rules:

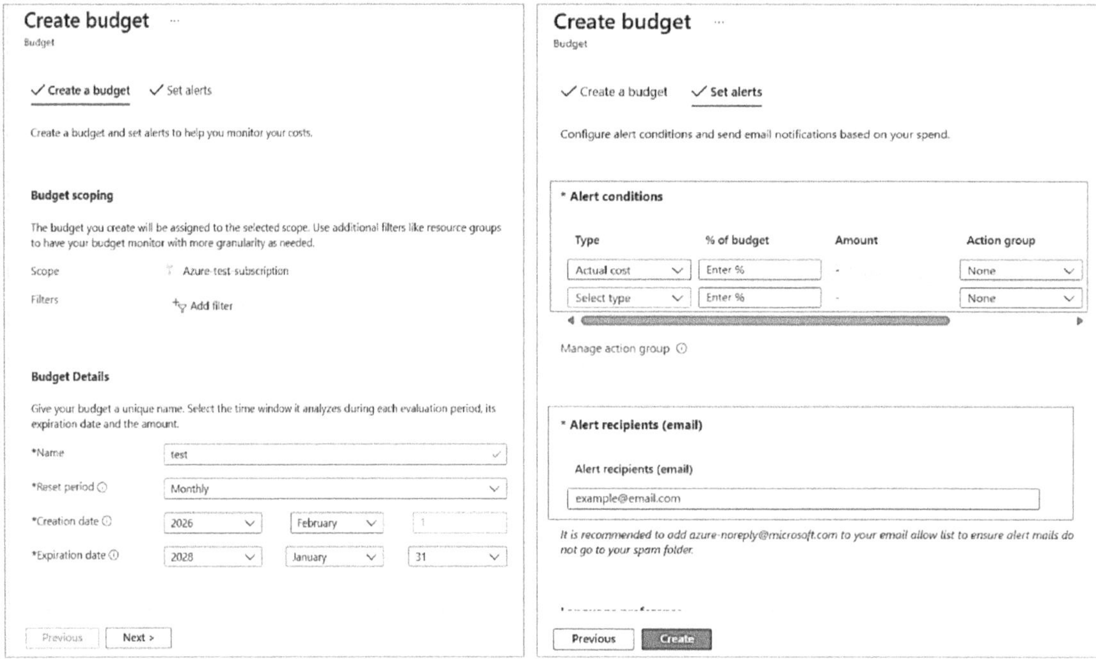

***Figure 11.10**: Setting up budget notification*

Once a budget is created, Azure automatically monitors spending against the defined thresholds. When an alert condition is met, notifications are sent to the recipients specified in the budget rule. These alerts typically arrive via email and include details such as the budget name, current spend, and percentage of the threshold reached. To view and manage alerts, return to the **Budgets** section in **Cost Management**, select the relevant budget, and review the alert history. This provides visibility into when alerts were triggered and helps track spending trends over time. Azure budgets are also integrated with Azure Monitor, allowing organizations to automate corrective actions when limits are exceeded.

Detecting anomalies in cloud usage and costs

Even with budgets in place, unusual spending and usage patterns may go undetected. For example:

- A monthly cost budget may not capture sudden spikes in a single service.
- An unnoticed configuration change could lead to disproportionate spending before being detected.

Anomaly detection systems are based on machine learning models and continuously monitor usage patterns, alerting teams to any detected outliers.

AWS Cost Anomaly Detection

AWS Cost Anomaly Detection uses ML models to analyze historical spending patterns and identify outliers. Unlike static budgets, it adapts dynamically to usage trends and provides intelligent alerts.

Benefits of using AWS Cost Anomaly Detection:

- Detects service-level anomalies (e.g., a sudden spike in AWS Glue costs).
- Provides root cause analysis, showing which service or account is driving the spike.
- Sends alerts in near real time to stakeholders.

AWS Cost Anomaly Detection is enabled by default, and the team needs to perform a few additional steps to get the required notification. The steps are as follows:

1. Go to AWS **Billing and Cost Management**.
2. From the left panel, launch **Cost Anomaly Detection**.
3. The summary page displays a list of anomalies detected for the month.
4. Review the **Detected Anomalies** tab for impacted services and root causes as shown in the following figure:

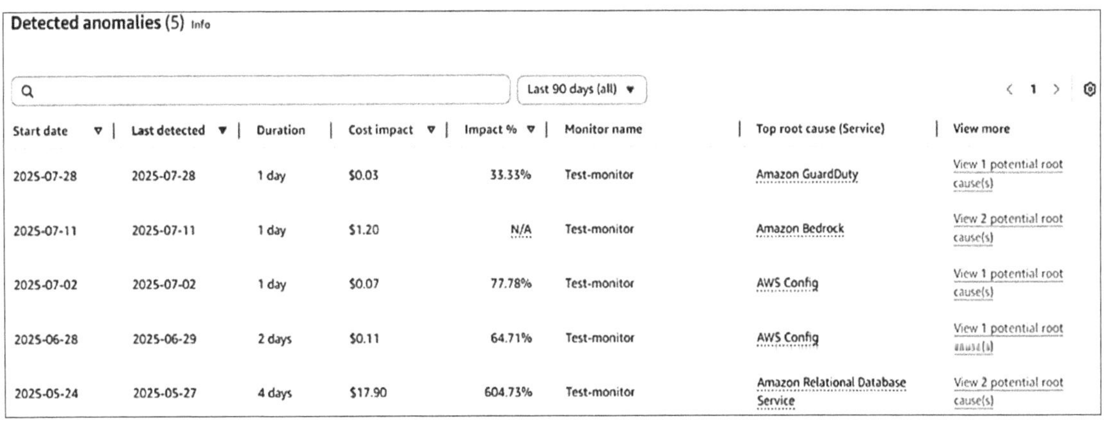

Detected anomalies (5) Info

Last 90 days (all)

Start date	Last detected	Duration	Cost impact	Impact %	Monitor name	Top root cause (Service)	View more
2025-07-28	2025-07-28	1 day	$0.03	33.33%	Test-monitor	Amazon GuardDuty	View 1 potential root cause(s)
2025-07-11	2025-07-11	1 day	$1.20	N/A	Test-monitor	Amazon Bedrock	View 2 potential root cause(s)
2025-07-02	2025-07-02	1 day	$0.07	77.78%	Test-monitor	AWS Config	View 1 potential root cause(s)
2025-06-28	2025-06-29	2 days	$0.11	64.71%	Test-monitor	AWS Config	View 1 potential root cause(s)
2025-05-24	2025-05-27	4 days	$17.90	604.73%	Test-monitor	Amazon Relational Database Service	View 2 potential root cause(s)

Figure 11.11: AWS Cost Anomaly Detection

5. Create a **Cost Monitor** to continuously track spend at an account or service level, as shown in the following figure:

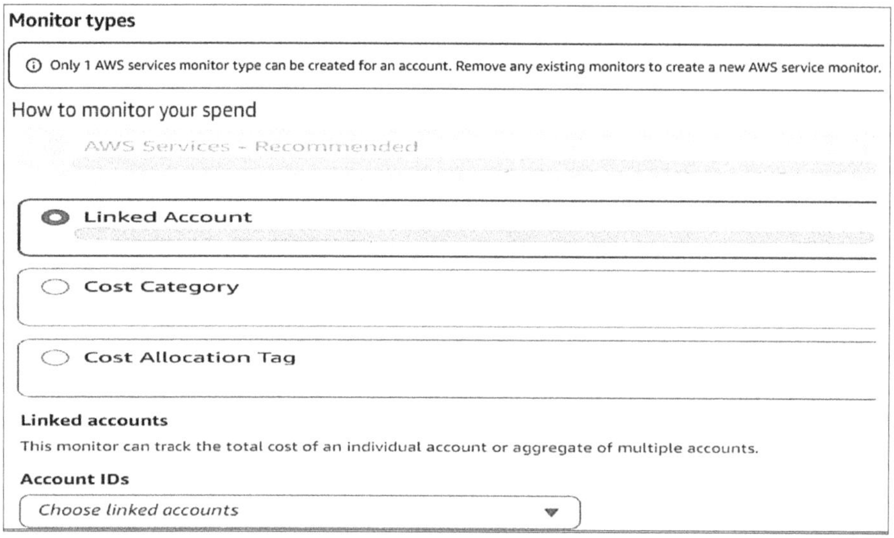

***Figure 11.12**: Create Cost Monitor*

6. Configure notifications to alert teams when anomalies occur. This ensures that the team is aware of the spike and can take measures to avoid cost overrun.

Azure Anomaly Detection

Similar to AWS Cost Anomaly Detection, Azure offers anomaly detection capabilities within **Cost Analysis** under the **Cost Management** section. Azure's ML-based models compare current usage against historical trends to detect outliers. This helps prevent bill shocks and ensures a proactive response.

Steps to create a cost alert rule for anomaly detection

To proactively monitor and receive notifications about anomalies, you can configure a cost alert rule in the Azure portal:

1. Sign in to the Azure portal and navigate to **Cost Management + Billing**.
2. Ensure the correct subscription scope is selected.
3. In the left navigation menu, select **Cost alerts**.
4. Click + **Add** to create a new alert rule.
5. On the alert configuration page, choose **Anomaly** as the alert type.
6. Provide the required alert details, including notification settings.
7. Select **Create** to activate the anomaly alert rule.

Once configured, Azure sends anomaly alert emails at the time of detection, summarizing cost deviations and providing links for further investigation. Refer to the following figure to create a cost alert:

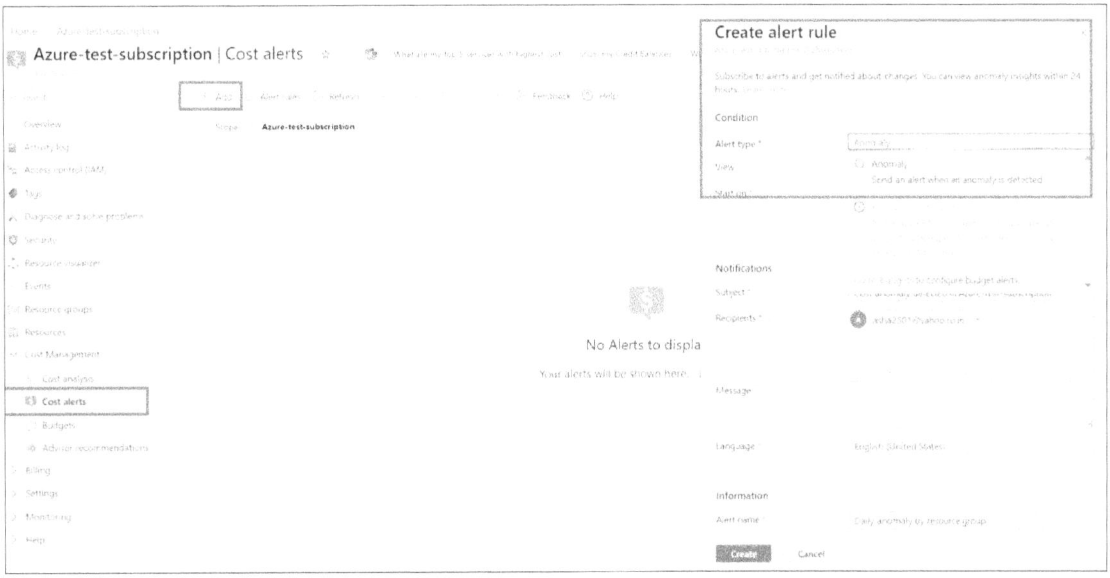

***Figure 11:13**: Azure Anomaly Detection*

Viewing anomalies in cost analysis smart views

Azure Cost Anomaly Detection provides valuable insights into unusual spending patterns across your subscriptions. To access anomaly insights, users can navigate to **Cost Management** from the Azure portal, select the required subscription scope, and open **Cost Analysis**. Under the **Smart Views** list, selecting views such as **Resources** displays anomaly indicators if unusual cost activity is detected. If no anomalies are present, Azure displays a **No anomalies detected** message along with the evaluated time range.

Comparing budgets and anomaly detection

While both budgets and Cost Anomaly Detection aim to control costs, they serve different purposes:

Feature	AWS/Azure budgets	AWS/Azure Anomaly Detection
Detection model	Static, rule-based	Dynamic, ML-driven models
Trigger	Threshold breach based on predefined rules (e.g., when spending crosses 80% of the allocated $100 budget). Budget alerts are dependent on rule configuration, i.e., if thresholds and alert rules are not defined, no alerts will be generated.	Deviation from historical usage patterns. Cost Anomaly Detection is driven by machine learning models that analyze historical usage and spending patterns to identify outliers. It does not rely on predefined thresholds or manual rule creation.

***Table 11.2**: Budget vs. Cost Anomaly Detection*

An organization can use budgets to set spending limits that are aligned with the IT budget allocated and use anomaly detection to flag unexpected deviations from expected usage patterns.

Enforcing guardrails using policies

Organizations can implement guardrails to define boundaries for resource deployment. These guardrails ensure all deployed resources comply with organizational security policies and cost governance requirements.

AWS service control policies

Service control policies (SCPs) are policies within AWS organizations that define the maximum permissions available to member accounts. They act as governance guardrails by restricting actions that could lead to cost spikes or compliance violations. Examples of SCP usage:

- Restrict launching of resources to certain regions (for example, only the Singapore region is allowed for the deployment of resources).
- Block provisioning of expensive EC2 instance (example, restriction on launching of GPU based instances).
- Enforce tagging policies to ensure all resources are properly tagged for cost allocation.

SCPs can be applied at the organization (Root), OU, or account level, ensuring consistent governance across environments.

Azure Policies

Azure Policies provide similar functionality by enforcing governance rules across Azure subscriptions. They ensure that only compliant resources are deployed and automatically remediate any detected violations. For example, policies can restrict deployments of resources to specific regions or enforce mandatory cost allocation tags (e.g., Department, Project). Azure Policy also supports bulk remediation, allowing organizations to automatically remediate existing resources and align them with compliance requirements.

Governing resource provisioning with AWS Service catalog

Even with budgets and policies in place, users may still deploy resources outside of approved configurations. AWS Service Catalog helps address this by providing a centralized catalog of pre-approved services. With Service Catalog, organizations can:

- Publish portfolios of approved AWS services, VM images, and applications.
- Control which teams or users have access to specific portfolios.
- Ensure deployments comply with security, cost, and governance policies.

This approach not only reduces the risk of cost overruns but also accelerates innovation by giving teams quick access to preconfigured, compliant resources.

Handling cost spikes

Even when an organization has well-established cost governance practices and required cost guardrails in place, an unexpected increase in cloud spending can still occur. These cost spikes may come from new deployments, misconfigurations, unplanned business activities, or even security incidents. The organization needs to have an effective mechanism to handle such situations. This section outlines a comprehensive approach to identifying, analyzing, allocating, and addressing unexpected cost increases in cloud infrastructure. A detailed step-by-step approach to handling an unexpected cost spike is given in the following section.

Early detection using proactive monitoring

The key to managing cost spikes effectively is early detection. Rather than discovering unexpected charges while reviewing monthly invoices, organizations should implement monitoring systems, such as budgets and anomaly detection, that provide alerts when spending deviates from expected patterns. Cloud providers offer native tools that help identify anomalies in near real-time, and we have explored these tools in the previous section:

- **Budgets**: Services like AWS budgets and Azure budgets allow teams to define spending thresholds at daily, monthly, or quarterly levels. When actual cloud charges approach or exceed these thresholds, the system sends notifications to designated recipients.
- **Anomaly detection**: Services such as AWS Cost Anomaly Detection use machine learning models to analyze historical usage patterns and send alerts when spending deviates from the expected pattern.

These services can help detect changes in cloud spending patterns that might go unnoticed in large cloud environments. Organizations not using these services should use alternate solutions for identifying deviations or conduct regular manual reviews using dashboards and reports (Example, reviewing AWS Cost Explorer or Azure Cost Analysis).

Allocating the cost to business units

Once a cost spike is detected, the next step is to determine which business unit, department, project, or application is responsible for the increased spending. Follow the cost allocation model defined in the previous section to allocate the cost to the business unit incurring the charges. The organization should implement a tagging strategy across all cloud resources, which will help in filtering the cost by tags and attributing the cost to specific projects, departments, or cost centers. The objective of cost allocation is to:

- **Assign ownership and accountability**: Business owners or application leaders can review the cost spike, correlate it with business growth or IT events, and take corrective measures if required.
- **Targeted optimization**: Granular cost allocation prevents situations where cost savings in one area are offset by increased spending in other areas. For example, if Team A reduces storage costs by archiving data, but Team B accidentally triggers an expensive migration, the overall cost may be the same and will not reflect the true scenario. Granular allocation ensures accountability at the application or department level.

This approach promotes fairness, assigns accountability, and ensures optimization efforts are not undermined by unrelated overspending.

Tracing the spike to services and features

After assigning ownership, the next step is to find which specific services and underlying components are responsible for the increased costs. To identify the services incurring the charges:

- The organization can review the budgets console to identify services breaching defined cost or usage thresholds.
- The anomaly detection console will also show detected anomalies and the root cause for the spike.
- Teams can leverage cost observability tools such as AWS Cost Explorer, AWS CUR, and Azure Cost Analysis to compare usage and cost from the previous periods and identify any spikes and deviations.

Once you have identified the services, you can analyze for any changes in usage patterns by asking questions, such as:

- *Has there been an increase in the number of resources being used?*
- *Have there been changes to the pricing structure or billing units?*
- *Have new features or components been enabled that incurred additional costs?*
- *Were any configuration changes performed for the services identified?*

Distinguishing genuine growth from misconfiguration

An organization may have business events such as new year sales campaigns or the onboarding of new customers to a SaaS platform, which can lead to a cost spike. Some common business events that can result in increased cloud cost include:

- Product launches or marketing campaigns driving higher user traffic.
- Expansion into new markets requiring additional infrastructure.
- Seasonal business fluctuations requiring temporary capacity increases.
- Data migration or transformation projects.
- New service adoption, such as analytics service deployment.

An increase in cloud costs due to business events is generally not a cause for concern. However, if the cost is increasing without any positive business growth, it may indicate misconfigurations or cost inefficiencies. To differentiate genuine cost increases from misconfigurations, organizations should investigate:

- **Business events**: Marketing campaigns, seasonal demand, or new product features.
- **IT changes**: Deployment of new features, activation of detailed logging, or changes to network routing.
- **Security events**: DDoS attacks or compromised credentials leading to unauthorized resource provisioning.

By correlating cloud spend with business and operational events, teams can identify whether the cost spike is due to positive business growth or is indicative of a bigger problem.

Applying optimization levers

Once the service and underlying resources responsible for the cost spike are identified, the next step is to optimize cost. We have discussed cost optimization levers for different services in previous chapters. Some common cost optimization levers include:

- **Rightsizing**: Scale down oversized compute instances, databases, or clusters.

- **Autoscaling**: Implement scaling policies so that resources adjust automatically based on demand.
- **Storage tiering**: Move infrequently accessed data to lower-cost storage classes.
- **Idle resource cleanup**: Terminate unused instances, snapshots, or orphaned storage volumes.
- **Data transfer optimization**: Use caching, **content delivery networks** (**CDNs**), or same-region architectures to reduce data transfer costs.

These cost optimization measures should balance cost savings with performance, security, and availability requirements of the application.

Change management

Implementing cost optimization measures requires careful planning to avoid disrupting business operations. Some of the key considerations are:

- Assess the potential impact of each proposed change on application performance, availability, and security.
- Prioritize changes based on their potential cost savings and implementation complexity.
- Follow established change management procedures, especially for changes that might affect production environments.
- Test changes in non-production environments before rollout.
- Schedule changes during maintenance windows when appropriate.
- Implement changes incrementally to minimize risk.
- Define rollback and mitigation measures to address any impact of changes implemented.

The goal is to implement cost savings recommendations without disrupting critical applications or user experience.

Escalating to cloud providers

In some scenarios, teams cannot identify the root cause of a cost spike and need specialized guidance on cost optimization. In such cases, it is advisable to engage the cloud provider. Options include:

- **Support cases**: Raise tickets through AWS, Azure, or GCP support portals.
- **Account teams**: Leverage customer success managers or technical account managers for expert advice.

- **Cost optimization programs**: Many providers offer free or subsidized reviews, such as AWS Well-Architected Reviews or Azure Advisor assessments, which help identify cost optimization opportunities.

Updating budgets and guardrails

After addressing the cost spike, the organization needs to improve Cost governance practices and guardrails to prevent similar issues from happening again. Teams should:

- **Refine budgets**: Adjust thresholds or create service-level budgets to catch similar issues earlier.
- **Strengthen guardrails**: Use SCPs in AWS Organizations or Azure Policy to restrict high-cost operations.
- **Automate actions**: Some budget alerts can trigger automated responses, such as stopping non-critical workloads once thresholds are crossed.

Building and updating a playbook

Finally, organizations should capture lessons learned from every cost increase incident in a cost management playbook. This playbook should include:

- **Detection processes**: The section should detail how to identify cost spikes and perform root cause analysis for cost spikes.
- **Ownership guidelines**: How to assign accountability for managing cost spikes by using cost allocation practices.
- **Optimization steps**: Leverage cost optimization levers to mitigate cost spikes and improve spending efficiency.
- **Escalation paths**: When and how to involve cloud providers for managing the cost spike incident.

The team should also share learnings across team members to improve organizational cost awareness. By continuously updating this playbook, organizations can move from a reactive management approach to a more proactive approach.

Creating a cost-aware culture

For the cost governance framework to succeed, it must be supported by a culture of cost awareness across the organization. In a traditional IT environment, the finance team controls the budget and makes purchasing decisions. However, the cloud model has shifted this paradigm. Different teams within an organization interact with the cloud in unique ways:

- **Application owners**: Focus on building and deploying applications, ensuring performance, and delivering a positive end-user experience.
- **Site reliability engineers (SREs)**: Ensure the application meets scalability, automation, and operational reliability requirements.
- **Security teams**: They are responsible for strengthening the security posture of the application and data hosted on the cloud.
- **Finance teams**: Aims to keep cloud spending aligned with the IT budget established at the start of the year.

While their priorities differ, all teams must share responsibility for managing cloud spend effectively. In the cloud world, it is important for every stakeholder, not just the finance team, to include cost considerations in their decision-making process. Building a cost-aware culture ensures accountability at every level and prevents costs from becoming an afterthought.

One approach many organizations are adopting is to create a **Cloud Center of Excellence (CCoE)**. A CCoE is a cross-functional team that brings together experts from finance, technology, business units, and executive leadership. By including diverse perspectives such as from corporate finance representatives, product owners, technology leads, business owners and cloud service champions, the CCoE bridges the gap between business goals and technical execution. The CCoE plays a key role in creating a culture of cost awareness:

- **Defining governance standards and tools**: To guide how cloud resources are deployed and audited across departments.
- **Sharing best practices**: For designing cloud-native architectures that balance performance, scalability, and cost efficiency.
- **Providing shared services**: Managing common resources like SCPs, centralized logging, or standardized monitoring frameworks to avoid duplication and reduce management expenses.
- **Creating reusable components**: Creating components like **infrastructure as code (IaC)** templates, IAM policies, and observability frameworks, which drive consistency and reduce operational overhead.
- **Implementing guardrails and controls**: Setting up guardrails for service selection and resource usage.
- **Cost attribution**: Managing showback and chargeback processes for different departments, allowing business units to have visibility into the costs they generate and bring accountability.

Beyond governance, a cost-aware culture also facilitates continuous improvement rather than a one-time cost optimization effort. Instead of treating cost optimization as a reactive exercise, organizations should include cost optimization in regular workflows. This might include setting up recurring reviews of unit costs, analyzing usage trends, or identifying underutilized resources for optimization.

The CCoE can help reinforce this mindset by publishing regular cost improvement reports, celebrating wins, and highlighting teams that successfully reduced spend while maintaining performance. Recognizing and rewarding cost-conscious behavior strengthens alignment with business objectives and ensures cost governance is not seen as restrictive but as a driver of sustainable growth. In summary, creating a cost-aware culture transforms cost management into a shared responsibility.

Conclusion

Cost governance is a foundational element of cloud cost optimization. It guides how an organization procures, consumes, and manages cloud resources to ensure that cloud spending remains predictable, accountable, and aligned with business priorities. Lack of cost governance in cloud deployment often leads to inefficiencies and budget overruns.

In this chapter, we explored the core pillars of cost governance—cost allocation, setting up cost controls and guardrails, handling cost spikes, and building a cost-aware culture. Cost allocation and tagging help organizations map cloud charges back to the right business units, projects, or applications, making it easier to analyze spending patterns and measure return on investment. Cost controls and guardrails, such as AWS Budgets, Anomaly Detection, Service Control Policies, and AWS Service Catalog, act as proactive mechanisms that bring financial discipline. Handling cost spikes through continuous monitoring ensures that sudden changes in usage are detected early, allowing teams to take corrective action. Finally, fostering a culture of cost awareness ensures that every team, not just the finance team, considers cost implications in their daily decisions.

In the concluding chapter of this book, we will bring the cost optimization journey together. We will revisit how cost observability, cost optimization, and cost governance work as interconnected levers for managing and optimizing cloud spend. We will also explore how generative AI solutions are making cost management easier by automating analysis and providing smarter recommendations.

CHAPTER 12
Advancing Cost Optimization Journey with GenAI

Introduction

Cost optimization in the cloud has moved beyond usual practices like rightsizing resources or purchasing Reserved Instances. Today, it has developed into a well-defined strategy that combines cost observability, advanced cost optimization techniques, and strong cost governance frameworks. Throughout this book, we have explored the lifecycle of **cloud financial management** (**CFM**), starting from understanding cloud pricing models to implementing governance structures that keep costs aligned with business objectives.

As we conclude, we will examine how organizations can put these strategies into practice while preparing to adopt emerging technologies and frameworks. **Generative AI** (**GenAI**) solutions from cloud platforms such as **Amazon Web Services** (**AWS**), Microsoft Azure, and **Google Cloud Platform** (**GCP**) are transforming cost optimization practices by delivering intelligent insights, predictive recommendations, and automated optimization actions. Alongside GenAI, open standards such as **FinOps Open Cost and Usage Specification** (**FOCUS**) are enabling the standardization of cost and usage data across cloud providers.

This chapter brings together the lessons learned throughout the book and connects them with emerging technologies and frameworks, demonstrating how organizations can leverage emerging technologies and apply insights to achieve smarter decision-making, faster optimization cycles, and more sustainable cloud cost management outcomes.

Structure

In this chapter, we will discuss the following topics:

- Indicators of effective cost optimization
- Summarizing the cost optimization framework
- Applying cost optimization framework in real-world examples

- Leveraging GenAI solutions for cost optimization
- Understanding FOCUS

Objectives

The goal of this chapter is to consolidate the concepts and techniques discussed throughout the book and demonstrate what effective cloud cost optimization looks like in practice through real-world examples. It also explores how GenAI is redefining cost optimization by making it easier to analyze complex usage data, identify cost savings opportunities, and automate optimization actions while supporting faster and more informed decision-making. Finally, the chapter introduces the FOCUS standard as a unifying framework for managing billing and usage data consistently across different cloud providers.

By combining proven cost optimization strategies with emerging technologies and open standards, organizations can advance their cost optimization journey while confidently adopting hybrid and multi-cloud platforms.

Indicators of effective cost optimization

When organizations begin their cloud cost optimization journey, one of the first questions that arises is: *What does success actually look like?* As discussed in earlier chapters, the answer is not as simple as reducing the monthly cloud bill. A lower bill may be good in the short term, but if that reduction comes at the expense of availability, performance, security, or growth, it can negatively impact the organization in the long run.

In a cost optimization journey, the ideal state is one in which costs are aligned with business value. Cloud spending should reflect the needs of the business, scaling up as the business grows, scaling down when resources are underutilized, and always ensuring that cloud spend is justified by a business value. *Figure 12.1* illustrates the relationship between cloud spend and unit cost, helping define the desired state of cost optimization:

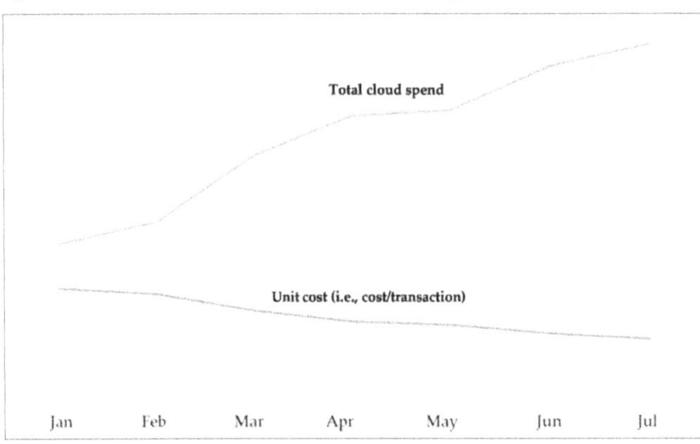

Figure 12.1*: Cloud spend vs. unit cost graph*

Many organizations track total monthly cloud spend and its alignment with the IT budget. While this metric provides visibility into how much cost is incurred per month, it does not indicate whether the increase or decrease is driven by business events. Cloud costs can increase for positive reasons, such as:

- Migration of workloads from an on-premises environment to the cloud.
- Expansion into new markets or geographies.
- Launch of new products or services that require additional cloud resources.
- Increase in user base as business scales.
- Automation of manual processes through the adoption of cloud-native services.

An increase in cloud spend that is directly linked to business growth is considered positive spend if the unit cost required to support the business remains stable or decreases as the business grows, and is illustrated in *Figure 12.1*.

Unit cost metrics

A better measure of cost optimization success is unit cost. Instead of focusing only on total spend, organizations should calculate the cost per unit of value delivered. The unit can be defined differently for each business, depending on its industry and applications. Examples include:

- **Software as a service (SaaS)**: Cost per user
- **Financial application**: Cost per transaction
- **Application programming interface (API) or digital services**: Cost per request
- **Insurance provider**: Cost per insurance policy
- **Data-intensive workloads**: Cost per gigabyte processed

Tracking unit cost allows organizations to understand whether their architecture and operations are becoming more efficient over time. For example, if overall cloud spend is increasing but the cost per user is decreasing, it indicates that the organization is supporting more users at a lower per-unit cost and that the increase in cloud spend is mainly due to more users getting onboarded to the cloud platform. This is a strong indicator of efficiency and maturity in cost optimization.

Summarizing the cost optimization framework

Throughout this book, we have explored different strategies, tools, and practices that enable organizations to shift from reactive cost management to proactive financial governance. At the heart of this journey lies a framework built on three pillars, which consists of cost observability, cost optimization, and cloud cost governance, as shown in the following figure:

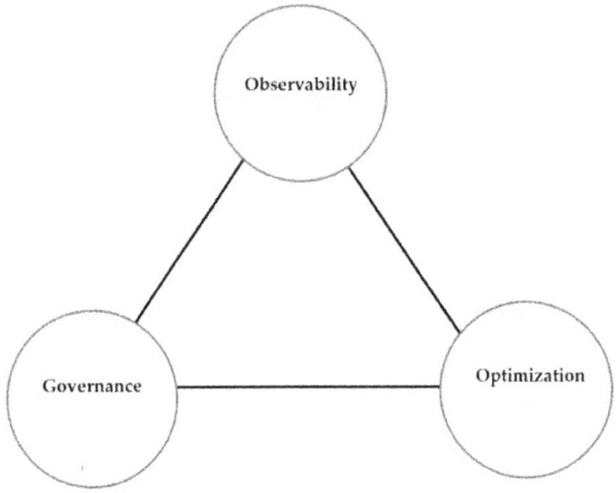

Figure 12.2: *Cost optimization framework*

Cost observability

The first step in cloud cost optimization is observability. With the right visibility into cloud usage and spend, organizations can make informed decisions about cost optimization activities. In the cost observability chapters, we discussed some of the key factors that can impact cloud billing, along with tools for cost and usage visibility. Some of the key points covered include:

- **Understanding pricing models**:
  - Cloud services have different pricing models, such as on-demand, spot, and commitment-based pricing models (like Reserved Instances or Savings Plan).
  - Pricing also varies by service type and billing unit. For example, compute is often billed per hour or per second of usage, storage per gigabyte of data stored, and data transfer per gigabyte transferred.
  - Other factors that impact cloud costs include the choice of region, whether services are cloud-managed or self-managed, and whether free-tier options are leveraged.
- **Using Pricing Calculators and forecasting tools**: Before workloads are deployed, organizations should use Pricing Calculators offered by cloud providers (such as the AWS Pricing Calculator or Azure Pricing Calculator) to estimate costs for workloads deployed on the cloud.
- **Leveraging cost observability tools**: Organizations have three main options for monitoring usage and spend:
  - **Cloud-native tools**: Cloud Providers such as AWS, Azure, and GCP offer native services for cost and usage visibility. Examples include AWS Cost Explorer, Azure Cost Analysis, and Google Cloud Billing Reports. More advanced tools, such as AWS CUR, can provide granular, resource-level data for in-depth analysis.

- **Customized tools**: Some organizations build their own reporting dashboards by extracting raw billing data and visualizing it using reporting tools such as Amazon QuickSight, Power BI, or Tableau. These solutions can be tailored to visualize and present business-specific metrics such as unit costs.
- **Third-party tools**: Several vendors offer comprehensive cost management solutions that combine cost visibility with optimization recommendations. Examples include platforms such as Apptio and CloudHealth.

With cost observability tools and practices in place, organizations get insights into what is driving the cloud cost and can prioritize optimization efforts accordingly.

Cost optimization

After getting insights into cloud usage and spend, the next step is to identify appropriate optimization levers and implement cost savings recommendations. Cost optimization involves finding the right balance between reducing costs and ensuring that workloads continue to meet business requirements for availability, performance, security, and resiliency. In the cost optimization chapters, we have discussed the following:

- **Using native tools**: Provided by cloud providers such as AWS Trusted Advisor, AWS Cost Optimization Hub, and Azure Advisor to identify levers for cost optimization. These services provide actionable recommendations for cost savings, such as:
  - Terminating unused resources.
  - Rightsizing underutilized instances.
  - Switching to more cost-effective purchase options.
- **Identifying optimization levers**: The organization needs to identify top services driving cloud costs and the associated levers for cost optimization. In previous chapters, we discussed cost optimization levers for different services such as compute, storage, databases, observability services, security services, and networking services.
- **Developing a prioritized action plan**: Organizations should develop a structured approach for implementing cost savings recommendations. By categorizing opportunities based on potential savings, associated risks, and ease of implementation, organizations can achieve quick wins while working toward longer-term improvements.

Cloud cost governance

The final pillar is governance, which ensures that cost optimization becomes part of the organization's culture and that appropriate guardrails are in place to prevent cost spikes. Key components of governance include:

- **Developing cost allocation models**: To ensure accountability, cloud costs must be allocated to the teams or business units responsible for them. This includes shared services costs, which should be distributed across the consuming teams. Cost allocation drives transparency and supports informed financial decisions about product profitability.

- **Cost guardrails**: Guardrails act as preventive controls to stop costs from spiraling. Examples include:
  - IAM policies for resource deployments.
  - Organization policies, such as SCPs, that restrict who can provision expensive resources.
  - Automated budget alerts and anomaly detection systems (like AWS Cost Anomaly Detection) that flag unexpected cost spikes.
  - Policies that block resource deployments once budgets are exceeded.
- **Building a cost-aware culture**: All stakeholders, from engineers to product managers, should consider cost implications when making design, configuration, or deployment decisions. Cost should be treated as a key metric alongside performance, security, and scalability.

Applying the cost optimization framework in real-world examples

In *Chapter 1, Introduction to Cloud Cost Optimization*, we looked at three examples where organizations faced unexpected increases in their cloud bills. Each example highlighted how missing one or more pillars of the cost optimization framework—cost observability, cost optimization, and cost governance can lead to cost spikes or failed cost optimization programs. Let us revisit these three examples and see how applying the cost optimization framework can help organizations in their cost optimization journey.

Unintended cost impact of network configuration changes

This example examines a cost spike caused by network configuration changes. An e-commerce company faced a sudden $100,000 cost increase due to a small change in network configuration. While the application was stable and met availability goals, the financial impact resulted from an overlooked data transfer configuration.

The following issues were identified during cost impact analysis:

- **Cost observability**: The e-commerce organization relied on end-of-month bills instead of proactive cost monitoring. The spike went unnoticed till the monthly invoice was generated.

- **Cost-aware culture**: Engineers focused only on performance and reliability. Cost impact analysis was not part of the design or architecture reviews.
- **Cost governance**: There are no guardrails, such as budgets or anomaly detection alerts, to trigger escalation when costs deviate significantly from expected levels.

This section demonstrates how the cost optimization framework discussed earlier can be applied in practice:

- **Cost observability**:
  - Use tools like Azure Cost Analysis, Budgets, and Anomaly Detection to continuously monitor costs and receive alerts when spending deviations occur.
  - Analyze the cost and usage data to identify the network cost increases and determine whether data transfer charges are related to Inter AZ, Inter-region, or outbound traffic to the internet.
- **Cost optimization**:
  - Before approving any architectural or configuration changes, review the cost impact analysis along with performance and security implications.
  - Encourage teams to perform cost estimation and forecasting using the Azure Pricing Calculator or other cost estimation tools for new solution designs, deployments, and major configuration changes.
  - As discussed in *Chapter 10, Optimizing Data Transfer Charges on Cloud,* review the appropriate cost optimization levers for data transfer and implement recommendations based on the prioritized action plan discussed in previous chapters.
- **Cost governance**:
  - Set up guardrails through Azure Policy and budgets to prevent uncontrolled cost increases.
  - Create a CCoE or a similar centralized review board. This team should review all proposed cloud deployments and changes and assist deployment teams in conducting cost impact assessments prior to rollout.
  - As discussed in the chapter on cloud cost governance, develop an incident handling mechanism to manage and respond to cost spikes.

Duplicate logging leading to unexpected costs

This example examines a cost increase in Amazon CloudWatch due to a lack of communication between teams.

Here, a fintech start-up faced a $15,000 increase in cloud costs when both the Security team and the DevOps team independently enabled AWS CloudTrail logging without knowing about each other's changes. The duplicate CloudTrail configurations led to excessive management event logging, exceeding the Free Tier limit and incurring significant logging charges.

The following issues were identified during analysis of usage and cost data:

- **Cost-aware culture**: Teams operated in silos without considering the financial impact of their technical decisions.
- **Cost governance**: There was no centralized review mechanism or CCoE to validate whether multiple trails were necessary.
- **Pricing understanding**: Teams lacked knowledge about the billing model of CloudTrail and CloudWatch, including Free Tier limits and applicable exclusions.
- **Cost observability**: There was limited visibility into how logging-related costs were accumulating over time.

Let us understand how the cost optimization framework discussed earlier can be applied in practice:

- **Cost observability**: Use native tools such as AWS Cost Explorer and CUR to monitor service-specific cost breakdowns and identify which service is contributing to unusual spikes. Also, leverage AWS budgets and anomaly detection to receive notifications for any deviations from expected usage.
- **Cost optimization**:
  - Use Pricing Calculators to estimate the cost of enabling services before deployment.
  - Implement right-sized logging strategies by capturing only the logs that are necessary for compliance and security rather than enabling all logging by default.
  - Follow the cost optimization levers discussed in *Chapter 8, Optimizing Cloud Observability Cost*. Consolidate CloudTrail logging trails wherever possible to avoid duplication.
- **Cost governance**:
  - Establish a change management process where all major service configurations are reviewed by a centralized team (like CCoE) before rollout.
  - Encourage cross-team communication. For example, when the security team enables a feature, DevOps should be notified to prevent duplicate setups.
  - Set up AWS budget and AWS anomaly detection to get notifications for any outliers at the earliest.

Challenges in cost allocation across business units

This example examines the difficulty in cost allocation across **business units** (**BUs**).

In this scenario, a CTO tried to incentivize different business units to reduce cloud costs by offering performance-based rewards. However, the initiative failed because the organization lacked the ability to accurately attribute cloud costs back to specific BUs. In the absence of consistent tagging, cost allocation models, and showback or chargeback mechanisms, costs appeared as a single aggregated amount, making accountability difficult. This lack of cost visibility and attribution made it difficult to establish accountability or measure the cost efficiency of individual business units.

The following issues were identified during analysis of cost and usage data:

- **Cost governance**: There was no formal cost allocation model, standardized tagging practice, or showback/chargeback mechanism defined for the organization.
- **Cost observability**: Finance teams could not drill down into cost data at the business unit or project level.
- **Cost-aware culture**: Without clear accountability, individual teams did not feel ownership for the cloud spend.

Let us understand how the cost optimization framework discussed earlier can be applied in practice:

- **Cost observability**:
  - Enforce resource tagging (e.g., BU, project, environment, owner) to ensure cloud usage can be tracked at the appropriate level of granularity.
  - Use reporting tools to generate showback reports, providing each BU visibility into their share of cloud costs.
- **Cost governance**:
  - Implement a chargeback and showback model to bring accountability into different teams.
  - Define policies and guardrails to enforce tagging at the point of resource creation.

There are many such examples where organizations face cost escalation due to not applying the cost optimization framework. By applying the three pillars of the cost optimization framework, organizations can:

- Detect issues early through cost observability.
- Make informed design and deployment decisions by incorporating cost optimization practices.
- Build accountability and alignment through cost governance structures.

Leveraging GenAI solutions for cost optimization

In previous chapters, we have seen how organizations can use various cost observability and cost optimization tools to get cost-related insights and generate cost savings recommendations. While these tools are effective, they require manual interpretation and deep technical knowledge. In recent years, emerging technologies such as GenAI have transformed the IT landscape by bringing intelligence, automation, and natural language interaction into technical and operational workflows. GenAI refers to a class of artificial intelligence models that can generate human-like responses, summarize large sets of data, and provide context-aware recommendations. Unlike traditional analytics tools that only display numbers and charts, GenAI solutions can interpret data, explain trends, and even suggest actions in natural language. GenAI-powered tools allow users to provide prompts in natural language and receive contextually relevant answers. The GenAI solutions can make cost optimization far more accessible for financial analysts, developers, operations teams, and executives who may not have specialized cloud expertise.

Today, all major cloud providers, such as Amazon Web Services and Microsoft Azure, offer integrated GenAI assistants that can help organizations optimize cloud costs. These assistants reduce the complexity of navigating multiple cost management tools and interpreting huge data sets, making it easier to identify savings opportunities, forecast expenses, and act on optimization strategies.

In this section, we will explore some of the GENAI solutions, such as Amazon Q from AWS and Microsoft Copilot, for cost optimization.

Amazon Q for cost optimization

Amazon Q is a generative AI assistant from AWS that helps simplify cloud operations by providing insights, recommendations, and automation support. It enables users to perform common tasks such as writing and testing code, troubleshooting technical issues, and summarizing documents. Amazon Q is tightly integrated with AWS Services and helps in analyzing and optimizing cloud costs through natural language queries. Amazon Q can access cost and usage data from sources such as AWS Cost Explorer, Cost Optimization Hub, and Trusted Advisor. Teams can ask Amazon Q about cost and usage-related information in natural language, such as:

- *Which AWS service incurred the highest cost last month?*
- *Why did my costs increase from November to December?*
- *What savings opportunities are available if I rightsize my EC2 instances?*
- *Which regions are driving the highest data transfer costs?*
- *How much can I save by purchasing Savings Plan?*

- *Which resources are underutilized?*

Instead of manually writing complex queries or navigating multiple dashboards, teams can use Amazon Q to get answers in natural language, backed by relevant data and direct links within the AWS management console.

Pricing for Amazon Q

Amazon Q has different subscription tiers for various use cases, and pricing is dependent on the selected subscription tier:

- **Amazon Q Business** has two subscription models—Amazon Q Business Lite and Amazon Q Business Pro. These tiers are designed for enterprise use, with features tailored to organizational needs. Pricing is shown in the following figure for reference, and you can refer to the AWS Pricing page for the latest information:

Amazon Q Business Lite	Amazon Q Business Pro
$3 per user/mo.	**$20 per user/mo.**
The Amazon Q Business Lite subscription provides users access to basic functionality such as asking questions and receiving permission-aware responses.	The Amazon Q Business Pro subscription provides users access to the full suite of Amazon Q Business capabilities, including access to Amazon Q Apps, and Amazon Q in QuickSight (Reader Pro).

Figure 12.3*: Amazon Q Business pricing*

- **Amazon Q Developer** is built for developers, offering two pricing tiers with access to development-focused features. Refer to the pricing for the Amazon Q developer, as shown in the following figure:

Free Tier: Advanced capabilities at zero cost	Pro Tier: Expanded limits $19/mo. per user
• Limited agentic requests per month • Access latest Claude models • Use in the IDE or CLI	Everything included in the Free tier, with • Increased limits of agentic requests • Increased limits for Java and .NET app transformation • Identity center support with admin dashboards and controls • IP indemnity

Figure 12.4*: Amazon Q Developer pricing*

- **Amazon Q in QuickSight** provides natural language querying within AWS QuickSight for analytics. Pricing differs for authors and readers:
    - **Author**: $24 per user/month
    - **Author Pro**: $50 per user/month
    - **Reader**: $24 per user/month
    - **Reader Pro**: $50 per user/month

The key point to note is that pricing depends on the chosen subscription tier and the type of usage. Organizations can choose the most suitable option depending on whether the primary users are developers, analysts, or business teams.

Comparing traditional and GenAI-enabled cost optimization

GenAI assistants such as Amazon Q and Microsoft Copilot integrate directly with cloud cost management platforms to provide intelligent, conversational cost insights. The following table compares how GenAI solutions such as Amazon Q and Microsoft Copilot provide advantages over traditional cost optimization tools and practices by supporting natural language interaction and enabling intelligent, conversational cost insights through deep integration with cloud cost management platforms:

Stages of cost optimization	Traditional approach	GenAI enabled approach (Amazon Q and Copilot)	Examples of GenAI in action
Cost observability (Monitoring cost and usage data)	Teams leverage cost observability tools such as AWS Cost Explorer, Azure Cost Management, and CUR to view and analyze cost and usage.	GenAI solutions such as Amazon Q and Microsoft Copilot are integrated with Cloud provider tools and fetch relevant data through natural language queries.	Teams can provide a prompt to get the required information. Example: *What was my total spend in August 2025?* *What are the top 5 services by cost for the month of August 2025?*

Stages of cost optimization	Traditional approach	GenAI enabled approach (Amazon Q and Copilot)	Examples of GenAI in action
Cost and usage data analysis (Understanding trends and anomalies)	The traditional model requires teams to manually review and filter data, write custom CUR queries, and export data into a visualization dashboard, often relying on BI tools for deeper analysis.	GenAI assistants interpret data trends and explain anomalies in natural language.	Use a prompt such as: *Which region had the biggest cost spike in August 2025?* *Which service had the highest percentage increase in cost from July 2025 to August 2025*
Recommendation (Identifying cost-saving opportunities)	Cloud providers offer tools such as AWS Trusted Advisor and Azure Advisor that provide rule-based recommendations. For example, idle RDS instances—a list of databases that have received no connections for 14 days or more are flagged for optimization. Beyond these automated recommendations, organizations can also develop additional optimization strategies by manually analyzing the usage data collected through cost observability tools.	GenAI assistants provide context-aware optimization recommendations based on actual usage patterns.	Use prompts like: *Suggest rightsizing opportunities for my virtual machines?* *Identify storage resources that can be moved to a cheaper tier?*

Stages of cost optimization	Traditional approach	GenAI enabled approach (Amazon Q and Copilot)	Examples of GenAI in action
Implementation guidance (How to implement cost-saving recommendations)	Teams require deep technical expertise and must manually search documentation and navigate console settings to implement recommendations.	GenAI assistants can provide step-by-step instructions on implementing the changes.	Teams can use prompts such as: *Provide step-by-step instructions for migrating Amazon EBS volumes from gp2 to gp3, including any prerequisites, cost implications, and performance considerations?*

***Table 12.1**: Using GenAI Assistants for cost optimization*

Prerequisites for using Amazon Q

Before you can use Amazon Q for cost optimization, check if the user has the required permissions for accessing Amazon Q and cost and usage data. Amazon Q uses AWS APIs to retrieve cost insights, so appropriate permissions and data visibility are essential. Before using Amazon Q for cost optimization, ensure that the following prerequisites are in place:

- **Permissions**: The IAM user accessing Amazon Q Developer must have permissions to retrieve cost and usage data from AWS Cost Explorer and have access to Amazon Q Developer.
- **Enable tools**: Make sure AWS Cost Explorer and AWS Cost Optimization Hub are enabled in your account.

Understanding how to use Amazon Q for cost queries

To get started with Amazon Q, follow the given steps:

1. Log in to the **AWS Management Console**.
2. Click the **Amazon Q icon** (located on the right side of the console).
3. Start asking questions such as: `What were my total AWS costs for the month of August 2025? What are the top 3 services by cost incurred for the month of August 2025?` Amazon Q will display the results, highlight the parameters used, and provide direct links to the relevant AWS console pages. You can validate the responses by clicking the AWS Cost Explorer link provided in the Amazon Q response. Refer to the following figure for the Amazon Q response:

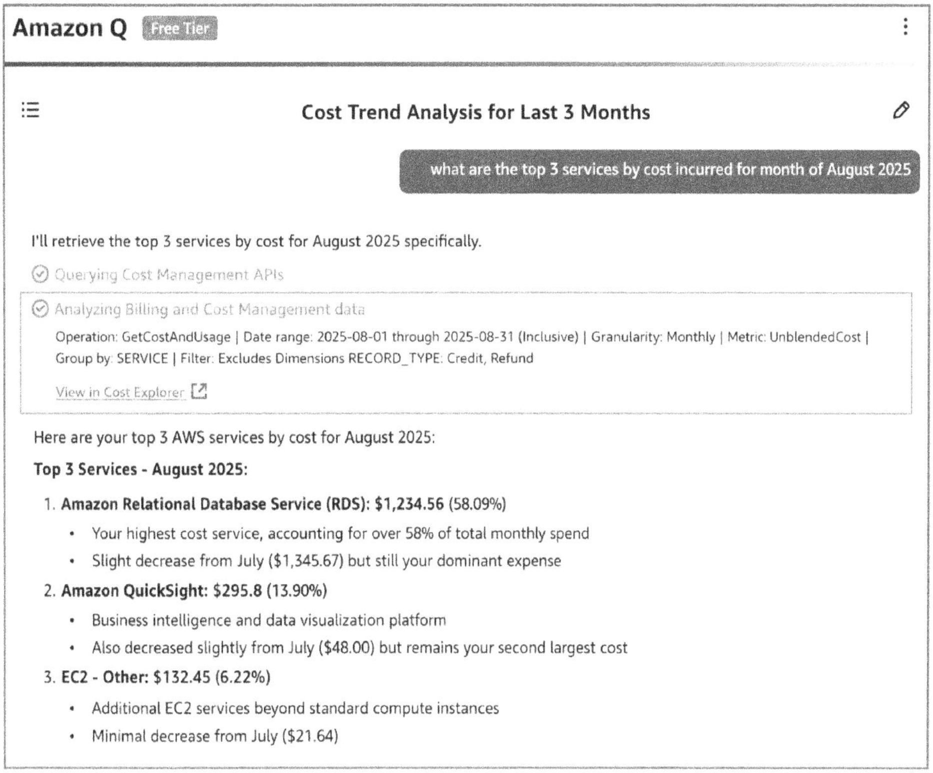

***Figure 12.5**: Amazon Q in action*

Microsoft Copilot for cost optimization

Microsoft Copilot is Azure's GenAI assistant, designed to help users interact with the platform using natural language. Just like Amazon Q, it makes it easier for organizations to understand costs and usage data and optimize cloud usage without requiring teams to have advanced technical expertise.

Copilot is integrated within the Azure portal, and you can launch it directly from the console (next to the search bar) or through the Azure Cost Management + Billing section. Refer to the following figure on launching Microsoft Copilot:

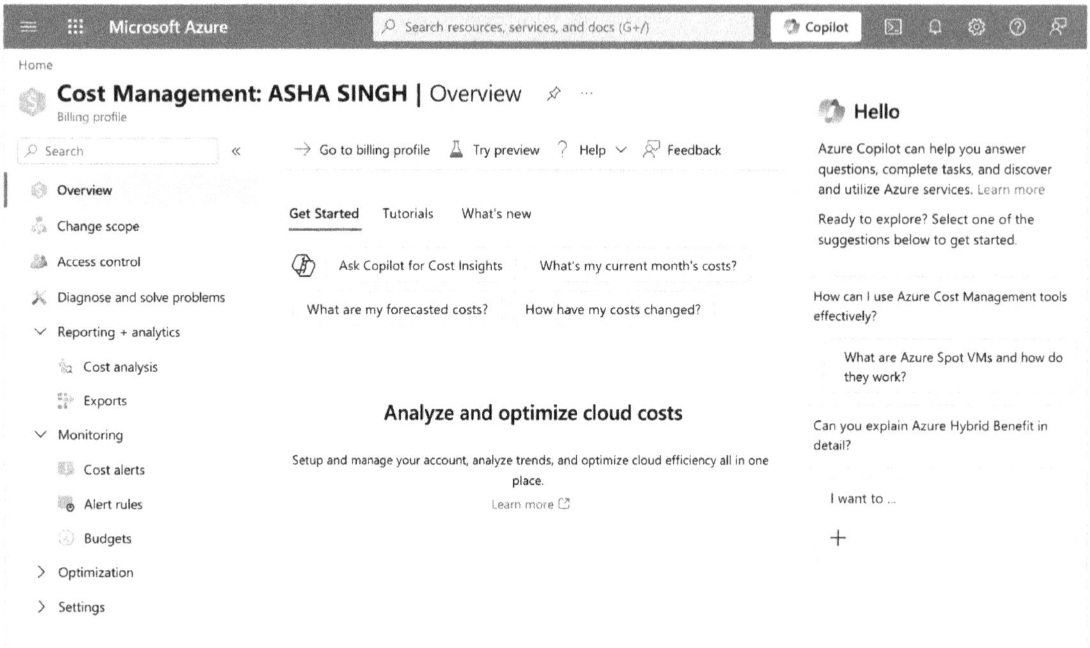

***Figure 12.6**: Microsoft Copilot for cost management*

Once launched, you can ask Copilot cost-related questions, and it will retrieve relevant data from Azure cost management tools. When asking cost-related questions, Copilot prompts you to select a scope (subscription, resource group, or management group). This ensures that the cost data you receive is specific to the level of detail you want.

Future of GenAI in cost optimization

GenAI is evolving at a rapid pace, and all cloud providers, such as AWS, Azure, and Google, are continuously enhancing their AI assistants. The organization needs to stay informed about new service launches and announcements to keep up with the latest GenAI solutions offered by cloud providers.

One important development is the introduction of the **Model Context Protocol** (**MCP**). MCP is an open standard designed to let AI assistants connect securely to external systems such as databases, APIs, or cloud billing platforms. Think of MCP servers as connectors that bridge AI models with enterprise systems in a structured and standardized way. With MCP, a GenAI assistant is not limited to pre-integrated tools like Cost Explorer or Azure Cost Management but can be extended to access additional data sources, including AWS CUR data, Azure Billing exports, as well as the organization's billing API or financial data source. With the introduction of MCP, you can connect to multiple cost and usage data sources to get meaningful insights and can also trigger actions to optimize the environment.

Understanding FOCUS

Managing cloud costs can be a challenge, especially for organizations using multiple cloud providers. Cloud providers such as AWS, Azure, and Google Cloud (GCP) provide cost management tools for getting insight into cloud spend. However, billing data formats differ across providers. For example, AWS provides billing data through CUR, which has a well-defined structure for capturing cost and usage details. In contrast, Azure provides billing data through Azure Cost Management exports, which deliver cost and usage details in a different schema, organized around subscriptions, resource groups, and resources. While both formats provide detailed billing insights, the structure, naming conventions, and level of granularity vary and require normalization when performing multi-cloud cost analysis. Dashboards and cost management solutions built for one provider often need to be redesigned and customized for another cloud provider. This increases the time and effort required to get a consolidated and consistent view of cloud spending in multi-cloud environments.

FOCUS addresses this challenge by providing a standardized specification for cloud billing and usage data.

Defining the FOCUS

FOCUS is an open standard developed by the FinOps Foundation to bring consistency to cloud billing and usage data. It defines a standardized specification for representing cost and usage information across cloud providers such as AWS, Azure, GCP, and OCI, enabling a common, provider-agnostic billing data model. By using FOCUS, organizations can simplify how they consume, analyze, and act on cloud financial data. Instead of spending hours interpreting and normalizing different billing formats, teams can work with a consistent, standardized dataset. This becomes valuable in a multi-cloud and SaaS environment, where cost visibility is often fragmented across providers and platforms.

Benefits of FOCUS

The following are the benefits of FOCUS:

- **Standardized cost visibility**: FOCUS provides a consistent way of representing cloud usage and spend, making it easier to interpret and analyze costs in a multi-cloud deployment. With a standardized format, organizations can quickly identify optimization opportunities.
- **Improved collaboration**: With FOCUS, different teams such as finance, engineering, and operations can work on the same dataset, reducing misunderstandings and aligning cloud spending with business goals.
- **Portable skills for practitioners**: As FOCUS is vendor-neutral, CFM practitioners who learn it can apply their skills across multiple cloud platforms without having to relearn billing structures for each provider.

- **Operational efficiency**: Activities like cost monitoring, cost analysis, and cost optimization can be standardized across providers. This reduces the need for manual data conversion and saves valuable time for cloud practitioners.
- **Simplify tooling and automation workflows**: As organizations are increasingly adopting multi-cloud strategies, FOCUS helps ensure that cost management tools and workflows remain consistent.

Enabling FOCUS data exports

Many cloud providers are members of the FinOps Foundation and have started supporting FOCUS-compatible data exports. For example, in AWS, you can generate billing data in FOCUS format by following the steps given as follows:

1. Go to the AWS console and open **Billing and Cost Management**.
2. From the left panel, click on **Data Exports**.
3. Click **Create** from **Data Exports** console.
4. In the **Standard data export** option, you can choose to extract data compliant with **FOCUS 1.0**.
5. Provide required details and click **Create**.

Once set up, AWS billing data is automatically formatted in FOCUS structure and can be integrated into compatible FinOps tools. Refer to the following figure for selecting FOCUS 1.0 as the output format from the **Data Exports** console:

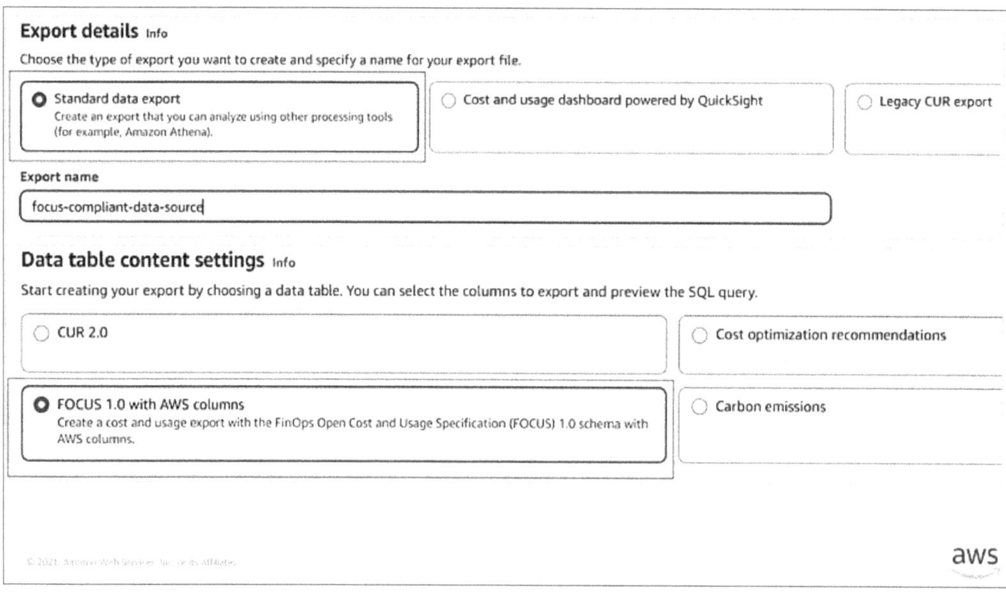

Figure 12.7: AWS Data Export—FOCUS

You can perform the following steps in Azure to extract billing data in FOCUS-compliant format:

1. In the Azure portal, go to **Cost Management + Billing** and choose the appropriate billing scope.
2. In the left-hand menu, click on **Exports.**
3. Select **+Create** to start a new export.
4. From the export options, select **Cost and usage (FOCUS)**. This ensures your data is formatted according to the FinOps Open Cost and Usage Specification. Refer to the following figure to create an export in FOCUS format:

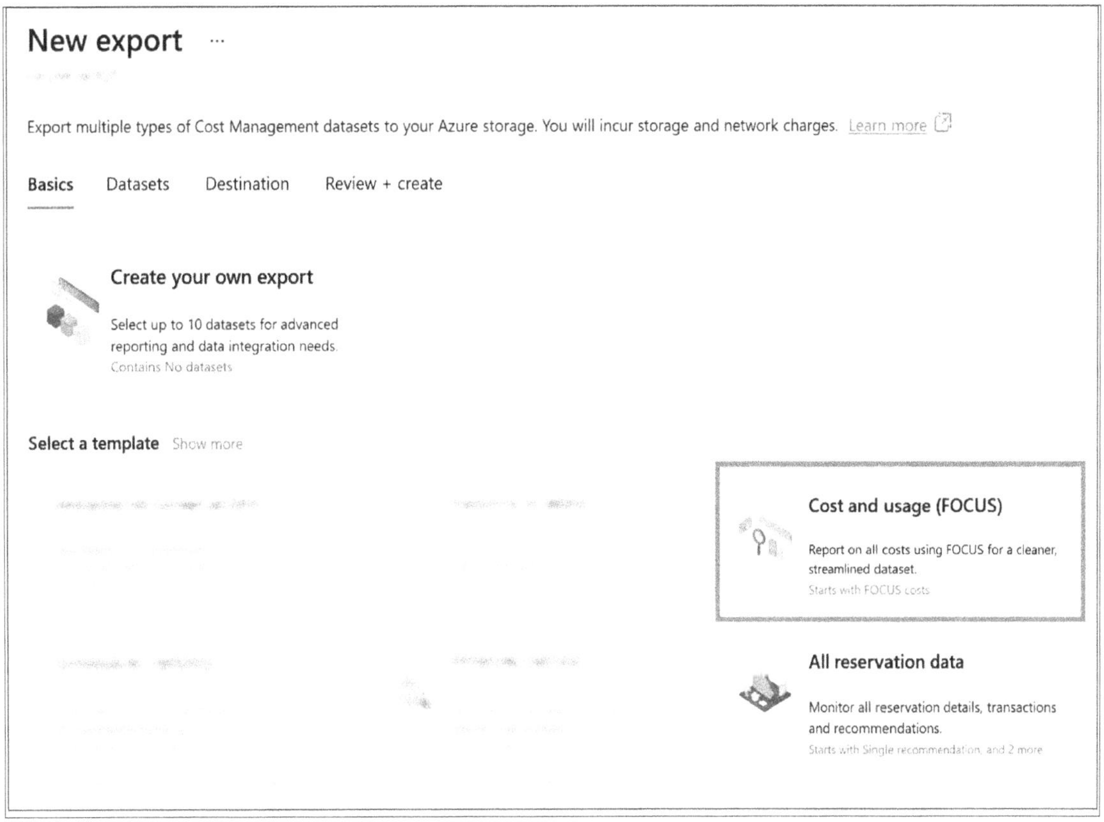

Figure 12.8: *Azure Data Export–FOCUS*

5. Provide the details such as **Export name, Dataset version, Output format, Destination,** and **Export frequency**.
6. Validate settings, then click **Create**. Exports will run automatically based on the chosen schedule. You can monitor the status under Exports.

Growing importance of FOCUS

FOCUS will continue to play a critical role in CFM, especially in multi-cloud environments. Standardized billing is essential for managing the increasing complexity of cloud costs. Cloud providers are increasingly adopting the FOCUS standard, and the FinOps Foundation continues to drive its adoption. FinOps Foundation has also introduced training and certification programs to help practitioners build expertise in using FOCUS and the FinOps domain.

For organizations struggling with the complexity of multi-cloud cost management, FOCUS represents a significant opportunity to simplify processes, improve visibility, and optimize cloud spending more effectively across their entire technology portfolio.

Conclusion

This chapter brings together the lessons learned throughout the book and connects them with emerging technologies and frameworks, demonstrating how organizations can apply these insights to achieve smarter decision-making, faster optimization cycles, and more sustainable cloud cost management outcomes.

Throughout this book, we have explored different strategies, tools, and practices that enable organizations to shift from reactive cost management to proactive financial governance. At the heart of this journey lies a framework built on three foundational pillars—cost observability, cost optimization, and cloud cost governance. Together, these pillars help organizations gain visibility into cloud spend, identify and implement optimization opportunities, and establish accountability through structured governance mechanisms.

Looking ahead, two major transformative trends are set to reshape the landscape of cloud cost optimization—FOCUS and GenAI.

The adoption of FOCUS represents a major shift in how organizations manage multi-cloud environments. By establishing a standard format for cloud billing and usage data across providers, FOCUS simplifies cost management in a multi-cloud environment.

At the same time, generative AI is fundamentally reshaping how organizations approach cloud cost optimization. Instead of spending hours interpreting data from cost management tools or writing custom queries, users can now rely on GenAI assistants like Amazon Q and Microsoft Copilot to get instant insights and actionable recommendations through natural language conversations. These tools not only democratize access to cost data across finance, operations, and development teams but also accelerate decision-making and unlock deeper savings opportunities. As GenAI continues to advance, it will move from being a reactive assistant to becoming a proactive partner in cost management, enabling organizations to achieve greater efficiency, predictability, and control over their cloud investments.

Together, FOCUS and GenAI signal the next phase of CFM, enabling organizations to achieve greater efficiency, predictability, and control over their cloud investments.

Index

A

Amazon Athena 55
Amazon Athena, use cases
  AWS S3 Costs 63
  AWS Services 61
Amazon CloudWatch 227
Amazon CloudWatch, implementing 227-229
Amazon Cognito 248
Amazon Cognito, configuring 249
Amazon Q 342
Amazon Q, prerequisites 346
Amazon Q, steps 346
Amazon Q, tiers 343, 344
Amazon QuickSight 64
Amazon Web Services (AWS) 211
AWS Billing Console 30
AWS Billing Console, configuring 30-32
AWS Billing Invoice 27
AWS Billing Invoice, components
  Credits/Discounts 28
  Monthly Charges 27
  Pricing Units 27
  Subscription-Based Charges 27
  Upfront Payments 27
AWS Billing Invoice, terms
  AWS Billing Console 30
  Cost Data 29
  Cost Management Dashboard 28
AWS Compute Optimizer 110
AWS Compute Optimizer, comparing 111
AWS Compute Optimizer, steps 110
AWS Cost Categories 311
AWS Cost Categories, steps 311, 312
AWS Cost Explorer 32, 106
AWS Cost Explorer, configuring 34, 35
AWS Cost Explorer, factors
  Data Granularity 33
  Lookback Period 33
AWS Cost Explorer, features 32
AWS Cost Explorer, illustrating 35-37
AWS Cost Explorer, steps 106-108
AWS Cost Management 219
AWS Cost Management, tools
  AWS Cost Explorer 219
  Billing Console 221
  Cost Usage Reports (CUR) 222
AWS CUR 38
AWS CUR, concepts
  AWS Data Exports 40
  Azure Cost Analysis 44
  Cost Management Billing 43
AWS CUR/Cost Explorer, differences 38
AWS CUR, features 38
AWS Data Exports 40
AWS Data Exports, configuring 41
AWS Data Exports, features
  Compatibility 40
  Data Management 40
  Integration 40
  S3 Export 40
  SQL Capabilities 40
AWS Data Exports, steps 42, 43
AWS Data Transfer 283
AWS Data Transfer, terms
  Billing Console 286
  CloudWatch 289
  Cost Explorer 284
  CUR 287
  SQL Query 287
  VPC Flow Logs 289
AWS Organizations 305
AWS Organizations, benefits 306

AWS Pricing Calculator 17
AWS Pricing Calculator, implementing 17-19
AWS Service Catalog 325
AWS, services
- Amazon CloudWatch 211
- CloudTrail 211
- Config 211
- Systems Manager 212

AWS Services 143
AWS Services, tools
- AWS Compute Optimizer 147
- AWS Cost Explorer 145
- Billing Console 146
- Cost Optimization Hub 148
- CUR Data 146
- S3 Inventory 151
- S3 Storage Class Analysis 150
- S3 Storage Lens 148
- Trusted Advisor 147

Azure Advisor 96
Azure Advisor, implementing 99
Azure Advisor, recommendations 98
Azure Advisor, steps 97
Azure Cost Analysis 112
Azure Cost Analysis, points
- Cost Analysis Dashboard 45
- Cost Analysis Views 46
- Export Cost Data 47

Azure Cost Analysis, steps 44, 45
Azure Data Transfer 290
Azure Data Transfer, terms
- Azure Cost Analysis 290
- Azure Monitor 291
- Billing Console 291

Azure Pricing Calculator 20
Azure Pricing Calculator, implementing 20-22
Azure Resource Hierarchy 306

C

CID, benefits
- Data Source 76
- Ease Deployment 76
- Pre-Built Visualization 76
- Resource-Level Visibility 76

CISO 48
CISO, points 51, 52
CISO, steps 48-51
Cloud Compute Pricing 103
Cloud Compute Pricing, elements
- Billing Units 103
- Instance Type 105
- Operating Systems 104
- Processor Type 104
- Purchage Options 104
- Region 103

Cloud Cost Management 2
Cloud Cost Management, configuring 4-6
Cloud Cost Management, ensuring 11-14
Cloud Cost Management, factors
- Application Licensing 8
- Cloud Service Model 7
- Free Tier 9
- Location-Based Pricing 7
- Scalability 9
- Self-Managed 8
- Service Consumed / Billing Units 8

Cloud Cost Management, features
- Elasticity / Scalability 4
- On-Demand Self-Service 4
- Pay-As-You-Go 4
- Resource Pooling / Multi-Tenant 4

Cloud Database Services 170
Cloud Database Services, models
- IaaS 170
- PaaS 170

Cloud Database Services, types
- Non-Relational 171
- Relational 171

Cloud Intelligence Dashboard (CID) 75
Cloud Observability 210
Cloud Observability, models
- Analytics / Insights Charges 218
- Commitment-Based Saving 218
- Component-Based Pricing 214
- Free Tier Inclusions 213

Regional Pricing Variation 218
Rule Evaluation 218
Storage/Retension Costs 217
Cloud Observability, principles
Cloud-Native 226
Commitment-Based Savings 227
Cost-Efficient 225
Environment-Based Configuration 225
Review Storage 227
Cloud Observability, services
Cost Management Billing 223
Log Analytics Workspace 223
Cloud Observability, tools
Amazon Web Services (AWS) 211
Google Cloud Platform (GCP) 212
Microsoft Azure 212
Cloud Security Services 238
Cloud Security Services, categories
Application Security 243
Data Protection 243
Detective Controls 242
Identity Access Management (IAM) 241
Incident Detection 243
Infrastructure Protection 242
Cloud Security Services, factors
Azure Firewall 253
Azure Key Vault 254
DDoS Protection 254
Microsoft Defender 252
Microsoft Sentinel 253
Cloud Security Services, methods
Amazon Cognito 248
DDoS Protection 252
GuardDuty 250
Security Hub 251
Cloud Security Services, models
Billing Units 247
Commitment-Based Saving 248
Component-Based Pricing 245
Free Tier Inclusions 244
Regional Price Variations 247
Cloud Security Services, principles
Cloud-Native 262
Commitment-Based Saving 263
Environment-Based Security 262
Free Tier Inclusions 263
Free Trials/Simulations 264
Logging 264
Right-Size Security 261
Cloud Security Services, strategies
Amazon Cognito 265
Amazon Inspector 266
AWS Security Hub 267
AWS Shield Advanced 267
Azure Firewall 268
Azure Key Vault 270
Data Protection Services 269
DDoS Protection 268
Detective Controls 265
GuardDuty 265
Identity Access Management (IAM) 264
Infrastructure Protection 267
Key Management Service (KMS) 269
Secrets Manager 269
WAF Pricing 268
Cloud Storage Cost 151
Cloud Storage Cost, principles
Access Patterns 160
API Calls 161
Data Protection 163
Idle Resources 154
Modernization 158
Reserved Capacity 164
Rightsizing Storage 156
Right Storage Types 152
Cloud Storage Portfolio 138
Cloud Storage Pricing 140

Cloud Storage Pricing, anatomy
 Backup Charges 143
 Billing Units 141
 Provisioned/Consumed Storage 140
 Region-Based Pricing 141
 Reserved Capacity 142
 Tiered Pricing Model 142
CloudTrail Optimization 230
CloudTrail Optimization, implementing 230-232
Compute Modernization 118
Compute Modernization, steps
 Assessment/ Prioritization 123
 Technical Evaluation 123
 Validation Testing 123
Compute Modernization, types
 Accelerate 122
 Identifying 120
 Instance 118
 Operating System (OS) 119
 Processor 119
 Quantifying 121
Compute Portfolio 102
Compute Portfolio, services
 Container Services 102
 Serverless Options 102
 Virtual Machines 102
Compute Resources 105
Compute Resources, tools
 AWS Compute Optimizer 110
 AWS Cost Explorer 106
 Azure Cost Analysis 112
 Cost Optimization Hub 109
 Cost Usage Reports (CUR) 109
 Trusted Advisor 109
Config Optimization 232
Cost Allocation 304
Cost Allocation, approach
 Consumption-Based 308
 Equal Distribution 308
 Fixed Ratio 308
Cost Allocation, concepts
 Chargeback 309
 Showback 308
Cost Allocation, purpose 305
Cost Allocation, tools 314
Cost Allocation, types
 Directly Attributable 307
 Shared 307
Cost Awareness 329
Cost Awareness, configuring 329-331
Cost Data 29
Cost Governance 302
Cost Governance, factors 303
Cost Governance, objectives 302, 303
Cost Governance, pillars
 Cost Allocation 304
 Cost-Aware Culture 304
 Cost Control/ Guardrails 304
 Incident Handling 304
Cost Governance, points
 Assign Ownership 326
 Budgets/ Guardrails 329
 Business Units 326
 Change Management 328
 Cloud Providers 328
 Cost Optimization Levers 327
 Indicate Misconfigurations 327
 Playbook 329
 Proactive Monitoring 325
Cost Guardrails 314
Cost Guardrails, policies
 Azure Policies 324
 Service Control Policies (SCPs) 324
Cost Guardrails, terms
 Anomaly Detection 320
 Budgets 314
Cost Management Billing 43
Cost Management Billing, features 43, 44
Cost Management Dashboard 28
Cost Management Dashboard, purpose
 Billing/Payments 28
 Budget/Planning 29
 Cost Organization 29
 Cost/Usage Analysis 29

Preferences 29
Cost Management, frameworks
Cloud Cost Governance 337
Cost Observability 336
Cost Optimization 337
Cost Management Tools 255
Cost Management Tools, foundation
AWS Cost Explorer 256
Billing Console 257
Cost Usage Reports (CUR) 258
Security Service 255
Cost Optimization 78
Cost Optimization, concepts
AWS Saving Plan 130
RI/SP Utilization 130
Cost Optimization Database, strategies
Commercial/Open-Source 186
Commitment-Based Savings 200
Database Type 185
Elasticity 196
Provisioned/Serverless 188
Query Optimization 204
Relational/Non-Relational 185
Reviewing 203
Rightsizing/Modernization 189
Self-Managed/Cloud-Managed 187
Storage/Backup Costs 198
Cost Optimization, factors
Cost Implementation 82
Dependency Management 83
Potential Saving 81
Timelines Implementation 82
Cost Optimization Hub 91, 109
Cost Optimization Hub, actions 95
Cost Optimization Hub, capabilities
Comprehensive Cost Recommendations 92
Prioritization 92
Cost Optimization Hub, configuring 94, 95
Cost Optimization Hub, features 93
Cost Optimization Hub, steps 93
Cost Optimization, levers
Alternative Services, leveraging 80
Deployment Configurations 79
Right Pricing Model 79
Waste/Idle Resources, eliminating 78
Cost Optimization, models
On-Demand Instances 128
Reserved Instances 130
Spot Instance 129
Cost Optimization, points
Business Units (BUs) 341
Duplicate Logging Leading 339
Network Configuration Changes 338
Cost Optimization, tools
Azure Advisor 96
Cost Optimization Hub 91
Trusted Advisor 86
Cost Usage Dashboard 64
Cost Usage Dashboard, concepts
Alerts/Notifications 69
Dashboard Customization 69
Stakeholders Sharing 69
Cost Usage Dashboard, configuring 67
Cost Usage Dashboard, features 65
Cost Usage Dashboard, steps 65-67
Cost Usage Reports (CUR) 109
Cost Visibility 26
CUR 2.0 55
CUR 2.0, options 56
CUR 2.0, steps 56-60
Custom Cost Analytics 54
Custom Cost Analytics, configuring 54, 55

D

Dashboard 74

Dashboard, configuring 74, 75
Database Costs 175
Database Costs, foundation
- Cost Optimization 181
- Pricing Models 183
- Visibility 177

Database Pricing 172
Database Pricing, anatomy
- Billing Units 175
- Database Cost 173
- Instance Types 174
- Processor Types 174
- Purchase Models 174
- Region-Based Pricing 174
- Self-Managed/Cloud-Managed Database 173

Data Transfer 274
Data Transfer, architecture 280
Data Transfer, categories
- Availability Zones 279
- Azure Services 277
- Cloud/Internet 275
- Regions 277

Data Transfer, concepts
- Commitment-Based Saving 282
- Free Tier Inclusions 281
- Regional Pricing Variation 282

Data Transfer, configuring 280
Data Transfer, factors 282, 283
Data Transfer, principles
- Free Tier 295
- Networking Services 295
- Network Services 293
- Right-Size Application 292
- Service Costs 294
- Terminate Idle Resources 294

Data Transfer, strategies
- Azure Blob Storage 296
- Azure Load Balancers 296
- Azure VMs 295

Data Transfer, types
- AWS 283
- Azure 290

DDoS Protection 252

E

Elasticity 115
Elasticity, architecture 115
Elasticity, configuring 116
Elasticity, practices 118
Elasticity, principles 115
Elasticity, solutions
- Auto Scaling Groups 117
- Instance Scheduler 117

F

FOCUS 349
FOCUS, architecture 349
FOCUS, benefits 349
FOCUS, illustrating 350, 351
FOCUS, practices 352

G

GCP, services
- Cloud Error Reporting 213
- Cloud Logging 213
- Cloud Monitoring 212
- Cloud Profiler 213
- Cloud Trace 213

GenAI 342
GenAI, practices 348
GenAI, solutions
- Amazon Q 342
- Microsoft Copilot 347

Google Cloud Platform (GCP) 212
GuardDuty 250

H

Hypothetical Food Tech 234

L

Log Analytics 234

M

Microsoft Azure 212
Microsoft Azure, services
- Activity Log 212
- Azure Monitor 212
- Azure Policy 212
- Logs Analytics Workspace 212

Microsoft Copilot 347

N

Non-Relational Databases 171
Non-Relational Databases, categories
- Document 171
- Graph 172
- In-Memory 172
- Key-Value Stores 171
- Time-Series 172

P

Pricing Calculators 16
Pricing Calculators, types
- AWS 17
- Azure 20

Prioritization Framework 84
Prioritization Framework, ensuring 84, 85
Prioritized Action Plan 133

Q

QuickSight Dashboard 69
QuickSight Dashboard, section
- Cost Linked Account 72
- Cost Service 73

QuickSight Dashboard, setup 69, 70
QuickSight Dashboard, steps 70-72

R

Relational Databases 171
Return On Investment (ROI) 83
Rightsizing 124
Rightsizing, services
- Compute Optimizer 125
- Trusted Advisor 124

Rightsizing, steps 127

S

Security Hub 251
Service-Specific Cost 227
Service-Specific Cost, strategies
- Amazon CloudWatch 227
- CloudTrail Optimization 230
- Config Optimization 232
- Hypothetical Food Tech 234
- Log Analytics 234

Shared Responsibility Model 238
Shared Responsibility Model, tips
- Cloud Security 239
- Organization Responsibilities 239

Storage Services, types
- Block 139
- Data Protection 140
- File 139
- Object 139

T

Tags 309
Tags, architecture 309
Tags, configuring 309, 310
Tags, implementing 312
Tags, steps 310
Third-Party Security Services 240
Third-Party Security Services, factors 240, 241
Third-Party Security Services, tools
- IAM 240
- Workload Protection 240

Trusted Advisor 86, 109
Trusted Advisor, architecture 87
Trusted Advisor, configuring 88, 89
Trusted Advisor, steps 87

U

Unit Cost 335

W

Workload Characteristics 114